LEARN JAPANESE

NEW COLLEGE TEXT   VOLUME II

John Young and Kimiko Nakajima-Okano

Published for
University of Maryland University College

University of Hawaii Press
Honolulu

This volume is another in a series of Japanese language text-
books prepared by the Asian Division of the University of
Maryland University College and published by the University of Hawaii Press.

Library of Congress Cataloging in Publication Data
(Revised for volume II)

Young, John, 1920–
    Learn Japanese.

    1.   Japanese language—Text-books for foreign speakers
—English.   I.   Nakajima-Okano, Kimiko.   II.   Title.
PL539.3.Y64   1984   495.68'3421   83–18060
    ISBN 0-8248-0859-2 (v. 1)
    ISBN 0-8248-0881-9 (v. 2)

LEARN JAPANESE
NEW COLLEGE TEXT

「満 林 花」 康 成

　written by Mr. Yasunari Kawabata, who is the author of many well-known novels, including *Yukiguni.* Mr. Kawabata received the "Bunka Kunshō," an imperial award to distinguished men of letters, in 1961 and the Nobel Prize in literature in 1968.

CONTENTS

ACKNOWLEDGMENTS

The authors are deeply indebted to the Japanese language faculty and administrative staff of the University of Maryland and of more than one hundred universities and schools who have used the original *Learn Japanese: College Text* and offered many invaluable comments in the preparation of this revised text. We are also very grateful to the staff members of the Institute of Far Eastern Studies and of the Asian Bilingual Curriculum Development Center at Seton Hall University for their assistance.

We also wish to mention the following people whose assistance was very valuable in the preparation of the original text, *Learn Japanese: College Text:* Ms. Yoshiko Andō, Dr. Edgar A. Austin, Dr. Ivan Benson, Dr. Keiichirō Okutsu, and Mr. Shōzō Kurokawa.

Shirayuri ya
Nikei utsurite
Ike kaoru
　　—Seien—

The elegant reflection
Of two white lilies;
Now the pond is fragrant.

INTRODUCTION

This is the second volume of *Learn Japanese: New College Text*. It begins where Volume I ends. The use of *roomaji*—romanized Japanese—is limited to a minimum, with *kana* and *kan'ji* used instead.

In this volume, a total of 100 *kan'ji* characters with 116 different readings are introduced. Any *kan'ji* that has appeared in a previous lesson with a different reading, or any compound *kan'ji* whose reading is especially derived as a result of a combination, is introduced with the number with which it was originally introduced. *Kan'ji* with different readings are assigned numbers (such as 中 12.6.c) which are different from those numbers (such as 小 5.6.9) assigned to newly introduced *kan'ji*. Most of the *kan'ji* first appear in presentations and dialogs, but there are some that first occur in notes or drills. They are identified with an asterisk.

In addition to the *kan'ji* for "active" learning, we are introducing *kan'ji* for "passive" learning, and to these *kan'ji, furigana*—readings of the *kan'ji* in small *hiragana* characters—are attached. The student is required to identify and possibly reproduce the "active" *kan'ji*, but the "passive" *kan'ji* need not be memorized until they are introduced as *kan'ji* for active learning.

Kan'ji have been classified according to radicals, shapes, categories, and elements. In many traditional *kan'ji* dictionaries they have been classified according to 214 *bushu*, or radicals, following the pre-1945 tradition. However, many *kan'ji* have been simplified, modified, or even changed since 1945, and some modified forms of classification systems have been introduced. For example, the Agency for Cultural Affairs' *Dictionary of Chinese Characters for Foreigners* classified *kan'ji* into five categories with 247 elements, or subcategories. Although there are many other reformed dictionaries that have classified *kan'ji* differently, for the purpose of convenience this text has used the following popular dictionary in classifying *kan'ji*: Kikuya Nagasawa, *Meikai Kan'wa Jiten,* 1959, San'seidoo, Tokyo.

It should be remembered that the introduction of *kan'ji* is not meant to interfere with the student's efforts in building his oral-aural capability, which is the focal target of this volume. Therefore, reproduction of *kan'ji* should not be overemphasized at this stage.

Lessons 1 and 2, 4 and 5, 7 through 9, and 11 through 13 constitute the main texts, while Lessons 3, 6, 10, and 15 are review lessons.

Review lessons have been constructed to (1) review sentence patterns introduced in previous lessons; (2) practice drills of a more complicated nature; (3) do more exercises; and (4) help the student to develop more aural comprehension with applied conversation under different situations. The student is also asked to listen to a passage and practice his/her hearing comprehension. Lesson 14 has been introduced for "passive" learning, and the student is not required to study the content for examination. If necessary, this lesson may be omitted.

The lesson arrangement of Volume I has been followed, with these exceptions:

1. A Presentation section has been introduced for each regular lesson, replacing the Useful Expression section of Volume I. This will enable the student to acquaint himself/herself with the narrative style, leading eventually to the written style.
2. The Hiragana Practice section has been replaced by a Kan'ji section.
3. The Pronunciation Drill has been omitted. However, pronunciation practice should be pursued continually and any error must be corrected immediately.
4. At the end of each main lesson, a section called Situational and Application Conversation has been added to make sure that the student does not stay at the mim-mem stage but goes beyond it. Unless the student develops the so-called selection ability in generating utterances, he has not yet learned the language. This section should help the student to develop this ability after learning the lesson through dialog and drills. The situation described in the section and the application conversation should be read by the student before he comes to his class and he should be able to enact and apply it in Japanese before his teacher.

LESSON 1
かいもの[1]

1.1 PRESENTATION

日本の デパート[2]などの 店員の ことばは たいへん ていねいです。 つぎは 店員と 客の かいわです。

1.2 DIALOG

店　員 「いらっしゃいませ[3]。 なにを さしあげましょう[4]か。」

女の客[5] 「ブーツが ほしい[6]んですが。」

店　員 「ブーツは こちらです。 どうぞ。」

女の客 「それを みせてください[7]。」

店　員 「これは 24ですが、 お客さま[8]の サイズ[9]は？」

女の客 「23はん[9]です。 一万五千円[10]ぐらい[11]のを かいたいんですが、
　　　　　それは おいくら[12]ですか。」

店　員 「これは 一万三千六百円です。 どうぞ はいてみて[13]ください。」

女の客 「すこし きついですね。」

店　員 「では、 これは いかがですか。 … ちょうど いいですね。」

女の客 「ええ。 じゃあ、 これを いただきます[14]。 それから、 くつずみを
　　　　　一つ ください[15]。」

店　員 「ありがとうございます。 ブーツは はこに[16] いれましょうか。」

女の客 「ええ、 そう してください。 それから、 レインコートは なんがい[17]ですか。」

店　員 「四かい[17]で うっています[18]。」

女の客 「じゃあ、 あとで いってみましょう。 ぜんぶで[19] いくらですか。」

店　員 「一万三千九百円です。 どうも ありがとうございました[20]。」

いちまんごせんえん 一万五千円	いちまんさんぜんろっぴゃくえん 一万三千六百円	ひと 一つ	よん 四かい
いちまんさんぜんきゅうひゃくえん 一万三千九百円			

1.3 PATTERN SENTENCES

1.3.1

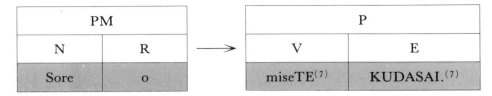

PM		→	P	
N	R		V	E
Sore	o		miseTE[7]	KUDASAI.[7]

1.3.2

SI	P		
	V	E	E
Doozo,	haiTE[13]	MIte[13]	kudasai.

1.4 NOTES

1.4.1 *Kaimono*

Most Japanese stores specialize in a particular item. In Japan, if a housewife needs vegetables, she goes to the *yaoya* (vegetable store). There are also *gyuunyuuya* (stores selling milk), *sakanaya* (fish stores), and *komeya* (rice stores). Because of the large number of different specialty food stores in Japan, one can usually purchase all of the food necessary for cooking within one's own neighborhood. Sometimes these goods can be delivered to the customer's home. Recently the supermarket has become more and more popular.

1.4.2 *Depaato* or Department Stores

Japanese department stores differ from the average American department store in that they are complete shopping districts in themselves. Usually comprising eight or nine floors, they are stocked with a wide range of products. Often the basement is similar to an American supermarket, selling canned foods and grocery items. Several of the remaining floors are usually organized by product. One floor might be a menswear department, while another floor might specialize in women's Western-style clothing. *Kimono*, furniture, household goods, electrical appliances, and so forth are also sold in the various departments. Often the top floor of the larger department stores has a restaurant, or a number of restaurants. In addition, hardware, stationery, kitchenware, china and crystal, musical instruments, and records are all available. Many stores also have travel agencies, florists, and departments featuring jewelry, optical equipment, leather goods, and art objects. Although a good number of large American stores carry many of the same products, most do not approach the volume and variety offered the Japanese customer.

All of the Japanese department stores, or *depaato*, open on Sundays. They are closed one day of the week.

1.4.3 *Irasshaimase* may be translated as "Welcome" or "Come in," but it occurs with a much greater frequency in Japan than its equivalent forms in America. Both the English and the Japanese expressions occur with about the same frequency when used to receive a guest into one's home. In Japan, however, *Irasshaimase* is mandatory for addressing each customer entering a restaurant,

bar, or shop. In department stores, for example, young women are usually stationed on each floor at the foot of the escalators to say *Irasshaimase* to customers going up to the next floor and to thank them when they leave. In the United States, a customer may or may not be welcomed into a store, and would not take it as exceptionally rude if he were not greeted accordingly.

1.4.4 *Sashiagemasu* is a very polite equivalent of *agemasu* "give." See Lesson 13 of Volume I in which *agemasu* and *sashiagemasu* are explained.

$$\mathbf{Noun}\ \mathbf{(person)} + ni + \mathbf{Noun}\ \mathbf{(object)} + o + \left\{ \begin{array}{l} agemasu \\ sashiagemasu \end{array} \right.$$

Ano kata ni kippu o sashiagemashita.	"I gave a ticket to that person."
Sen'sei ni kore o sashiagemasu.	"I will give this to you [my teacher]."

Sashiagemashoo ka? means in this instance "Shall I give it?" In some such situations, *-mashoo ka?* may refer to the speaker's doing something without involving the hearer and means "Shall I . . . ?" instead of "Shall we . . . ?" The affirmative answer to this question is often an expression of "please do such and such," which is introduced in Note 1.4.7.

Nani o sashiagemashoo ka?	"What shall I give to [you]?"
Hako ni iremashoo ka?	"Shall I put it into a box?"
Watakushi ga ikimashoo ka?	"Shall I go?"
Moo ichido iimashoo ka?	"Shall I say it once more?"
Ee, moo ichido itte kudasai.	"Yes, please say it once more."

1.4.5 *On'na no kyaku* means "lady customer." *On'na* "female" and *otoko* "male" form many phrases as follows:

otoko on'na } no {	hito	{ "man" "woman" }
	kata	{ "gentleman" "lady" }
	sen'sei	{ "male teacher" "female teacher" }
	gakusei	{ "boy student" "girl student" }
	tomodachi	{ "male friend" "female friend" }
	ko	{ "boy" "girl" }
	kyoodai	{ "brothers" "sisters" }

Female Customer

In this dialog, the level of politeness of the customer's speech toward the salesclerk indicates that the customer is most likely a woman. The comparable speech of a male customer in the same or similar situation would be considerably less polite. Evidence of this politeness on the part of a female customer can be seen in the following breakdown of the conversation in question. The polite forms or markers are italicized.

Clerk	Female customer
irasshai*mase*	
sashiagemashoo ka	mise*te kudasai*
okyaku*sama* no	o*ikura desu* ka
ikaga desu ka	kitsui *desu ne*
arigatoo *gozaimasu*	*itadakimasu*
doomo arigatoo *gozaimashita*	

1.4.6 *Hoshii* is an Adjective meaning "something is wanted," "desire to have something," or "want." Therefore, like ~ *ga suki desu*, an item that is wanted is followed by the Relational *ga*. The one who wants to have something is followed by the Relational *wa*.

Noun (person) + *wa* + **Noun (object)** + *ga* + *hoshii desu*

| (watakushi wa) | {rein'kooto / okane} | ga | hoshii (n) desu
hoshiku arimasen
hoshiku nai (n) desu
hoshikatta (n) desu
hoshiku arimasen deshita
hoshiku nakatta (n) desu | "a raincoat"
"money" | is
is not
is not
was
was not
was not | wanted (by me)" |

Eiga no kippu ga nimai hoshii n desu ga, arimasu ka?	"I want two movie tickets; do you have any?"
Watashitachi wa okashi ga hoshii n desu.	"We want some candy."

The item that is not wanted, however, is usually followed by the Relational *wa*, not the Relational *ga* unless the item which is not wanted must be emphasized.

Noun (object) + *wa* + *hoshiku* + { *arimasen* / *nai (n) desu* }

Ima ocha wa *hoshiku arimasen*.	"I don't want tea now."

Hoshii means "I desire to have something." Usually this word is not used to refer to a second-person or third-person subject, and especially not in referring to a second person. Therefore, when serving a customer as a waiter or waitress, one would never use *hoshii* in asking the customer "What do you wish to have?" *Hoshii* is most appropriately used in the first person, referring to what "I, myself, desire to have."

In the expression *hoshii n desu ga*, *ga* is relatively meaningless in the context. Literally *ga* means "but" or "although." Here, however, it serves as a softener; by using it to terminate the sentence, it softens the abruptness of the desire or hope of the subject person in a fashion characteristic of the Japanese. The meaning of the sentence, however, is that the customer does want a raincoat.

1.4.7 *Misete* is the TE form of the Verb *misemasu←miseru* "show." This form is used in various patterns, some of which are introduced in this lesson and in some of the following lessons, and it is important for you to familiarize yourself with this form. A grammatical note is given in Note 1.4.21 to explain how the TE forms are formed.

Here is a list of the TE forms of the Verbs you have studied in Volume I and in this lesson.

agemasu	"give"	⟶	agete
ben'kyoo shimasu	"study"	⟶	ben'kyoo shite
dekakemasu	"go out"	⟶	dekakete
den'wa shimasu	"make a phone call"	⟶	den'wa shite
hairimasu	"enter"	⟶	haitte
hakimasu	"put on"	⟶	haite
hanashimasu	"talk"	⟶	hanashite
iimasu	"say"	⟶	itte
ikimasu	"go"	⟶	itte
imasu	"be"	⟶	ite
iremasu	"put in"	⟶	irete
itadakimasu	"receive"	⟶	itadaite
kaerimasu	"go back"	⟶	kaette
kaimasu	"buy"	⟶	katte
kaimono shimasu	"do shopping"	⟶	kaimono shite
kakimasu	"write"	⟶	kaite
karimasu	"borrow"	⟶	karite
ken'butsu shimasu	"see the sights of"	⟶	ken'butsu shite
kikimasu	"listen"	⟶	kiite
kimasu*1	"come"	⟶	kite
kimasu*1	"wear"	⟶	kite
machimasu	"wait"	⟶	matte
mimasu	"see"	⟶	mite
misemasu	"show"	⟶	misete
moraimasu	"receive"	⟶	moratte
naraimasu	"learn"	⟶	naratte
nomimasu	"drink"	⟶	non'de
oyogimasu	"swim"	⟶	oyoide
ryokoo shimasu	"travel"	⟶	ryokoo shite
sagashimasu	"look for"	⟶	sagashite
sashiagemasu	"give"	⟶	sashiagete
shimasu	"do"	⟶	shite
shokuji shimasu	"have a meal"	⟶	shokuji shite
shookai shimasu	"introduce"	⟶	shookai shite
tabemasu	"eat"	⟶	tabete
urimasu	"sell"	⟶	utte
yarimasu	"give"	⟶	yatte
yobimasu	"call"	⟶	yon'de
yomimasu	"read"	⟶	yon'de
(arimasu*2	"be"	⟶	atte*2)
(furimasu*2	"fall"	⟶	futte*2)
(kudasaimasu*2	"give"	⟶	kudasatte*2)
(kuremasu*2	"give"	⟶	kurete*2)

*1The Verb *kimasu* "come" has the same TE form, *kite*, as the Verb *kimasu* "wear." The accent patterns and the Predicate Modifiers preceding *kite kudasai* will make it clear which meaning is called for.

Kore o kite kudasai.	"Please wear this."
Uchi e kite kudasai.	"Please come to my house."

*²TE forms of these Verbs are listed here, but the use of them is rather limited. They seldom occur in the patterns introduced in this lesson.

Misete kudasai means "Please show it to me or us." The TE form of a Verb plus the Predicate Extender *kudasai*, Verb(*-te*)+*kudasai*, formulates the polite imperative "please do such and such."

Verb(*-te*) + *kudasai*

Han'kachi to nekutai o misete kudasai.	"Please show me handkerchiefs and ties."
Kore o tabete kudasai.	"Please eat this."
Chotto matte kudasai.	"Please wait for a minute."

1.4.8 The *-sama* is a polite equivalent of the dependent Noun *-san*. The *-sama* is used in very polite speech or regularly used in superscribing a letter. As already explained in Note 7.4.8, Volume I, *okyakusama* may be said directly to the second person who is a customer or a guest.

okyakusan	okyakusama	otoosan	otoosama
okusan	okusama	Ishii san	Ishii sama

The Japanese, in order to gain the favor of others in such situations as selling goods or attempting to obtain a job, use extremely polite forms of expression. This is the case with clerks in department stores, as this dialog evidences. The salesman or merchant is always the inferior in a buying-selling relationship, while the customer is the superior. Thus, the customer uses less polite styles and levels of speech, while the salesman uses polite forms of address such as: *okusama, goshujin'sama, okyakusama*. The suffix *-sama* distinguishes these as polite forms.

In the dialog, the salesclerk asks *Okyakusama no saizu wa?* meaning "What is your size?" The prefix *o-* and the suffix *-sama* raise the level of politeness. *Kyaku* does not, however, mean "you." *Okyakusama* is in this case a way of addressing a customer or a guest.

Use of *anata* is considered impolite if the person has a title. "Customer" is a title, as is "teacher," "company president," "section chief," and so forth.

1.4.9 *-Han* is a dependent Noun meaning "half," and is often attached to numbers such as *goji* "five o'clock," *ichinen* "one year," to express the meaning "five-thirty," "one year and a half," and so on.

Watashi no kutsu no saizu wa nijuu san-han desu.	"The size of my shoes is twenty-three and a half."
Ima nan'ji desu ka?	"What time is it now?"
Yojihan desu.	"It's four-thirty."

The metric system is the standard for measurement used in Japan, and it is important that the American shopping in Japan familiarize himself or herself with this system. Otherwise one might be completely baffled in finding that an American size nine shoe is a size twenty-seven in Japan. One meter is approximately thirty-nine inches.

Due to differences in the average build of the Japanese as compared to the average American build, a large size in Japan would probably fit someone of an American medium size.

1.4.10 *-En* is the counter for "yen," the unit for Japanese currency. Counters for American currency units are *-doru* "dollar" and *-sen'to* "cent."

Sore wa ikura desu ka?	"How much is that?"
Gosen'en desu.	"It is five thousand yen."
Chichi kara hyakudoru moraimashita.	"I was given a hundred dollars by my father."
Gosen'to kudasai.	"Give me five cents."

Like *-satsu* and *-sai*, some of the combinations of a numeral and *-sen'to* make sound changes as follows:

1	issen'to	5	gosen'to	9	kyuusen'to
2	nisen'to	6	rokusen'to	10	jissen'to; jussen'to
3	san'sen'to	7	nanasen'to		
4	yon'sen'to	8	hassen'to; hachisen'to		

1.4.11 The *-gurai* used immediately after a number is a dependent Noun that indicates an approximate number or amount. *-Gurai* will correspond to "about" or "approximately." *-Gurai* may sometimes be pronounced *-kurai* by some Japanese. Even if the number or amount is definite, the Japanese may still use *-gurai* to indicate the speaker's consideration toward the listener.

Hyakuen gurai desu.	"It is about a hundred yen."
Kono hen ni gakusei ga nan'nin imasu ka?	"How many students are there in this area?"
Juunin gurai imasu.	"There are about ten."
Sono zasshi wa ikura desu ka?	"How much is that magazine?"
Happyakuen gurai deshoo.	"I presume it will cost about eight hundred yen."

Note that *-gurai* is never used to indicate approximate point of time. (See Note 2.4.13.)

1.4.12 *Ikura* is the interrogative Noun meaning "how much?" The way *ikura* is used is the same as that of *ikutsu* "how many?" The prefix *o-* may be added to *ikura* to make the word more polite.

Kono rein'kooto wa ikura desu ka?	"How much is this raincoat?"
Kore wa oikura deshita ka?	"How much was this?"
Okane ga ikura arimasu ka?	"How much money is there?" "How much money do you have?"
Ikura kaimashita ka?	"How much did you buy?"

1.4.13 *Haite mite kudasai* here means "Please try them on." The TE form plus the Predicate Extender *mimasu*←*miru* "try" forms the connotation "someone will do something and find out." The Extender *mimasu* conjugates like a Verb.

$$\textbf{Verb}(\textit{-te}) + \begin{cases} \textit{mimasu} \\ \textit{mimasen} \\ \textit{mimashita} \\ \textit{mimasen deshita} \\ \textit{mimashoo} \\ \textit{mite kudasai} \end{cases}$$

Chotto kite mimashoo.	"I think I'll try it on for a short time."
Sushi o tabete mimashoo.	"Let's eat *sushi* and find out how it is."
Kono waishatsu o kite mimasen ka?	"Won't you wear this dress shirt and see how it fits you?"
Sono sake o non'de mite kudasai.	"Please drink that wine and find out how it is."

1.4.14 *Itadakimasu* means "I'll receive it." *Itadakimasu* is a polite equivalent of *moraimasu* "receive; get." This word may be used when a giver is a superior or even an equal to show politeness. (See Note 13.4.1, Volume I.)

$$\textbf{Noun}\begin{pmatrix}\textbf{person}\end{pmatrix} + \textit{kara} + \textbf{Noun}\begin{pmatrix}\textbf{object}\end{pmatrix} + \textit{o} + \begin{cases} \textit{moraimasu} \\ \textit{itadakimasu} \end{cases}$$

Kore o itadakimasu.	"I will get [take] this one."
Donata kara itadakimashita ka?	"From whom did you get it?"
Sen'sei kara itadakimashita.	"I got it from the teacher."

1.4.15 When *kudasai* is used as a Predicate by itself, without being preceded by the TE form, it is the imperative form of the Verb *kudasaimasu*, the polite equivalent of *kuremasu* "give to me," which has been introduced in Note 13.4.8, Volume I. *Kudasai* without being preceded by the TE form means "please give me or us." The direct object of the Predicate *kudasai* will be followed by the Relational *o* and the indirect object will be followed by *ni*.

$$\textbf{Noun}\begin{pmatrix}\textbf{person}\end{pmatrix} + \textit{ni} + \textbf{Noun}\begin{pmatrix}\textbf{object}\end{pmatrix} + \textit{o} + \begin{cases} \textit{kuremasu} \\ \textit{kudasaimasu} \\ \textit{kudasai} \end{cases}$$

Kutsuzumi o hitotsu kudasai.	"Please give me a shoe polisher."
Watakushi ni sore o kudasai.	"Please give that to me."
Mittsu kudasai.	"Please give me three."
Nani o sashiagemashoo ka?	"What shall I give to you?"
Koohii o kudasai.	"Please give me coffee."
Sore o kudasaimasu ka?	"Would you please give it to me?"
Sen'sei ga watashitachi ni hon o kudasaimashita.	"The teacher gave us books."

As explained in Lesson 13 of Volume I (see Note 13.4.8), when the second person is involved either as a giver or as a receiver, more polite expressions are employed, indicating that Japanese is a language that is second-person centered. This is called heteronomy. The polite version is also used when the third person is present.

The words in Group A are used among peer or in-group members, while the words in Group B are used for superior or out-group members, although hierarchical consideration must be given.

A	B
kuremasu	*kudasaimasu*
agemasu	*sashiagemasu*
moraimasu	*itadakimasu*

1.4.16 *Iremasu* in *Hako ni iremashoo ka?* is a transitive Verb meaning "to put [a thing] in." The place in which something is put is followed by the Relational *ni* "into." The Verb *hairimasu*, on the other hand, is an intransitive Verb. The place where someone enters is also followed by the Relational *ni*.

Watashi wa heya ni hairimashita.   "I entered the room."

Watashi wa buutsu o heya ni iremashita.   "I put the boots in the room."

1.4.17 *Nan'gai* is the combination of *nan* "which" and *-gai*, a voiced version of *-kai*, counter for "floor" or "story" as in "second floor" or "two-storied house." *-Kai* may mean either a specific floor or number of floors.

1	ikkai*	5	gokai	9	kyuukai
2	nikai	6	rokkai*	10	jikkai*; jukkai
3	san'gai	7	nanakai; shichikai	?	nan'gai
4	yon'kai	8	hakkai*; hachikai		

*The combination for these numbers is always *-kkai*.

The basement is called *chika*: Basement 2 is *chika nikai*.

Nikai de utte imasu.   "They sell it on the second floor."

San'gai e ikimashoo.   "Let's go to the third floor."

Ano tatemono wa nanakai desu.   "That building has seven floors."

Pan ya koohii wa chika ni arimasu.   "Bread and coffee are in the basement."

Similarly, *-hon* is the counter for long and slender objects like thread, pencils, cigarettes, bottles, pillars, belts, and neckties.

1	ippon*	3	san'bon	5	gohon
2	nihon	4	yon'hon	6	roppon*

7	nanahon; shichihon	9	kyuuhon
8	happon*; hachihon	10	jippon*; juppon*

? nan'bon

*The combination of these numbers is always -ppon.

Also, -hai is the counter for cupfuls, glassfuls, and spoonfuls.

1	ippai*	5	gohai	9	kyuuhai
2	nihai	6	roppai*; rokuhai	10	jippai*; juppai*
3	san'bai	7	nanahai; shichihai	?	nan'bai
4	yon'hai	8	happai*; hachihai		

*The combination for these numbers is always -ppai.

1.4.18 *Utte imasu* means ''(they) sell.'' The pattern, the TE form plus *imasu*, will be explained in Note 2.4.2.

1.4.19 *Zen'bu de* means ''for everything'' or ''for all.'' The function of the Relational *de* after a quantity Noun is often to totalize.

Zen'bu de ikura desu ka?	''How much for everything?''
Ichidaasu de sen gohyakuen desu.	''They are fifteen hundred yen for a dozen.''
Kore wa mittsu de hyakuen desu.	''These cost a hundred yen for three.''

1.4.20 *Doomo arigatoo gozaimashita* means ''Thank you very much for what you have done.'' This expression is the perfect tense form of *Doomo arigatoo gozaimasu* and is used to express someone's having done something (here, for the customer's having bought some articles).

1.4.21 Verb Classification

All Verbs are classified into the following four categories:

1. Vowel Verb: the ending of the Base*¹ form is a vowel.

2. Consonant Verb: the ending of the Base form is a consonant. (When Verbs are *naraimasu, kaimasu,* and the like, only the Pre-Nai*² form of these Verbs contains a consonant as the ending of the Base. These Verbs should still be classified as Consonant Verbs.)

3. *shimasu* ← *suru* (Irregular Verb)

4. *kimasu* ← *kuru* (Irregular Verb)

The following is a list of some forms of Vowel Verbs and Consonant Verbs:

classification	Dictionary*3 form	Base form	Stem*4 form	Pre-Nai form
Vowel Verb	taberu	tabe	tabe(masu)	tabe(nai)
	miru	mi	mi(masu)	mi(nai)
Consonant Verb	ka(w)u	ka(w)	ka(w)i(masu)	kawa(nai)
	kaku	kak	kaki(masu)	kaka(nai)
	oyogu	oyog	oyogi(masu)	oyoga(nai)
	matsu /matu/	mat /mat/	machi(masu) /mati/	mata(nai)
	kaeru	kaer	kaeri(masu)	kaera(nai)
	hanasu	hanas	hanashi(masu) /hanasi/	hanasa(nai)
	yobu	yob	yobi(masu)	yoba(nai)
	nomu	nom	nomi(masu)	noma(nai)
	shinu*5	shin	shini(masu)	shina(nai)

*1 The Base of each Verb is the part that stays constant, after deleting the inflected part.
*2 The Pre-Nai form is the form that appears before -nai.
*3 The Dictionary form is the form that appears in dictionaries.
*4 The Stem or Pre-Masu form of a Verb is the form that occurs with -masu.
*5 "die"

The student may have difficulty making a distinction between a Consonant Verb and a Vowel Verb. Some hints for the classification are given as follows:

1. If the Dictionary form of a Verb does not end in -eru or -iru, it is a Consonant Verb (except suru and kuru).
2. If a Verb ends in -eru or -iru, you cannot immediately know whether it is a Consonant Verb or a Vowel Verb until you check the TE form or the plain perfect tense form (TA form) of the Verb.
3. The Derivatives -masu and -nai can be used as criteria for determining whether a Verb is a Vowel Verb or a Consonant Verb. If the two forms before -masu and -nai are identical, it is a Vowel Verb. If the two forms are not identical, the Verb is classified as a Consonant Verb.

The TE form of each Verb is formed in one of the following manners:

1. Vowel Verb......Stem form + te

    example: age(masu) ⟶ agete
    dekake(masu), i(masu), ire(masu), kari(masu), ki(masu) "wear," mi(masu), mise(masu), sashiage(masu), tabe(masu), kure(masu)

2. Consonant Verb depends on the final syllable of the Stem form of the Verb. When the final syllable of the Stem form is:

    a)   *-i(masu)*......*tte* replaces *i*

        example: *ii(masu)* ⟶ *itte*

                   kai(masu), morai(masu), narai(masu)

    b)   *-ki(masu)*......*ite* replaces *ki*

        example: *haki(masu), itadaki(masu), kaki(masu), kiki(masu)*

         Iki(masu) is the only exception to this rule and becomes *itte*.

    c)   *-gi(masu)*......*ide* replaces *gi*

        example: *oyogi(masu)* ⟶ *oyoide*

    d)   *-chi(masu)* or *-ri(masu)*......*tte* replaces *chi* or *ri*

        example: *hairi(masu)* ⟶ *haitte*

                   kaeri(masu), machi(masu), uri(masu), yari(masu), ari(masu), furi(masu)

    e)   *-shi(masu)*......add *te* to *shi*

        example: *hanashi(masu)* ⟶ *hanashite*

                   sagashi(masu)

    f)   *-bi(masu), -mi(masu),* or *-ni(masu)*......*n'de* replaces *bi, mi,* or *ni*

        example: *nomi(masu)* ⟶ *non'de*

                   yobi(masu), yomi(masu), shini(masu)

3. Irregular Verb

    a)   *shi(masu)* ⟶ *shite* "do"

         ben'kyoo shi(masu), den'wa shi(masu), kaimono shi(masu), kekkon shi(masu), ken'butsu shi(masu), ryokoo shi(masu), shokuji shi(masu), shookai shi(masu)

    b)   *ki(masu)* ⟶ *kite* "come"

1.5   VOCABULARY

Presentation

など	-nado	......	Nd	etc.; and the like
店員	ten'in	......	N	(shop) clerk
ことば	kotoba	......	N	speech; word; language
たいへん	taihen	......	Adv.	very (formal equivalent of *totemo*)
ていねい	teinei	......	Na	polite
つぎ	tsugi	......	N	next; following
客	kyaku	......	N	customer; guest; visitor
かいわ	kaiwa	......	N	dialog; conversation

Dialog

いらっしゃいませ。	Irasshaimase.	......	(exp.)	Welcome. (see 1.4.3)
さしあげましょう	sashiagemashoo	......	V	I shall give (OO form of *sashiagemasu←sashiageru*) (polite equivalent of *agemasu*) (see 1.4.4)
女 (おんな)	on'na	......	N	female (see 1.4.5)
ブーツ	buutsu	......	N	boots
ほしい	hoshii	......	A	want; is desirous (see 1.4.6)
みせて	misete	......	V	TE form of *misemasu←miseru*—show (see 1.4.7)
ください	kudasai	......	E	please (do) (see 1.4.7)
さま	-sama	......	Nd	polite equivalent of *-san* (see 1.4.8)
サイズ	saizu	......	N	size (see 1.4.9)
はん	-han	......	Nd	half (see 1.4.9)
一万五千円	ichiman gosen'en	......	N	fifteen thousand yen (see 1.4.10)
ぐらい	-gurai	......	Nd	about; approximately (see 1.4.11)
いくら	ikura	......	Ni	how much? (see 1.4.12)
一万三千六百	ichiman san'zen roppyaku	......	N	thirteen thousand and six hundred
はいて	haite	......	V	TE form of *hakimasu←haku*—put on (shoes, pants, a skirt, socks, etc.)
みて	mite	......	E	TE form of *mimasu←miru*—try; (do and) see (see 1.4.13)
きつい	kitsui	......	A	tight
ちょうど	choodo	......	Adv.	just; exactly
いただきます	itadakimasu	......	V	get; receive (normal form of *itadaku*) (polite equivalent of *moraimasu*) (see 1.4.14)
くつずみ	kutsuzumi	......	N	shoe polisher
ください	kudasai	......	V	please give me (see 1.4.15)
はこ	hako	......	N	box; case
に	ni	......	R	into (see 1.4.16)
いれましょう	iremashoo	......	V	I shall put it in (OO form of *iremasu←ireru*)
して	shite	......	V	TE form of *shimasu←suru*—do

レインコート	rein'kooto	......	N	raincoat
なんがい	nan'gai	......	Ni	which floor? (see 1.4.17)
四かい	yon'kai	......	N	fourth floor (see 1.4.17)
うって	utte	......	V	TE form of *urimasu←uru*—sell
います	imasu	......	E	(see 1.4.18)
あとで	ato de	......	Adv.	later
いって	itte	......	V	TE form of *ikimasu←iku*—go
みましょう	mimashoo	......	E	I think I'll try (OO form of *mimasu←miru*) (see 1.4.13)
ぜんぶ	zen'bu	......	N	all; everything
で	de	......	R	totalizing (see 1.4.19)
一万三千九百	ichiman san'zen kyuuhyaku	......	N	thirteen thousand and nine hundred
どうも ありがとう ございました。	Doomo arigatoo gozaimashita.	......	(exp.)	Thank you very much for what you have done for me. (see 1.4.20)

Notes

おとこ	otoko	......	N	male (see 1.4.5)
こ	ko	......	N	child (usually preceded by a modifier, e.g., *otoko no ko* "boy")
きます	kimasu	......	V	wear (normal form of *kiru*)
ハンカチ	han'kachi	......	N	handkerchief
ネクタイ	nekutai	......	N	necktie
くつ	kutsu	......	N	shoes
円	-en	......	Nd	unit for Japanese currency (see 1.4.10)
ドル	-doru	......	Nd	dollar(s) (see 1.4.10)
セント	-sen'to	......	Nd	cent(s) (see 1.4.10)
くらい	-kurai	......	Nd	about; approximately (see 1.4.11)
すし	sushi	......	N	vinegar-treated rice, flavored primarily with sea food, usually raw
ワイシャツ	waishatsu	......	N	dress shirt
（お）さけ	(o)sake	......	N	rice wine; liquor
くださいます	kudasaimasu	......	V	give me (or us) (polite equivalent of *kuremasu*) (normal form of *kudasaru*) (see 1.4.15)
かい	-kai	......	Nd	floor; stories (see 1.4.17)
はい	-hai	......	Nd	counter for cupfuls; glassfuls (see 1.4.17)

ほん	-hon	......	Nd	counter for long and thin objects (see 1.4.17)
ちか	chika	......	N	basement (lit. underground)
ダース	-daasu	......	Nd	dozen

Drills

セーター	seetaa	......	N	pullover
かたかな	katakana	......	N	the square Japanese syllabary
ひらがな	hiragana	......	N	the cursive Japanese syllabary
かんじ	kan'ji	......	N	Chinese character

1.6   KAN'JI

As stated in Volume I, Lesson 2, there were no writing symbols in Japan before the introduction of Chinese characters, which are called *kan'ji*. After *kan'ji* were introduced, however, the Japanese started to use them to write their language.

ON and *KUN*

One way of reading Chinese characters was to attach a Chinese character to the original Japanese word, which in turn has become the pronunciation of that Chinese character. Such pronunciation is known as the *kun* reading. This reading is strictly Japanese in origin and represents the affixing of a Japanese ''word'' to the Chinese character with a roughly corresponding meaning. There are variations, however, and the current Japanese meaning is not necessarily identical to the meaning of the same character in China, nor was it necessarily identical at the time of its adoption.

The following are examples of *kun* readings:

国（くに）、口（くち）、上（うえ）、下（した）、人（ひと）、東（ひがし）、外（そと）、

木（き）、話（はな）す、食（た）べる

ON Reading

Kan'ji were also introduced and pronounced according to their original Chinese sounds. Such pronunciations were used either as phonetic symbols or as meaningful words, and are called *on* readings. *Kan'ji* were introduced into Japan over an extended time, however, and the original Chinese pronunciations differed, depending on the time and place of origin. Thus, not only the southern Chinese sounds were introduced but also the northern sounds.

Roughly speaking, in addition to the *Kan'yoo On*, or the derived *on*, there are three major *on* readings, namely *Go On* (Wu), *Kan On* (Han), and *Too On* (T'ang). For example, the character 明 is pronounced differently as follows:

Kan'yoo On .... *mei*

Go On .... *myoo*

Kan On .... *bei*

Too On .... *min*

Stroke Order

Kan'ji are written according to stroke order. The following are two basic principles of stroke order:

1. From top to bottom
   Example: 1.6.3 (most examples listed below are found in the following section, ''*Kan'ji* For This Lesson'')

2. From left to right
   Example: 1.6.8

Other principles are described below:

1. The horizontal is written first when both horizontal and vertical strokes cross.
   Example: 1.6.10
   Exceptions: 田 and 王 related *kan'ji* (such as 玉)

2. The center stroke is written first when it is flanked on left and right by 1 or 2 strokes.
   Example: 4.6.1; 5.6.9
   Exceptions: 性 and 火

3. Outside enclosure is written first.
   Example: 7.6.5
   Exceptions: 区 and 医

4. When slanting strokes cross, the one which curves away to the left comes first.
   Example: 1.6.9

5. A vertical bar which protrudes through the top or the bottom of the entire character is written last.
   Example: 2.6.9

6. A horizontal bar which protrudes through the entire left and right strokes is written last.
   Example: 4.6.2; 8.6.3
   Exception: 世

7. When a long horizontal bar and a short stroke curving away to the left cross, then the slanting stroke is to be written first.
   Example: 13.6.7

8. When a short horizontal bar and a long stroke curving away to the left cross, then the horizontal stroke is to be written first.
   Example: 13.6.6

Kan'ji For This Lesson

Each of the *kan'ji* is introduced for:

1. reading: *on* pronunciation in capitals, *kun* pronunciation in italics. Sound change is shown in brackets and *hiragana* following *kan'ji* in parentheses.
2. meaning
3. classifier and/or phonetic element (some books call these forms ''radicals''). The dictionary used in determining classifiers is Kikuya Nagasawa, *Meikai Kan'wa Jiten,* 1959, San'seidoo, Tōkyō. The classifier in parentheses is that appearing in traditional dictionaries.
4. stroke order
5. examples of usage
6. other useful notes (Origins indicated below may not be historically accurate, but are useful for identification.)

1.6.1　一　(1) ICHI, *hito*(*tsu*)　(2) one　(3) forms the classifier 一　(4) 一

(5) 一ドル、一まい、一つ、一ぱい *ippai*、一ぽん *ippon*、一かい *ikkai*

1.6.2 二 (1) NI, *futa(tsu)* (2) two (3) forms the classifier 一 (二) (4) ⊡ ⊡
(5) 二じ、二円、二つ (6) homonym 仁

1.6.3 三 (1) SAN, *mit(tsu)* (2) three (3) classifier 一
(4) ⊡ ⊡ ⊡ (5) 三にん、三さい、三つ

1.6.4 四 (1) SHI, *yon, yo-, yot(tsu)* (2) four (3) classifier 口 [enclosure]
(4) ⊡ ⊡ ⊡ ⊡ ⊡ (5) 四セント、四にん、四つ

1.6.5 五 (1) GO, *itsu(tsu)* (2) five (3) classifier 一(二) (4) ⊡ ⊡ ⊡ ⊡
(5) 五はい、五じ、五つ (6) three horizontal lines and two vertical lines;
homonym 吾、語、悟

1.6.6 六 (1) ROKU, *mut(tsu)* (2) six (3) classifier 宀(八) (4) ⊡ ⊡ ⊡ ⊡
(5) 六さい、六にん、六つ、六ぱい *roppai*、六ぽん *roppon*、六かい *rokkai*

1.6.7 七 (1) SHICHI, *nana(tsu)* (2) seven (3) classifier 一
(4) ⊡ ⊡ (5) 七まい、七はい、七つ

1.6.8 八 (1) HACHI, *yat(tsu)* (2) eight (3) forms the classifier 八 (4) ⊡ ⊡
(5) 八円、八にん、八つ、八ぱい *happai*、八ぽん *happon*、八かい *hakkai*

1.6.9 九 (1) KU, KYUU, *kokono(tsu)* (2) nine (3) classifier ノ(乙)
(4) ⊡ ⊡ (5) 九にん、九じ、九つ

1.6.10 十 (1) JUU, *too* (2) ten (3) forms the classifier 十 (4) ⊡ ⊡
(5) 十円、十ドル、十ぱい *jippai; juppai*、十ぽん *jippon; juppon*、十かい
jikkai; jukkai (6) ten fingers of two crossed hands; homonym 汁

1.6.11 百 (1) HYAKU [-BYAKU] [-PYAKU] (2) hundred (3) classifier 白
(4) ⊡ ⊡ ⊡ ⊡ ⊡ ⊡ (5) 二百、三百、八百

1.6.12 千 (1) SEN [-ZEN] (2) thousand (3) classifier 十
(4) ⊡ ⊡ ⊡ (5) 千五百、千にん、三千

1.6.13 万 (1) MAN (2) ten thousand (3) classifier 一 (4) ⊡ ⊡ ⊡
(5) 四万、九万ドル

1.7 DRILLS

1.7.1 Transformation Drill

1. はこに いれます。 ⟶ はこに いれてください。
2. ちょっと まちます。 ⟶ ちょっと まってください。

3. この　セーターを　うります。　⟶　この　セーターを　うってください。

4. デパートで　かいます。　⟶　デパートで　かってください。

5. 日本語で　はなします。　⟶　日本語で　はなしてください。

6. あなたのを　みせます。　⟶　あなたのを　みせてください。

7. あした　うちに　います。　⟶　あした　うちに　いてください。

8. ここへ　きます。　⟶　ここへ　きてください。

9. もう一ど　いいます。　⟶　もう一ど　いってください。

10. タクシーを　よびます。　⟶　タクシーを　よんでください。

11. よく　ききます。　⟶　よく　きいてください。

12. すぐ　うちへ　かえります。　⟶　すぐ　うちへ　かえってください。

13. この　ブーツを　はいてみます。　⟶　この　ブーツを　はいてみてください。

14. ワイシャツを　きてみます。　⟶　ワイシャツを　きてみてください。

15. これを　たべてみます。　⟶　これを　たべてみてください。

1.7.2　Transformation Drill

1. ちょっと　これを　はきましょう。　⟶　ちょっと　これを　はいてみましょう。

2. てんぷらを　たべました。　⟶　てんぷらを　たべてみました。

3. ブラウンさんと　いきました。　⟶　ブラウンさんと　いってみました。

4. ネクタイを　みましょう。　⟶　ネクタイを　みてみましょう。

5. あの　きっさ店に　はいりました。　⟶　あの　きっさ店に　はいってみました。

6. かたかなで　かきませんか。　⟶　かたかなで　かいてみませんか。

7. 店員を　よびましょう。　⟶　店員を　よんでみましょう。

8. うちで　さがしましょう。　⟶　うちで　さがしてみましょう。

9. あした　でんわしてください。　⟶　あした　でんわしてみてください。

10. その　本を　よんでください。　⟶　その　本を　よんでみてください。

11. 日本語で　はなしました。　⟶　日本語で　はなしてみました。

12. おさけを　一ぱい　のみました。　⟶　おさけを　一ぱい　のんでみました。

13. あっちで　およぎましょう。　⟶　あっちで　およいでみましょう。

14. もう一ど　きてください。　⟶　もう一ど　きてみてください。

1.7.3　Transformation Drill

A. 1. なにを　あげますか。　⟶　なにを　さしあげますか。

2. せんせいに　これを　あげます。　⟶　せんせいに　これを　さしあげます。

3. ごしゅじんに　おちゃを　あげました。　⟶　ごしゅじんに　おちゃを　さしあげました。

4. 五千円の　ネクタイを　　　　⟶　五千円の　ネクタイを　さしあげましょう。
　　あげましょう。

5. あとで　お客さまに　　　　　⟶　あとで　お客さまに　さしあげてください。
　　あげてください。

B. 1. わたしに　なに を　<u>くれますか</u>。　⟶　わたしに　なに を　<u>くださいますか</u>。

2. この　かたが　くれました。　　⟶　この　かたが　くださいました。

3. せんせいが　しけんの　かみを　⟶　せんせいが　しけんの　かみを
　　くれませんでした。　　　　　　　　くださいませんでした。

4. ハンカチを　くれませんか。　　⟶　ハンカチを　くださいませんか。

5. ともだちの　おとうさんが　　　⟶　ともだちの　おとうさんが　これを
　　これを　くれました。　　　　　　　くださいました。

C. 1. あなたの　おとうさんから　　　⟶　あなたの　おとうさんから　<u>いただきました</u>。
　　<u>もらいました</u>。

2. あの　女の　かたから　　　　　⟶　あの　女の　かたから　いただきませんか。
　　もらいませんか。

3. おくさんから　すこし　　　　　⟶　おくさんから　すこし　いただきました。
　　もらいました。

4. これを　もらいましょう。　　　⟶　これを　いただきましょう。

5. お客さまから　おかしの　　　　⟶　お客さまから　おかしの　はこを
　　はこを　もらいました。　　　　　　いただきました。

1.7.4　E-J Mixed Drill

1. ほしいんです。

　　tea　　　　　　　……　おちゃが　ほしいんです。

　　I　　　　　　　　……　わたしは　おちゃが　ほしいんです。

　　wanted　　　　　……　わたしは　おちゃが　ほしかったんです。

2. ほしかったんです。

　　what　　　　　　……　なにが　ほしかったんですか。

　　yesterday　　　　……　きのう　なにが　ほしかったんですか。

　　you　　　　　　　……　あなたは　きのう　なにが　ほしかったんですか。

3. ほしいです。

　　don't want　　　　……　ほしくありません。

　　not very much　　……　あまり　ほしくありません。

　　money　　　　　　……　おかねが　あまり　ほしくありません。

　　I　　　　　　　　……　わたくしは　おかねが　あまり　ほしくありません。

4. ほしくありません。

didn't want	……	ほしくありませんでした。
sweater	……	セーターが　ほしくありませんでした。
I	……	わたしは　セーターが　ほしくありませんでした。

1.7.5　Substitution Drill

A.　さけを　一ぱい　のみました。

1.	三ばい	……	さけを　三ばい　のみました。
2.	おちゃ	……	おちゃを　三ばい　のみました。
3.	六ぱい	……	おちゃを　六ぱい　のみました。
4.	二はい	……	おちゃを　二はい　のみました。
5.	みず	……	みずを　二はい　のみました。
6.	九はい	……	みずを　九はい　のみました。
7.	コーヒー	……	コーヒーを　九はい　のみました。
8.	四はい	……	コーヒーを　四はい　のみました。
9.	十ぱい	……	コーヒーを　十ぱい　のみました。
10.	なんばい	……	コーヒーを　なんばい　のみましたか。

B.　ペンが　三ぼん　ほしいんです。

1.	一ぽん	……	ペンが　一ぽん　ほしいんです。
2.	えんぴつ	……	えんぴつが　一ぽん　ほしいんです。
3.	四ほん	……	えんぴつが　四ほん　ほしいんです。
4.	六ぽん	……	えんぴつが　六ぽん　ほしいんです。
5.	十ぽん	……	えんぴつが　十ぽん　ほしいんです。
6.	五ほん	……	えんぴつが　五ほん　ほしいんです。
7.	ネクタイ	……	ネクタイが　五ほん　ほしいんです。
8.	八ぽん	……	ネクタイが　八ぽん　ほしいんです。
9.	一ダース	……	ネクタイが　一ダース　ほしいんです。
10.	なんぼん	……	ネクタイが　なんぼん　ほしいんですか。

C.　レインコートは　二かいで　うっていますか。

1.	五かい	……	レインコートは　五かいで　うっていますか。
2.	七かい	……	レインコートは　七かいで　うっていますか。
3.	一かい	……	レインコートは　一かいで　うっていますか。
4.	ちか　二かい	……	レインコートは　ちか　二かいで　うっていますか。

5. レコード　　　　……　レコードは　ちか　二かいで　うっていますか。

6. 四かい　　　　　……　レコードは　四かいで　うっていますか。

7. 三がい　　　　　……　レコードは　三がいで　うっていますか。

8. 六かい　　　　　……　レコードは　六かいで　うっていますか。

9. 八かい　　　　　……　レコードは　八かいで　うっていますか。

10. なんがい　　　　……　レコードは　なんがいで　うっていますか。

1.7.6　Response Drill

1. この　本を　かいましょうか。　　　……　ええ、（この　本を）かってください。

2. 日本語を　べんきょうしましょうか。　……　ええ、（日本語を）べんきょうしてください。

3. あした　きましょうか。　　　　　　……　ええ、（あした）きてください。

4. しんぶんを　よみましょうか。　　　……　ええ、（しんぶんを）よんでください。

5. わたなべさんを　まちましょうか。　……　ええ、（わたなべさんを）まってください。

6. すずきさんに　あげましょうか。　　……　ええ、（すずきさんに）あげてください。

7. ひらがなで　かきましょうか。　　　……　ええ、（ひらがなで）かいてください。

8. お客さまに　さしあげましょうか。　……　ええ、（お客さまに）さしあげてください。

9. デパートへ　いってみましょうか。　……　ええ、（デパートへ）いってみてください。

10. 一ぱい　のんでみましょうか。　　　……　ええ、（一ぱい）のんでみてください。

1.7.7　E-J Substitution Drill

ハンカチを　三まい　ください。

1. one　　　　　　　……　ハンカチを　一まい　ください。

2. four　　　　　　　……　ハンカチを　四まい　ください。

3. water　　　　　　……　みずを　四はい　ください。

4. one　　　　　　　……　みずを　一ぱい　ください。

5. three　　　　　　……　みずを　三ばい　ください。

6. dictionary　　　　……　じしょを　三さつ　ください。

7. four　　　　　　　……　じしょを　四さつ　ください。

8. one　　　　　　　……　じしょを　一さつ　ください。

9. candy　　　　　　……　おかしを　一つ　ください。

10. four　　　　　　　……　おかしを　四つ　ください。

11. necktie　　　　　……　ネクタイを　四ほん　ください。

12. one　　　　　　　……　ネクタイを　一ぽん　ください。

1.7.8 E-J Response Drill

1. サイズは　いくつですか。

   twenty-six and a half　　　　　……　26はんです。

2. ハンカチは　はこに　いれましようか。

   please do so　　　　　　　　……　そう　してください。

3. これは　女の　このですか。

   no, boy's　　　　　　　　　　……　いいえ、おとこの　この　です。

4. いくらですか。

   ten thousand yen for everything　……　ぜんぶで　一万円です。

5. どなたに　あげましようか。

   please give it to me　　　　　　……　わたくしに　ください。

6. いくらの　ネクタイが　ほしいんですか。

   three thousand yen　　　　　　……　三千円のが　ほしいんです。

7. なにを　さしあげましようか。

   please give me three pencils　　……　えんぴつを　三ぼん　ください。

8. なにを　たべてみましたか。

   tempura　　　　　　　　　　　……　てんぷらを　たべてみました。

9. どなたが　くださいましたか。

   that lady　　　　　　　　　　　……　あの　女の　かたが　くださいました。

10. どなたから　いただきますか。

    Mr. Watanabe's wife　　　　　……　わたなべさんの　おくさんから
    　　　　　　　　　　　　　　　　　いただきます。

1.7.9 Expansion Drill

1. 一万円のを　ください。　　　　……　一万円ぐらいのを　ください。
2. おさけを　二はい　のみました。　……　おさけを　二はいぐらい　のみました。
3. いくらの　ネクタイを　かいましたか。……　いくらぐらいの　ネクタイを
   　　　　　　　　　　　　　　　　　　　　かいましたか。
4. 三千円のを　みせてください。　……　三千円ぐらいのを　みせてください。
5. サイズは　たぶん　25です。　　……　サイズは　たぶん　25ぐらいです。
6. はこが　二十　あります。　　　……　はこが　二十ぐらい　あります。
7. ぜんぶで　いくらでしたか。　　……　ぜんぶで　いくらぐらいでしたか。
8. あの　たてものは　なんがいですか。……　あの　たてものは　なんがいぐらいですか。

1.8   EXERCISES

1.8.1   Transform the following into the polite imperative …てください：

    1.　まいにち　日本語を　べんきょうします。

    2.　その　レインコートを　みせます。

    3.　あした　うちへ　きます。

    4.　ひらがなで　かきます。

    5.　セーターを　はこに　いれます。

    6.　あとで　さがします。

    7.　この　かんじを　よみます。

    8.　もうすこし　まちます。

    9.　ぜんぶ　あげます。

  10.　この　ワイシャツを　きてみます。

1.8.2   Express the following in Japanese:

    1.　Let's go to the third floor of that building and see.

    2.　I don't want coffee.

    3.　I think I will try these shoes on.

    4.　I will have [receive] tea later.

    5.　I want handkerchiefs and a lady's sweater.

    6.　I want three pencils.

    7.　The size is just right.

    8.　This sweater is a little (too) tight.

    9.　Shall I put these in a box?

  10.　Please read [the book on] page 10.

1.8.3   Combine each of the left-hand Predicate Modifiers with an appropriate Verb:

    1.　お客さまが　わたしに　おかしを

    2.　あなたに　これを

    3.　ちちは　せんせいから　てがみを　　　　　　くださいました。

    4.　わたしは　スミスさんから　プレゼントを　　さしあげました。

    5.　せんせいは　わたしたちに　ほんを　　　　　いただきました。

    6.　わたしは　お客さまに　コーヒーを

1.8.4 What would you say when you ask the hearer:

1. to give you a dollar and fifty cents?
2. to write it two more times?
3. to show you a sweater for about 4,500 yen?
4. to telephone you tomorrow morning?
5. to try speaking Japanese?
6. to try eating *sushi*?

1.8.5 Answer the following questions in Japanese:

1. これは　いくらですか。

   670 yen

2. いくらの　セーターが　ほしいんですか。

   for about 3,500 yen

3. ぜんぶで　いくらですか。

   $425.25

4. そこに　おかねが　いくら　ありますか。

   $83.10

1.8.6 Write the following in *kan'ji*:

1. せん　きゅうひゃく　ろくじゅう　しち
2. はっぴゃく　よんじゅう　いち
3. ごせん　さんびゃく　じゅう　に
4. よんまん　ななせん　ろくじゅう　はち

1.8.7 Write in *katakana*:

1. saizu
2. rein'kooto
3. doru
4. nekutai
5. daasu
6. han'kachi
7. waishatsu
8. sen'to
9. seetaa
10. buutsu

1.8.8 Which expression would a Japanese salesclerk at a department store use? Choose one out of each of the following:

1. Arigatoo gozaimasu.

   Arigatoo.

   Doomo.

   Sumimasen.

2. Irasshai.

   Irasshaimase.

3. Nani ga hoshii n desu ka?

   Nani o sashiagemashoo ka?

4. Kore wa doo desu ka?

   Kore wa ikaga desu ka?

5. Okyakusama no saizu wa ikutsu desu ka?

   Anata no saizu wa ikutsu desu ka?

1.8.9 Which one of the following three expressions is the most polite form?

1. Sore o kuremasen ka?

2. Sore o kudasai.

3. Sore o kudasaimasen ka?

1.8.10 When you tell your teacher that you received something from his wife, which of the following would be the most appropriate?

1. Okusama kara moraimashita.

2. Okusama kara itadakimashita.

1.8.11 Your teacher asks ''Shall I give it to you?'' Which of the following would he be more likely to use?

1. Agemashoo ka?

2. Sashiagemashoo ka?

1.8.12 Express the following in Japanese:

1. What do you want to have?

2. I want to have . . .

1.8.13 In what cases is the use of *anata* considered impolite?

1.8.14 By making the customer in the dialog of this lesson male rather than female, make the appropriate changes in the conversation forms employed by the customer.

1.9   SITUATIONAL AND APPLICATION CONVERSATION

Using the patterns and expressions of this lesson, carry on the following conversations:

1.9.1 A salesclerk greets a customer.

The customer wants to buy a raincoat for himself.

The customer tries on one and finds it is a little small.

The clerk recommends a larger one.

The customer decides to buy it.

The clerk tells its price.

1.9.2   A customer asks for two handkerchiefs and a tie.

A salesclerk shows them to the customer and the customer decides to buy them.

The customer asks the total price. Then the customer asks where he can find shoes.

1.9.3   Clerk: Irasshaimase. Nani o sashiagemashoo ka?

Customer: Shatsu ga hoshii n desu ga.

Clerk: Okyakusama no desu ka?

Customer: Iie, kono ko no desu.

Clerk: Okosama no desu ka? Okosama no wa nikai desu ga.

1.9.4   Customer: Kore wa doo?

Clerk: Sore wa chotto ookii desu nee. Kore wa ikaga deshoo ka?

Customer: Soo ne. Sore o moraimashoo.

Clerk: Hai, arigatoo gozaimasu.

LESSON 2
大学生

2.1 PRESENTATION

一郎は　大学の　四年生[1]です。　きょういく学を　べんきょうしています[2]。

日本の　大学生は　なつ休みに[3]　よく　アルバイトを　します[4]。　大学の　なつ休みは　七月[5]と　八月です。　一郎は　七月に　デパートで　はたらきました[4]。

2.2 DIALOG

林　「一郎くん[6]　しばらく。」

一郎　「あ、　せんぱい[6]　しばらくです。」

林　「きみ[6]は　まだ　学生でしょう？」

一郎　「ええ、　四年です。　林さんは　いま　なんの　しごとを　していますか。」

林　「かいしゃに　つとめています[4]。」

一郎　「そうですか。　かいしゃへは　車で　かよって[7]いますか。」

林　「いいえ、　車は　もっていません[8]。　バスで　かよっています。　一郎くん、　あしたの　ばん　うちへ　きませんか。　ゆっくり　はなしましょう。」

一郎　「ええ、　ぜひ　うかがいます[9]。」

林　「ぼくの　ところは　しっていますね[10]。　いまも　まえの　アパートに　すんでいます[11]。」

一郎　「ええと…。　しぶやでした[12]ね。　なん時に[3]　うかがいましょうか。」

林　「五時はんは　どうですか。」

一郎　「ええ、　いいです。」

林　「では、　五時はんごろ[13]　まっていますよ[14]。」

一郎　「ええ。　たのしみに　しています[15]。」

大学生 だいがくせい	一郎 いちろう	大学 だいがく	四年生 よねんせい	きょういく学 きょういくがく
日本 にほん	なつ休み なつやすみ	七月 しちがつ	八月 はちがつ	車 くるま　なん時 なんじ
五時はん ごじはん				

2.3 PATTERN SENTENCES

2.3.1

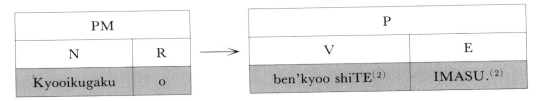

2.3.2

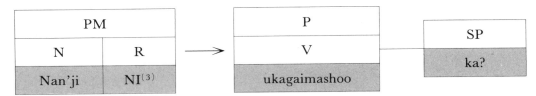

2.4 NOTES

2.4.1 *Yonen'sei* means "fourth-year student," or "senior in college." *Yonen'sei* can be shortened to *yonen*. *-Nen* is a counter for "year." *Nan'nen* may mean either "how many years?" or "what year?"

1	ichinen	5	gonen	9	kyuunen; kunen
2	ninen	6	rokunen	10	juunen
3	san'nen	7	shichinen; nananen	?	nan'nen
4	yonen	8	hachinen		

Boku wa Tookyoo Daigaku no yonen'sei desu.	"I am a senior at Tōkyō University."
Ima nan'nen'sei desu ka?	"What year are you in?"
Sen kyuuhyaku hachijuu ichinen ni Nihon e kimashita.	"He came to Japan in 1981."
Nan'nen Nihon ni imasu* ka?	"How many years have you been in Japan?"

*As explained in Note 3.4.2, Volume I, the imperfect tense form indicates that an action or a status has not been completed. Since the person is still in Japan, *imasu* is used. When he is not in Japan any more, *imashita* will be used.

The College System

Normally, the Japanese semester system at a college is as follows: first semester begins in April and ends in October, second semester begins in November and ends in March, which is the end of the school year.

Entrance into a Japanese university is considerably more difficult for the Japanese student than entrance into an American university is for the American student. In Japan, acceptance is based on scores achieved in a special entrance examination, and not necessarily on the student's past academic record. Competition for entrance into the better schools is extremely fierce. The student who fails to achieve acceptance into the school of his choice may then take the examination for another school, or wait and take the examination the next year. For this reason, students in Japan may often be *roonin*, that is a student without a school and preparing for admission. A by-product of this examination system is that once accepted into a school, a student need not study as hard; if he should fail a test he merely pays a fee and retakes the test.

The lives of Japanese students are mainly occupied with study and financial concerns as a majority of them must work part-time in order to meet the costs of their education, food and living expenses, as well as recreational activities.

Another strong point of contrast between American and Japanese universities is their respective alumni associations, or *doosookai*. Such organizations are much stronger in terms of power and influence in Japan than they are in the United States. In many respects they resemble American fraternities or clubs, or secret societies. Business may be conducted with a particular company only because its president graduated from the same university as the head or president of the other firm. Jobs are often given on the same basis. Such practices serve to increase the intensity of competition for enrollment in the better universities, and it is clear that one's choice of schools will affect not only the quality of one's education, but one's future career, since that is the time and place where valuable contacts are made.

Students have to apply for jobs with companies before they graduate. This is done through their school office. Each of the various companies sets up testing times. The large numbers of students desiring a job upon graduation must first pass or excel in these rather strict exams.

Thus, the best time for seeking job opportunities is upon graduating from college, because once out of school the graduate is no longer considered as a potential candidate.

2.4.2   *Ben'kyoo shite imasu* means "is studying," and is the combination of the TE form of the Verb *ben'kyoo shimasu ← ben'kyoo suru* and the imperfect tense form of the Predicate Extender *imasu ← iru*. The Extender *imasu* conjugates as the Verb *imasu* does.

$$(\textbf{Predicate Modifier}) + \textbf{Verb}(\textit{-te}) + \begin{cases} \textit{imasu} \\ \textit{imasen} \\ \textit{imashita} \\ \textit{imasen deshita} \\ \textit{imashoo} \\ \textit{ite kudasai} \end{cases}$$

This combination conveys either one of the following two meanings. The first meaning of the two should be studied thoroughly in this lesson. Only some of the second will be introduced at this time. Verbs such as *arimasu* and *imasu* do not have this combination however.

1.   An action is continuing or going on: "someone is doing such and such." Here is a list of *-te imasu* combinations that carry this connotation:

agemasu	⟶ agete imasu	"is giving"
arubaito shimasu	⟶ arubaito shite imasu	"is doing a side-job"
ben'kyoo shimasu	⟶ ben'kyoo shite imasu	"is studying"
den'wa shimasu	⟶ den'wa shite imasu	"is making a phone call"
furimasu	⟶ futte imasu	"is raining" ["snowing," etc.]
hanashimasu	⟶ hanashite imasu	"is talking"

hatarakimasu	⟶ hataraite imasu	"is working"
iimasu	⟶ itte imasu	"is saying"
iremasu	⟶ irete imasu	"is putting in"
kaimasu	⟶ katte imasu	"is buying"
kaimono shimasu	⟶ kaimono shite imasu	"is shopping"
kakimasu	⟶ kaite imasu	"is writing"
kayoimasu	⟶ kayotte imasu	"is commuting"
ken'butsu shimasu	⟶ ken'butsu shite imasu	"is sightseeing"
kikimasu	⟶ kiite imasu	"is listening"
kimasu	⟶ kite imasu	"is wearing"
machimasu	⟶ matte imasu	"is waiting"
mimasu	⟶ mite imasu	"is watching"
misemasu	⟶ misete imasu	"is showing"
naraimasu	⟶ naratte imasu	"is learning"
nomimasu	⟶ non'de imasu	"is drinking"
oyogimasu	⟶ oyoide imasu	"is swimming"
ryokoo shimasu	⟶ ryokoo shite imasu	"is traveling"
sagashimasu	⟶ sagashite imasu	"is looking for"
shigoto shimasu	⟶ shigoto shite imasu	"is working"
shimasu	⟶ shite imasu	"is doing"
sumimasu	⟶ sun'de imasu	"is living"
tabemasu	⟶ tabete imasu	"is eating"
tsutomemasu	⟶ tsutomete imasu	"is employed"
urimasu	⟶ utte imasu	"is selling" "sell"
yobimasu	⟶ yon'de imasu	"is calling"
yomimasu	⟶ yon'de imasu	"is reading"

2. The result of an action exists or the state resulting from an action exists: "something has been done, and the result of that action exists," or "something is done." This usage is common among Verbs which are not continuative.

hairimashita	⟶ haitte imasu	"is in"
hakimashita*	⟶ haite imasu	"wear" "is wearing"
karimashita	⟶ karite imasu	"have borrowed"
kekkon shimashita	⟶ kekkon shite imasu	"is married"
kikimashita*	⟶ kiite imasu	"have heard"
kimashita*	⟶ kite imasu	"wear"
mochimashita	⟶ motte imasu	"have"
shirimashita	⟶ shitte imasu	"know"

*Some Verbs such as *hakimasu* above may indicate both "an action is going on" and "the result of an action" under certain limited circumstances. Verbs such as *kikimasu* and *kimasu*, however, are used in either one of the two meanings rather regularly. The context usually makes it clear which meaning is called for.

Chichi wa ima gin'koo ni tsutomete imasu.	"My father is working for the bank now."
Boku wa ima arubaito o shite imasen.	"I'm not working (I don't have a part-time job) now."

Yamamoto san wa mae Kyooto ni sun'de imashita.	"Mr. Yamamoto was living (used to live) in Kyōto before."
Eki de matte ite kudasai.	"Please be waiting at the station."
Kinoo no kuji goro nani o shite imashita ka?	"What were you doing around nine o'clock yesterday?"
Terebi o mite imashita.	"I was watching television."
Hayashi san wa kekkon shite imasu ka?	"Is Mr. Hayashi married?"

2.4.3 The Relational *ni* as in *natsuyasumi ni* or *nan'ji ni* is used to indicate a specific point of time. *Ni* corresponds to "at" as in "at three o'clock," "in" as in "in 1979," or "on" as in "on Monday." The Relational *wa* or *mo* may follow *ni*, forming multiple Relationals.

yasumi		"on vacation" "on a holiday"
haruyasumi		"during the spring vacation"
natsuyasumi		"during the summer vacation"
akiyasumi		"during the fall vacation"
fuyuyasumi		"during the winter vacation"
kugatsu	*ni*	"in September"
nan'gatsu		"in what month?"
yoji		"at four o'clock"
nan'ji		"at what time?"
sen kyuuhyaku nanajuu kunen		"in 1979"
nan'nen		"in what year?"

Natsuyasumi ni nani o shimasu ka?	"What are you going to do during the summer vacation?"
Nan'nen ni sono kaisha ni hairimashita ka?	"In what year did you join that company?"
Kuji ni mo kite kudasai.	"Please come at nine o'clock also."

Note the difference between time Nouns that require the time Relational *ni* and those which are used alone, such as *kinoo*, *rainen*, and so on.

2.4.4 *Arubaito (o) shimasu* means "(a student's) work (for money)," or "do a side-job." *Arubaito* comes from *arbeit*, a German word for "work." *Hatarakimasu* is a word for "work" or "labor." While *tsutomete imasu* means "is employed (by an organization) and work (for it)," *hataraite imasu* merely means "is working" and often "is working physically." *Hatarakimasu* cannot be used in the meaning of "study."

| Depaato de hatarakimashita. | "I worked at a department store." |
| Haha wa ima niwa de hataraite imasu. | "My mother is now working in the garden." |

The Verb *tsutomemasu* means "is employed," "serve in," or "work for (an organization)." The organization such as *depaato* "department store," *gin'koo* "bank" is always followed by *ni*.

Anata wa doko ni tsutomete imasu ka?	"What (organization, company, bank) are you working for?"
Tookyoo Gin'koo ni tsutomete imasu.	"I am working for the Bank of Tōkyō."

2.4.5 *Shichigatsu* means "July," and *hachigatsu* "August." The name of months is the combination of a numeral and the dependent Noun *-gatsu*.

ichigatsu	一月	"January"	gogatsu	五月	"May"	kugatsu	九月 "September"
nigatsu	二月	"February"	rokugatsu	六月	"June"	juugatsu	十月 "October"
san'gatsu	三月	"March"	shichigatsu	七月	"July"	juuichigatsu	十一月 "November"
shigatsu	四月	"April"	hachigatsu	八月	"August"	juunigatsu	十二月 "December"

Nan'gatsu is the word for "what month?"

Nan'gatsu ni ryokoo shimashoo ka?	"In what month shall we take a trip?"
Kon'getsu wa nan'gatsu desu ka?	"What month is this month?"
Kon'getsu wa kugatsu desu yo.	"This month is September."
Sen kyuuhyaku hachijuu ichinen（no）shigatsu ni Yooroppa e ikimashita.	"I went to Europe in April 1981."

The days of the month:

1	tsuitachi	一日	11	juu ichinichi	十一日	21	nijuu ichinichi	二十一日
2	futsuka	二日	12	juu ninichi	十二日	22	nijuu ninichi	二十二日
3	mikka	三日	13	juu san'nichi	十三日	23	nijuu san'nichi	二十三日
4	yokka	四日	14	juu yokka	十四日	24	nijuu yokka	二十四日
5	itsuka	五日	15	juu gonichi	十五日	25	nijuu gonichi	二十五日
6	muika	六日	16	juu rokunichi	十六日	26	nijuu rokunichi	二十六日
7	nanoka	七日	17	juu shichinichi	十七日	27	nijuu shichinichi	二十七日
8	yooka	八日	18	juu hachinichi	十八日	28	nijuu hachinichi	二十八日
9	kokonoka	九日	19	juu kunichi	十九日	29	nijuu kunichi	二十九日
10	tooka	十日	20	hatsuka	二十日	30	san'juunichi	三十日
						31	san'juu ichinichi	三十一日

The counter for "day" is *-nichi*. Except *tsuitachi*, the above words may be used also for the number of days; *futsuka* can be "the second day of the month," or "two days," *mikka* "the third day," or "three days." *Ichinichi* is used for "a day." *Nan'nichi* can be "what day of the month?" or "how many days?" The *kan'ji* for *tsuitachi, futsuka, mikka,* and the like, are all written 一、二、三、 and so forth, plus 日、 regardless of their pronunciation. To tell the date, the year comes first, and then comes the month, and the day comes last. If the day of the week occurs, it comes after the day.

一九七七年十二月二十四日

八月五日木<ruby>曜<rt>よう</rt></ruby>日

Anata no tan'joobi wa itsu desu ka?	"What day is your birthday?"
Juuichigatsu juu san'nichi desu.	"It's November 13."
Kon'getsu no itsuka ni shiken ga arimasu.	"We'll have an exam on the fifth of this month."
Nan'nichi gurai Kyooto ni imasu ka?	"About how many days are you staying in Kyōto?"

2.4.6 Suffixes

The choice of one of the suffixes, *-kun*, *-san*, or *-sama*, exhibits the relationship between speaker and listener. *-Kun* is addressed to a close male friend, or to someone of a lower social status. *-San*, the most common of the three, would be chosen for an acquaintance one does not know well, a peer, or one's superior. *-Sama* is very formal and generally occurs more often with titles or other words of address rather than with proper names.

Kimi and *Anata*

Kimi is a less polite version of *anata*, which means "you." *Kimi* is mainly used by men toward either peers, inferiors, or intimate friends. *Anata* is used with a more formal tone and tends to be used more frequently by women than by men. When a woman uses *anata* to another woman, it sounds quite natural for any informal occasion, but it is not so when a woman uses this word to a man.

However, the Japanese do not use the word "you," in quite the same way as the English equivalent implies, due to the indirectness of address which they favor. The problem which arises concerning second-person address, then, may be handled in one of two ways: If it is understood that the second person is in fact being referred to, "you" may be omitted entirely. Such omissions of what is understood in the context of the conversation is peculiar to the Japanese language. On the other hand, the name, title, or other words including particular grammatical structures may often be employed to indicate reference to the second person, thereby avoiding the direct confrontation of second-person address.

It is interesting to note that Japanese contains numerous forms of second-person address (referents), and yet such forms have an extremely low frequency of use due to the tendency toward indirectness. The hierarchy of Japanese society necessitates the great number of such forms, yet Japanese indirectness and vagueness precludes their extensive use.

Sen'pai

By comparing the different forms employed by Ichirō and Hayashi, one can deduce the relationship existing between them. For example, Hayashi uses such terms as *Ichiroo kun*, *shibaraku*, and *kimi wa*. On the other hand, Ichirō uses the more polite forms of *sen'pai*, *shibaraku desu*, and *ukagaimasu*. These clearly indicate that Hayashi is Ichirō's superior. *Sen'pai* usually means an "older graduate from one's alma mater." It may also mean a senior, a superior or an elder outside of the alumni relationship. *Sen'pai* normally expects *koohai* (a junior) to show respect and deference.

Address: First Names

Toward an inferior member of the same family or its equivalent (e.g., children, young unmarried women), toward *koohai*, and toward an intimate friend, the first name may be used. At elementary school, first names may be used by teachers; however, at the secondary school level first names are almost never used and one is addressed by his last name, which is more formal. On the other hand, a private tutor in the house may call the child by his first name. Childhood friends may also call each other by first names.

The following chart indicates some rough differences between Japanese and American customs, although they only show some general trends.

talking to	culture	A	J
S	F	+	−
S	L	+	+
P	F	+	+
P	L	−	+
I	F	+	+
I	L	East coast + / West coast −	+

S = superior; P = peer; I = inferior
F = first name; L = last name
A = American; J = Japanese
+ = used; − = not used

2.4.7 *Kayoimasu* means "living out," or "come to work [from elsewhere]."

Uchi kara kayotte imasu.	"I go to work from home."
Kuruma de kayoimasu.	"I come to work by car."
Nan de kayotte imasu ka?	"How do you go to work?"

2.4.8 *Motte imasen* means "do not have," and is a transitive Verb. Note that the Verb *mochimasu ← motsu* means an action, "hold," "own," and so on. Therefore, the state of "have" would be expressed by *motte imasu,* the result of *motsu* "hold."

Kuruma o motte imasen.	"I don't have a car."
Anata wa okane o motte imasu ka?	"Do you have some money?"
Iie, motte imasen.	"No, I don't."

2.4.9 *Ukagaimasu* here is a polite equivalent of "visit (someone else's house)," or "go (to someone else's house)." *Ukagaimasu* is a motion Verb and is used like *ikimasu.*

| Zehi (anata no uchi e) ukagaimasu. | "I will visit (your house) by all means." |
| Kinoo sen'sei no tokoro e ukagaimashita. | "I went to the teacher's (place) yesterday." |

2.4.10 *Shitte imasu* means "[I] know it." The Verb *shirimasu←shiru* is somewhat different in usage from other Verbs. *Shirimasu* means "get to know," or "come to know." Therefore, the state "someone does not know it" is expressed by the negative imperfect *shirimasen* "you haven't come to know," but never *shitte imasen*. Note that the negative expressions of "know" are formed differently from the affirmative expressions.

shitte imasu	"know"
shirimasen	"do not know"
shitte imashita	"knew"
shirimasen deshita	"did not know"
Okusan wa nihon'go o shitte imasu ka?	"Does your wife know the Japanese language?"
Hai, sukoshi shitte imasu.	"Yes, she knows a little."
Iie, shirimasen.	"No, she doesn't know it."

2.4.11 The expression "is living in (a place)" is expressed as ~ *ni sun'de imasu*. The Verb *sumimasu* "live" does not need any specific action except to be in that place, and it represents something inactive like *imasu* and *arimasu*. Consequently, a place where one lives is never followed by *de* but by *ni*. (See Note 5.4.2, Volume I.)

Doko ni sun'de imasu ka?	"Where are you living?"
Ima Oosaka ni sun'de imasu.	"I am now living in Ōsaka."
Kyonen wa apaato ni sun'de imashita.	"I was living in an apartment last year."

2.4.12 *Shibuya deshita ne?* may mean not only "It WAS Shibuya, wasn't it?" but it can also mean "It IS Shibuya, isn't it?" The reason this Japanese sentence has the Predicate in the perfect tense is that it carries the connotation of "that WAS my understanding or memory."

Anata wa daigakusei deshita ne?	(1) "You were a college student, weren't you?"
	(2) "According to my understanding, you are a college student. Am I right?"
Sumisu san wa amerikajin deshita ne?	(1) "Mr. Smith, you were an American, weren't you?"
	(2) "Mr. Smith, you are an American, aren't you?"

2.4.13 *-Goro* is a dependent Noun that occurs immediately after a time expression, and means an approximate point of time or "about." The time Relational *ni* that has been introduced in Note 2.4.3 may be replaced by *-goro*, or both *-goro* and *ni* may occur. In the latter case, *-goro* always precedes *ni*.

Nan'ji ni kimashita ka?	"What time did you come?"
Niji goro (ni) kimashita.	"I came here about two o'clock."

Do not confuse the *-goro* ''approximate point of time'' with *-gurai* and *-kurai* ''approximate amount or number.''

Ohiru goro uchi e kaerimasu.	''I am going home about noon.''
Gohyakunin gurai imashita.	''There were about five hundred persons.''

2.4.14 *Ne(e)* and *Yo*

Ending a statement with *ne(e)* or *yo* is somewhat less polite than ending simply with the Predicate. For example, *Shibaraku deshita* is more formal than *Shibaraku deshita nee*. When the speaker wishes to convey a more personal tone toward the listener, the speaker tends to add *ne(e)* or *yo*. Hayashi's use of *yo* in *matte imasu yo* is a good example of this situation.

Japanese levels and styles of speech are so explicit that in many Japanese novels the relationship between two persons and shifts or changes in that relationship, whether temporary or long-term, need not be described by the writer. The reader can immediately recognize such shifts or changes through the different usages employed by the characters in conversation. Similarly, without any subject or reference to the speaker, readers can readily identify the sex, age, and status of the speaker just from the forms he or she uses in the context of the situation.

2.4.15 *Tanoshimi ni shite imasu* is an idiomatic expression meaning ''anticipating with pleasure.''

Kodomo wa tan'joobi o tanoshimi ni shite imasu.	''My child is looking forward to [celebrating] his birthday.''

2.5 VOCABULARY

Presentation

大学生	daigakusei	......	N	college student
一郎	Ichiroo	......	N	boy's first name
四年生	yonen'sei	......	N	a senior student; fourth-year student (see 2.4.1)
きょういく学	kyooiku-gaku	......	N	study of education; pedagogy
べんきょうして	ben'kyoo shite	......	V	TE form of *ben'kyoo shimasu*←*ben'kyoo suru*—study (see 2.4.2)
います	imasu	......	E	normal form of *iru* (see 2.4.2)
に	ni	......	R	at; in; on (time Relational) (see 2.4.3)
アルバイト	arubaito	......	N	(student's) work (for money) (see 2.4.4)
アルバイト（を）します	arubaito (o) shimasu	......	V	do a side-job (see 2.4.4)
七月	shichigatsu	......	N	July (see 2.4.5)
八月	hachigatsu	......	N	August
はたらきました	hatarakimashita	......	V	worked; labored (TA form of *hatarakimasu*←*hataraku*) (see 2.4.4)

Dialog

林 (はやし)	Hayashi	......	N	family name
せんぱい	sen'pai	......	N	senior member at school, etc.
まだ	mada	......	Adv.	still
四年	yonen	......	N	fourth year (see 2.4.1)
しごと	shigoto	......	N	work; job
しごと（を）します	shigoto (o) shimasu	......	V	work; do one's job (see 2.4.4)
かいしゃ	kaisha	......	N	company
つとめて	tsutomete	......	V	TE form of *tsutomemasu*←*tsutomeru*—is employed; work (see 2.4.4)
かよって	kayotte	......	V	TE form of *kayoimasu*←*kayou*—commute; go to and from (see 2.4.7)
もって	motte	......	V	TE form of *mochimasu*←*motsu*—have; hold; possess (see 2.4.2 and 2.4.8)
ゆっくり	yukkuri	......	Adv.	leisurely; slowly; take one's time
ぜひ	zehi	......	Adv.	by all means; without fail
うかがいます	ukagaimasu	......	V	visit; go (to someone's house) (normal form of *ukagau*) (see 2.4.9)
ところ	tokoro	......	N	place; address
しって	shitte	......	V	TE form of *shirimasu*←*shiru*—know (see 2.4.10)
アパート	apaato	......	N	apartment
すんで	sun'de	......	V	TE form of *sumimasu*←*sumu*—live (see 2.4.11)
ええと	eeto	......	SI	let me see; well
しぶや	Shibuya	......	N	a district of Tōkyō
五時はん	gojihan	......	N	five-thirty
ごろ	-goro	......	Nd	about (time); approximately (see 2.4.13)
まって	matte	......	V	TE form of *machimasu*←*matsu*—wait
たのしみにしています。	Tanoshimi ni shite imasu.	......	(exp.)	Looking forward to (〜ing). (see 2.4.15)

Notes

年生	-nen'sei	......	Nd	(〜th) year student (see 2.4.1)
けっこん	kekkon	......	N	marriage
けっこん（を）します	kekkon (o) shimasu	......	V	marry (normal form of *kekkon (o) suru*)

一月	ichigatsu	......	N	January (see 2.4.5)
二月	nigatsu	......	N	February
三月	san'gatsu	......	N	March
四月	shigatsu	......	N	April
五月	gogatsu	......	N	May
六月	rokugatsu	......	N	June
九月	kugatsu	......	N	September
十月	juugatsu	......	N	October
十一月	juuichigatsu	......	N	November
十二月	juunigatsu	......	N	December
なん月	nan'gatsu	......	Ni	what month
一日	tsuitachi	......	N	the first day of the month (see 2.4.5)
二日	futsuka	......	N	the second day of the month; two days
三日	mikka	......	N	the third day of the month; three days
四日	yokka	......	N	the fourth day of the month; four days
五日	itsuka	......	N	the fifth day of the month; five days
六日	muika	......	N	the sixth day of the month; six days
七日	nanoka	......	N	the seventh day of the month; seven days
八日	yooka	......	N	the eighth day of the month; eight days
九日	kokonoka	......	N	the ninth day of the month; nine days
十日	tooka	......	N	the tenth day of the month; ten days
十四日	juu yokka	......	N	the fourteenth day of the month; fourteen days
二十日	hatsuka	......	N	the twentieth day of the month; twenty days
二十四日	nijuu yokka	......	N	the twenty-fourth day of the month; twenty-four days
日	-nichi	......	Nd	day (see 2.4.5)
一日	ichinichi	......	N	a day
なん日	nan'nichi	......	N	what day of the month?; how many days?
たんじょう日	tan'joobi	......	N	birthday
こうはい	koohai	......	N	junior member of school, etc.

Drills

大阪	Oosaka	......	N	the biggest city in western Japan

2.6 KAN'JI

2.6.1 大 (1) DAI (2) big; large; great (3) forms the classifier 大
(4) 一 ナ 大 (5) 大すき、大きらい
(6) a person stretching his arms and legs. See 5.6.9

2.6.2 学 (1) GAKU (2) learning; study (3) classifier 子
(4) ⺍ ⺍ ⺍ ⺍ 龸 学 学 学 (5) 大学、メリーランド大学、ハワイ大学

2.6.3 生 (1) SEI (2) beings; life; birth; person (3) classifier ⺧ (生)
(4) ノ ⺧ 牛 牛 生 (5) 先生、学生
(6) homonym 性、姓、牲、星; shape of a growing plant

2.6.4 年 (1) NEN (2) year (3) classifier ⺧ (干) (4) ノ ⺧ ⺧ 乍 年 年
(5) 一年、四年生、なん年、まい年 (6) a good harvest once a year

2.6.5 日 (1) NICHI [NI for NIHON] (2) sun; day; daytime
(3) forms the classifier 日 (4) 丨 冂 日 日
(5) まい日、日本 (6) shape of the sun

2.6.6 本 (1) HON [-BON, -PON] (2) origin; book (3) classifier 木
(4) 一 十 才 木 本 (5) 日本、本屋、日本語の本、一本、二本、三本
(6) the short horizontal line at the bottom indicates the bottom of the root of a tree. See 4.6.9

2.6.7 休 (1) *yasu(mi)* (2) rest; leave (3) classifier 亻 (4) 亻 休
(5) 冬休み、学校を休む、あっちで休みましょう
(6) a man resting beside a tree

2.6.8 月 (1) -GATSU (2) counter for name of month; moon—*tsuki*
(3) forms the classifier 月 (4) ノ 冂 月 月 (5) 七月、九月、十二月、
なん月 (6) a picture of the crescent moon

2.6.9 車 (1) *kuruma* (2) automobile (3) forms the classifier 車
(4) 一 ⺨ 冎 百 亘 亘 車 (5) 車にのります、車で行きましょう
(6) the shape of a cart

2.6.10 時 (1) JI (2) time; o'clock (3) classifier 日
(4) 丨 冂 日 日 旪 旪 昖 昿 時 時 (5) 九時、十一時、なん時
(6) homonym 寺、持、侍

2.7   DRILLS

2.7.1   Transformation Drill

1. きょういく学を　<u>べんきょうします</u>。　⟶　<u>いま</u>　きょういく学を
  　　　　　　　　　　　　　　　　　　　　　　　　　　<u>べんきょうしています</u>。

2. ちちは　ぎんこうに　つとめます。　⟶　いま　ちちは　ぎんこうに　つとめています。

3. がいこくじんが　日本語で　　　　⟶　いま　がいこくじんが　日本語で
  　　はなします。　　　　　　　　　　　　　はなしています。

4. うちで　おんがくを　ききます。　⟶　いま　うちで　おんがくを　きいています。

5. 大阪を　けんぶつします。　　　　⟶　いま　大阪を　けんぶつしています。

6. ともだちが　えきで　まちます。　⟶　いま　ともだちが　えきで　まっています。

7. 日本語の　本を　さがします。　　⟶　いま　日本語の　本を　さがしています。

8. ゆっくり　しんぶんを　よみます。　⟶　いま　ゆっくり　しんぶんを　よんでいます。

9. ドイツ語を　ならいます。　　　　⟶　いま　ドイツ語を　ならっています。

10. おとこの　こが　にわで　　　　　⟶　いま　おとこの　こが　にわで
  　　はたらきます。　　　　　　　　　　　　はたらいています。

11. でんしゃで　かよいます。　　　　⟶　いま　でんしゃで　かよっています。

12. あには　アメリカに　すみます。　⟶　いま　あには　アメリカに　すんでいます。

13. あの　みせで　うります。　　　　⟶　いま　あの　みせで　うっています。

14. わたしは　アルバイトを　します。　⟶　いま　わたしは　アルバイトを　しています。

15. あめが　ふります。　　　　　　　⟶　いま　あめが　ふっています。

2.7.2   Response Drill

1. いま　日本語を　ならっていますか。

  　はい　　　　　　　……　はい、いま　日本語を　ならっています。

  　いいえ　　　　　　……　いいえ、いま　日本語を　ならっていません。

2. きょ年　ハワイに　すんでいましたか。

  　はい　　　　　　　……　はい、きょ年　ハワイに　すんでいました。

  　いいえ　　　　　　……　いいえ、きょ年　ハワイに　すんでいませんでした。

3. いま　かいしゃで　はたらいていますか。

  　はい　　　　　　　……　はい、いま　かいしゃで　はたらいています。

  　いいえ　　　　　　……　いいえ、いま　かいしゃで　はたらいていません。

4. ごしゅじんは　ぎんこうに　つとめていますか。

  　はい　　　　　　　……　はい、しゅじんは　ぎんこうに　つとめています。

  　いいえ　　　　　　……　いいえ、しゅじんは　ぎんこうに　つとめていません。

5. かんじを　しっていますか。

   はい   …… はい、かんじを　しっています。

   いいえ   …… いいえ、かんじを　しりません。

6. レインコートを　もっていますか。

   はい   …… はい、レインコートを　もっています。

   いいえ   …… いいえ、レインコートを　もっていません。

7. あなたは　けっこんしていますか。

   はい   …… はい、けっこんしています。

   いいえ   …… いいえ、けっこんしていません。

2.7.3　Substitution Drill

一九八一年に　ここへ　きましたか。

1. 九月   …… 九月に　ここへ　きましたか。
2. 一九八一年九月 …… 一九八一年九月に　ここへ　きましたか。
3. なん年   …… なん年に　ここへ　きましたか。
4. なん月   …… なん月に　ここへ　きましたか。
5. 四月   …… 四月に　ここへ　きましたか。
6. 十一月ごろ   …… 十一月ごろ(に)　ここへ　きましたか。
7. 二時   …… 二時に　ここへ　きましたか。
8. 二時はん   …… 二時はんに　ここへ　きましたか。
9. 四時はんごろ …… 四時はんごろ(に)　ここへ　きましたか。
10. なん時   …… なん時に　ここへ　きましたか。
11. 休み   …… 休みに　ここへ　きましたか。
12. ふゆ休み   …… ふゆ休みに　ここへ　きましたか。

2.7.4　E-J Transformation Drill

1. じむしょで　はたらきます。

   I'm working   …… じむしょで　はたらいています。

   I'm not working   …… じむしょで　はたらいていません。

   I was working   …… じむしょで　はたらいていました。

   please be working …… じむしょで　はたらいていてください。

2. しります。

   do you know   …… しっていますか。

   I don't know   …… しりません。

I knew	……	しっていました。
I didn't know	……	しりませんでした。

3. 大阪（おおさか）に　すみます。

I'm not living	……	大阪（おおさか）に　すんでいません。
I was living	……	大阪（おおさか）に　すんでいました。
are you living	……	大阪（おおさか）に　すんでいますか。
I was not living	……	大阪（おおさか）に　すんでいませんでした。

4. 車を　もちます。

I have	……	車を　もっています。
I don't have	……	車を　もっていません。
did you have	……	車を　もっていましたか。
I didn't have	……	車を　もっていませんでした。

5. デパートで　うります。

(they) were selling	……	デパートで　うっていました。
(they) are not selling	……	デパートで　うっていません。
(they) are selling	……	デパートで　うっています。
(they) were not selling	……	デパートで　うっていませんでした。

6. ともだちの　ところで　まちます。

I will be waiting	……	ともだちの　ところで　まっています。
I was waiting	……	ともだちの　ところで　まっていました。
please be waiting	……	ともだちの　ところで　まっていてください。

2.7.5　E-J Response Drill

1. なん年に　日本へ　きましたか。

   in 1979　　　　　　　　　　　　……　一九七九年に　きました。

2. いつ　アルバイトを　しましたか。

   during the spring vacation　　　　……　はる休みに　しました。

3. いつ　きょうとへ　いきますか。

   next month　　　　　　　　　　　……　らいげつ　いきます。

4. なん時に　うちへ　きますか。

   about six o'clock　　　　　　　　　……　六時ごろ（に）　きます。

5. いつ　ぎんこうで　はたらいていましたか。

   last year　　　　　　　　　　　　……　きょ年　はたらいていました。

6. なん月に　りょこうしますか。

    in October   ……　十月に　りょこうします。

7. いつ　先生の　ところへ　うかがいましょうか。

    tomorrow   ……　あした　うかがいましょう。

8. なつ休みは　いつですか。

    June, July, and August   ……　六月と　七月と　八月です。

2.7.6　E-J Response Drill

1. いま　なんの　しごとを　していますか。

    working for a bank   ……　ぎんこうに　つとめています。

2. あなたは　まえ　どこに　すんでいましたか。

    Shinjuku   ……　しんじゅくに　すんでいました。

3. きのうの　よる　七時ごろ　なにを　していましたか。

    watching TV   ……　テレビを　みていました。

4. きょ年の　ふゆ　なにを　べんきょうしていましたか。

    studying Japanese at the University ……　大阪大学で　日本語を
      of Ōsaka   べんきょうしていました。

5. あなたは　まだ　学生ですか。

    yes, a junior at the University of Hawaii……　はい、ハワイ大学の　三年（生）です。

6. やまださんの　ところを　しっていますか。

    no   ……　いいえ、しりません。

7. 車を　もっていますか。

    no   ……　いいえ、もっていません。

8. いま　なにを　していますか。

    reading a newspaper   ……　しんぶんを　よんでいます。

9. 林さんは　けっこんしていますか。

    no   ……　いいえ、けっこんしていません。

10. くだものは　どこで　うっていますか。

    basement   ……　ちかで　うっています。

2.7.7　Transformation Drill

1. ここで　<u>はたらいています</u>。　　　⟶　ここで　<u>はたらいていてください</u>。

2. えきで　まっています。　　　⟶　えきで　まっていてください。

3. コーヒーを　のんでいます。　　　⟶　コーヒーを　のんでいてください。

4. テープを　きいています。　　　——→　テープを　きいていてください。

5. この　本を　よんでいます。　　　——→　この　本を　よんでいてください。

6. うちで　べんきょうしています。　——→　うちで　べんきょうしていてください。

7. テレビを　みています。　　　　　——→　テレビを　みていてください。

8. あの　レストランで　たべています。　——→　あの　レストランで　たべていてください。

2.8　EXERCISES

2.8.1　Insert an appropriate form in each blank according to the English equivalent:

1. けさ　なにを（　　　　　　　　　　）。

   What were you doing this morning?

2. にわで（　　　　　　　　　　）。

   He is not working in the garden.

3. だれを（　　　　　　　　　　）。

   Whom are you waiting for?

4. テープを（　　　　　　　　　　）。

   I was not listening to the tape.

5. 二かいで（　　　　　　　　　　）。

   They are selling it on the second floor.

6. やまださんは　おちゃを（　　　　　　　　　　）。

   Mr. Yamada is not drinking tea.

7. なに語を（　　　　　　　　　　）。

   What language do you know?

8. ほっかいどうでは　いま　ゆきが（　　　　　　　　　　）。

   It is snowing in Hokkaidō now.

2.8.2　Answer the following questions in Japanese:

1. あなたは　大学生ですね。

2. どこの　学生ですか。

3. いま　なん年生ですか。

4. ドイツ語を　しっていますか。

5. いま　なに語を　ならっていますか。

6. なつ休みは　なん月ですか。

7. きょ年の　なつ休みに　アルバイトを　しましたか。

8. いま　どこに　すんでいますか。

9. かぞくと　いっしょに　すんでいますか。

10. 車を　もっていますか。

11. 学校へ　なんで　かよっていますか。

2.8.3　Insert an appropriate Relational in the blank, if necessary:

1. 一九七五年（　　）　日本（　　）　きました。

2. 休み（　　）　どこ（　　）　はたらきましたか。

3. かずおさんが　四時（　　）　えき（　　）　まっていますよ。

4. きょ年（　　）　どこ（　　）　すんでいましたか。

5. けさ（　　）　七時はん（　　）　大阪（　　）　でかけました。

6. なん月（　　）　くに（　　）　かえりますか。

7. 五月（　　）　六月（　　）　学校（　　）　アルバイト（　　）　しました。

8. まい日（　　）　コーヒー（　　）　ほしいですねえ。

9. いま（　　）　どこ（　　）　つとめていますか。

10. 林さん（　　）　なん（　　）　かよっていますか。

2.8.4　Write the underlined *hiragana* in *kan'ji*:

1. わたしは　<u>くがつ</u>に　<u>だいがく</u>へ　いきます。

2. 一郎は　<u>だいがくせい</u>です。いま、<u>よねんせい</u>です。

3. いつ　<u>にほん</u>へ　きましたか。<u>きょねん</u>の　<u>じゅうにがつ</u>に　きました。

4. <u>くるま</u>で　かよっていました。

5. <u>ごじ</u>ごろ　いきましょう。

6. しごとは　あした　<u>やすみ</u>です。

2.8.5　Answer the following questions on the basis of the Presentation and the Dialog:

1. だれが　一郎くんの　せんぱいですか。

2. 林さんは　いま　なにを　していますか。

3. 一郎くんは　まえ　林さんの　アパートに　いきましたか。

4. 一郎くんは　いつ　林さんの　ところへ　いきますか。

5. 一郎くんは　どこで　アルバイトを　しましたか。

6. 一郎くんは　大学で　なにを　べんきょうしていますか。

2.8.6　Explain under what situation(s) a male student can use the following expressions:

1. kimi
2. anata

2.8.7 Fill in the blanks with *shitte imasu* or *gozon'ji desu*.

1. Gakusei: Sen'sei, watakushi no tokoro o _____ ka?
   Sen'sei: Ee, _____ .

2. Gakusei: Boku no tokoro o _____ ka?
   Gakusei: Ee, _____ .

3. Sen'sei: Watashi no tokoro o _____ ka?
   Gakusei: Hai, _____ .

2.8.8 Instead of *anata* in such sentences as *Anata no tokoro wa doko desu ka?* various substitutions are possible. What substitutions for *anata* may be used in the following cases?

1. a student talking to Professor Tanaka
2. Professor Tanaka's male friend talking to Professor Tanaka
3. Tanaka's child talking to Mr. Tanaka
4. Professor Tanaka's acquaintance talking to Professor Tanaka
5. a salesclerk talking to a customer

2.8.9 Describe the relationship between the people in the following dialogs, giving the age, sex, and so forth when possible.

1. B: Hayashi san, watashi no jimusho e kite kudasai.
   H: Hai, sugu ukagaimasu. Ohanashi wa nan deshoo ka?
   B: Jimusho de iimasu.

2. Watanabe: A, min'na shibaraku.
   Toshio: Watanabe san, shibaraku desu.
   A: Shibaraku nee.
   B: Watanabe san, shibaraku desu.
   C: Doo? Gen'ki?

2.8.10 Match the situations in the left-hand column with the appropriate form of address presented in the column on the right. Remember that there may be more than one possibility for each situation.

1. man to close male friend	a. Hayashi sama
2. woman to male friend	b. Hayashi san
3. man to close female friend	c. Hayashi kun
4. male teacher to college student	d. Hayashi
5. student to teacher	e. Ichiroo sama
6. employer to employee	f. Ichiroo san
7. man to wife	g. Ichiroo kun
8. male teacher to grammar school student	h. Ichiroo
9. tutor to child	i. Kanai
10. man to older brother's friend	j. Okusama
11. child to parents' friend	k. Okusan
12. man to acquaintance	l. Michiko sama
13. employer to employee's wife	m. Michiko san
14. man to close friend's wife	n. Michiko
15. female teacher to student	o. Sen'sei
16. woman to close female friend	

2.9 SITUATIONAL AND APPLICATION CONVERSATION

2.9.1 Two friends meet in the street.

They haven't seen each other for a long time.

They ask each other what they are doing and where they are living.

One is a sophomore at college and one is a bank employee.

The student had a part-time job at a restaurant during the winter vacation.

The bank employee invites the student for dinner at his home.

They set a time and day for dinner.

2.9.2 Same as 2.9.1. Change the two friends' profession or job, living place, and the like.

2.9.3 Free conversation on the topic of college life.

2.9.4 Talk about your school or office, annual schedule, vacations, Christmas holidays, and so forth.

2.9.5 The following three entries contain words or expressions you have not studied yet (indicated by *). Try to identify the speaker's relationship.

1. A: Hayashi sen'sei (wa) irasshaimasu* ka? (knocking on the door)

   B: Ohairi nasai.*

   A: Hai, shitsurei shimasu.

   B: Kinoo kimi no repooto* o yomimashita. Totemo yokatta desu yo.

   A: Arigatoo gozaimasu.

   B: Kimi wa eigo mo joozu desu nee.

   A: Iie, mada . . .

2. Male: Kojima san, kyoo no kurasu wa nan desu ka?

   Female: Kyoo wa eigo dake* desu. Ishii san wa eigo ga joozu desu kara*, ii desu nee.

   Male: Iie, boku mo eigo wa mada heta desu yo.

3. A: Katoo kun, kimi wa kyoo isogashii desu ka?

   Katō: Iie, amari isogashiku arimasen.

   A: Jaa, watashi no heya e chotto kite kudasai. Kimi no repooto o yomimashita yo.

   Katō: Soo desu ka? Sugu ukagaimasu. Sen'sei no heya wa Kimura sen'sei no tonari* deshoo ka?

   A: Ee, soo desu. Jaa, matte imasu yo.

   Katō: Hai.

LESSON 3
REVIEW AND APPLICATION

3.1　　**PREDICATES**

3.1.1　　**TE form ＋ *imasu***

a.　　"is doing"

ひるごはんを　たべます	⟶	ひるごはんを　たべて
テレビを　みます	⟶	テレビを　みて
ぎんこうに　つとめます	⟶	ぎんこうに　つとめて
くつを　うります	⟶	くつを　うって
あめが　ふります	⟶	あめが　ふって
セーターを　かいます	⟶	セーターを　かって
かいしゃに　かよいます	⟶	かいしゃに　かよって
かんじを　ならいます	⟶	かんじを　ならって
ちかで　まちます	⟶	ちかで　まって
日本語を　かきます	⟶	日本語を　かいて
東京で　はたらきます	⟶	東京で　はたらいて
まだ　ききます	⟶	まだ　きいて
ちゅうごく語で　はなします	⟶	ちゅうごく語で　はなして
ざっしなど　さがします	⟶	ざっしなど　さがして
コーヒーを　のみます	⟶	コーヒーを　のんで
しんぶんを　よみます	⟶	しんぶんを　よんで
しぶやに　すみます	⟶	しぶやに　すんで
ちちが　よびます	⟶	ちちが　よんで
プールで　およぎます	⟶	プールで　およいで
大阪で　アルバイトします	⟶	大阪で　アルバイトして
車で　りょこうします	⟶	車で　りょこうして

います
いません
いました
いませんでした

b.　　"is done"　"has done"

林さんは　けっこんします	⟶	林さんは　けっこんして
その　店に　はいります	⟶	その　店に　はいって
本を　かります	⟶	本を　かりて
ワイシャツを　きます	⟶	ワイシャツを　きて
ブーツを　はきます	⟶	ブーツを　はいて
カメラを　もちます	⟶	カメラを　もって

います
いません
いました
いませんでした

3.1.2 TE form + *kudasai* "please do"

うちへ　かえります	⟶	うちへ　かえって
あとで　きます	⟶	あとで　きて
ぜひ　いきます	⟶	ぜひ　いって
六時に　でかけます	⟶	六時に　でかけて
お客さまに　いいます	⟶	お客さまに　いって
ゆっくり　はなします	⟶	ゆっくり　はなして
としょかんに　つとめます	⟶	としょかんに　つとめて
ぜんぶ　かいます	⟶	ぜんぶ　かって
その　カメラを　うります	⟶	その　カメラを　うって
くつを　はきます	⟶	くつを　はいて
学生を　よびます	⟶	学生を　よんで
これを　もちます	⟶	これを　もって
ネクタイを　みせます	⟶	ネクタイを　みせて
二かいで　まちます	⟶	二かいで　まって
四月に　はたらきます	⟶	四月に　はたらいて
しょくどうで　アルバイトします	⟶	しょくどうで　アルバイトして
すぐ　でんわします	⟶	すぐ　でんわして
一ど　たべます	⟶	一ど　たべて
せんぱいに　あげます	⟶	せんぱいに　あげて
はこに　いれます	⟶	はこに　いれて

ください

3.1.3 TE form + *mimasu* "do and find out"

ちかへ　いきます	⟶	ちかへ　いって
この　レインコートを　きます	⟶	この　レインコートを　きて
日本の　カメラを　かいます	⟶	日本の　カメラを　かって
てんぷらを　たべます	⟶	てんぷらを　たべて
テープを　ききます	⟶	テープを　きいて
その　ざっしを　よみます	⟶	その　ざっしを　よんで
一郎くんを　まちます	⟶	一郎くんを　まって
おさけを　のみます	⟶	おさけを　のんで
しょくどうで　はたらきます	⟶	しょくどうで　はたらいて
なつ休みに　アルバイトします	⟶	なつ休みに　アルバイトして

みます
みません
みました
みませんでした
みましょう
みてください

ゆっくり　はなします	⟶	ゆっくり　はなして
ドイツ語で　いいます	⟶	ドイツ語で　いって
この　くつを　はきます	⟶	この　くつを　はいて

3.2　OTHERS

3.2.1　Time Relational *ni*

一九八二年		日本へ　きました
一九七六年四月		がいこくへ　いきました
一月		
二月		
三月		りょこうを　しましょう
・		いってみたいです
・		
・		
十一月		
十二月	に	
一日	ごろ(に)	
二日		
三日		でかけました
・		うちへ　きてください
・		
・		
三十一日		
十一時		としょかんで　べんきょうしていました
九時はん		きてください
なつ休み	に	ハワイへ　いきます
休み		アルバイトを　したいです

↓

なん年		....	
なん月	に	....	
なん日	ごろ(に)	....	か
なん時			
いつ	(ごろ)	....	

3.2.2 Relational of totalizing *de*

		で		です でした
（これは）	ぜんぶ		一万三千八百円	
（この　おかしは）	五つ		六百円	
（えんぴつは）	一ダース		三百円	
（この　ハンカチは）	三まい		五ドルぐらい	
（その　アルバムは）	二さつ		一ドル二十セント	
（ビールは）	六本		千八百円ぐらい	
（コーヒーは）	二はい		六百円	

↓

		で	いくら（ぐらい）	です でした	か
（……………）	…………	で	いくら（ぐらい）	です でした	か

3.2.3 Giving and Receiving (polite)

a. ''giving to someone else''

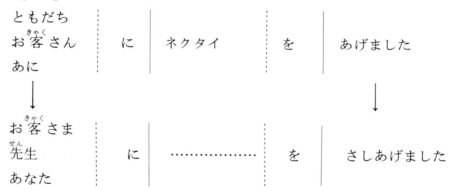

ともだち お客さん あに	に	ネクタイ	を	あげました

↓

お客さま 先生 あなた	に	………………	を	さしあげました

b. ''giving to me or to us''

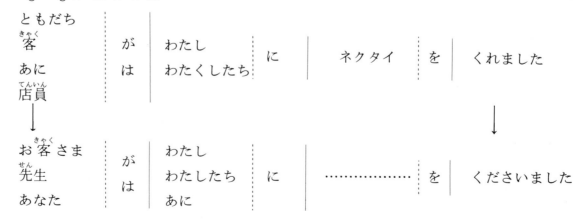

ともだち 客 あに 店員	が は	わたし わたくしたち	に	ネクタイ	を	くれました

↓

お客さま 先生 あなた	が は	わたし わたしたち あに	に	………………	を	くださいました

c.　"receiving"

わたし / わたしたち	は	ともだち / 客（きゃく） / あに / 店員（てんいん）	から	ネクタイ	を	もらいました
わたし / わたしたち	は	お客さま（きゃく） / 先生（せん）	から	…………	を	いただきました

3.2.4　Numbers

a.

主	数	（ぐらい）	動
いま	七百五十円（えん）		もっています
おかねが	十五ドル八セント		ありました
	一本		くれます
みずを	二本		くださいました
ビールを	三本		ください
えんぴつを	・		あげましょうか
ネクタイを	・		さしあげます
おさけを	・		もらいたいんです
	十本	（ぐらい）	いただきたいんです
	一ぱい		
コーヒーが	二はい		
ビールが	三ばい		ほしいです
ごはんが	・		あります
ぎゅうにゅうが	・		
おちゃが	・		
	十ぱい		
日本語の　本を	十さつ		かいました
かみを	二十まい		もらいました
			くださいました
	いくら		
	なん円（えん）		
…………	なんドル	（ぐらい）	…………　か
…………	なんセント		

b.

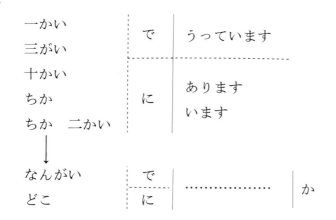

3.3　REVIEW DRILLS (Lessons 1 and 2)

3.3.1　Transformation Drill (want to try 〜ing)

1. おすしを　たべます。　　　　　　　⟶　　おすしを　たべてみたいです。
2. おさけを　のみます。　　　　　　　⟶　　おさけを　のんでみたいです。
3. にっこうへ　いきます。　　　　　　⟶　　にっこうへ　いってみたいです。
4. この　ブーツを　はきます。　　　　⟶　　この　ブーツを　はいてみたいです。
5. きものを　きます。　　　　　　　　⟶　　きものを　きてみたいです。
6. ぎんざで　しょくじを　します。　　⟶　　ぎんざで　しょくじを　してみたいです。
7. 日本語の　しんぶんを　よみます。　⟶　　日本語の　しんぶんを　よんでみたいです。
8. としょかんで　はたらきます。　　　⟶　　としょかんで　はたらいてみたいです。

3.3.2　Response Drill

1. はこに　いれましょうか。　　　　……　はい、はこに　いれてください。
2. ビールを　かいましょうか。　　　……　はい、ビールを　かってください。
3. ひらがなで　かきましょうか。　　……　はい、ひらがなで　かいてください。
4. アルバムを　みせましょうか。　　……　はい、アルバムを　みせてください。
5. もう一ど　いいましょうか。　　　……　はい、もう一ど　いってください。
6. えい語で　はなしましょうか。　　……　はい、えい語で　はなしてください。
7. 山田さんを　よびましょうか。　　……　はい、山田さんを　よんでください。

8.　そう　してみましょうか。　　　……　はい、そう　してみてください。

9.　もうすこし　まっていましょうか。　……　はい、もうすこし　まっていてください。

10.　あの　カメラを　うりましょうか。　……　はい、あの　カメラを　うってください。

3.3.3　Relational Checking Drill (with or without the time Relational *ni*)

<u>なつ休みに</u>　いきましたか。

1.　いつ　　　　　　　　　　……　いつ　いきましたか。

2.　なん月　　　　　　　　　……　なん月に　いきましたか。

3.　九月　　　　　　　　　　……　九月に　いきましたか。

4.　きのう　　　　　　　　　……　きのう　いきましたか。

5.　なん年　　　　　　　　　……　なん年に　いきましたか。

6.　なん時　　　　　　　　　……　なん時に　いきましたか。

7.　一九八十年　　　　　　　……　一九八十年に　いきましたか。

8.　きょ年　　　　　　　　　……　きょ年　いきましたか。

9.　しゅうまつ　　　　　　　……　しゅうまつに　いきましたか。

10.　けさ　　　　　　　　　　……　けさ　いきましたか。

11.　まい日　　　　　　　　　……　まい日　いきましたか。

12.　七時はん　　　　　　　　……　七時はんに　いきましたか。

13.　四月　　　　　　　　　　……　四月に　いきましたか。

14.　まいしゅう　　　　　　　……　まいしゅう　いきましたか。

15.　まい年　　　　　　　　　……　まい年　いきましたか。

3.3.4　Relational Checking Drill (*ni* or *de*)

1.　デパート、はたらきました　　　　　……　デパート<u>で</u>　はたらきました。

2.　アパート、すんでいます　　　　　　……　アパート<u>に</u>　すんでいます。

3.　ぎんこう、つとめています　　　　　……　ぎんこうに　つとめています。

4.　うち、しごとを　しています　　　　……　うちで　しごとを　しています。

5.　どこ、すんでいましたか　　　　　　……　どこに　すんでいましたか。

6.　かいしゃ、まっていてください　　　……　かいしゃで　まっていてください。

7.　どの　かいしゃ、つとめていますか　……　どの　かいしゃに　つとめていますか。

8.　ゆうびんきょく、アルバイトしたいです　……　ゆうびんきょくで　アルバイトしたいです。

3.3.5　Substitution and Transformation Drill
（Substitute the underlined parts with the given words, making necessary changes.）

1.　A:　　ブーツを　はこに　いれましょうか。

　　　B:　　ええ、いれてください。

　　　　　1.　もう一ど　いう　　　　　　2.　タクシーを　よぶ
　　　　　3.　もうすこし　まっている　　4.　くつを　はいてみる
　　　　　5.　ハンカチを　みせる　　　　6.　この　レインコートを　きてみる

2.　店員:　　いらっしゃいませ。なにを　さしあげましょうか。

　　　客:　　ブーツが　ほしいんですが。

　　　店員:　　これは　いかがでしょうか。二万円ですが。

　　　客:　　ちょうど　いいです。これを　いただきます。

　　　　　1.　くつ、五千円　　　　　　2.　セーター、八千円
　　　　　3.　レインコート、三万円　　4.　ワイシャツ、六千円
　　　　　5.　ティーシャツ*、三千円

　　　　　　* "T-shirt"

3.　客:　　あの　レインコートを　みせてください。

　　　店員:　　これですね。どうぞ　きてみてください。

　　　客:　　ちょっと　きついですね。

　　　店員:　　では、これを　きてみてください。

　　　客:　　ちょうど　いいです。　これを　ください。

　　　　　1.　くつ、はきます　　　　　2.　コート、きます
　　　　　3.　ブーツ、はきます　　　　4.　ジャケット*¹、きます
　　　　　5.　ガウン*²、きます　　　　6.　サンダル*³、はきます

　　　　　　*¹"jacket"　*²"gown"　*³"sandals"

4.　A:　かずこさんを　しっていますか。

　　　B:　いいえ、どの　かたですか。

　　　A:　あそこで　おんなの　ひとが　はなしていますね。

　　　　　あの　ひとです。しょうかいしましょうか。

　　　B:　ぜひ　しょうかいしてください。

　　　　　1.　本を　よんでいます　　　2.　コーヒーを　のんでいます
　　　　　3.　しごとを　しています　　4.　およいでいます
　　　　　5.　はたらいています　　　　6.　テレビを　みています

5. C: あなたは　きっぷを　もっていますか。

   D: いいえ、もっていません。なんがいで　うっていますか。

   C: 二かいで　うっていますよ。いってみましょうか。

   D: ええ、いっしょに　きてください。

     1.　カード*¹、三がい   2.　フイルム*²、一かい

     3.　おかし、ちか   4.　きっぷ、五かい

     *¹"card"   *²"film"

3.4　REVIEW EXERCISES

3.4.1　Choose the appropriate word for each of the following sentences.

  1. わたしは　先生に　えんぴつを　（くださいました、さしあげました）。

  2. お客さまが　わたしたちに　おかしを　（くださいました、さしあげました、いただきました）。

  3. いもうとは　お客さまに　おちゃを　（くださいました、さしあげました、いただきました）。

  4. おとうとは　ぼくに　おかしを　（くださいました、くれました）。

  5. わたくしは　先生から　本を　（くださいました、さしあげました、いただきました）。

  6. わたしは　お客さまに　おつり*を　（さしあげました、あげました）。

  7. 先生は　おとうとに　えんぴつを　（さしあげました、くださいました、いただきました）。

  8. ぼくは　せんぱいに　てがみを　（さしあげました、あげました）。

  9. わたくしは　先生に　おてがみを　（さしあげました、あげました）。

 10. 先生は　みのるくんから　かみを　（いただきました、もらいました）。

    * "change"

3.4.2　Combine each of the words in the A, B, and C groups:

A	B	C
1. ハンカチが	二十五はん	うっています。
2. みずを	いくつ	ありますか。
3. えんぴつを	九百円	もっていますか。
4. おかねが	三がいで	ください。
5. はこが	二まい	です。
6. ざっしなどは	なん本	あります。
7. ネクタイを	一ぱい	

8. ごはんを

9. くつの　サイズは

3.4.3　Fill in the blanks with Relationals:

1. この　ネクタイ（　　）二本（　　）五千円^{えん}です。やすいでしょう。

2. わたし（　　）コーヒー（　　）ほしいんです。

3. どこ（　　）すんでいますか。

4. ごしゅじんは　どこ（　　）つとめていますか。

5. ごしゅじんは　どこ（　　）はたらいていますか。

6. こどもたちは　まい日　バス（　　）かよっています。

7. 四時はん（　　）うかがいます。

8. スミスさんは　大学（　　）一年です。

9. あめが　ふっていますね。シャツ（　　）セーターなどを　うち（　　）いれて
　　ください。

10. ぜんぶ（　　）いくらですか。

3.4.4　Insert *-goro* or *-gurai* in each blank:

1. いま　なん時（　　）ですか。

2. まい日　コーヒーを　三ばい（　　）のみます。

3. 日本では　六月（　　）に　あめが　よく　ふります。

4. あしたの　ひる（　　）きてください。

5. いくら（　　）の　セーターが　ほしいんですか。

6. ペンを　なん本（　　）もっていますか。

7. いつ（　　）京都^{きょうと}へ　いきたいですか。

8. 千ドル（　　）のを　かいたかったんです。

3.4.5　What would you say:

1. when you want to see a certain tie in the showcase?

2. when you see your customer coming into your shop?

3. when you suggest nine-thirty (for a meeting time)?

4. when you are looking forward to doing something?

5. when you meet one of your old friends after a long absence?

6. when you know something?

7. when you don't know?

3.5 AURAL COMPREHENSION

3.5.1　店員　「いらっしゃいませ。」

　　　　　客　「ボールペン*を　ください。」

　　　　店員　「はい、こちらです。どれを　さしあげましょうか。」

　　　　　客　「その　ボールペンは　いくらですか。」

　　　　店員　「これですか。これは　百五十円ですが。」

　　　　　客　「じゃあ、それを　三本　ください。」

　　　　店員　「ありがとうございます。四百五十円　いただきます。」

　　　　　　　　　　* ''ball-point pen''

3.5.2　男の客　「すみません。」

　　　　　店員　「はい、いらっしゃいませ。」

　　　　男の客　「ハンカチは　どこですか。」

　　　　　店員　「男の　かたのですか。男の　かたの　ハンカチは　三がいで　うって
　　　　　　　　　います。」

　　　　男の客　「どうも。」

3.5.3　A　「はじめまして。」

　　　　B　「どうぞ　よろしく。」

　　　　A　「あなたは　大学生ですか。」

　　　　B　「はい、そうです。三年です。」

　　　　A　「どちらの？」

　　　　B　「京都大学です。」

　　　　A　「なにを　べんきょうしていますか。」

　　　　B　「きょういく学を　べんきょうしています。」

　　　　A　「ごかぞくと　いっしょに　すんでいますか。」

　　　　B　「いいえ、京都の　アパートに　すんでいます。」

3.5.4　青木　「山田さんじゃありませんか。」

　　　　山田　「やあ、しばらく。おげんきですか。」

　　　　青木　「ええ、おかげさまで。おしごとは　いそがしいですか。」

　　　　山田　「ええ、とても。」

　　　　青木　「しぶやの　デパートに　つとめていましたね。」

　　　　山田　「ええ。でも、いまは　しんじゅくの　デパートに　つとめています。青木さん、
　　　　　　　うちは　かんだでしたね。」

青木　「いいえ、いまは　しぶやの　アパートに　すんでいます。」
山田　「そうですか。ごけっこんは？」
青木　「まだ　けっこんしていません。こんど　うちへ　きてください。」
山田　「ええ、ぜひ　うかがいます。」

3.5.5　　ぼくは　大学の　二年生です。いま　学校で　フランス語や　ちゅうごく語を
べんきょうしています。とても　むずかしいです。きょ年の　はる休みは
アルバイトを　しませんでしたが、ことしの　はるは　デパートで　はたらきます。
なつに　ほっかいどうへ　いきたいんです。それで、おかねが　ほしいんです。
　　ちちは　先月　アメリカへ　いきました。ちちは　ぼくたちに　アメリカの
おみやげ*¹を　くれました。ぼくは　ちちから　ジャズ*²の　レコードを
もらいました。
　　*¹''souvenir''　*²''jazz''

3.5.6　　わたしと　かないは　きのう　はじめて*¹　日本レストランへ　いきました。日本人
や　アメリカ人などが　おおぜい　しょくじを　していました。わたしは　はじめて
おすしを　たべてみましたが、とても　おいしかったです。ぜんぶで　十　たべました。
かないは　てんぷらを　たべました。　レストランでは　日本の　女の　ひとが
おおぜい　はたらいていました。　その　ひとたちは　みんな　きもの*²を　きて
いました。
*¹ ''for the first time''　　　*² ''Japanese clothes''

3.5.7　　スミスさんは　きのう　ぎんざの　デパートへ　いきました。　デパートの　二かい
では　おとこの　ひとの　レインコートや　セーターなどを　うっていました。
スミスさんは　レインコートが　ほしかったんです。それで、くろい*　レインコートを
きてみました。　ちょうど　よかったです。　スミスさんは　それを　かいました。
それから　ネクタイも　一本　かいました。その　ネクタイは　フランスのでしたが、
一万円でした。
* ''black''

LESSON 4
で ん わ[1]

4.1   PRESENTATION

　井上さんは　水曜日[2]の　クラスを　とっています。　よし子さんも　その　クラスに　くる[3]
はず[3]でしたが、　きませんでした。　それで、　つぎの　日に、　井上さんは　よし子さんの
うちに[4]　でんわを　かけました。　よし子さんの　うちの　でんわばんごう[5]は
０３－４５１－５７９２[5]（ゼロさんの　よんごういちの　ごうななきゅうにい）　です。

4.2   DIALOG

井　上　「もしもし[6]、　森さんの　おたく[7]ですか。」

よし子　「はい、　そうです[8]。」

井　上　「よし子さん[9]、　いらっしゃいます[10]か。」

よし子　「わたくしですが…[11]。」

井　上　「あ、　ぼく[9]、　井上です。」

よし子　「あら[12]、　こんにちは。」

井　上　「きのう　あい[13]たかったんですけど、　学校に[14]　きませんでした[15]ね。」

よし子　「ええ[15]、　行きませんでした[15]。　ちょっと　気分が　わるかったんですが、　もう
　　　　　だいじょうぶです。　あしたは　休まない[16][3]つもり[17]です。」

井　上　「そうですか。　じつは[18]、　土曜日に　いもうとを　かぶき[19]に　つれて行く[20]つもりです
　　　　　けど、　よし子さんも　見たくありませんか[21]。」

よし子　「ええ、　見たいです。　ぜひ　つれて行ってください。」

井　上　「じゃあ、　ごご[22]　四時十五分[23]ごろ　かぶきざで　あいましょう。」

よし子　「わかりました[24]。　どうも　ありがとう。　そうそう、　かぶきは　なん時ごろ
　　　　　おわりますか。」

井　上　「九時半ごろ　おわるはずですけど。」

よし子　「そうですか。　では、　土曜日に。」

井　上　「じゃあ、　また。」

水曜日	よし子	つぎの　日	行きませんでした
気分	土曜日	見たくありません	四時十五分
九時半			

4.3 PATTERN SENTENCES

4.3.1

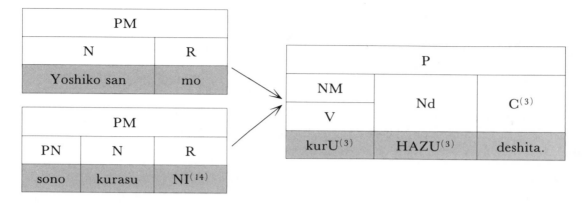

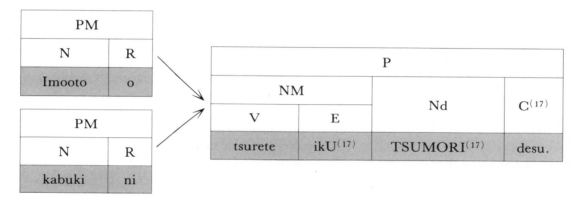

4.3.2

4.3.3

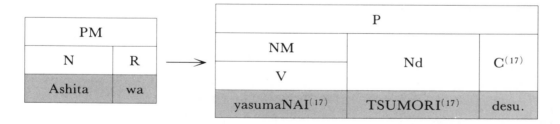

4.4 NOTES

4.4.1 The Telephone

Japan ranks near the top in the number of public telephones and sixth in the world in the per person ratio of private telephones. There are four kinds of public phones, each designated by a different color. The two biggest differences between Japanese and U.S. pay telephones are: (1) Collect calls are less frequent in Japan. (2) When you dial direct, the fee is based on the ten-yen unit. This means the minimum fee is always ten yen wherever you call.

4.4.2 *Suiyoobi* is a Noun meaning "Wednesday." The days of the week are as follows:

nichiyoobi	日曜日	"Sunday"		mokuyoobi	木曜日	"Thursday"
getsuyoobi	月曜日	"Monday"		kin'yoobi	金曜日	"Friday"
kayoobi	火曜日	"Tuesday"		doyoobi	土曜日	"Saturday"
suiyoobi	水曜日	"Wednesday"				

"What day of the week?" is *nan'yoobi*. In this series of words *-yoobi* may be shortened into *-yoo*, as in *nichiyoo, getsuyoo,* and so on. These days of the week are usually followed by the time Relational *ni*, but they may sometimes occur without *ni*.

Nichiyoobi ni Tookyoo e ikimashita.	"I went to Tōkyō on Sunday."
Raishuu no kayoobi, kabuki o mitai desu.	"Next Tuesday I want to see *kabuki*."
Kayoo to mokuyoo ni nihon'go no kurasu ga arimasu.	"I have Japanese classes on Tuesdays and Thursdays."

4.4.3 *Kuru* is the Dictionary form of *kimasu* "come." This is so called because it is the basic form of Verbs as you find them in dictionaries.

The Dictionary form of Verbs is formulated in one of the following ways:

1. When a Verb is a Vowel Verb, the Dictionary form is formed by attaching *-ru* to the Stem form of the Verb. Vowel Verbs that have been introduced so far are as follows:

age-masu	⟶	age-ru	mise-masu	⟶	mise-ru
dekake-masu	⟶	dekake-ru	ne-masu	⟶	ne-ru
i-masu	⟶	i-ru	oki-masu	⟶	oki-ru
ire-masu	⟶	ire-ru	sashiage-masu	⟶	sashiage-ru
kake-masu	⟶	kake-ru	tabe-masu	⟶	tabe-ru
ki-masu "wear"	⟶	ki-ru	tsure-masu	⟶	tsure-ru
kure-masu	⟶	kure-ru	tsutome-masu	⟶	tsutome-ru
mi-masu	⟶	mi-ru			

2. The Dictionary form of a Consonant Verb is formed by attaching *-u* to the Base form of the Verb. Some of the Consonant Verbs are shown below:

ar-imasu	⟶	ar-u	ma/t/-imasu	⟶	ma/t/-u
fur-imasu	⟶	fur-u	mo/t/-imasu	⟶	mo/t/-u
hair-imasu	⟶	hair-u	hak-imasu	⟶	hak-u
hajimar-imasu	⟶	hajimar-u	hatarak-imasu	⟶	hatarak-u
kaer-imasu	⟶	kaer-u	ik-imasu	⟶	ik-u
owar-imasu	⟶	owar-u	itadak-imasu	⟶	itadak-u
shir-imasu	⟶	shir-u	kak-imasu	⟶	kak-u
tor-imasu	⟶	tor-u	kik-imasu	⟶	kik-u
ur-imasu	⟶	ur-u	hana/s/-imasu	⟶	hanas-u
wakar-imasu	⟶	wakar-u	saga/s/-imasu	⟶	sagas-u
yar-imasu	⟶	yar-u			

a-imasu	$\longrightarrow$	a-u	nom-imasu	$\longrightarrow$	nom-u
chiga-imasu	$\longrightarrow$	chiga-u	sum-imasu	$\longrightarrow$	sum-u
i-imasu	$\longrightarrow$	i-u	yasum-imasu	$\longrightarrow$	yasum-u
ka-imasu	$\longrightarrow$	ka-u	yom-imasu	$\longrightarrow$	yom-u
kayo-imasu	$\longrightarrow$	kayo-u			
mora-imasu	$\longrightarrow$	mora-u	yob-imasu	$\longrightarrow$	yob-u
nara-imasu	$\longrightarrow$	nara-u	oyog-imasu	$\longrightarrow$	oyog-u
ukaga-imasu	$\longrightarrow$	ukaga-u			

3. Irregular Verbs

kimasu	$\longrightarrow$	kuru
shimasu	$\longrightarrow$	suru

Kuru hazu desu means "[someone] is supposed to come," or "[someone] is expected to come." The *hazu* is a dependent Noun meaning "expectation," and is always followed by a Noun Modifier. In general, it indicates the objective "expectation" of the speaker concerning some action, happening, state, and so on, outside the speaker's immediate control.

In other words, the use of *hazu* does not reflect subjective "guesswork," but rather reflects some objective understanding on the part of the speaker. The *hazu* is usually used to state the speaker's expectation of someone else's doing such and such or being such and such, but it can also refer to, on some limited occasions, the speaker's own doing or being such and such.

This pattern of expectation often will be equivalent to "is expected to," "is supposed to," "should (not in the meaning of obligation)," and the like. The *hazu* may occur in various structural environments, but only the following will be introduced in this lesson. Not only a Verb but also an Adjective may occur as a Noun Modifier before *hazu*, while an Adjective usually does not occur before *tsumori*, but only *hazu* with a Verb will be introduced in this lesson.

In addition to the Dictionary form of Verbs, the plain negative imperfect tense form (the -*nai* form) may also occur before *hazu*. The -*nai* form (-*nai* is the adjectival Derivative attached to the Pre-Nai form Verb) is formed as follows:

1. When a Verb is a Vowel Verb, the Stem form (or the Pre-Nai form) plus -*nai*:

age-masu	$\longrightarrow$	age-ru	$\longrightarrow$	age-nai
dekake-masu	$\longrightarrow$	dekake-ru	$\longrightarrow$	dekake-nai
i-masu	$\longrightarrow$	i-ru	$\longrightarrow$	i-nai
ire-masu	$\longrightarrow$	ire-ru	$\longrightarrow$	ire-nai
kake-masu	$\longrightarrow$	kake-ru	$\longrightarrow$	kake-nai
ki-masu "wear"	$\longrightarrow$	ki-ru	$\longrightarrow$	ki-nai
kure-masu	$\longrightarrow$	kure-ru	$\longrightarrow$	kure-nai
mi-masu	$\longrightarrow$	mi-ru	$\longrightarrow$	mi-nai
mise-masu	$\longrightarrow$	mise-ru	$\longrightarrow$	mise-nai
ne-masu	$\longrightarrow$	ne-ru	$\longrightarrow$	ne-nai
oki-masu	$\longrightarrow$	oki-ru	$\longrightarrow$	oki-nai
sashiage-masu	$\longrightarrow$	sashiage-ru	$\longrightarrow$	sashiage-nai
tabe-masu	$\longrightarrow$	tabe-ru	$\longrightarrow$	tabe-nai
tsure-masu	$\longrightarrow$	tsure-ru	$\longrightarrow$	tsure-nai
tsutome-masu	$\longrightarrow$	tsutome-ru	$\longrightarrow$	tsutome-nai

2. When a Verb is a Consonant Verb, the Pre-Nai form (or the Base form plus -*a*) plus -*nai*:

fur-imasu	$\longrightarrow$	fur-u	$\longrightarrow$	fur-anai
hair-imasu	$\longrightarrow$	hair-u	$\longrightarrow$	hair-anai
hajimar-imasu	$\longrightarrow$	hajimar-u	$\longrightarrow$	hajimar-anai

kaer-imasu	⟶	kaer-u	⟶	kaer-anai
owar-imasu	⟶	owar-u	⟶	owar-anai
shir-imasu	⟶	shir-u	⟶	shir-anai
tor-imasu	⟶	tor-u	⟶	tor-anai
ur-imasu	⟶	ur-u	⟶	ur-anai
wakar-imasu	⟶	wakar-u	⟶	wakar-anai
yar-imasu	⟶	yar-u	⟶	yar-anai
a(w)-imasu	⟶	a(w)-u	⟶	aw-anai
chiga(w)-imasu	⟶	chiga(w)-u	⟶	chigaw-anai
i(w)-imasu	⟶	i(w)-u	⟶	iw-anai
ka(w)-imasu	⟶	ka(w)-u	⟶	kaw-anai
kayo(w)-imasu	⟶	kayo(w)-u	⟶	kayow-anai
mora(w)-imasu	⟶	mora(w)-u	⟶	moraw-anai
nara(w)-imasu	⟶	nara(w)-u	⟶	naraw-anai
ukaga(w)-imasu	⟶	ukaga(w)-u	⟶	ukagaw-anai
ma/t/-imasu	⟶	ma/t/-u	⟶	mat-anai
mo/t/-imasu	⟶	mo/t/-u	⟶	mot-anai
hak-imasu	⟶	hak-u	⟶	hak-anai
hatarak-imasu	⟶	hatarak-u	⟶	hatarak-anai
ik-imasu	⟶	ik-u	⟶	ik-anai
itadak-imasu	⟶	itadak-u	⟶	itadak-anai
kak-imasu	⟶	kak-u	⟶	kak-anai
kik-imasu	⟶	kik-u	⟶	kik-anai
hana/s/-imasu	⟶	hanas-u	⟶	hanas-anai
saga/s/-imasu	⟶	sagas-u	⟶	sagas-anai
nom-imasu	⟶	nom-u	⟶	nom-anai
sum-imasu	⟶	sum-u	⟶	sum-anai
yasum-imasu	⟶	yasum-u	⟶	yasum-anai
yom-imasu	⟶	yom-u	⟶	yom-anai
yob-imasu	⟶	yob-u	⟶	yob-anai
oyog-imasu	⟶	oyog-u	⟶	oyog-anai

3. Irregular Verbs:

| kimasu | ⟶ | kuru | ⟶ | konai |
| shimasu | ⟶ | suru | ⟶ | shinai |

(Predicate Modifier)＋Dictionary form
(Predicate Modifier)＋plain negative imperfect form } **of Verb＋*hazu*＋** { *desu* *deshita*

ame ga furu
Inoue san wa imooto o tsurete kuru
ano hito wa kekkon shite iru
- } hazu { desu deshita
ame ga furanai
Inoue san wa imooto o tsurete konai
ano hito wa kekkon shite inai

$$\left.\begin{array}{l}\text{''it is supposed that}\\\text{''it was expected that}\end{array}\right\}\left\{\begin{array}{l}\text{it will rain''}\\\text{Mr. Inoue is coming with his sister''}\\\text{that person is married''}\\\text{------------------------------------}\\\text{it will not rain''}\\\text{Mr. Inoue is not coming with his sister''}\\\text{that person is not married''}\end{array}\right.$$

Buraun san wa rainen kekkon
suru hazu desu.

"Mr. Brown is supposed to get married next
year."

Kyoo tomodachi ga san'nin uchi
e kuru hazu deshita.

"Three friends were expected to come to my
house today."

Yamamoto san wa kyoo gakkoo
o yasumu hazu desu.

"Mr. Yamamoto is supposed to be absent from
school today."

Inoue san wa yasumi ni
arubaito o shinai hazu desu yo.

"Mr. Inoue supposedly does not do any part-
time job during the vacation."

Ano kodomotachi wa kan'ji o
shiranai hazu desu kedo.

"I suppose those children would not know any
kan'ji."

4.4.4 *Ni* in *Yoshiko san no uchi ni den'wa o kakemashita* is a Relational indicating that the preceding word is the recipient of an action. Verbs of "giving" are not necessarily the only ones to occur in this sentence pattern. The following Verbs may also occur.

$$\textbf{Noun}\text{ (indirect object)} + ni + \textbf{Noun}\text{ (direct object)} + o + \left\{\begin{array}{l}\textit{kakemasu}\\\textit{iimasu}\\\textit{hanashimasu}\\\textit{kakimasu}\\\textit{misemasu}\\\textit{urimasu}\end{array}\right.$$

Yamada san ni soo iimashita.

"I said so to Mr. Yamada."

Watashitachi ni mo sono arubamu
o misete kudasai.

"Please show that album to us also."

Kon'ban haha ni tegami o kaku
tsumori desu.

"I am going to write a letter to my mother
tonight."

4.4.5 In giving a telephone number, one-syllable numerals such as *ni, shi, go* are preferably replaced by *nii, yon, goo,* with *shichi* replaced by *nana* to avoid possible confusion.

zero, ichi, nii, san, yon, goo, roku, nana, hachi, kyuu, juu

Tookyoo nii-yon-ichi no nana-goo-nii-kyuu   Tōkyō 241-7529

zero-san no yon-hachi-ichi no
nii-roku-goo-nana

03-481-2657

To ask one's telephone number, *Den'wa (ban'goo) wa nan'ban desu ka?* is used.

66

4.4.6 *Moshi moshi* is largely reserved for telephone conversations. It is a greeting like ''hello'' and is used by the person making the telephone call. *Moshi moshi* is also used to get the attention of a stranger as when, for instance, someone walking ahead of you on the street drops something and you want to let him know.

4.4.7 The addition of the prefix *o-* to the word *taku* (house, home) serves either to give this particular word more elegance, or shows that the house referred to is either the second or third person's house and not that of the speaker. Inoue could have said either *Mori san no otaku desu ka?* or *Mori san no uchi desu ka?* His use, however, of the more commonly employed *otaku desu ka?* demonstrates his respect, especially since Inoue—as the caller—would not know who would be answering the telephone.

4.4.8 *Hai, soo desu* means ''Yes, it is correct.'' However, if it were a misdialed call, then you would say *Iie, chigaimasu* meaning ''(It is) wrong'' or ''Wrong number.''

4.4.9 **Omission of Relationals**

In conversation, Relationals, such as *wa* and *o,* are sometimes dropped.

Watakushi, Yoshiko desu.   ''I'm Yoshiko.''

Boku, Inoue desu.   ''I'm Inoue.''

In the following, the Relationals in parentheses are omitted: *Boku (wa) Inoue desu, Yoshiko san (wa) irasshaimasu ka?* These Relationals are omitted because the relationship between the preceding Nouns and the Predicate is clear and understood. Normally, the Relationals *wa, e,* and *o,* may be omitted in colloquial speech when their presence is understood. However, *o* and *wa* omission occurs even in less colloquial or less informal talk. Nevertheless, Relationals are never omitted in written documents or papers.

4.4.10 *Irasshaimasu* is a polite equivalent of *imasu. Irasshaimasu* is used only to mean ''someone else's being (in a place),'' and the speaker cannot use it for his own ''being (in a place).'' Nor can he use this expression in referring to his own in-group or family members.

Yoshiko san wa irasshaimasu ka?   ''Is Yoshiko there (at home, etc.)?''

Soko ni donata ga irasshaimashita ka?   ''Who was there?''

Goshujin wa irasshaimasu ka?   ''Is your husband home?''

Hierarchy and in-groupness are involved in differentiating the uses of *irasshaimasu* and *imasu.* The following factors must be considered: (1) who is the listener, and (2) who is the person referred to. Therefore, in-group superior, out-group superior, or in-group peer distinction would make a difference. Normally *irasshaimasu* may be used to your superior (in age, rank, or title) or to the listener's superior. However, *irasshaimasu* becomes *imasu* in referring to your superior within the in-group, but talking to an outsider.

4.4.11 *Watakushi desu ga . . .* is often used in telephone conversation to mean ''she (or he) is speaking,'' ''this is she (he) speaking,'' or ''this is she (he).''

Inoue san to hanashitai n desu ga,   ''I'd like to talk with Mr. Inoue, but is he
   irasshaimasu ka?   there?''

(Inoue wa) boku desu kedo . . .   "This is he."
Watakushi desu ga . . .

The clause Relationals *ga* or *kedo* may be used for two reasons: (1) one does not want to make a direct, clear-cut statement, or one does not wish to appear too self-aggrandizing or definitive; (2) to encourage the other party to start speaking, to urge others to reply or continue the conversation. Therefore, in this dialog, Yoshiko says *Watakushi desu ga . . .* meaning literally, "Yes, it's me, but [who is calling please?]."

4.4.12 *Ara* means "Oh!" or "Dear me!" Traditionally, *ara* is used more by women than men.

Ara, maa!	"Dear me!"
Ara! Nan deshoo?	"There! What's that?"
Ara! Soo desu ka?	"Oh, really?" or "Oh, is that so?"

4.4.13 *Aimasu* is a Verb meaning "meet." As this Verb is an intransitive Verb, "the person seen" is not followed by *o* but instead by the Relational *ni*.

Daigaku no sen'pai ni aimashita ka?	"Did you meet our university *sen'pai*?"
Eki de dare ni aimasu ka?	"Whom are you going to meet at the station?"
Anata ni aitakatta n desu.	"I wanted to see you."

4.4.14 In the place of the direction Relational *e*, *ni* is often used (in the same meaning) with such Verbs as *ikimasu, kimasu, kaerimasu, hairimasu, iremasu.*

Gakkoo ni kimasen deshita ne?	"You didn't come to school, did you?"
Doko ni ikitai desu ka?	"Where do you want to go?"

4.4.15 Negative Question (1)

When a Japanese is asked a negative question such as *Gakkoo ni kimasen deshita ne?* "You did not come to school, did you?" his answer is *hai* or *ee* if he confirms or agrees with the idea of the question, namely, if he did not go to school, *Ee, kimasen deshita* will be said. But his answer must be *Iie (kimashita yo)* if he did go to school. This tendency indicates the Japanese people's inclination to respond to the questioner's idea first, and then proceed to make his/her statement (see Note 4.4.21 for (2)).

Kinoo uchi ni imasen deshita ne?	"You weren't home yesterday, were you?"
Iie, imashita yo.	"Yes, I was."
Ee, imasen deshita.	"No, I wasn't."
Kibun ga yoku nai n desu ka?	"Don't you feel well?"
Iie, daijoobu desu.	"Yes, I am all right."
Ee, yoku nai n desu.	"No, I don't feel well."

68

4.4.16 *Yasumanai* is the plain equivalent of *yasumimasen.* (See Note 4.4.3.) *Yasumimasu* is "miss (class)," or "take leave." Since *yasumimasu* is a transitive Verb, the Relational *o* precedes *yasumimasu.* The Noun that precedes *o* can be a place or an event. The Dictionary form of *yasumimasu* is *yasumu.*

gakkoo		"do not go to school"
jimusho		"do not go to the office to work" or "take (a day) off"
daigaku	*o yasumimasu*	"do not go to the university"
--------		--
arubaito		"do not go to one's part-time job"
shigoto		"take (a day) off from work" or "do not (go to) work"
ben'kyoo		"do not (go to) study"

When *yasumimasu* is used as an intransitive Verb, it means "rest."

Yamamoto san wa kinoo shigoto o yasumimashita.	"Mr. Yamamoto took a day off yesterday."
Chotto sono hen de yasumimashoo.	"Let's take a rest around there for a while."

4.4.17 *Tsumori desu* means "I intend to." The *tsumori* is a dependent Noun meaning "intention," "will," "plan," and so on, and it is always preceded by a Noun Modifier. The Noun Modifier preceding *tsumori* can be the Dictionary form of a Verb, or the plain negative form of a Verb. The *tsumori* may be followed by the Copula *desu* or *deshita.* When the *deshita* is used after *tsumori* the context usually implies that a person had the intention of doing such and such in the past but failed to do it. When the sentence of intention is a statement, it is normally the speaker's intention, but it can be that of a second or a third person. *Tsumori* in other structural environments will be introduced in later volumes.

(Predicate Modifier)+Dictionary form of Verb
(Predicate Modifier)+plain negative form of Verb } + ***tsumori*** + { ***desu*** / ***deshita***

kuni e kaeru		"I am planning to"	"go home"
seetaa o kau		"I was planning to"	"buy a sweater"
den'wa o suru		------------------------	"telephone"
Nakamura san ni au	*tsumori* { *desu* / *deshita* }	"I am not planning to"	"meet Mr. Nakamura"
umi de oyogu		"I wasn't planning to"	"swim in the sea"
--------------------			
kuni e kaeranai			
seetaa o kawanai			
den'wa o shinai			
Nakamura san ni awanai			
umi de oyoganai			

Raishuu no nichiyoobi ni doko e iku tsumori desu ka?	"Where do you intend to go next Sunday?"
Kyoo wa gojikan gurai uchi de ben'kyoo suru tsumori deshita ga, dame deshita.	"I was planning to study for about five hours at home today, but I couldn't."
Boku wa kotoshi no natsuyasumi ni wa kuni e kaeranai tsumori desu.	"I do not intend to go home during this summer vacation."
Kon'ban wa dekakenai tsumori desu.	"I don't intend to go out tonight."

4.4.18 *Jitsu wa*

In conversation, the traditional-minded Japanese tend to leave the most important matters until last. This is especially so if the purpose of the conversation is to make a request or seek a favor. The use of *jitsu wa* signals that such business is about to be brought up. *Jitsu wa*—"as a matter of fact"—is a convenient expression to change the tone of the conversation from preliminaries to the actual business in mind, the true reason for coming, and so forth. This is evidenced by Inoue's use of *jitsu wa* to introduce his request that Yoshiko join him in seeing a *kabuki* play. Note its occurrence toward the end of the dialog, and its function to smooth what might be an otherwise abrupt transition from chatting to the actual reason for his call. In American society, where one "gets to the point" right away, such a custom is hard to comprehend. It may even be termed devious or sly by a culture that lacks an understanding of Japanese culture; that is, that in Japan the very directness and openness sought in American society would be considered rude, if not somewhat vulgar.

4.4.19 *Kabuki*

Kabuki was first developed at the beginning of the seventeenth century and immediately gained the support of the common people in general and members of the wealthy merchant and artisan class in particular. The *samurai* and noble classes, however, despised it as a low form of amusement, or *goraku*.

In the West, acting was traditionally an all-male profession. The early development of *kabuki* was, however, just the opposite. *Kabuki*'s originator is commonly thought to have been a woman named Okuni of Izumo, who was a performer of the *nen'butsu-odori*, a popular Japanese folk dance. Her troupe consisted only of women and thus the early *kabuki* had women playing the male parts. In 1629 the Tokugawa government banned the *kabuki* of its time, a form known as *on'na kabuki*, or women's *kabuki*, because it was performed by courtesans. In 1707 another law prohibited all women from performing on the *kabuki* stage on the grounds that it had an undesirable influence upon public morals. Thereafter, only male actors were allowed to perform in public, and since that time female parts have been played by specially trained male actors, or *oyama*.

Gradually the original *kabuki* developed into a form of classical theater as the emphasis on mere dance was replaced by plays with realistic plots.

In *kabuki* the beauty of form is an important characteristic. Another indication of this emphasis on form is *kabuki* makeup. The actors paint their faces with exaggerated lines and color to create a highly stylized makeup. The accompaniment of music, the enrichment of the color schemes, and this beauty of form all interweave to make the art of *kabuki* a unified entity.

4.4.20

Imooto o tsurete iku tsumori desu means "I intend to take my sister with me," or literally it means "I intend to go accompanying my sister." *Tsurete* is the TE form of the Verb *tsuremasu* meaning "accompany" or "lead." When someone leads someone else to a certain place, one of the Extenders *ikimasu*, *kimasu*, and *kaerimasu* will be used after the TE form of *tsuremasu*, depending upon where the speaker is. *Tsurete ikimasu* is equivalent to "take a person (or an animal) with one (to a place)," *tsurete kimasu* is "bring a person with one (to a place)," and *tsurete kaerimasu* "take or bring a person back with one."

$$\begin{matrix} \textbf{Noun} \\ \textbf{(animate)} \end{matrix} + o + tsurete + \left\{ \begin{matrix} ikimasu \\ kimasu \\ kaerimasu \end{matrix} \right.$$

otooto			ikimasu	"take		my younger brother	
tomodachi						my friend	
kodomo	} o tsurete {		kimasu	"bring	}	a child	} (with me)"
otoko no ko			kaerimasu	"take (bring) back		a boy	
inu						a dog	

Uchi e tomodachi o tsurete ikimashoo.   "I think I'll take a friend of mine with me to my house."

Otooto wa inu o tsurete kaerimashita.   "My younger brother brought a dog back with him."

When a thing or a plant is taken or brought with someone, *motte* "hold" is used in the place of *tsurete*.

Noun (inanimate) + *o* + *motte* + { *ikimasu* / *kimasu* / *kaerimasu* }

kippu			ikimasu	"take		a ticket	
okane	} o motte {		kimasu	"bring	}	some money	} (with me)"
miyage			kaerimasu	"take (bring) back		souvenir	

Gakkoo e jisho o motte ikimasen deshita.   "I did not take a dictionary with me to school."

Sono hako o motte kite kudasai.   "Please bring that box to me."

Suzuki san wa Amerika kara kuruma o motte kaerimashita.   "Mr. Suzuki brought a car back from the States."

4.4.21 Negative Question (2)

In the dialog Inoue asks *Yoshiko san mo mitaku arimasen ka?* The literal English translation, "Don't you want to see *kabuki?*" might seem to imply that Inoue has reason to suspect that Yoshiko does not want to go. In Japanese, however, this is not the case. It is simply a question, and the negative form is felt to have a softening effect.

As discussed before, the appropriate response to a negative question in Japanese is the reverse of the English convention. For example, *Kinoo gakkoo e ikimasen deshita ka?* is answered with *Hai, ikimasen deshita.* One exception to this rule, however, is if the negative question is an invitation, the answer would be the same as it is in English. For example, "Won't you go to school with me tomorrow?" *Ashita gakkoo e ikimasen ka?* is answered with *Hai, ikimashoo,* "Yes, I will," or *Iie, ikimasen,* "No, I won't." In English, "Won't you go to school with me tomorrow?" means "Will you please go to school with me tomorrow," and the expression "Aren't you going to school tomorrow?" implies that the speaker feels the listener will not be going to school the next day. The former is an invitation but the latter is not.

4.4.22

Gogo means "P.M." as in "5:15 P.M." or "in the afternoon" when used by itself. Likewise, *gozen* is used in the meaning of "A.M.," but *gozen* is not normally used to mean "in the morning"; *asa* is used instead.

Kinoo wa gogo kuji ni nemashita.   "I went to bed at 9 P.M. yesterday."

Ashita no gogo ukagaimasu.   "I will visit you tomorrow afternoon."

Eiga wa gozen kujihan ni hajimarimasu.   "The movie will start at 9:30 A.M."

4.4.23 *Juugofun* is "fifteen minutes." The *-fun* is a counter for "minute(s)." Depending upon the numeral that precedes *-fun*, *-fun* sometimes changes into *-pun*.

1	ippun	5	gofun	9	kyuufun
2	nifun	6	roppun	10	jippun; juppun
3	san'pun	7	nanafun; shichifun	?	nan'pun
4	yon'pun	8	happun; hachifun		

"How many minutes?" is *nan'pun*.

In telling time, "o'clock" is always said first and then "minutes." However, *gozen* or *gogo* should always be placed before time.

Yoji juugofun ni owarimasu.	"It will be over at four-fifteen."
Juuniji yon'juppun goro aimashoo.	"Let's meet at about twelve-forty."
Nan'pun hanashite imashita ka?	"How many minutes were you talking?"
San'jippun gurai hanashite imashita.	"I was talking about thirty minutes."
Gozen kuji gofun desu.	"It's five minutes past nine in the morning."

4.4.24 *Wakarimasu* means "comprehend," "understand," "grasp," or "is clear." This is an intransitive Verb and the thing which is understood is followed by *ga*. The person who understands is followed by *ni*.

Nihon'go ga wakarimasen.	"[I] do not understand Japanese."

Shirimasu "know" or "get to know" is a transitive Verb and the thing a person gets to know is followed by *o*. The person who gets to know (something) is followed by *ga* or *wa*.

Yamada san wa Nihon o shirimasen.	"Mr. Yamada does not know Japan."

Foreigners tend to confuse *Wakarimasen* and *Shirimasen* in giving a reply "I don't know." Since *shirimasu* only refers to "knowledge," this cannot be used when asked something concerning the speaker himself. He should instead answer *Wakarimasen*.

Koyama san, natsuyasumi ni doko e iku tsumori desu ka?	"Where are you planning to go during the summer vacation, Miss Koyama?"
Mada wakarimasen.	"I don't know yet."
Yoshiko san wa yasumi ni nani o shimasu ka?	"What will Yoshiko be doing during the vacation?"
Shirimasen. *or* Wakarimasen.	"I don't know."

4.5   VOCABULARY

Presentation

井上	Inoue	......	N	family name
水曜日	suiyoobi	......	N	Wednesday (see 4.4.2)

とって	totte	......	V	TE form of *torimasu* ← *toru*—take
よし子	Yoshiko	......	N	girl's first name
くる	kuru	......	V	come (Dictionary form of *kimasu*) (see 4.4.3)
はず	hazu	......	Nd	expected to (do); supposed to (do) (see 4.4.3)
日	hi	......	N	day
かけました	kakemashita	......	V	turned on; dialed (TA form of *kakemasu* ← *kakeru*)
ばんごう	ban'goo	......	N	(sequential) number (see 4.4.5)
ゼロ	zero	......	N	zero

Dialog

もしもし	moshi moshi	......	SI	hello (regularly used in telephone conversation) (see 4.4.6)
森	Mori	......	N	family name
おたく	(o)taku	......	N	house; home (polite equivalent of *uchi*) (see 4.4.7)
いらっしゃいます	irasshaimasu	......	V	exist; is (normal form of *irassharu*; polite equivalent of *imasu*) (see 4.4.10)
あら	ara	......	SI	oh; ah (used by women) (see 4.4.12)
あい（たかった）	ai(takatta)	......	V	Stem form of *aimasu* ← *au*—meet (see 4.4.13)
に	ni	......	R	to (a place) (see 4.4.14)
気分	kibun	......	N	feeling (cf. feel sick, feel fine)
だいじょうぶ	daijoobu	......	Na	all right; safe (this word is used to allay fear or doubt)
休まない	yasumanai	......	V	not be absent; take leave (plain negative imperfect tense form of *yasumu*) (see 4.4.3 and 4.4.16)
つもり	tsumori	......	Nd	intention; planning (see 4.4.17)
土曜日	doyoobi	......	N	Saturday
かぶき	kabuki	......	N	*kabuki* performance (performed only by men)
つれて	tsurete	......	V	TE form of *tsuremasu* ← *tsureru*—take (with); bring (with); accompany (see 4.4.20)
行く	iku	......	E	go (〜ing) (see 4.4.20)

ごご	gogo	......	N	P.M.; in the afternoon (see 4.4.22)
分	-fun	......	Nd	minute (see 4.4.23)
かぶきざ	Kabukiza	......	N	*Kabuki* Theater, near the Ginza
わかりました	wakarimashita	......	V	understood (TA form of *wakarimasu* ← *wakaru*) (intransitive Verb) (see 4.4.24)
そうそう	soosoo	......	SI	oh, yes (used when something comes into one's mind)
おわります	owarimasu	......	V	end; finish (intransitive Verb) (normal form of *owaru*)
おわる	owaru	......	V	end; finish (Dictionary form of *owarimasu*)

Notes

日曜日	nichiyoobi	......	N	Sunday
月曜日	getsuyoobi	......	N	Monday
火曜日	kayoobi	......	N	Tuesday
木曜日	mokuyoobi	......	N	Thursday
金曜日	kin'yoobi	......	N	Friday
曜（日）	-yoo(bi)	......	Nd	day of the week (see 4.4.2)
なん曜日	nan'yoobi	......	Ni	what day of the week?
おきます	okimasu	......	V	get up (normal form of *okiru*)
ない	-nai	......	Da	negative Derivative (see 4.4.3)
ばん	-ban	......	Nd	counter for naming numbers in succession (see 4.4.5)
ちがいます	chigaimasu	......	V	differ; is different (normal form of *chigau*) (see 4.4.8)
きます	kimasu	......	E	come (～ing) (see 4.4.20)
かえります	kaerimasu	......	E	go (come) (～ing) back (see 4.4.20)
（お）みやげ	(o)miyage	......	N	souvenir; gift
ごぜん	gozen	......	N	A.M.
ねます	nemasu	......	V	go to bed; sleep (normal form of *neru*)
はじまります	hajimarimasu	......	V	begin (normal form of *hajimaru*) (intransitive Verb)

Drills

すきやき	sukiyaki	......	N	*sukiyaki*; beef cooked with vegetables

4.6 KAN'JI

4.6.1 水 （1） SUI （2） water （3） forms the classifier 水

（4） | 丿 | 才 | 刃 | 水 | （5） 水曜日 （6） flowing water in a river

4.6.2 子 （1） *ko* （2） child （3） forms the classifier 子 （4） | フ | 了 | 子 |

（5） 子ども、よし子、女の子 （6） a swaddled baby

4.6.a 日 [2.6.5] （1） *bi; hi* （5） 金曜日、日曜日、たんじょう日 [birthday]、
出かける日、日と時間

4.6.3 行 （1） *i(kimasu)* （2） go （3） forms the classifier 彳(行)

（4） | 丿 | 彡 | 彳 | 行 | 行 | 行 | （5） 行きました、行ってください

（6） a crossroad; 街 is the widened crossroad with plenty of soil added. See 4.6.4

4.6.4 土 （1） DO （2） earth; soil （3） forms the classifier 土 （4） | 一 | 十 | 土 |

（5） 土曜日 （6） a flower sprouting from the soil

4.6.5 見 （1） *mi(masu)* （2） see; watch; look （3） classifier 目(見)

（4） | | | 冂 | 冃 | 月 | 目 | 尸 | 見 | （5） 見ます、見ましょう、見せます

（6） a man with eyes. See 11.6.2

4.6.6 分 （1） FUN [-PUN] （2） minute （3） classifier 八(刀) （4） | 丷 | 八 | 今 | 分 |

（5） 二分、三分、十五分 （6） homonym 紛、粉、雰; a knife 刀 divided

4.6.7 半 （1） HAN （2） half （3） classifier ソ(十) （4） | 丶 | 丷 | 丷 | 半 | 半 |

（5） 五時半、半ダース （6） homonym 判、伴、畔; an object cut in two

4.6.b 月 [2.6.8] （1） GETSU （5） 月曜日、せん月、こん月、らい月、まい月

4.6.8 火 （1） KA （2） fire （3） forms the classifier 火 （4） | 丶 | 丷 | 少 | 火 |

（5） 火曜日、火事 [a fire] （6） shape of a flame

4.6.9 木 （1） MOKU （2） tree; wood （3） forms the classifier 木

（4） | 一 | 十 | 才 | 木 | （5） 木曜日 （6） the horizontal line represents branches,
the vertical line the trunk, and the diagonal lines the roots

4.6.10 金 （1） KIN （2） gold （3） forms the classifier 金

（4） | 丿 | 八 | 今 | 今 | 全 | 全 | 全 | 金 | （5） 金曜日、金ぱつ [blond]

4.7 DRILLS

4.7.1 Transformation Drill

1.	あげます	⟶	あげる	21.	ふります	⟶	ふる
2.	でかけます	⟶	でかける	22.	はいります	⟶	はいる
3.	かけます	⟶	かける	23.	はじまります	⟶	はじまる
4.	ねます	⟶	ねる	24.	かえります	⟶	かえる
5.	おきます	⟶	おきる	25.	おわります	⟶	おわる
6.	たべます	⟶	たべる	26.	しります	⟶	しる
7.	いれます	⟶	いれる	27.	とります	⟶	とる
8.	見ます	⟶	見る	28.	うります	⟶	うる
9.	あいます	⟶	あう	29.	わかります	⟶	わかる
10.	ちがいます	⟶	ちがう	30.	やります	⟶	やる
11.	もらいます	⟶	もらう	31.	さがします	⟶	さがす
12.	うかがいます	⟶	うかがう	32.	はなします	⟶	はなす
13.	かよいます	⟶	かよう	33.	よびます	⟶	よぶ
14.	はきます	⟶	はく	34.	のみます	⟶	のむ
15.	はたらきます	⟶	はたらく	35.	すみます	⟶	すむ
16.	行きます	⟶	行く	36.	休みます	⟶	休む
17.	かきます	⟶	かく	37.	よみます	⟶	よむ
18.	およぎます	⟶	およぐ	38.	きます	⟶	くる
19.	まちます	⟶	まつ	39.	します	⟶	する
20.	もちます	⟶	もつ				

4.7.2 Transformation Drill

1.	あげる	⟶	あげない	11.	もらう	⟶	もらわない
2.	でかける	⟶	でかけない	12.	うかがう	⟶	うかがわない
3.	かける	⟶	かけない	13.	かよう	⟶	かよわない
4.	ねる	⟶	ねない	14.	はく	⟶	はかない
5.	おきる	⟶	おきない	15.	はたらく	⟶	はたらかない
6.	たべる	⟶	たべない	16.	行く	⟶	行かない
7.	いれる	⟶	いれない	17.	かく	⟶	かかない
8.	見る	⟶	見ない	18.	およぐ	⟶	およがない
9.	あう	⟶	あわない	19.	まつ	⟶	またない
10.	ちがう	⟶	ちがわない	20.	もつ	⟶	もたない

21. ふる	⟶	ふらない		31. さがす	⟶	さがさない
22. はいる	⟶	はいらない		32. はなす	⟶	はなさない
23. はじまる	⟶	はじまらない		33. よぶ	⟶	よばない
24. かえる	⟶	かえらない		34. のむ	⟶	のまない
25. おわる	⟶	おわらない		35. すむ	⟶	すまない
26. しる	⟶	しらない		36. 休む	⟶	休まない
27. とる	⟶	とらない		37. よむ	⟶	よまない
28. うる	⟶	うらない		38. くる	⟶	こない
29. わかる	⟶	わからない		39. する	⟶	しない
30. やる	⟶	やらない				

4.7.3　Transformation Drill

1. いもうとを　かぶきに　つれて行きます。　⟶　いもうとを　かぶきに　つれて行くつもりです。
2. あした　しごとを　休みます。　⟶　あした　しごとを　休むつもりです。
3. 七時十五分に　おきます。　⟶　七時十五分に　おきるつもりです。
4. こんばん　うちに　でんわを　かけます。　⟶　こんばん　うちに　でんわを　かけるつもりです。
5. 四時半ごろ　ともだちに　あいます。　⟶　四時半ごろ　ともだちに　あうつもりです。
6. あしたの　ばん　おたくに　うかがいます。　⟶　あしたの　ばん　おたくに　うかがうつもりです。
7. 日本語の　クラスを　とります。　⟶　日本語の　クラスを　とるつもりです。
8. らい年　車を　もちます。　⟶　らい年　車を　もつつもりです。
9. いもうとを　つれて行きます。　⟶　いもうとを　つれて行くつもりです。
10. クラスへ　じしょを　もって行きます。⟶　クラスへ　じしょを　もって行くつもりです。
11. 車で　かいしゃに　かよいます。　⟶　車で　かいしゃに　かようつもりです。
12. タクシーを　よびます。　⟶　タクシーを　よぶつもりです。

4.7.4　Transformation Drill

1. あしたは　休みません。　⟶　あしたは　休まないつもりです。
2. バスで　かよいません。　⟶　バスで　かよわないつもりです。
3. きっぷを　井上さんから　もらいません。　⟶　きっぷを　井上さんから　もらわないつもりです。
4. せんぱいに　でんわを　かけません。　⟶　せんぱいに　でんわを　かけないつもりです。

5. この　なつは　およぎません。　　⟶　　この　なつは　およがないつもりです。

6. きょうは　十二時に　ねません。　　⟶　　きょうは　十二時に　ねないつもりです。

7. くにに　てがみを　かきません。　　⟶　　くにに　てがみを　かかないつもりです。

8. 休みに　アルバイトを　しません。　　⟶　　休みに　アルバイトを　しないつもりです。

9. 森さんに　それを　はなしません。　　⟶　　森さんに　それを　はなさないつもりです。

10. わたしは　いぬを　つれてきません。　⟶　　わたしは　いぬを　つれてこないつもりです。

4.7.5　Transformation Drill

1. かぶきは　九時半ごろ　<u>おわります</u>。　⟶　かぶきは　九時半ごろ　<u>おわるはずです</u>。

2. 六月には　あめが　たくさん　　　　⟶　六月には　あめが　たくさん　ふるはずです。
　　ふります。

3. かぶきは　五時に　はじまります。　⟶　かぶきは　五時に　はじまるはずです。

4. 林さんは　まだ　しぶやに　　　　⟶　林さんは　まだ　しぶやに　すんでいる
　　すんでいます。　　　　　　　　　　　　はずです。

5. 森さんは　えい語が　わかります。　⟶　森さんは　えい語が　わかるはずです。

6. ばんごうが　ちがいます。　　　　　⟶　ばんごうが　ちがうはずです。

7. きょう　よし子さんは　学校に　　　⟶　きょう　よし子さんは　学校に　くるはず
　　きます。　　　　　　　　　　　　　　　です。

8. としょかんで　先生に　あいます。　⟶　としょかんで　先生に　あうはずです。

9. あの　女の　子は　わたしを　　　⟶　あの　女の　子は　わたしを　しっている
　　しっています。　　　　　　　　　　　はずです。

10. あの　人は　カメラを　もっています。⟶　あの　人は　カメラを　もっているはずです。

4.7.6　Transformation Drill

1. あの　人は　日本語が　<u>わかりません</u>。⟶　あの　人は　日本語が　<u>わからないはずです</u>。

2. えいがは　三時に　おわりません。　⟶　えいがは　三時に　おわらないはずです。

3. きょうは　あめが　ふりません。　　⟶　きょうは　あめが　ふらないはずです。

4. 井上さんは　でんわばんごうを　　　⟶　井上さんは　でんわばんごうを　しらない
　　しりません。　　　　　　　　　　　　はずです。

5. かぶきは　まだ　はじまりません。　⟶　かぶきは　まだ　はじまらないはずです。

6. ブラウンさんは　すしを　たべません。⟶　ブラウンさんは　すしを　たべないはずです。

7. よし子さんは　きょう　クラスに　　⟶　よし子さんは　きょう　クラスに　こない
　　きません。　　　　　　　　　　　　　はずです。

8. よし子さんは　おさけを　のみません。⟶　よし子さんは　おさけを　のまないはずです。

9. 井上さんは　おとうとさんを　　　　──→　　井上さんは　おとうとさんを
　　つれて行きません。　　　　　　　　　　　つれて行かないはずです。

10. タクシーは　よびません。　　　　　──→　　タクシーは　よばないはずです。

4.7.7　Response Drill（short answer）

1. きのう　学校に　きませんでしたね。

　　はい　　　　　　　　　　　……　はい、きませんでした。

2. かぶきは　すきじゃありませんね。

　　いいえ　　　　　　　　　　　……　いいえ、すきです。

3. あなたは　水曜日の　クラスを　とっていませんね。

　　ええ　　　　　　　　　　　　……　ええ、とっていません。

4. きのう　よし子さんに　あいませんでしたね。

　　ええ　　　　　　　　　　　　……　ええ、あいませんでした。

5. かぶきは　十時には　おわりませんか。

　　いいえ　　　　　　　　　　　……　いいえ、おわります。

6. その　くつは　きつくないでしょう？

　　ええ　　　　　　　　　　　　……　ええ、きつくないです。

7. かいしゃを　休みたくありませんね。

　　はい　　　　　　　　　　　　……　はい、休みたくありません。

8. 林さんの　でんわばんごうを　ききませんでしたか。

　　いいえ　　　　　　　　　　　……　いいえ、ききました。

9. あそこは　本屋じゃありませんね。

　　ええ　　　　　　　　　　　　……　ええ、本屋じゃありません。

10. スミスさんに　でんわを　かけませんでしたね。

　　いいえ　　　　　　　　　　　……　いいえ、かけました。

4.7.8　Substitution Drill

A.　本を　もってきました。

　　1.　はし　　　　　　　　　……　はしを　もってきました。

　　2.　行きます　　　　　　　……　はしを　もって行きます。

　　3.　行きましょう　　　　　……　はしを　もって行きましょう。

　　4.　きてください　　　　　……　はしを　もってきてください。

　　5.　くつ　　　　　　　　　……　くつを　もってきてください。

　　6.　かえりました　　　　　……　くつを　もってかえりました。

7. おみやげ …… おみやげを　もってかえりました。

8. かえりませんでした …… おみやげを　もってかえりませんでした。

B. 学生を　つれて行きます。

1. いぬ …… いぬを　つれて行きます。

2. かえります …… いぬを　つれてかえります。

3. きましょう …… いぬを　つれてきましょう。

4. 女の人 …… 女の人を　つれてきましょう。

5. きますか …… 女の人を　つれてきますか。

6. 子ども …… 子どもを　つれてきますか。

7. 行ってください …… 子どもを　つれて行ってください。

8. 行きませんでした …… 子どもを　つれて行きませんでした。

4.7.9　Substitution Drill

A. よし子さんに　あいませんでした。

1. あいたかったんです …… よし子さんに　あいたかったんです。

2. きみ …… きみに　あいたかったんです。

3. あわないつもりです …… きみに　あわないつもりです。

4. 森さん …… 森さんに　あわないつもりです。

5. あうつもりです …… 森さんに　あうつもりです。

6. あってください …… 森さんに　あってください。

B. かずおさんは　クラスを　休みました。

1. かいしゃ …… かずおさんは　かいしゃを　休みました。

2. 休むはずです …… かずおさんは　かいしゃを　休むはずです。

3. 学校 …… かずおさんは　学校を　休むはずです。

4. 休まないはずです …… かずおさんは　学校を　休まないはずです。

5. しごと …… かずおさんは　しごとを　休まないはずです。

6. 休んでいます …… かずおさんは　しごとを　休んでいます。

C. うちに　でんわを　かけました。

1. ともだち …… ともだちに　でんわを　かけました。

2. そう　いってください …… ともだちに　そう　いってください。

3. スミスさん …… スミスさんに　そう　いってください。

4. わたしの　えを　見せました…… スミスさんに　わたしの　えを　見せました。

5. はなすつもりです …… スミスさんに　はなすつもりです。

6. てがみを　かくつもりです…… スミスさんに　てがみを　かくつもりです。

4.7.10 E-J Response Drill

1. いま　なん時ですか。

　　　six thirty　　　　　　　　　　　　……　六時三十分です。

2. まい日　なん時に・大学へ　行きますか。

　　　at eight fifteen　　　　　　　　　　……　八時十五分に　行きます。

3. なん時に　あいたいですか。

　　　about three twenty　　　　　　　　……　三時二十分ごろ（に）　あいたいです。

4. なん曜日に　アルバイトを　していますか。

　　　on Wednesday and Friday　　　　　……　水曜日と　金曜日に　しています。

5. きょう　なん時に　おきましたか。

　　　at 5: 30 A.M.　　　　　　　　　　　……　ごぜん　五時三十分に　おきました。

6. なん時ごろ　ねるつもりでしたか。

　　　at half past nine　　　　　　　　　……　九時半に　ねるつもりでした。

7. アルバイトは　なん時ごろに　おわりますか。

　　　about 4 P.M.　　　　　　　　　　　……　ごご　四時ごろ（に）　おわります。

8. バスは　なん時ごろに　くるはずですか。

　　　about two-twelve　　　　　　　　　……　二時十二分ごろに　くるはずです。

4.7.11 Response Drill

1. あなたは　八月に　りょこうしますか。

　　　はい/つもり　　　　　　　　　　　……　はい、りょこうするつもりです。

2. えいがは　なん時に　はじまりますか。

　　　二時十五分/はず　　　　　　　　　……　二時十五分に　はじまるはずです。

3. あさって　学校を　休みますか。

　　　いいえ/つもり　　　　　　　　　　……　いいえ、休まないつもりです。

4. なん曜日に　しけんが　ありますか。

　　　火曜日/はず　　　　　　　　　　　……　火曜日に　あるはずです。

5. いつ　にわで　はたらきますか。

　　　ごご/つもり　　　　　　　　　　　……　ごご　はたらくつもりです。

6. でんわばんごうが　ちがいますか。

　　　いいえ/はず　　　　　　　　　　　……　いいえ、ちがわないはずです。

7. おにいさんは　なんの　クラスを　とりますか。

　　　ちゅうごく語/はず　　　　　　　　……　ちゅうごく語の　クラスを　とるはずです。

8. こんばん　でかけますか。

　　いいえ/つもり　　　　　　　　……　いいえ、でかけないつもりです。

9. なにを　かいますか。

　　車/つもり　　　　　　　　　　……　車を　かうつもりです。

10. いしいさんは　きょう　としょかんへ　きますか。

　　いいえ/はず　　　　　　　　　……　いいえ、こないはずです。

4.8　EXERCISES

4.8.1　Transform each of the given Verbs as shown in the example:

　　　　Example:　休みます/つもり　⟶　休むつもりです

1.　たべます/はず	7.　よびます/つもり
2.　つとめています/はず	8.　さがします/つもり
3.　はきます/つもり	9.　します/はず
4.　およぎます/つもり	10.　わかります/はず
5.　うかがいます/つもり	11.　きます "come"/つもり
6.　もちます/はず	12.　すみます/つもり

4.8.2　Insert an appropriate Relational in blank, if necessary:

1. 土曜日（　　）　よし子さん（　　）　あいます。

2. じゅぎょう（　　）　休みたくありませんでした（　　）、学校（　　）
　　行きませんでした。

3. ごご（　　）　三時（　　）　学校（　　）　もって行きますよ。

4. 三月（　　）　くに（　　）　かえります。そして、らい年（　　）　また　きます。

5. ともだち（　　）　でんわ（　　）　かけましたが、るすでした。

4.8.3　Make an appropriate question that fits each of the following answers:

1. いいえ、こないはずです。

2. ごご　四時五分に　はじまります。

3. はい、もってきませんでした。

4. 045-851-6792 です。

5. いいえ、日本語の　クラスを　とっています。

6. ともだちに　あうつもりでした。

7. いもうとか　おとうとを　つれて行くつもりです。

8. いいえ、ちがいます。こちらは　井上です。

9. 月曜日に　休みました。

4.8.4　Carry on the following telephone conversation in Japanese:

Mori:　　　Hello, is this the Yamada home?

Kazuko:　　Yes, it is.

Mori:　　　Is Kazuko there?

Kazuko:　　This is she speaking.

Mori:　　　Good afternoon. This is Mori.

Kazuko:　　Good afternoon.

Mori:　　　I want to see you at school tomorrow. Are you going to school at about ten o'clock?

Kazuko:　　Yes, I am.

Mori:　　　Then please bring my German language dictionary. I want to study German tomorrow night.

Kazuko:　　All right. I'll take it with me to school.

Mori:　　　Then let's meet at school around ten o'clock tomorrow.

Kazuko:　　OK.

Mori:　　　Well, so long.

Kazuko:　　Good-bye.

4.8.5　Answer the following questions in Japanese:

1. 日曜日は　なん時ごろ　おきますか。

2. きのうは　なん時に　ねましたか。

3. 日本語の　クラスは　まいしゅう　なん曜日に　ありますか。

4. いつも　学校へ　なにを　もって行きますか。

5. 土曜日に　どこへ　行きたいですか。

6. 日本語の　クラスは　なん時ごろ　おわりますか。

7. おたくの　でんわばんごうは　なんばんですか。

8. ときどき　がいこくへも　でんわを　かけますか。

4.8.6　Write the underlined *hiragana* in *kan'ji*:

1. よしこさんは　きん曜びに　かぶきを　みます。

2. ごじ　にじっぷんに　ともだちが　きます。それから、いっしょに　ほん屋へ　いきます。

3. にち曜び、 げつ曜び、 か曜び、 すい曜び、 もく曜び、 ど曜び

4. つぎの ひは やすみでした。 くじはんに おきました。

4.8.7 Which is more polite? Choose one expression out of each set.

1. Moshi moshi, Mori san no uchi desu ka?

   Moshi moshi, Mori san no otaku desu ka?

2. Yoshiko san imasu ka?

   Yoshiko san irasshaimasu ka?

4.8.8 If when making a phone call to your close friend Keiko, her mother answers the phone, you might use *Keiko san irasshaimasu ka?* instead of *Keiko san imasu ka?* What makes you decide to use *irasshaimasu* instead of *imasu?*

4.8.9 What is the function of *ga* at the end of a sentence?

For example: Tanaka san to hanashitai n desu ga.

Rein'kooto ga hoshii n desu ga.

Inoue wa watakushi desu ga.

4.8.10 Hearing comprehension:

1. —Moshi moshi, Inoue san no otaku desu ka?

   —Hai, Inoue desu ga.

   —Kazuko san irasshaimasu ka?

   —Ima dekakete imasu ga, donata desu ka?

2. —Moshi moshi. Kazuko desu ga, Yoshiko san irasshaimasu ka?

   —Hai, imasu. Shooshoo omachi kudasai.

3. —Moshi moshi. Itoo san desu ka?

   —Iie, chigaimasu. Mori desu ga.

   —Doomo sumimasen.

4. —Moshi moshi, Waseda Daigaku desu.

   —Anoo, naisen no 115 (o) onegai shimasu.

   —Hanashichuu desu*. Shibaraku omachi kudasai.

   *"line is busy"

4.9 SITUATIONAL AND APPLICATION CONVERSATION

4.9.1 Telephone conversation (1)

A boy telephones a girl friend's home.

The girl answers the phone.

Talking to the girl friend, the boy asks why she didn't come to school on Thursday.

She answers she was sick but has recovered now.

The boy wants to take her to a movie on Sunday.

She agrees to go.

They fix the place and time to meet on Sunday.

4.9.2 Telephone conversation (2)

    A: Hello, is this the Yamada residence?

    B: No, you have a wrong number. (lit. It's wrong.)

    A: I'm sorry.

    ....

    A: Hello, is this the Yamada residence?

    C: Yes, it is.

    A: Is Ikuo there, please?

    C: Ikuo is out now. He will be back around four o'clock.

    A: Then I'll call back later.

4.9.3 Develop your own telephone conversation on the basis of the following entries.

    1. A: Moshi moshi, Yamada san no otaku desu ka?

         B: Hai, soo desu ga.

         A: Otoosan irasshaimasu ka?

         B: Iie, chichi wa imasen ga. Donata desu ka?

         A: Shitsurei shimashita. Watakushi (wa) Yoshida desu.

    2. A: Yamada san. Kurashikku on'gaku o kikitaku arimasen ka?

         B: Ee, on'gaku wa suki desu ga.

         A: Jitsu wa, kippu (o) nimai tomodachi kara moraimashita ga, watashi (wa) kon'shuu isogashii n desu. Yamada san, ikimasen ka?

    3. Hayashi: Moshi moshi, Hayashi desu ga.

         Yoshida: Moshi moshi, Hayashi san? Watashi (wa) Yoshida desu.

         Hayashi: A. Yoshida san, shibaraku desu. Sen'shuu otaku e ukagaimashita ga, irasshaimasen deshita ne.

         Yoshida: Sore wa doomo sumimasen deshita. Jitsu wa, raishuu Minami sen'sei ga uchi e irasshaimasu. Yoshida san mo irasshaimasen ka?

         Hayashi: Soo desu ka? Watashi mo zehi ukagaitai desu nee.

LESSON 5
花見[1]

5.1   PRESENTATION

さくらは　ゆうめいな[2]　日本の　花です。　東京（とうきょう）では　だいたい　四月の　はじめに
さきます。　日本の　人たちは　よく　いろいろな　花を　見に[3]　行きますが、　とくに
さくらが　好きです。

5.2   DIALOG

みち子　「きょうは　いい[4]　お天気ですね。」

ジョージ　「ほんとに　すばらしい　日ですね。　みち子さんは　きょう　なにを　するつもり
　　　　　ですか。」

みち子　「べつに…[5]。　でも、　どうして？」

ジョージ　「ごご　さんぽに[3]　行きませんか。」

みち子　「いいですね[6]。　行きましょう[6]。」

ジョージ　「いい　所を　知っていますか。」

みち子　「上野（うえの）[7]は　どうですか。　ちょうど　今　さくらが　さいていますから[8]、　お花見に[3]
　　　　　行きましょうか。」

ジョージ　「ああ、　花見ですね。　さくらは　大好きな　花ですから[8]、　見に　行きたいです。
　　　　　でも、　そこは　どんな[9]　所ですか。」

みち子　「そうですねえ…[10]。　とても　大きい　公園（こうえん）です。　びじゅつかんや　どうぶつ園（えん）
　　　　　などが　ありますから、　おとなも[11]　小さい　子どもも[11]　おおぜい　あそび[12]
　　　　　に　行きます。　上野（うえの）の　山は　さくらで[13]　ゆうめいですよ。」

ジョージ　「じゃあ、　今は　花見の　きせつですから[8]　人が　おおい[14]でしょうね。」

みち子　「ええ。　じゃあ、　ジョージさん、　こう　しましょう。　はじめに、　どうぶつ
　　　　　園（えん）へ　行きませんか。　そして、　ゆうがた　お花見を　しましょう。」

ジョージ　「それが　いいですね。　ゆうがたは　人が　すくないでしょうから、　たぶん
　　　　　ゆっくり　お花見を　することが　できます[15]ね。」

花見（はなみ）	花（はな）	四月（しがつ）	人（ひと）	好き（すき）	天気（てんき）	所（ところ）
知（し）っています	今（いま）	大好（だいす）き	大（おお）きい	小（ちい）さい	山（やま）	

5.3 PATTERN SENTENCES

5.3.1

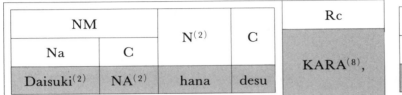
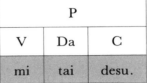

P		
NM	N[4]	C
Adv. → A		
Taihen → II[4]	TEN'KI	desu.

5.3.2

NM		N[2]	C	Rc	P		
Na	C				V	Da	C
Daisuki[2]	NA[2]	hana	desu	KARA[8],	mi	tai	desu.

5.3.3

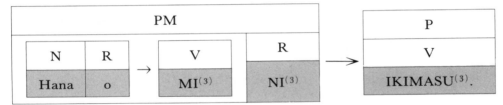

PM					→	P
N	R	V	R			V
Hana	o	→ MI[3]	NI[3]			IKIMASU[3].

5.3.4

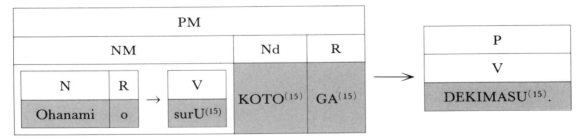

PM						→	P
NM			Nd	R			V
N	R	V					
Ohanami	o	→ surU[15]	KOTO[15]	GA[15]			DEKIMASU[15].

5.4 NOTES

5.4.1 *Hanami*

Hanami, or cherry blossom viewing, has been enjoyed in Japan throughout most of her written history. Records indicate that *hanami* parties were common among the upper classes more than fifteen centuries ago. It was not, however, until about three hundred years ago that such parties became popular among the general public. The *sakura* had a particular significance for the *samurai*. The *samurai* saw their very existence symbolized in the *sakura*—a few days of glory and then certain destruction.

Today, when the *sakura* are in bloom, hundreds of thousands of Japanese flock to Yoshino Mountain, Ueno Park, and many other popular *hanami* areas. Most go in groups, taking large amounts of food and *sake* along, and the parties that follow are often quite lively, with singing and dancing. Before the *sakura* are in bloom, the Japanese enjoy viewing the *ume*, or plum, flower. Atami and Mito are among the most famous *umemi* (plum flower viewing) places.

A significant characteristic of recreation and amusement in Japan lies in the close relation both have with nature. The appreciation of natural beauty and the changes of season directly or indirectly underlie many forms of recreation. *Hanami* is just one example of this deep involvement with nature. In looking for reasons behind their naturalistic emphasis, the fact that the Japanese are surrounded by scenic beauty that is never stagnant, constantly changing and providing a panorama of colors, forms, tastes, and smells, is an obvious consideration.

Furthermore, the Japanese people being agricultural rather than pastoral, they tend to attach deep significance to the land, settling in one place to till the soil, to raise animals, and to grow crops. An intimate sentiment runs deep within the Japanese approach to nature and prevents resentment or anger against it. Thus, although Japan is often the victim of natural catastrophes that ravage the land such as typhoons, earthquakes, and tidal waves, the people traditionally feel resigned to such calamities and indeed feel close to and very much a part of nature.

5.4.2   *Yuumei na* means "(something) which is famous," and, together with *Nihon no*, modifies *hana; yuumei na Nihon no hana* "famous Japanese flower."

Yuumei "famous," *iroiro* "various," *kirei* "pretty," *shizuka* "quiet," and so on are adjectival Nouns, and are normally used as equivalents of English adjectives. In most cases, they behave like other ordinary Nouns. However, when an adjectival Noun is used as a Noun Modifier, that is, before another Noun, it cannot occur as a Modifier of the Noun by itself, but *na*, a conjugated form of the Copula—NA form, occurs immediately after the adjectival Noun.

adjectival Noun + *desu* ⟶ adjectival Noun + *na* + Noun

suki desu	"is fond of"	suki		on'gaku	"favorite music"
yuumei desu	"is famous"	yuumei		kooen	"famous park"
iroiro desu	"is various"	iroiro		hana	"various flowers"
hen desu	"is strange"	hen	*na*	ten'ki	"strange weather"
shitsurei desu	"is rude"	shitsurei		hito	"rude person"
teinei desu	"is polite"	teinei		kotoba	"polite speech"

The following are more adjectival Nouns that have appeared in the text so far: *daikirai, daisuki, dame, gen'ki, heta, hima, joozu, kirai, kirei, nigiyaka, rippa, shizuka.*

Sakura wa yuumei na Nihon no hana desu.	"Cherry blossoms are famous Japanese flowers."
Suki na supootsu wa nan desu ka?	"What is your favorite sport?"

When there is also a Pre-Noun modifying the Noun, the Pre-Noun normally precedes an adjectival Noun.

Ano kirei na tatemono ni hairimashoo.	"Let's go into that pretty building."

An Adverb or other Predicate Modifiers may modify an adjectival Noun that precedes a Noun.

Totemo shizuka na tokoro desu.	"It is a very quiet place."

Chotto hen na ten'ki desu nee.	"It's a little strange weather, isn't it?"
Jooji wa itsumo gen'ki na otoko no ko desu.	"George is a boy who is always full of pep."

5.4.3 *Mi ni ikimasu* means "go to see." The Relational *ni* as in *mi ni ikimasu* denotes the purpose of action, normally that of motion Verbs, such as *ikimasu, kimasu, kaerimasu*. *Ni* is used after the Stem form (Pre-Masu form) of a Verb, such as *mi(masu), ne(masu), san'po shi(masu)*.

Stem form (Pre-Masu form) of Verb + *ni* + motion Verb

~e	mi kiki hanashi hataraki ai asobi yobi	ni	ikimasu kimasu kaerimasu	"go "come "go back	to	see listen talk work meet play call	to (a place)"

Eiga o mi ni ikimasen ka?	"Won't you go to see a movie?"
Ueno e on'gaku o kiki ni ikimashita.	"I went to Ueno to listen to music."
Hirugohan o tabe ni kaerimashoo.	"I think I'll go home to eat lunch."

When it is necessary to indicate a place where one goes, comes, and so forth, the place may precede either the phrase meaning "to see (it)," or be used immediately before the motion Verb, but the former case is more common.

Ueno Kooen e sakura o mi ni ikimashoo. *or* Sakura o mi ni Ueno Kooen e ikimashoo.	"Let's go to Ueno Park to see the cherry blossoms."

In the above pattern, a Noun may replace the Stem form of a Verb if that Noun should connote action (such as *san'po* "a walk," *ben'kyoo* "study," *ken'butsu* "sightseeing," *hanami* "flower viewing") which is normally followed by *shimasu*.

san'po shimasu ben'kyoo shimasu ken'butsu shimasu hanami o shimasu ⟶ kaimono o shimasu shigoto o shimasu shokuji o shimasu	san'po ben'kyoo ken'butsu hanami kaimono shigoto shokuji	ni	ikimasu kimasu kaerimasu	"go "come "go back	for a walk" to study" sightseeing" flower viewing" shopping" to work" for a meal"

Hiru wa uchi e shokuji ni kaerimasu.	"I go home for lunch."
Kinoo Mori san to issho ni Tookyoo e kaimono ni ikimashita.	"I went shopping to Tōkyō with Mr. Mori yesterday."
Sumisu san wa sen'getsu Nihon e ben'kyoo ni kimashita.	"Mr. Smith came to Japan for study last month."

5.4.4 *Ii ten'ki* means "good weather." As in English, an Adjective may precede a Noun and modify it. As explained in Note 5.4.2, an Adverb or other Predicate Modifiers may modify the Adjective, and a Pre-Noun may usually precede the Adjective when both the Pre-Noun and the Adjective modify the following Noun.

(Predicate Modifier)＋Adjective＋Noun

(Pre-Noun)＋Adjective＋Noun

atatakai hi	"warm day"
tsumetai mizu	"cold water"
subarashii tokoro	"wonderful place"
utsukushii Fujisan	"beautiful Mt. Fuji"
hoshii hon	"books I want"
kawaii on'na no ko	"cute girl"
furui tatemono	"old building"
atarashii sen'sei	"new teacher"
Totemo ii ten'ki desu nee.	"It's a very good day [weather], isn't it?"
Kono utsukushii hana wa nan desu ka?	"What is this beautiful flower?"
Kyooto ni wa furui tera ga takusan arimasu.	"There are many old temples in Kyōto."

5.4.5 *Betsu ni* originally means "particularly" and is usually followed by a negative statement. Therefore, it is not necessary for Michiko to make a complete sentence such as *Betsu ni nani mo shimasen* "[I] have nothing to do in particular."

Nani o shitai desu ka?	"What do you want to do?"
Betsu ni.	"Nothing particular."

5.4.6 Michiko's attitude toward George is revealed in her conversation. She seems to dominate, take over the conversation, and actively make suggestions. Michiko is more outspoken than is usual for a traditional Japanese woman, although it is quite normal for her to be talkative because she is the one who knows more about Tōkyō.

5.4.7 Ueno Park

Ueno Park was first created during the Edo period. Today it includes a museum of natural history, a science and technology museum, a modern art museum, a zoo, a concert hall, ponds, trees, and so forth. Within its vicinity there are shopping centers as well as the Ueno station, which is the gateway to Tōkyō from the northeastern part of Japan.

5.4.8 *Kara* immediately after a Predicate is the clause Relational meaning "reason," or "cause," and is often translated as "so," "because," or "since." In normal spoken style, the Predicate occurring before the "reason" or "cause" Relational *kara* is either in normal forms or in plain forms. (Plain forms with *kara* will be introduced later, and only the normal form, such as *desu, deshita, -masu, -mashita,* will be drilled in this lesson.) Note that when an Adjective occurs in the "reason" clause, the Copula *desu* may be rather freely omitted.

Sentence 1 ⎫
Sentence 2 ⎬ ⟶ Sentence 1 + *kara,* Sentence 2
‎ ⎭

Sakura ga saite imasu. ⎫
Mi ni ikimashoo. ⎬ ⟶ Sakura ga saite imasu kara, mi ni ikimashoo.

   "Cherry blossoms are in bloom."   "Cherry blossoms are in bloom, so let's go
   "Let's go to see them."   to see them."

Ima wa hanami no kisetsu desu. ⎫ ⟶ Ima wa hanami no kisetsu desu kara, hito ga
Hito ga ooi deshoo.   ooi deshoo.

   "Now is the flower viewing season."   "Now is the flower viewing season,
   "There probably are many people there."   so there must be many people there."

Kibun ga warui (desu) kara, shigoto   "I don't feel well, so I won't go to work."
  o yasumimasu.

Ten'ki ga yokatta (desu) kara,   "Since the weather was good, we had a very
  totemo tanoshikatta desu.   good time."

Chuugokugo wa naraimasen deshita   "I haven't studied Chinese, so I don't
  kara, wakarimasen.   understand it."

San'po wa suki ja arimasen kara,   "As I don't like taking a walk, I will
  uchi ni imasu.   stay home."

Ashita wa hima desu kara, asobi   "As I won't be busy tomorrow,
  ni kite kudasai.   come and visit me."

5.4.9 *Don'na* is a Pre-Noun meaning "what sort of?" Like *kono, sono, ano,* and *dono,* here is another group of Pre-Nouns:

kon'na   "this sort of"   an'na   "that sort of"
son'na   "that sort of"   don'na   "what sort of?"

Sono kooen wa don'na tokoro desu ka?   "What sort of place is that park?"

Totemo shizuka na tokoro desu.   "It is a very quiet place."

Yoshiko san wa don'na kata desu ka?   "What sort of person is Yoshiko?"

Utsukushii kata desu yo.   "She is a beautiful lady."

5.4.10 *Soo desu nee* . . . is an expression used in the meaning of "Let me see . . . " or "What shall I say?"

5.4.11 *Otona mo chiisai kodomo mo* means "both adults and little children." When the Relational *mo* is repeated in a sentence, it means "both . . . and . . . " or "either . . . or . . . " in negatives. It should be noted that *mo* replaces *ga* and *o,* and it may also follow a phrase with Relationals such as *kara, e, ni,* and so forth.

Noun + *mo* + Noun + *mo*   "both . . . and . . . " or
Noun + Relational + *mo* + Noun + Relational + *mo*   "(not) either . . . or . . . "

Otona mo kodomo mo asobi ni ikimasu.	"Both adults and children visit there."
Koohii mo koocha mo nomimasen.	"I don't drink either coffee or black tea."
Bijutsukan e mo doobutsuen e mo ikimashita.	"I went to the art museum as well as the zoo."
Ichiroo wa uchi ni mo gakkoo ni mo imasen.	"Ichirō is neither at home nor at school."

5.4.12 *Asobimasu* is a Verb that may be interpreted in various ways, and is just the opposite of *hatarakimasu*, *ben'kyoo shimasu*, or *shigoto shimasu*. The following are some of the interpretations of *asobimasu*:

1. "play"

| Kodomotachi ga kooen de ason'de imasu. | "Children are playing in the park." |

2. "enjoy oneself," "have a good time"

| Ashita uchi e asobi ni kimasen ka? | "Won't you come to my house tomorrow (for chatting)?" |
| Kyoo shiken ga owarimashita kara, kon'ban wa asobitai desu. | "Today the exam was over, so I would like to enjoy myself this evening." |

3. "do nothing"

| Ima don'na shigoto o shite imasu ka? | "What sort of work are you doing now?" |
| Ason'de imasu. | "I have no job." "I am loafing." |

Asobimasu cannot be used for "play cards," "play tennis," or "play a musical instrument." Verbs such as *shimasu* (for games) or *hikimasu* (for musical instruments) are used instead.

5.4.13 *Sakura de yuumei desu* means "[this place] is (also) famous for its cherry blossoms." *De* in *sakura de* is a Relational meaning "cause."

| Kan'da wa nan de yuumei desu ka? | "What is Kanda famous for?" |
| Hon'ya de yuumei desu. | "It's famous for bookstores." |

5.4.14 The Adjective *ooi* "are many; is much" or *sukunai* "is few; is little" may not normally occur as a Noun Modifier. A Noun Modifier *takusan* or *oozei* plus *no* may be used instead.

tatemono
ame
kodomo   } ga ooi   *but*   takusan no { tatemono / ame
hito   oozei no { kodomo / hito

gakkoo
hana   } ga sukunai   *but*   sukoshi no { gakkoo / hana / otoko no ko
otoko no ko

Quantity Adverbs such as *oozei, takusan, sukoshi,* may modify a Noun, but when the Relational *no* occurs between it and a Noun, *oozei, takusan,* and so forth are classified as Nouns.

oozei no otona	"many adults"
takusan no kuruma	"a lot of cars"
sukoshi no ame	"a little rain"
san'mai no kami	"three sheets of paper"
gosatsu no jisho	"five dictionaries"

5.4.15 *Ohanami o suru koto ga dekimasu ne* means "[We] will probably be able to see cherry blossoms." The Verb *dekimasu* means "be able to (do)," "be possible," "can (do)," and the one who can do it, if there is one, is followed by *wa;* the thing that one can do is followed by the Relational *ga.* However, the thing that one can do may be expressed either by a Noun or by a Verb plus *koto.*

$$\textbf{Noun (person)} + \textit{wa} + \left\{ \begin{matrix} \textbf{Noun} \\ \textbf{Dictionary form of a Verb} + \textit{koto} \end{matrix} \right\} + \textit{ga} + \textit{dekimasu}$$

Koto is a dependent Noun or a nominalizer meaning "act." It is always preceded by a Noun Modifier—the Dictionary form of a Verb—and together they behave as a Noun.

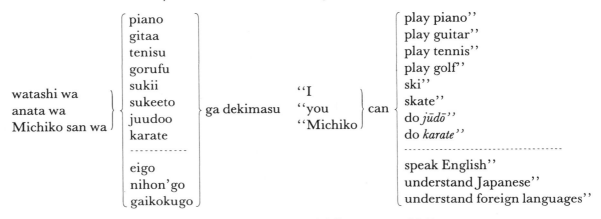

Michiko san wa sukii ga dekimasen.   "Michiko cannot ski."

Ichiroo kun wa karate ga dekimasu ka?   "Can Ichirō do *karate?*"

Ano kata wa eigo ga yoku dekimasu.   "That person has a good command of English."

Ashita san'ji goro uchi ni kuru koto ga dekimasu ka?   "Can you come to my home at about three o'clock tomorrow?"

Iie, isogashii kara, iku koto wa dekimasen.   "No, I'm busy so I can't go."

Nihon'go de hanasu koto ga dekimasen ka?   "Can't you speak in Japanese?"

Ee, dekimasen.   "No, I can't."

Eki de au koto ga dekimasu ka?   "Can I meet with you at the station?"

Dekimasu yo!   "Yes, you can!"

Kan'ji o ikutsu kaku koto ga
dekimasu ka?

"How many *kan'ji* can you write?"

Gojuu gurai kaku koto ga dekimasu.

"I can write about fifty."

5.5 VOCABULARY

Presentation

花見	hanami	......	N	flower viewing (usually cherry blossom viewing) (see 5.4.1)
さくら	sakura	......	N	cherry (tree or blossoms)
ゆうめい	yuumei	......	Na	famous; noted
な	na	......	C	(see 5.4.2)
花	hana	......	N	flower; blossom
だいたい	daitai	......	Adv.	roughly speaking; mostly; approximately
はじめ	hajime	......	N	beginning
さきます	sakimasu	......	V	bloom (normal form of *saku*)
いろいろ	iroiro	......	Na	various
見（に）	mi (ni)	......	V	Stem form of *mimasu* ← *miru*—see; view (see 5.4.3)
に	ni	......	R	Relational of purpose (see 5.4.3)
とくに	toku ni	......	Adv.	especially

Dialog

みち子	Michiko	......	N	girl's first name
ジョージ	Jooji	......	N	George
ほんとに	hon'to ni	......	Adv.	really; truly
さんぽ	san'po	......	N	a stroll; a walk
上野	Ueno	......	N	a district of Tōkyō (see 5.4.7)
さいて	saite	......	V	TE form of *sakimasu* ← *saku*—bloom
から	kara	......	Rc	because; since (see 5.4.8)
ああ	aa	......	SI	oh; ah
どんな	don'na	......	PN	what sort of? (see 5.4.9)
そうですねえ。	Soo desu nee.	......	(exp.)	Well.; Let me see. (see 5.4.10)
公園	kooen	......	N	park; public garden
びじゅつかん	bijutsukan	......	N	art museum
どうぶつ園	doobutsuen	......	N	zoo

おとな	otona	......	N	adult; grown-ups
あそび	asobi	......	V	Stem form of *asobimasu* ← *asobu*—play (see 5.4.12)
で	de	......	R	(famous) for (see 5.4.13)
きせつ	kisetsu	......	N	season
おおい	ooi	......	A	are many; is much (see 5.4.14)
ゆうがた	yuugata	......	N	late afternoon; early evening
すくない	sukunai	......	A	is few; is little (opposite of *ooi*—are many; is much)
こと	koto	......	Nd	act or fact (see 5.4.15)
できます	dekimasu	......	V	is able to; can (do); is possible (see 5.4.15)

Notes

へん	hen	......	Na	strange; unusual; funny
しつれい	shitsurei	......	Na	rude
さんぽ（を）します	san'po (o) shimasu	......	V	stroll; take a walk
うつくしい	utsukushii	......	A	is beautiful
ふじ山	Fujisan	......	N	Mt. Fuji
かわいい	kawaii	......	A	is cute
ふるい	furui	......	A	is old (thing)
あたらしい	atarashii	......	A	is new; is fresh
（お）てら	(o)tera	......	N	temple
こんな	kon'na	......	PN	this sort of (see 5.4.9)
そんな	son'na	......	PN	that sort of
あんな	an'na	......	PN	that sort of
こうちゃ	koocha	......	N	English tea
ピアノ	piano	......	N	piano
ギター	gitaa	......	N	guitar
テニス	tenisu	......	N	tennis
ゴルフ	gorufu	......	N	golf
スキー	sukii	......	N	ski
スケート	sukeeto	......	N	skate
じゅうどう	juudoo	......	N	*jūdō*; a Japanese art of self-defense
からて	karate	......	N	*karate*; an art of self-defense originated in the Ryūkyū Islands

5.6   KAN'JI

5.6.1 花   (1) *hana*   (2) flower   (3) classifier 艹 [grass]

(4) 一 ⼗ 艹 扩 扩 花 花 (5) 花見、花屋、いけ花 [flower arrangement]

(6) shapes of plants 艹 plus a phonetic sign 化（KA）

5.6.2 人   (1) *hito*   (2) person   (3) forms the classifier 人   (4) ノ 人

(5) あの人、 日本の人たち、 おとこの人 (6) the human form

5.6.3 好   (1) *su(ki)*   (2) like   (3) classifier 女   (4) く 乆 女 奵 好

(5) 好きです、大好き   (6) a woman and a child together, signifying love and care. See 4.6.2 and 8.6.3

5.6.4 天   (1) TEN   (2) sky; heaven   (3) classifier 大   (4) 一 二 テ 天

(5) 天気、天こう [climate]、天皇 [Emperor]

5.6.5 気   (1) KI   (2) spirit; mind; energy   (3) classifier 𠂉（气）

(4) ノ 𠂉 𠂉 气 気 気   (5) 天気、気分、げん気、びょう気

5.6.6 所   (1) *tokoro*   (2) place; address   (3) classifier 戸

(4) 一 ヲ ㇕ 戸 戸 所 所 所   (5) きれいな所、先生の所

(6) 戸 means a door, 斤 is the shape of a hacksaw

5.6.7 知   (1) *shi(rimasu)*   (2) know   (3) classifier 矢

(4) ノ ㇒ 乍 チ 矢 知 知 知   (5) 知っています、知りません

5.6.8 今   (1) *ima*   (2) now; present   (3) classifier へ

(4) へ 仐 今   (5) 今、なん時ですか

5.6.a 大[2.6.1]   (1) *oo(kii)*   (5) 大きいうち、大きい子ども

5.6.9 小   (1) *chii(sai)*   (2) small   (3) forms the classifier 小

(4) 亅 小 小   (5) 小さい公園[こうえん]

(6) a person with his/her arms and legs pulled in toward his/her sides. See 2.6.1

5.6.10 山   (1) *yama*   (2) mountain   (3) forms the classifier 山

(4) l 山 山   (5) 山のぼり、山やうみへ行きます、あの山はたかい、中山さん

(6) a shape of a range of mountains with peaks

5.7   DRILLS

5.7.1   Substitution Drill

A. <u>大きい</u>　はこを　ください。

    1.　小さい　　　　　　　　……　小さい　はこを　ください。

    2.　あたらしい　　　　　　……　あたらしい　はこを　ください。

    3.　ふるい　　　　　　　　……　ふるい　はこを　ください。

    4.　その　やすい　　　　　……　その　やすい　はこを　ください。

    5.　その　きたない　　　　……　その　きたない　はこを　ください。

    6.　とても　大きい　　　　……　とても　大きい　はこを　ください。

    7.　その　とても　かわいい　……　その　とても　かわいい　はこを　ください。

B. みち子さんは　<u>いい</u>　人です。

    1.　かわいい　　　　　　　……　みち子さんは　かわいい　人です。

    2.　うつくしい　　　　　　……　みち子さんは　うつくしい　人です。

    3.　おもしろい　　　　　　……　みち子さんは　おもしろい　人です。

    4.　すばらしい　　　　　　……　みち子さんは　すばらしい　人です。

    5.　わるい　　　　　　　　……　みち子さんは　わるい　人です。

    6.　とても　かわいい　　　……　みち子さんは　とても　かわいい　人です。

    7.　たいへん　うつくしい　……　みち子さんは　たいへん　うつくしい　人です。

5.7.2   Substitution Drill

A. あの　人は　<u>ゆうめいな</u>　人ですね。

    1.　げん気な　　　　　　　……　あの　人は　げん気な　人ですね。

    2.　ていねいな　　　　　　……　あの　人は　ていねいな　人ですね。

    3.　きれいな　　　　　　　……　あの　人は　きれいな　人ですね。

    4.　しずかな　　　　　　　……　あの　人は　しずかな　人ですね。

    5.　りっぱな　　　　　　　……　あの　人は　りっぱな　人ですね。

    6.　しつれいな　　　　　　……　あの　人は　しつれいな　人ですね。

    7.　とても　ゆうめいな　　……　あの　人は　とても　ゆうめいな　人ですね。

    8.　へんな　　　　　　　　……　あの　人は　へんな　人ですね。

B. さくらは　<u>ゆうめいな</u>　花です。

    1.　きれいな　　　　　　　……　さくらは　きれいな　花です。

    2.　大好きな　　　　　　　……　さくらは　大好きな　花です。

3. きらいな   …… さくらは きらいな 花です。

4. 好きな   …… さくらは 好きな 花です。

5. ゆうめいな   …… さくらは ゆうめいな 花です。

5.7.3   Mixed Transformation Drill

A. それは <u>きれいな</u> 花です。

1. ゆうめい   …… それは ゆうめいな 花です。

2. うつくしい   …… それは うつくしい 花です。

3. 大好き   …… それは 大好きな 花です。

4. 大きい   …… それは 大きい 花です。

5. 好き   …… それは 好きな 花です。

6. たかい   …… それは たかい 花です。

7. すばらしい   …… それは すばらしい 花です。

8. きらい   …… それは きらいな 花です。

B. あの <u>うつくしい</u> 人は わたしの ともだちです。

1. かわいい   …… あの かわいい 人は わたしの ともだちです。

2. しずか   …… あの しずかな 人は わたしの ともだちです。

3. げん気   …… あの げん気な 人は わたしの ともだちです。

4. しつれい   …… あの しつれいな 人は わたしの ともだちです。

5. 大きい   …… あの 大きい 人は わたしの ともだちです。

6. ていねい   …… あの ていねいな 人は わたしの ともだちです。

7. きれい   …… あの きれいな 人は わたしの ともだちです。

8. 小さい   …… あの 小さい 人は わたしの ともだちです。

C. そこは とても <u>大きい</u> 公園です。

1. しずか   …… そこは とても しずかな 公園です。

2. うつくしい   …… そこは とても うつくしい 公園です。

3. あたらしい   …… そこは とても あたらしい 公園です。

4. ゆうめい   …… そこは とても ゆうめいな 公園です。

5. きれい   …… そこは とても きれいな 公園です。

6. 小さい   …… そこは とても 小さい 公園です。

7. ふるい   …… そこは とても ふるい 公園です。

8. いい   …… そこは とても いい 公園です。

5.7.4 Transformation Drill

1. みち子さんは 女の 人です。　　　　⎫　　みち子さんは きれいな 女の 人です。
   きれいです。　　　　　　　　　　　⎭ ⟶

2. ここは きっさ店です。　　　　　　　⎫　　ここは しずかな きっさ店です。
   しずかです。　　　　　　　　　　　⎭ ⟶

3. きのう えいがを 見ました。　　　　⎫　　きのう つまらない えいがを 見ました。
   つまらないです。　　　　　　　　　⎭ ⟶

4. さくらは 日本の 花です。　　　　　⎫　　さくらは ゆうめいな 日本の 花です。
   ゆうめいです。　　　　　　　　　　⎭ ⟶

5. 公園へ 行ってみました。　　　　　　⎫　　とても とおい 公園へ 行ってみました。
   とても とおいです。　　　　　　　⎭ ⟶

6. ジョージさんは 日本語を はなします。⎫　ジョージさんは じょうずな 日本語を
   じょうずです。　　　　　　　　　　⎭ ⟶　　　　はなします。

7. まい日 おんがくを ききます。　　　⎫　　まい日 好きな おんがくを ききます。
   好きです。　　　　　　　　　　　　⎭ ⟶

8. おてらを けんぶつしました。　　　　⎫　　いろいろな おてらを けんぶつしました。
   いろいろです。　　　　　　　　　　⎭ ⟶

5.7.5 Combination Drill

1. 上野へ 行きましょう。　　　　　　　⎫　　上野へ 花見に 行きましょう。
   花見に 行きましょう。　　　　　　⎭ ⟶

2. 日本へ きました。　　　　　　　　　⎫　　日本へ けんぶつに きました。
   けんぶつに きました。　　　　　　⎭ ⟶

3. みち子さんと いっしょに でかけます。⎫　みち子さんと いっしょに かいものに
   かいものに でかけます。　　　　　⎭ ⟶　　　　でかけます。

4. 先生の 所へ うかがいたいんです。　⎫　　先生の 所へ べんきょうに
   べんきょうに うかがいたいんです。⎭ ⟶　　　　うかがいたいんです。

5. ごご 公園へ 行くつもりです。　　　⎫　　ごご 公園へ さんぽに 行くつもりです。
   さんぽに 行くつもりです。　　　　⎭ ⟶

6. うちへ かえりましたか。　　　　　　⎫　　うちへ しょくじに かえりましたか。
   しょくじに かえりましたか。　　　⎭ ⟶

7. 東京へ きました。　　　　　　　　　⎫　　東京へ しごとに きました。
   しごとに きました。　　　　　　　⎭ ⟶

8. 学校の しょくどうへ きてください。⎫　　学校の しょくどうへ アルバイトに
   アルバイトに きてください。　　　⎭ ⟶　　　　きてください。

5.7.6　Transformation Drill

1. ともだちと　いっしょに　くつを
　　<u>かいます</u>。　⎫
　　行きました。　　⎭ ⟶ ともだちと　いっしょに　くつを　<u>かいに</u>
　　　　　　　　　　　　行きました。

2. 土曜日に　よし子さんに　あいます。　⎫
　　行きましょう。　　　　　　　　⎭ ⟶ 土曜日に　よし子さんに　あいに
　　　　　　　　　　　　　　　　　　行きましょう。

3. 本屋が　じしょを　うります。　⎫
　　学校へ　くるはずです。　　　⎭ ⟶ 本屋が　じしょを　うりに　学校へ
　　　　　　　　　　　　　　　　くるはずです。

4. らい月　はたらきます。　⎫
　　大阪へ　きてください。　⎭ ⟶ らい月　はたらきに　大阪へ
　　　　　　　　　　　　　　きてください。

5. ゆうがた　アルバイトを　します。　⎫
　　でかけます。　　　　　　　　　⎭ ⟶ ゆうがた　アルバイトを　しに
　　　　　　　　　　　　　　　　　でかけます。

6. おおぜいの　学生が　本を　かります。　⎫
　　きます。　　　　　　　　　　　　　⎭ ⟶ おおぜいの　学生が　本を　かりに
　　　　　　　　　　　　　　　　　　　きます。

7. きょういく学を　べんきょうします。　⎫
　　アメリカへ　かえりたいんです。　　⎭ ⟶ きょういく学を　べんきょうしに
　　　　　　　　　　　　　　　　　　アメリカへ　かえりたいんです。

8. いもうとを　よびます。　⎫
　　へやへ　行きました。　　⎭ ⟶ いもうとを　よびに　へやへ　行きました。

9. えを　見ます。　　　　　　　⎫
　　上野の　びじゅつかんへ　　⎬ ⟶ えを　見に　上野の　びじゅつかんへ
　　　　行きましょう。　　　⎭ 　　　　行きましょう。

10. あそびます。　　　　　⎫
　　うちへ　きてください。　⎭ ⟶ あそびに　うちへ　きてください。

5.7.7　Combination Drill

1. さくらが　さいています。　⎫
　　見に　行きませんか。　　⎭ ⟶ さくらが　さいています<u>から</u>、見に
　　　　　　　　　　　　　　行きませんか。

2. 花見の　きせつです。　　　　⎫
　　たぶん　人が　おおいでしょう。⎭ ⟶ 花見の　きせつですから、たぶん　人が
　　　　　　　　　　　　　　　　おおいでしょう。

3. しごとが　たくさん　あります。⎫
　　いそがしいです。　　　　　⎭ ⟶ しごとが　たくさん　ありますから、
　　　　　　　　　　　　　　　いそがしいです。

4. ドイツ語は　ならいませんでした。⎫
　　わかりません。　　　　　　　⎭ ⟶ ドイツ語は　ならいませんでしたから、
　　　　　　　　　　　　　　　　わかりません。

5.　かぶきの　きっぷを　もらいました。　　⎫　　　かぶきの　きっぷを　もらいましたから、
　　あなたに　さしあげましょう。　　　　　⎬　⟶
　　　　　　　　　　　　　　　　　　　　　　⎭　　　　あなたに　さしあげましょう。

6.　気分が　わるいです。　　　　　　　　　⎫　　　気分が　わるい（です）から、
　　休みたいです。　　　　　　　　　　　　⎬　⟶
　　　　　　　　　　　　　　　　　　　　　　⎭　　　　休みたいです。

7.　車を　もっていません。　　　　　　　　⎫　　　車を　もっていませんから、でんしゃで
　　でんしゃで　かえりましょう。　　　　　⎬　⟶
　　　　　　　　　　　　　　　　　　　　　　⎭　　　　かえりましょう。

8.　ハワイは　あたたかいです。　　　　　　⎫　　　ハワイは　あたたかい（です）から、
　　すみたいです。　　　　　　　　　　　　⎬　⟶
　　　　　　　　　　　　　　　　　　　　　　⎭　　　　すみたいです。

5.7.8　Substitution Drill

A.　上野公園で　お花見が　できますか。

　　1.　しょくじ　　　　　　……　上野公園で　しょくじが　できますか。

　　2.　さんぽ　　　　　　　……　上野公園で　さんぽが　できますか。

　　3.　かいもの　　　　　　……　上野公園で　かいものが　できますか。

　　4.　およぎ　　　　　　　……　上野公園で　およぎが　できますか。

　　5.　アルバイト　　　　　……　上野公園で　アルバイトが　できますか。

　　6.　テニス　　　　　　　……　上野公園で　テニスが　できますか。

　　7.　ゴルフ　　　　　　　……　上野公園で　ゴルフが　できますか。

B.　ジョージさんは　ゴルフが　できます。

　　1.　およぎ　　　　　　　……　ジョージさんは　およぎが　できます。

　　2.　日本語　　　　　　　……　ジョージさんは　日本語が　できます。

　　3.　べんきょう　　　　　……　ジョージさんは　べんきょうが　できます。

　　4.　ピアノ　　　　　　　……　ジョージさんは　ピアノが　できます。

　　5.　スケートと　スキー　……　ジョージさんは　スケートと　スキーが　できます。

　　6.　ドイツ語の　かいわ　……　ジョージさんは　ドイツ語の　かいわが　できます。

5.7.9　Transformation Drill

1.　わたしは　かんじを　よみます。　　　⟶　　わたしは　かんじを　よむことが　できます。

2.　ちちは　ドイツ語を　はなします。　　⟶　　ちちは　ドイツ語を　はなすことが
　　　　　　　　　　　　　　　　　　　　　　　　　　できます。

3.　こんばん　えいがを　見ますか。　　　⟶　　こんばん　えいがを　見ることが
　　　　　　　　　　　　　　　　　　　　　　　　　　できますか。

4.　いっしょに　花見に　行きます。　　　⟶　　いっしょに　花見に　行くことが　できます。

5.　あなたは　二時に　きますね。　　　　⟶　　あなたは　二時に　くることが　できますね。

6. 学生も　デパートで　はたらきます。　──→　学生も　デパートで　はたらくことが
　　　　　　　　　　　　　　　　　　　　　　　　　　　　できます。

7. 千円で　きっぷを　かいます。　　　──→　千円で　きっぷを　かうことが　できます。

8. わたしは　はしで　たべません。　　──→　わたしは　はしで　たべることが
　　　　　　　　　　　　　　　　　　　　　　　　　　　　できません。

5.7.10 Expansion Drill

1. かいたいです。　　　　　……　かいたいです。
　　花を　　　　　　　　　……　花を　かいたいです。
　　きれいな　　　　　　　……　きれいな　花を　かいたいです。
　　あの　　　　　　　　　……　あの　きれいな　花を　かいたいです。

2. だれですか。　　　　　　……　だれですか。
　　女の　人は　　　　　　……　女の　人は　だれですか。
　　大きい　　　　　　　　……　大きい　女の　人は　だれですか。
　　あの　　　　　　　　　……　あの　大きい　女の　人は　だれですか。

3. 見に　行きました。　　　……　見に　行きました。
　　おてらを　　　　　　　……　おてらを　見に　行きました。
　　いろいろな　　　　　　……　いろいろな　おてらを　見に　行きました。

4. ききました。　　　　　　……　ききました。
　　おんがくを　　　　　　……　おんがくを　ききました。
　　きっさ店で　　　　　　……　きっさ店で　おんがくを　ききました。
　　きれいな　　　　　　　……　きれいな　きっさ店で　おんがくを　ききました。

5. よみました。　　　　　　……　よみました。
　　ざっしを　　　　　　　……　ざっしを　よみました。
　　おもしろい　　　　　　……　おもしろい　ざっしを　よみました。
　　とても　　　　　　　　……　とても　おもしろい　ざっしを　よみました。
　　きのう　　　　　　　　……　きのう　とても　おもしろい　ざっしを　よみました。

5.7.11 Transformation Drill（〜も〜も）

1. おとなが　見に　きます。　　　　　──→　おとなも　子どもも　見に　きます。
　　子どもが　見に　きます。

2. びじゅつかんに　いませんでした。　　──→　びじゅつかんにも　どうぶつ園にも
　　どうぶつ園に　いませんでした。　　　　　　　　いませんでした。

3. きのう　花見に　行きました。　　　　──→　きのうも　きょうも　花見に　行きました。
　　きょう　花見に　行きました。

4. みち子さんに　レコードを　あげました。
　　ジョージさんに　レコードを
　　　　あげました。　　　　　　　　　⟶　　みち子さんにも　ジョージさんにも
　　　　　　　　　　　　　　　　　　　　　　　　レコードを　あげました。

5. 月曜日に　でんわを　かけました。
　　木曜日に　でんわを　かけました。　⟶　　月曜日にも　木曜日にも　でんわを
　　　　　　　　　　　　　　　　　　　　　　　　かけました。

6. コーヒーは　ほしくありません。
　　こうちゃは　ほしくありません。　　⟶　　コーヒーも　こうちゃも
　　　　　　　　　　　　　　　　　　　　　　　　ほしくありません。

7. ハンカチは　二かいで　うっています。
　　ハンカチは　三がいで　うっています。⟶　ハンカチは　二かいでも　三がいでも
　　　　　　　　　　　　　　　　　　　　　　　　うっています。

8. にっこうへ　りょこうしました。
　　京都へ　りょこうしました。　　　　⟶　　にっこうへも　京都へも
　　　　　　　　　　　　　　　　　　　　　　　　りょこうしました。

5.7.12 Substitution Drill

日本は　さくらで　ゆうめいです。

1. 日本、ふじ山　　　　　　　……　日本は　ふじ山で　ゆうめいです。
2. 京都, ふるい　おてら　　　……　京都は　ふるい　おてらで　ゆうめいです。
3. かんだ、古本屋　　　　　　……　かんだは　古本屋で　ゆうめいです。
4. この　店、おいしい　　　　……　この　店は　おいしい　コーヒーで　ゆうめいです。
　　　　　コーヒー
5. 上野、どうぶつ園　　　　　……　上野は　どうぶつ園で　ゆうめいです。
6. 上野、花見　　　　　　　　……　上野は　花見で　ゆうめいです。
7. りょうあんじ、いしの　にわ……　りょうあんじは　いしの　にわで　ゆうめいです。
8. この　公園、うつくしい　花……　この　公園は　うつくしい　花で　ゆうめいです。

5.7.13 E-J Response Drill

1. ハワイは　どんな　所ですか。
　　a pretty place　　　　　　　……　きれいな　所です。
2. その　えいがは　どんな　えいがでしたか。
　　a very interesting movie　……　とても　おもしろい　えいがでした。
3. どんな　はこが　ほしいですか。
　　a big box　　　　　　　　　……　大きい　はこが　ほしいです。
4. どんな　本を　よみたいですか。
　　a famous book　　　　　　　……　ゆうめいな　本を　よみたいです。
5. ほっかいどうは　どんな　天気でしたか。
　　wonderful weather　　　　　……　すばらしい　天気でした。

6.　あの　学生は　どんな　人ですか。

a quiet man　　　　　　　　……　しずかな　人です。

7.　どんな　うちに　すみたいですか。

a new house　　　　　　　　……　あたらしい　うちに　すみたいです。

5.7.14　E-J Response Drill

1.　きのう　どうして　しごとを　休みましたか。

I didn't feel well　　　　　……　気分が　わるかったから、休みました。

2.　あなたは　どうして　日本語を　ならっていますか。

I want to go to Japan　　　　……　日本へ　行きたいから、ならっています。

3.　どうして　よし子さんを　知っていますか。

I met Yoshiko before　　　　……　まえ　よし子さんに　あいましたから、　知っています。

4.　どうして　ゆうがた　花見に　行きますか。

there are few people　　　　……　人が　すくないから、行きます。

5.　せんしゅう　どうして　きませんでしたか。

I was busy　　　　　　　　……　いそがしかったから、きませんでした。

6.　どうして　えい語で　はなしますか。

I cannot speak French　　　……　フランス語を　はなすことが　できませんから、

　　　　　　　　　　　　　　　　　　えい語で　はなします。

7.　どうして　森さんに　あいませんでしたか。

I didn't have free time　　　……　ひまが　ありませんでしたから、あいませんでした。

8.　どうして　上野の　山へ　行きますか。

cherry blossoms are in bloom　……　さくらが　さいていますから、　行きます。

5.8　　EXERCISES

5.8.1　Transform the following sentences into ～に　行きます ending:

Example:　いっしょに　あそびます。　──→　いっしょに　あそびに　行きます。

1.　あした　よし子さんに　あいます。

2.　かぶきの　きっぷを　もらいました。

3.　森先生を　よびます。

4.　日本語の　本を　かりました。

5.　ちちも　わたしも　まい日　はたらきます。

6.　さくらの　きせつですから、見ましょう。

5.8.2　Fill in each blank with a *hiragana*:

1. あなた（　　）テニス（　　）できますか。
2. デパート（　　）ギター（　　）かい（　　）行きました。
3. この　公園は　花（　　）ゆうめいです。
4. まい日　どこ（　　）さんぽ（　　）行きますか。
5. ゆうがたは　人（　　）すくない（　　）（　　）、しずかでしょう。
6. 好き（　　）山は　ふじ山です。
7. わたしは　スキーは　できます（　　）、スケート（　　）できません。でも、
　　　ジョージさんは　スキー（　　）スケート（　　）じょうずです。
8. おねえさん（　　）ひらがな（　　）かくこと（　　）できますか。

5.8.3　Answer the following questions according to the instructions given:

1. どうして　ぎんざへ　あそびに　行きませんでしたか。

   because I was not free

2. ブラウンさんは　どんな　外国語を　はなすことが　できますか。

   Japanese and Chinese

3. きのう　どんな　所で　しょくじを　しましたか。

   a very pretty restaurant in the Ginza

4. どうして　コーヒーを　のみませんでしたか。

   because I couldn't buy it

5. どんな　えいがを　見ましたか。

   an interesting American movie

5.8.4　Answer the following questions:

1. おくには　どこですか。（おくに―"the place where you are from"）
2. そこは　どんな　所ですか。
3. そこは　なんで　ゆうめいですか。
4. そこでは　どんな　花が　さきますか。
5. 今　なにが　さいていますか。
6. あなたの　くにで　スキーを　することが　できますか。

5.8.5 Write the underlined *hiragana* in *kan'ji*:

1. いい <u>てんき</u>ですから、<u>はなみ</u>に <u>い</u>きましょう。
2. あの <u>おおきい</u> <u>ひと</u>を <u>し</u>っていますか。
3. どんな <u>ところ</u>が すきですか。
4. わたしは <u>いま</u> <u>ちいさい</u> うちに すんでいます。
5. <u>つぎ</u>の <u>ひ</u>は <u>やま</u>で あそびました。

5.8.6 Write in *katakana*:

1. tenisu	3. gorufu	5. sukii	7. gitaa
2. piano	4. sukeeto	6. Jooji	

5.8.7 Explain the significance of flower viewing to the Japanese.

5.8.8 Explain the difference between Japanese and American expressions for describing wonderful weather.

5.8.9 Show how George betrays his foreignness in the dialog.

5.9 SITUATIONAL AND APPLICATION CONVERSATION

5.9.1 Going to the park

Mr. A and Mr. B want to see the cherry blossoms.

Mr. A recommends that they go to a good park where the cherry blossoms are in bloom.

Mr. B asks about the park and Mr. A describes the park for Mr. B.

They decide to go to the park to see the cherry blossoms in the evening.

5.9.2 Talk about going somewhere to enjoy an evening.

5.9.3 Invite your friend to go to a famous spot you are familiar with and describe the place for your friend.

5.9.4 A: Ima isogashii desu ka?

B: Ee, totemo. Suzuki san wa?

A: Boku wa amari isogashiku arimasen. Kore kara ocha o nomi ni iku tsumori desu.

B: Soo. Watashi mo issho ni ikitai n desu kedo nee.

5.9.5   Foreigner: Keiko san, ashita boku to eiga o mi ni ikimasen ka?

Keiko: Ashita wa chotto tsugoo ga warui n desu.

Foreigner: Jaa, asatte wa ikaga desu ka?

Keiko: Watashi amari eiga wa suki ja nai n desu. Gomen nasai.

5.9.6   Yasuko: Kazuko san, gogo aitai n desu kedo.

Kazuko: Ee. Doko de aimashoo ka?

Yasuko: Itsumo no kissaten de niji goro matte imasu.

5.9.7   George: Kon'nichi wa.

Mrs. Katō: Irasshai, Jooji san. Doozo.

George: Kyoo eiga no kippu o nimai moraimashita kara, Michiko san to mi ni ikitai n desu.

Mrs. Katō: Michiko ima imasen kedo.

LESSON 6
REVIEW AND APPLICATION

6.1 CONJUGATION

6.1.1 Verbs of plain imperfect tense form

a. Vowel Verb

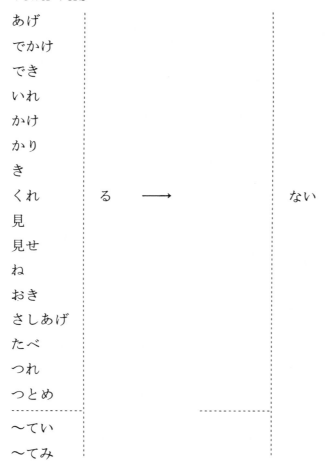

あげ			
でかけ			
でき			
いれ			
かけ			
かり			
き			
くれ	る	⟶	ない
見			
見せ			
ね			
おき			
さしあげ			
たべ			
つれ			
つとめ			
〜てい			
〜てみ			

b. Consonant Verb

ふ			
はい			
はじま			
かえ			
おわ	る	⟶	らない
知			
と			

う わか や	る	→	らない
は はたら 行 いただ か き さ	く		かない
もって行 つれて行			
ま も	つ		たない
あ ちが い か かよ もら なら うかが	う	→	わない
はな さが	す		さない
の す 休 よ	む		まない
あそ よ	ぶ		ばない
およ	ぐ		がない

c. Irregular Verbs *kuru* and *suru*

くる	こない
もってくる	もってこない
つれてくる ⟶	つれてこない
する	しない

アルバイト	りょこう
べんきょう	さんぽ
でんわ	しょくじ
かいもの	しょうかい
けんぶつ	しごと
けっこん	

6.2 PATTERNS

6.2.1 Noun Modifier—adjectival Noun

にぎやか		にぎやか	所 店(みせ)
しずか		しずか	
きれい		きれい	しょくどう
いろいろ		いろいろ	花
ゆうめい		ゆうめい	学校(こう)
げん気		げん気	子ども
しつれい		しつれい	ことば
ていねい		ていねい	てがみ
ひま	です ⟶	ひま	な 学生
だめ		だめ	日
りっぱ		りっぱ	たてもの
好き		好き	人
きらい		きらい	しごと
大好き		大好き	え
大きらい		大きらい	ことば
へん		へん	天気

110

じょうず へた	です →	じょうず へた	な	日本語 かいわ
		どんな		…………

6.2.2 Noun Modifier—Adjective

あたらしい		あたらしい	図書館
ふるい		ふるい	おてら
きたない		きたない	たてもの
うつくしい		うつくしい	女の人
大きい		大きい	山
小さい		小さい	公園
うるさい		うるさい	人
かわいい		かわいい	花
いそがしい		いそがしい	店員
おそい		おそい	バス
はやい		はやい	クラス
おもしろい	です →	おもしろい	しごと
つまらない		つまらない	ざっし
まずい		まずい	しょくじ
おいしい		おいしい	すきやき
むずかしい		むずかしい	かいわ
わるい		わるい	ことば
いい、よい		いい、よい	天気
つめたい		つめたい	ビール
ない		ない	おかね
きつい		きつい	くつ
ほしい		ほしい	おみやげ

ちかい とおい		ちかい とおい	うち おたく
やすい たかい		やすい たかい	きっぷ アルバム
すばらしい たのしい	です ⟶	すばらしい たのしい	りょこう おんがく
すずしい あたたかい むしあつい あつい さむい		すずしい あたたかい むしあつい あつい さむい	日
		↓	
		どんな	……………

6.2.3 Pre-Noun and Predicate Modifier in Noun Modifier

a.

	ゆうめいな しずかな しつれいな うつくしい	人 学生 ともだち
この その あの		
	へんな おもしろい うるさい いい	所 店_{みせ}

b.

	ゆうめいな しずかな しつれいな うつくしい	人 学生 ともだち
とても ちょっと たいへん		

とても ちょっと たいへん	へんな おもしろい うるさい いい	所 店(みせ)

c.

この その あの	とても ちょっと たいへん	ゆうめいな しずかな しつれいな うつくしい	人 学生 ともだち
		へんな おもしろい うるさい いい	所 店(みせ)

6.2.4 Subject in Noun Modifier

うち		とおい ちかい	人 子ども
え		好きな	ともだち
ことば		ふるい すくない	じしょ
え	が の	きれいな	え本
あめ ゆき		おおい ない	きせつ ふゆ
てんぷら		おいしい ゆうめいな	所 店(みせ)
たてもの		あたらしい	図書館(としょかん)

↓

どんな | ………

6.2.5 Intention ''intend to; planning to''

プレゼントを	あげる			あげない	
六時に	おきる			おきない	
あの　店に	はいる			はいらない	
おかねを	いただく			いただかない	
花を	もって行く			もって行かない	
バスを	まつ			またない	
ともだちに	あう	つもりです ⟶ ～	あわない	つもりです
えい語で	はなす			はなさない	
しごとを	休む			休まない	
そとで	あそぶ			あそばない	
プールで	およぐ			およがない	
しょくじに	くる			こない	
けっこんを	する			しない	

↓　　　　　　　　　↓

～ ｜…………… ｜つもりでした　　　～ ｜……………｜ つもりでした

わたくし		きょう　さんぽに　行く		です
しゅじん	は		つもり	
いもうと		よし子さんに　それを　はなさない		でした

6.2.6 Expectation ''supposed to; expected to''

からてが	できる			できない	
あめが	ふる			ふらない	
花が	さく			さかない	
さんぽに	行く	はずです ⟶ ～	行かない	はずです
車を	もつ			もたない	
なまえが	ちがう			ちがわない	
東京に	すむ			すまない	
タクシーを	よぶ			よばない	
うみで	およぐ			およがない	

↓　　　　　　　　　↓

～ ｜………… ｜はずでした　　　～ ｜……………｜ はずでした

6.2.7 Potential ''be able to''

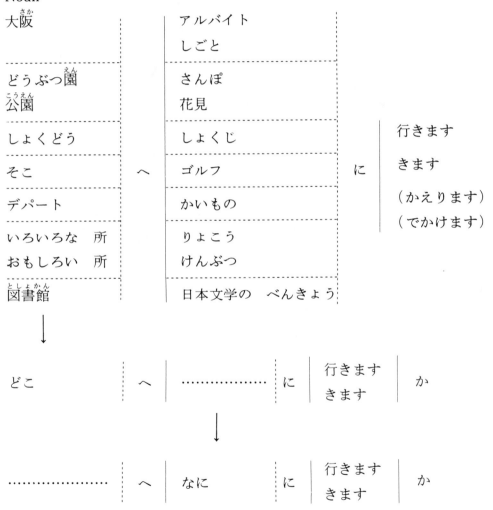

ぼく 林さん ともだち	は	ドイツ語を　はなす フランス語を　よむ バイオリンを　ひく あさ　三時に　おきる ふゆ　アルバイトする	こと	が （は）	できます

6.2.8 Purpose of a motion

a.　Noun

大阪	へ	アルバイト しごと	に	行きます きます （かえります） （でかけます）
どうぶつ園 公園		さんぽ 花見		
しょくどう		しょくじ		
そこ		ゴルフ		
デパート		かいもの		
いろいろな　所 おもしろい　所		りょこう けんぶつ		
図書館		日本文学の　べんきょう		

どこ	へ	…………………	に	行きます きます	か

…………………	へ	なに	に	行きます きます	か

b.　Verb

かぶきざ	へ	かぶきを　見	に	行きます きます （かえります） （でかけます）
そと		でんわを　かけ		
びじゅつかん		えを　見		

ともだちの　所		じしょを　もらい ノートを　かり			
うち		おとうとを　よび			行きます
大学		日本語を　べんきょうし			きます
きっさ店	へ	レコードを　きき	に		（かえります）
えき		せんぱいに　あい			（でかけます）
どうぶつ園		いもうとと　あそび			
学校		本を　さがし			

↓

どこ	へ	…………………………	に	行きます きます	か

↓

………………	へ	なにを　し	に	行きます きます	か

6.2.9　Intransitive Verbs with Relational *ga*

さくら 花		さきます
えいが しごと かいわ 学校		はじまります おわります
フランス語 日本人の　ことば	が	わかります
日本語の　かいわ からて じゅうどう ギター		できます
でんわばんごう なまえ		ちがいます

6.2.10 Clause Relational *kara* "because"

花見の　きせつです		人が　おおいでしょう
すきやきは　好きじゃありません		たべたくありません
あの　人は　ゆうめいでした		知っています
スケートは　じょうずではありません　でした		しませんでした
サイズが　ちょうど　いい（です）		これを　かうつもりです
バスは　はやくありません	から、	タクシーで　行きましょう
天気が　よかった（です）		さんぽに　行きました
気分が　よくありませんでした		学校を　休みました
日本語を　ならっています		ときどき　日本の　えいがを　見ます
よく　わかりませんでした		もう一ど　いってみてください
一日じゅう　うちに　いました　あめが　ふっていました		こんばん　でかけたいです　でかけませんでした

↓

どうして　………………………………　か

6.2.11 Indirect Relational *ni*

わたし あなた よし子さん	は	ジョージさん せんぱい 森さん	に	でんわを　かける　つもりです そう　いっています ひらがなで　かきました はなして　みました でんわばんごうを　見せます きっぷを　うりました

6.2.12 Relationals ～*mo* ～*mo* "both ～ and ～" "(not) either ～ or ～"

おとな わたし	も	子ども あなた	も	知っています 知りません

えいが		かぶき		見たいです
あさ ごぜん	も	ゆうがた ごご	も	さんぽしました でかけませんでした
土曜日に どうぶつ園へ 天気の いい 日に		日曜日に びじゅつかんへ わるい 日に		カメラを もって行きます いぬを つれて行きません

6.3　REVIEW DRILLS

6.3.1　E-J Substitution Drill

A.　<u>いい</u>　人に　あいましたか。

1.	very nice	……	とても　いい　人に　あいましたか。
2.	very pretty	……	とても　きれいな　人に　あいましたか。
3.	who likes *jūdō*	……	じゅうどうが　好きな　人に　あいましたか。
4.	who is good at tennis	……	テニスの　じょうずな　人に　あいましたか。
5.	that polite	……	あの　ていねいな　人に　あいましたか。
6.	that very famous	……	あの　とても　ゆうめいな　人に　あいましたか。
7.	what sort of	……	どんな　人に　あいましたか。

B.　<u>おもしろい</u>　本を　かいました。

1.	very difficult	……	とても　むずかしい　本を　かいました。
2.	a little expensive	……	すこし　たかい　本を　かいました。
3.	my favorite	……	わたしの　好きな　本を　かいました。
4.	that I want	……	わたしが　ほしい　本を　かいました。
5.	various	……	いろいろな　本を　かいました。
6.	very old	……	とても　ふるい　本を　かいました。

C.　<u>きれいな</u>　所へ　行きましょうか。

1.	various	……	いろいろな　所へ　行きましょうか。
2.	that has little rain	……	あめの　すくない　所へ　行きましょうか。
3.	where fruit is delicious	……	くだものが　おいしい　所へ　行きましょうか。
4.	famous for cherry blossoms	……	さくらで　ゆうめいな　所へ　行きましょうか。
5.	very warm	……	とても　あたたかい　所へ　行きましょうか。
6.	what sort of	……	どんな　所へ　行きましょうか。

6.3.2　Substitution Drill

A.　上野へ　さくらを　見に　行きましょうか。

1.　えを　見ます　　　　……　上野へ　えを　見に　行きましょうか。

2.　さんぽ　　　　　　　……　上野へ　さんぽに　行きましょうか。

3.　公園　　　　　　　　……　公園へ　さんぽに　行きましょうか。

4.　あそびます　　　　　……　公園へ　あそびに　行きましょうか。

5.　ともだちの　所　　　……　ともだちの　所へ　あそびに　行きましょうか。

6.　先生の　おたく　　　……　先生の　おたくへ　あそびに　行きましょうか。

7.　どこ　　　　　　　　……　どこへ　あそびに　行きましょうか。

B.　うちへ　あそびに　きてください。

1.　東京　　　　　　　　……　東京へ　あそびに　きてください。

2.　べんきょうします　　……　東京へ　べんきょうしに　きてください。

3.　図書館　　　　　　　……　図書館へ　べんきょうしに　きてください。

4.　本を　かります　　　……　図書館へ　本を　かりに　きてください。

5.　うち　　　　　　　　……　うちへ　本を　かりに　きてください。

6.　しょくじ　　　　　　……　うちへ　しょくじに　きてください。

7.　あいます　　　　　　……　うちへ　あいに　きてください。

C.　うちへ　しょくじに　かえりましたか。

1.　ごはんを　たべます　……　うちへ　ごはんを　たべに　かえりましたか。

2.　ねます　　　　　　　……　うちへ　ねに　かえりましたか。

3.　おかねを　もらいます　……　うちへ　おかねを　もらいに　かえりましたか。

4.　くに　　　　　　　　……　くにへ　おかねを　もらいに　かえりましたか。

5.　かぞくに　あいます　……　くにへ　かぞくに　あいに　かえりましたか。

6.　あそびます　　　　　……　くにへ　あそびに　かえりましたか。

7.　なにを　します　　　……　くにへ　なにを　しに　かえりましたか。

6.3.3　Relational Checking Drill（から or けど）

1.　天気が　いいです。　　　　　　天気が　いい（です）から、さんぽに
　　さんぽに　行きましょう。　　　　行きましょう。

2.　あの　公園は　ゆうめいじゃ　　　あの　公園は　ゆうめいじゃありませんけど、
　　　　ありません。　　　　　　　　わたしたちは　よく　知っています。
　　わたしたちは　よく　知っています。

3.　えいがは　四時半に　はじまります。　えいがは　四時半に　はじまりますから、
　　四時ごろ　きてください。　　　　　四時ごろ　きてください。

4. 気分が　わるいです。
　　学校は　休まないつもりです。 ⟶ 気分が　わるい（です）けど、学校は
　　　　　　　　　　　　　　　　　　　　休まないつもりです。

5. せんぱいに　でんわを　かけました。 ⟶ せんぱいに　でんわを　かけましたけど、
　　るすでした。 　　　　　　　　　　　　　るすでした。

6. びじゅつかんに　好きな　えが
　　　あります。 ⟶ びじゅつかんに　好きな　えが
　　よく　見に　行きます。 　　　　　あ';ますから、よく　見に　行きます。

7. かいものに　でかけました。 ⟶ かいものに　でかけましたけど、
　　かいませんでした。 　　　　　　　　かいませんでした。

8. えいがの　きっぷを　もらいました。 ⟶ えいがの　きっぷを　もらいましたけど、
　　見に　行きませんでした。 　　　　　　見に　行きませんでした。

9. えいがの　きっぷを　もらいました。 ⟶ えいがの　きっぷを　もらいましたから、
　　子どもを　つれて行くつもりです。 　　　子どもを　つれて行くつもりです。

10. カメラを　すぐ　もってきます。 ⟶ カメラを　すぐ　もってきますから、
　　ちょっと　まっていてください。 　　　　ちょっと　まっていてください。

6.3.4　Substitution and Transformation Drill

1. A: あなたは　さんぽに　行きますね。
　 B: ええ、行くつもりです。
　 A: 井上さんも　行きますか。
　 B: 行くはずですけど、よく　わかりません。
　　　 1. カメラを　もって行きます　　　2. 日本語の　クラスを　とります
　　　 3. あした　きます　　　　　　　　4. らい年　けっこんします
　　　 5. 日本語の　じしょを　かいます

2. A: みち子さんは　月曜日には　休みませんね。
　 B: ええ、休まないはずですけど。
　 A: なん曜日に　休みますか。
　 B: 火曜日に　休むはずです。
　　　 1. 火曜日、水曜日、アルバイトします　　2. 水曜日、木曜日、くにへ　かえります
　　　 3. 木曜日、金曜日、あいに　きます　　　4. 金曜日、土曜日、はたらきます
　　　 5. 土曜日、日曜日、あそびます

3. A: 日本へ　なにを　しに　きましたか。
　 B: べんきょうしに　きました。

A: どこで　べんきょうする<u>つもりですか。</u>

B: <u>東京大学で</u>　べんきょうするつもりです。

1. はたらきます、大阪の　かいしゃ　　2. しごとを　します、東京

3. あそびます、京都　　　　　　　　　4. 日本語を　ならいます、日本語学校

5. さくらを　見ます、京都

6.4　REVIEW EXERCISES

6.4.1　Insert a Relational in each blank:

1. なつ休み（　　）は　山へ（　　）　うみへ（　　）　あそび（　　）　行きたい
   です。

2. 「からて（　　）　できますか。」「いいえ。でも、じゅうどう（　　）
   できます。」

3. ともだち（　　）　あいたかった（　　）、ともだちの　うち（　　）　でんわ（　　）
   かけました（　　）、るすでした。

4. スキー（　　）　ゆうめいな　所（　　）　知っていますか。

5. 先生（　　）　そう　はなしてみてください。

6. おとうさん（　　）　おたく（　　）　いらっしゃるはずですよ。

7. なん曜日（　　）　かいしゃ（　　）　休みましたか。

8. ちゅうごく語（　　）　わかりますか。

9. しゅじんは　ドイツ（　　）　はたらき（　　）　行きました。

10. わたしは　公園（　　）　いぬ（　　）　つれて行きました。

11. つごう（　　）　いい　日は　いつですか。

12. でんわばんごう（　　）　ちがいますよ。もう一ど　かけてみてください。

13. 四月（　　）　はじめ（　　）　どんな　花（　　）　さきますか。

14. 小さい　子ども（　　）　おとな（　　）　おおぜい　います。

15. かぶきは　四時半（　　）　はじまります（　　）、四時十五分（　　）
    あいましょう。

6.4.2　Complete each of the following:

1. いろいろな　花が　ほしい（です）から、＿＿＿＿＿＿＿＿＿＿＿＿＿。

2. いろいろな　花が　ほしい（です）けど、＿＿＿＿＿＿＿＿＿＿＿＿＿。

3. 天気が　よくありませんから、＿＿＿＿＿＿＿＿＿＿＿。

4. 天気が　よくありませんけど、＿＿＿＿＿＿＿＿＿＿＿。

5. 木曜日に　しけんが　ありますから、＿＿＿＿＿＿＿＿＿＿＿。

6. 木曜日に　しけんが　ありますけど、＿＿＿＿＿＿＿＿＿＿＿＿。

7. さくらが　さきましたから、＿＿＿＿＿＿＿＿＿＿。

8. さくらが　さきましたけど、＿＿＿＿＿＿＿＿＿＿。

9. ここでは　日本語を　はなすことが　できませんから、＿＿＿＿＿＿＿＿＿＿＿。

10. ここでは　日本語を　はなすことが　できませんけど、＿＿＿＿＿＿＿＿＿＿。

6.4.3 Answer the following questions:

1. いつも　あなたは　だいたい　なん時ごろ　おきますか。

2. こんばん　なん時ごろ　ねるつもりですか。

3. おしごとは　なん時に　はじまりますか。

4. どうして　日本語を　ならっていますか。

5. かんじを　いくつぐらい　かくことが　できますか。

6. 好きな　きせつは　いつですか。

7. その　きせつに　どんな　スポーツが　できますか。

8. あなたの　くにでは　お花見に　行きませんね。

9. あなたの　くには　どんな　花で　ゆうめいですか。

10. あなたは　つぎの　クラスを　休みませんね。

6.5   AURAL COMPREHENSION

6.5.1　A　「もしもし、井上さんの　おたくですか。」

　　　　B　「いいえ、ちがいますけど。」

　　　　A　「どうも　すみません。」

6.5.2　A　「もしもし、井上さんの　おたくですか。」

　　　　C　「いいえ、ちがいます。」

　　　　A　「03の　941の　4589ではありませんか。」

　　　　C　「いいえ、941の　4588ですけど。」

　　　　A　「あ、どうも　しつれいしました。」

6.5.3　すずき　「もしもし、森さんですか。」

　　　　森　　　「はい、そうですが。」

　　　　すずき　「東京大学の　すずきですが、けい子さん、いらっしゃいますか。」

　　　　森　　　「今　ちょっと　いません。おひるごろには　かえるはずですが。」

　　　　すずき　「そうですか。じゃ、また　あとで　でんわしますから。」

森　　　「こちらから　かけましょうか。」

すずき　「いいえ、けっこうです。では、また。」

6.5.4　けい子　「もしもし、森です。」

すずき　「もしもし、けい子さん？」

けい子　「ええ、けい子ですけど。すずきさん？」

すずき　「そう。じつは、きょうの　クラスを　休みますから、先生に　そう　いって
　　　　くださぃ。」

けい子　「わかりました。でも、どうして？」

すずき　「ちょっと　気分が　わるいから、これから　びょういんへ　行くつもり
　　　　です。」

けい子　「それは　いけませんね*1。おだいじに*2。」

　　　　　　　*1"That's too bad."　　*2"Please take good care of yourself."

6.5.5　井上　「もしもし、林さんの　おたくですか。」

林　　　「はい、そうです。」

井上　　「ごしゅじんは　いらっしゃいますか。」

林　　　「いま　ちょっと　るすですが、どなたでしょうか。」

井上　　「井上です」

林　　　「ああ、井上さんですか。しばらくです。」

井上　　「おくさんですか。みなさん、お元気ですか。」

林　　　「ええ、おかげさまで。」

井上　　「じつは、あした　ぜひ　ごしゅじんに　あいたいんですが。」

林　　　「あしたは　土曜日ですね。今　ちょっと　しゅじんの　あしたの　つごうは
　　　　わかりませんが。」

井上　　「じゃあ、また　あとで　でんわを　してみます。」

林　　　「ええ、おねがいします。八時半ごろ　かえるはずですから。」

井上　　「そうですか。では、また。」

6.5.6　A　「かいものですか。」

B　「ええ、きょうは　かないの　たんじょう日ですから、プレゼントを　かいに
　　きました。」

A 「そうですか。」

B 「ネックレス*1か イヤリング*2を かうつもりですが、いい 店を
  知っていますか。」

A 「あの デパートで バーゲンセール*3を していますよ。」

B 「そうですか。どうも。あなたの たんじょう日は いつですか。」

A 「十一月三日です。」

B 「じゃあ、もうすぐですね。おくさんから なにを もらいますか。」

A 「とけい*4を くれるはずですけど、わかりません。たかいですからね。じゃあ、
  行ってらっしゃい。」

    *1"necklace" *2"earring" *3"bargain sale" *4"watch"

6.5.7　　わたしは この しゅうまつに 京都けんぶつに 行きました。かないも 子どもも
いっしょでした。すぐ けんぶつを するつもりでしたが、みんな おなかが すいて
いました*1から、はじめに しょくじを しに てんぷら屋へ はいりました。てんぷら
の とても おいしい 店でした。

　　ごご いろいろな おてらを 見に 行きました。りょうあんじへは まえ 行きました
から、こんどは 行かないつもりでした。でも、まだ ゆうがた はやかったから、
行ってみました。しずかな にわが とても よかったです。

　　つぎの 日も いろいろな ゆうめいな おてらや じんじゃ*2を けんぶつしまし
た。つぎの 休みに また ゆっくり 京都へ 行ってみたいです。

*1"was hungry" *2"shrines"

LESSON 7
のりもの[1]

7.1   PRESENTATION

東京から　大阪まで[2]　五百五十六キロ[3]（三百四十六マイル）ありますが、　むかしは　はやい
のりものが　ありませんでしたから、　りょこう　するの[4]は　たいへんでした。　今は　ひこうき
では　一時間、　しんかん線[5]では　三時間で[6]　行くこと[7]が　できます。

7.2   DIALOG

外国人　「ちょっと　うかがいますが[8]、　新潟行[9]の　急行は　どれでしょうか。」

日本人　「さあ[10]、　よく　わかりません。　あそこに　いる　駅員[11]に　聞いて[12]みてください。」

外国人　「はい、　どうも。」

. . . .

外国人　「あのう[13]、　新潟行の　急行に　のり[14]たいんですが、　なん番線[15]から　出ますか。」

駅員　　「二十三時二十分に　出る[11]　急行ですか。　七番線からです[16]。」

外国人　「新潟まで　どのくらい[17]　かかりますか。」

駅員　　「急行が　新潟に　つく[18]　時間[19]は　あしたの　ごぜん　五時十五分ですから、五時間[19]
　　　　　五十五分　かかります。」

外国人　「そうですか。　グリーンけんを　中で　かうことが　できますか。」

駅員　　「さあ、　わかりませんね。　のってから[20]、　しゃしょうに　聞いてみてください。
　　　　　たまに　のらない　人[21]や　すぐ　おりる[22]　人が　いますから。」

外国人　「じゃあ、　そう　します。　どうも　ありがとう。」

とうきょう	おおさか	いちじかん	がいこくじん	にいがたゆき	にほんじん
東京	大阪	一時間	外国人	新潟行	日本人

えきいん	き	で	なか
駅員	聞いて	出ます	中

7.3 PATTERN SENTENCES

7.3.1

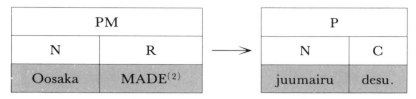

7.3.2

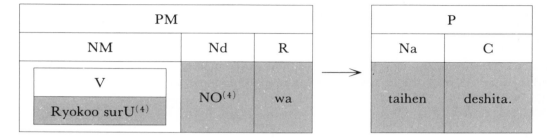

7.3.3

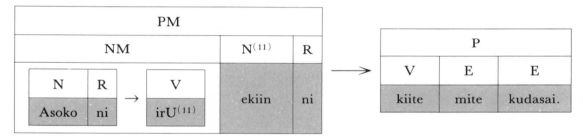

7.3.4

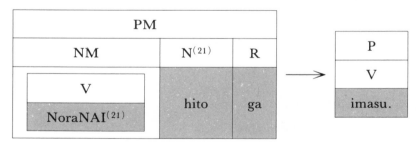

7.4 NOTES

7.4.1 *Norimono* means "vehicle" or "transportation facility." The following two are also commonly used words of the same kind: *tabemono* "food," *nomimono* "a drink."

Norimono ga arimasu ka?   "Do you have transportation?"

Don'na tabemono ga suki desu ka?   "What sort of food do you like?"

Nomimono ga hoshii n desu kedo.   "I'd like to have something to drink."

7.4.2 *Made* in *Oosaka made* means "as far as (a place)" or "up to and including (a place)." The Predicate Modifier with *made* often follows the Predicate Modifier with *kara* "from."

$$\left.\begin{array}{l}\textbf{Noun}+\textbf{\textit{kara}}\\\textbf{Noun}+\textbf{\textit{made}}\end{array}\right\}+\textbf{Predicate}\longrightarrow(\textbf{Noun}+\textbf{\textit{kara}})+\textbf{Noun}+\textbf{\textit{made}}+\textbf{Predicate}$$

Tookyoo kara Oosaka made gohyaku gojuu rokkiro arimasu.	"It is five hundred and fifty-six kilometers from Tōkyō to Ōsaka."
Shin'juku kara Shibuya made den'sha de jippun gurai kakarimasu.	"It takes about ten minutes from Shinjuku to Shibuya by train."
Maiasa uchi kara eki made arukimasu.	"I walk from my house to the station every morning."
Kooen made takushii ni norimashoo.	"Let's take a taxi to the park."

The difference between *made* and *e* is that *e* "to" or "toward" merely represents direction while *made* is used in sentences referring to distance, the time required to go, or the means by which one goes the distance.

Compare:

Kono den'sha wa Ueno made ikimasu.	"This train goes as far as Ueno."
Kono den'sha wa ima Kan'da kara Ueno e hashitte imasu.	"This train is now running from Kanda toward Ueno."

The *made* can also be used in the meaning of "until, including the time," with or without *kara*.

Kyoo wa kuji kara niji made kurasu ga arimasu.	"I have classes from nine to two o'clock today."
Itsu made koko ni imasu ka?	"Until when (how long) are we going to be here?"
Doyoobi made koko ni imasu.	"We'll be here until Saturday."

7.4.3 *-Kiro* here is the shortened equivalent of *-kiromeetoru*. *-Meetoru* and *-sen'chi* (*meetoru*) are also used to state length. Japan has been using the metric system for some time. The following is a conversion table showing U.S. equivalents.

Conversion of Metric to U.S. System

	Metric	U.S. equivalents
length	1 meter	3.28084 feet
	1 kilometer	0.62137 mile
area	1 hectare	2.47105 acres
	1 square meter	1.19599 square yards
capacity	1 liter	0.21998 Imp. gallon
		0.26418 U.S. gallon
	1 cubic meter	35.31467 cubic feet
weight	1 gram	0.03527 ounce
	1 metric ton	0.98419 long ton
		1.10231 short tons

7.4.4 *Ryokoo suru no wa taihen deshita* means "It was very hard to travel." The *no* after the plain form of a Verb is a dependent Noun or a nominalizer meaning "act." *No* is always preceded by a Noun Modifier—in this lesson, the Dictionary form of a Verb—and the combination *ryokoo suru no* serves as a Noun equivalent to "to travel," or "traveling."

The Dictionary form of Verbs has been introduced in Lesson 4. (See Note 4.4.3.) Here are some Verbs in the Dictionary form:

1. Vowel Verb

deki-masu	⟶	deki-ru	i-masu	⟶ i-ru
de-masu	⟶	de-ru	dekake-masu	⟶ dekake-ru
ori-masu	⟶	ori-ru	tabe-masu	⟶ tabe-ru

2. Consonant Verb

hashir-imasu	⟶	hashir-u	aruk-imasu	⟶ aruk-u
kakar-imasu	⟶	kakar-u	hik-imasu	⟶ hik-u
nor-imasu	⟶	nor-u	kik-imasu	⟶ kik-u
hair-imasu	⟶	hair-u	sak-imasu	⟶ sak-u
kaer-imasu	⟶	kaer-u	tsuk-imasu	⟶ tsuk-u
ukaga-imasu	⟶	ukaga-u	kak-imasu	⟶ kak-u
a-imasu	⟶	a-u	ik-imasu	⟶ ik-u
ka-imasu	⟶	ka-u	hana/s/-imasu	⟶ hana/s/-u
ma/t/-imasu	⟶	ma/t/-u	saga/s/-imasu	⟶ saga/s/-u
mo/t/-imasu	⟶	mo/t/-u	nom-imasu	⟶ nom-u
			yasum-imasu	⟶ yasum-u
			asob-imasu	⟶ asob-u
			yob-imasu	⟶ yob-u
			isog-imasu	⟶ isog-u

3. Irregular Verb

kimasu	⟶	kuru	shimasu	⟶ suru

The *no* may be used in several patterns, but only the following use of *no* will be dealt with in this lesson:

(Predicate Modifier)＋Dictionary form of Verb＋*no*＋ $\left\{ \begin{array}{l} \textit{wa} \\ \textit{ga} \end{array} \right\}$ **. . .**

Oosaka made ryokoo suru			taihen desu
issho ni iku	*no*	wa	tanoshii desu
gaikokugo o narau		ga	yasashii desu
fune ni noru			suki desu

		hard	travel to Ōsaka"
"it's	pleasant	to	go together"
	easy		learn a foreign language"
"[I]	like		take a ship"

Maiasa aruku no wa tanoshii desu.   "To walk every morning is pleasant."

Ima kyuukoo ni noru no wa
    muzukashii deshoo.   "It must be difficult to catch an express now."

Kan'ji o ben'kyoo suru no wa taihen desu ga, omoshiroi desu yo.	"It is hard to study Chinese characters, but it is interesting."
Suujii san wa nihon'go de hanasu no ga joozu desu.	"Susie is good at speaking Japanese."
Nani o suru no ga suki desu ka?	"What do you like to do?"
Boku wa piano o hiku no ga suki desu.	"I like to play the piano."

7.4.5 *Shin'kan'sen*—the new trunk line—with its "bullet" train, is known to be the fastest and safest train in the world. The new expresses run between Tōkyō and Hakata, Ōmiya and Nīgata, and Ōmiya and Morioka at an average speed exceeding 100 MPH, and have been known to go as fast as 158 MPH.

In Japan, trains are relied upon for transportation to a much greater extent than in America. However, with the rapid development of highways and expressways, privately owned automobiles are becoming increasingly important as a mode of transportation. Air transportation is presently heavily utilized, and air traffic more congested than ever before.

The subway system is amazingly efficient. Trains are well maintained, lacking the graffiti which is the trademark of the New York subway.

7.4.6 *San'jikan de* means "in three hours." The *de* after a number that shows length of time is the Relational meaning "in," as in "in a year," or "within," as in "within two hours."

gofun nijikan yonen	de	"in" "within"	five minutes" two hours" four years"

Juugofun de soko e ikimasu kara, matte ite kudasai!	"I'll be there in fifteen minutes, so please wait for me!"
Watakushi wa nijikan de soko ni tsuku koto ga dekimasu.	"I can reach there in two hours."
Oosaka e wa ichijikan de ikimasu.	"It takes one hour to go to Ōsaka."

7.4.7 *Iku koto ga dekimasu* is "(we) can go," or literally means "going is possible." As already introduced in Note 5.4.15, *dekimasu* is an intransitive Verb meaning "is possible" or "can," and what one can do is followed by the subject Relational *ga*. Like *no* introduced in Note 7.4.4, *koto* preceded by the Dictionary form of a Verb behaves as a Noun meaning "to (do)," or "(do)ing." Although *koto* and *no* are similar in their function and meaning and are sometimes interchangeable, *koto* cannot be replaced by *no* in the pattern ~ *koto ga dekimasu*.

7.4.8 *Chotto ukagaimasu ga,* . . . is used when the speaker needs some information and starts talking, usually with a stranger. This expression corresponds to "Excuse me, but may I ask you a question?" *Ukagaimasu* here is a polite equivalent of *kikimasu* "hear" or "inquire."

Chotto ukagaimasu ga, . . . provides further illustration of two points that have been mentioned previously. *Chotto* softens the expression, and *ukagaimasu* is the polite form of *kikimasu* meaning "to inquire." The speech level is raised in this instance because the utterance is being addressed to a stranger. The softener—in this case *chotto*—is frequently used to avoid abruptness, and in this instance functions similarly to the expression *Sumimasen ga*.

Ukagaimasu is a far more polite version of *kikimasu*: *kikimasu* and *shitsumon shimasu* are differentiated in that *kikimasu* means "ask" as well as "listen," whereas the latter expression means only "question." *Ukagaimasu* is the polite counterpart of both questioning and, to a lesser degree, listening, as well as "visit." (See Lesson 2.)

7.4.9   *Niigata-yuki no kyuukoo* means "express bound for Nīgata." The *-yuki* is derived from *yuki(masu)*, which is an alternative form of *iki(masu)* "go." Sometimes *-iki* is used instead of *-yuki*.

Nyuu Yooku yuki no hikooki	"airplane for New York"
Kono fune wa San Furan'shisuko yuki desu ka?	"Is this ship bound for San Francisco?"
Are wa doko yuki no basu desu ka?	"Where does that bus go?"

7.4.10   *Saa* indicates that you are thinking, that it is not very clear in your mind. Therefore, when *saa* is followed by *wakarimasen*, it means "Well, I don't know or understand it too well." *Saa* can also be used independently, in which case it carries the meaning that you are pondering something. *Saa* has a very high frequency of usage.

Shin'bun wa doko desu ka?	"Where is the newspaper?"
Saa, shirimasen.	"Well, I don't know."
Saa . . .	"Well . . ."

7.4.11   *Asoko ni iru ekiin* means "a station employee who is over there." When a Verb modifies or describes the following Noun, the Verb is in the Dictionary form. The Dictionary forms of Verbs have been introduced in Note 4.4.3. Depending upon what the Noun modified by the preceding Predicate represents, the English equivalent will be "something which or that does such and such," "one who does such and such," "the time when one does such and such," and so on. While a Noun Modifier in English may precede or follow the Noun modified, the Noun Modifier in Japanese always precedes the Noun directly. Thus:

Noun Modifier + Noun

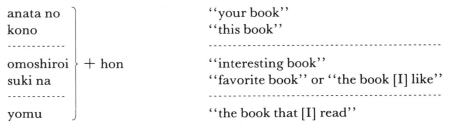

anata no	"your book"
kono	"this book"
omoshiroi + hon	"interesting book"
suki na	"favorite book" or "the book [I] like"
yomu	"the book that [I] read"

The verbal Noun Modifier that precedes a Noun can be a single Verb or have Predicate Modifiers:

(Predicate Modifier)+Verb (normal form)⟶
　　　　　　　　(Predicate Modifier)+Verb (plain form)+ Noun

asoko ni iru ekiin	"a station employee who is over there"
ryokoo suru hito	"a person who travels"
nijuu ichiji ni deru kyuukoo	"an express train that leaves at 2100"
Oosaka ni tsuku jikan	"the time when it arrives at Ōsaka"
sugu oriru hito	"a person who will get off soon"
mainichi kaimono o suru mise	"the store where I do some shopping every day"
yuki ga furu kisetsu	"the season when it snows"
kuni e kaeru hi	"the day when I go home"
Asoko ni iru on'na no gakusei wa dare desu ka?	"Who is the girl student over there?"
Watakushi wa rokuji ni deru kyuukoo ni norimasu.	"I will take an express train that leaves at six o'clock."
Hayashi san ga Oosaka ni tsuku jikan o shitte imasu ka?	"Do you know the time when Mr. Hayashi arrives at Ōsaka?"

When a sentence that modifies a Noun includes the subject, the subject is followed either by the subject Relational *ga* or by *no*. *No* can replace *ga* in the Noun Modifier. Note that the Relational *wa* never replaces *ga* in this case; in other words, when a sentence has *wa* following the subject, *wa* should be changed into *ga* or *no*.

Noun+*ga*+Predicate
　　　　　　　　⟶ Noun+*ga* or Noun+*no* } **+Predicate+Noun**
Noun+*wa*+Predicate

kyuukoo ga tsukimasu ⟶ kyuukoo { ga / no } tsuku jikan

"an express arrives" "time when an express arrives"

hana ga ooi desu ⟶ hana { ga / no } ooi kooen

"there are many flowers" "a park where there are many flowers"

on'gaku ga suki desu ⟶ on'gaku { ga / no } suki na hito

"he likes music" "a person who likes music"

Michiko san wa on'gaku ga suki desu ⟶ Michiko san { ga / no } suki na on'gaku

"Michiko likes music" "the music which Michiko likes"

The following examples show how to form a Noun Modifier plus a Noun:

gakusei / kodomo } *ga* { ikimasu / aruite imasu / nete imasu ⟶ iku / aruite iru / nete iru } gakusei / kodomo

"a student { "goes"
"a child   { "is walking"
            { "is sleeping"

"a student } who { "goes"
"a child   }   { "is walking"
                  { "is sleeping"

kuruma   } ga { kimasu
kyuukoo }   { demasu
              { hashitte imasu

⟶

kuru   } kuruma
deru   } kyuukoo
hashitte iru }

"a car   { comes"
"an express { leaves"
            { is running"

"a car   } that { comes"
"an express }   { leaves"
                   { is running"

watakushi wa { tegami o kakimasu
             { zasshi o yomimasu
             { ben'kyoo o shite imasu

⟶

watakushi ga/no { kaku tegami
                { yomu zasshi
                { shite iru ben'kyoo

"I { write a letter"
   { read a magazine"
   { am studying"

"a letter   } which I { write"
"a magazine }   { read"
"study   }   { am doing"

inu ga
----
shokudoo ga } kooen ni { imasu
----------   { ----------
basu ga   { arimasu
                       { ----------
                       { tsukimasu

⟶

inu ga/no iru
shokudoo ga/no aru } kooen
basu ga/no tsuku

"a dog is   } in a park"
"an eating house is } (at)
"a bus arrives   }

"a park where { there is a dog"
              { there is an eating house"
              { a bus arrives"

Sumisu san ga eki de { machimasu
                     { hataraite imasu

⟶

Sumisu san ga/no { matsu
                 { hataraite iru } eki

"Mr. Smith { waits
           { is working } at the station"

"the station where Mr. Smith { waits"
                             { is working"

boku wa { mise e kimasu
(ga)   { daigaku e kaerimasu
         { yuumei na tokoro e ikimasu

⟶

boku ga/no { kuru mise
           { kaeru daigaku
           { iku yuumei na tokoro

"I { come to the store"
   { return to the college"
   { go to a famous place"

"the store   } where { I come"
"the college   }   { I return"
"a famous place   }   { I go"

Daigaku e iku gakusei wa nan'nin imasu ka?

"How many students are there going to the college?"

Sumisu san ga hataraite iru eki wa doko desu ka?

"Where is the station Mr. Smith is working at?"

Michiko san ga matte iru tokoro wa ano kissaten desu.

"The place where Michiko is waiting is that coffee shop."

7.4.12 The Verb *kikimasu* has another meaning, "inquire," in addition to "listen" or "hear." The person of whom one inquires is followed by the Relational *ni*, and what one inquires is followed by *o*.

Shashoo ni kiite mite kudasai.	"Please ask a conductor and find out."
Inoue san ni ano gakusei no namae o kikimashita.	"I asked Mr. Inoue that student's name."

As already introduced in Note 7.4.8, *ukagaimasu* is a polite equivalent of *kikimasu*.

Sen'sei ni ukagaimashoo.	"Let's ask the teacher about it."

7.4.13 *Anoo* is a Sentence Interjective meaning "Say" or "Er-r-r-r." It is more casual and informal than *Sumimasen ga . . .* or *Chotto ukagaimasu ga. . . .* It implies hesitation, allows one time to think and thus avoids abruptness. English expressions similar to *Anoo* might be "Well . . . ," "Let me see . . . ," or "Hmm. . . ." Such expressions stall for time while one thinks.

7.4.14 *Nori(masu)* is a Verb meaning "get on (a vehicle)" or "take (a train)." This Verb is an intransitive Verb, and what one gets on or takes is followed by the Relational *ni*.

Den'sha ni norimasu ka, basu ni norimasu ka?	"Are you going to take a train or a bus?"
Guriin'sha ni norimashoo.	"Let's ride in a green car."

7.4.15 *Nan'ban'sen* is "what track number?" The *-ban* is a counter for naming numbers in succession, and *sen* means "track" or "line." *Nanaban'sen* is "track number seven."

Nan'ban'sen kara demasu ka?	"What track (number) does it leave from?"
Ichiban'sen kara demasu.	"It leaves from track number one."

7.4.16 *Nanaban'sen kara desu* is a variation of *Nanaban'sen kara demasu*. A Predicate Modifier can be used alone as a short reply to a question. In this case, the Predicate Modifier is usually followed by the Copula *desu* in normal speech.

Kono kyuukoo wa doko made ikimasu ka?	"How far does this express go?"
Oosaka made desu.	"It goes to Ōsaka."

7.4.17 *Dono gurai* (or *kurai*) means here "how long?" Depending upon the situation and the Predicate following it, *dono gurai* (*kurai*) may mean "how long?" "how far?" "how much?" and so on. When the Verb following *dono gurai* is *kakarimasu* "require," *dono gurai* means "how long?" or "how much?" and *dono gurai* with *arimasu* means "how far?" or "how much?" *Desu* can be used in place of *arimasu* and *kakarimasu*.

Tookyoo kara Oosaka made dono gurai kakarimasu ka?	"How long does it take from Tōkyō to Ōsaka?"
San'jikan gurai kakarimasu.	"It takes about three hours."

Tookyoo kara Oosaka made dono gurai arimasu ka?	"How far is it from Tōkyō to Ōsaka?"
San'byaku yon'juu rokumairu arimasu.	"It is 346 miles."
Sumisu san wa dono gurai Nihon ni imashita ka?	"How long did Mr. Smith stay in Japan?"
San'nen gurai imashita.	"He stayed about three years."
Anata no sei wa dono gurai arimasu ka?	"How tall are you?"
Ichimeetoru hachijissen'chi gurai arimasu.	"I am about one meter and eighty centimeters tall."

7.4.18 *Niigata ni tsuku jikan* means "the time when [the train] arrives at Nīgata." The destination is followed by *ni*, which precedes the Verb *tsuku*.

Uchi ni tsuku jikan wa osoi deshoo.	"The time when we arrive home will be late."
Kono basu wa eki no doko ni tsukimasu ka?	"Where does this bus arrive (stop) at in the station?"

7.4.19 *Jikan,* when used as an independent Noun, means "hour" or "time."

shokuji ben'kyoo nihon'go } no jikan	"time for { a meal" study" Japanese"
gakkoo { e iku ni tsuku kara kaeru } jikan	"time { to go to to arrive at to return from } school"
Jikan ga kakarimasu.	"It takes time."
Neru jikan wa hayai desu ka?	"Is your bedtime early?"

The *-jikan* preceded by numerals is a counter meaning "hour." *Nan'jikan* is "how many hours?"

Nan'jikan kakarimasu ka?	"How many hours does it take?"
Juujikan'han kakarimasu.	"It takes ten hours and a half."
Mainichi gojikan nihon'go o ben'kyoo shimasu.	"I study Japanese five hours every day."

7.4.20 *Notte kara* means "after getting on (a train)." This usage will be introduced in Volume III.

7.4.21 *Noranai hito* means "a person who does not get on (a train)." Like the pattern already introduced in Note 7.4.11, *hito* is described or modified by *noranai. Noranai* is the plain negative imperfect tense, and the plain equivalent of *norimasen* which has been introduced in Note 4.4.3.

Here are some Verbs in the plain negative imperfect tense form:

1. Vowel Verb

deki-masu	⟶	deki-ru	⟶ deki-nai
de-masu	⟶	de-ru	⟶ de-nai
ori-masu	⟶	ori-ru	⟶ ori-nai
i-masu	⟶	i-ru	⟶ i-nai
dekake-masu	⟶	dekake-ru	⟶ dekake-nai
tabe-masu	⟶	tabe-ru	⟶ tabe-nai

2. Consonant Verb

hashir-imasu	⟶	hashir-u	⟶ hashir-anai
kakar-imasu	⟶	kakar-u	⟶ kakar-anai
nor-imasu	⟶	nor-u	⟶ nor-anai
hair-imasu	⟶	hair-u	⟶ hair-anai
kaer-imasu	⟶	kaer-u	⟶ kaer-anai
ukaga(w)-imasu	⟶	ukaga(w)-u	⟶ ukagaw-anai
a(w)-imasu	⟶	a(w)-u	⟶ aw-anai
ka(w)-imasu	⟶	ka(w)-u	⟶ kaw-anai
ma/t/-imasu	⟶	ma/t/-u	⟶ mat-anai
mo/t/-imasu	⟶	mo/t/-u	⟶ mot-anai
aruk-imasu	⟶	aruk-u	⟶ aruk-anai
hik-imasu	⟶	hik-u	⟶ hik-anai
kik-imasu	⟶	kik-u	⟶ kik-anai
sak-imasu	⟶	sak-u	⟶ sak-anai
tsuk-imasu	⟶	tsuk-u	⟶ tsuk-anai
kak-imasu	⟶	kak-u	⟶ kak-anai
ik-imasu	⟶	ik-u	⟶ ik-anai
hana/s/-imasu	⟶	hanas-u	⟶ hanas-anai
saga/s/-imasu	⟶	sagas-u	⟶ sagas-anai
nom-imasu	⟶	nom-u	⟶ nom-anai
yasum-imasu	⟶	yasum-u	⟶ yasum-anai
asob-imasu	⟶	asob-u	⟶ asob-anai
yob-imasu	⟶	yob-u	⟶ yob-anai
isog-imasu	⟶	isog-u	⟶ isog-anai

3. Irregular Verb

kimasu	⟶	kuru	⟶ konai
shimasu	⟶	suru	⟶ shinai

The structural environment is the same as that of the affirmative form in Note 7.4.11.

kyuukoo ni { noru / noranai } hito   "a person who { gets on / does not take } an express"

watashi { ga / no } { motte iru / motte inai } hon   "the book that I { have / do not have }"

watashi { ga / no } { oriru / orinai } eki   "a station where { I get off / I don't get off }" ame ga $\left\{ \begin{array}{l} \text{furu} \\ \text{furanai} \end{array} \right\}$ kisetsu   "the season when $\left\{ \begin{array}{l} \text{it rains"} \\ \text{it doesn't rain"} \end{array} \right.$

Takushii ni noru hito ga san'nin imasu.   "There are three persons who take a taxi."

Den'sha ni noranai hito wa imasen.   "There are no persons who do not get on (ride) a train."

Chichi ga ima yon'de iru shin'bun wa Asahi Shin'bun desu.   "The newspaper my father is reading now is the Asahi Newspaper."

Chichi ga ima yon'de inai shin'bun wa Mainichi Shin'bun desu.   "The newspaper my father is not reading now is the Mainichi Newspaper."

7.4.22 The opposite of *norimasu* is *orimasu* "get off," and what one gets off is followed by the Relational *kara*.

Oosaka de kyuukoo kara orimashita.   "I got off an express at Ōsaka."

Hikooki kara orimashita. Soshite, sugu takushii ni norimashita.   "I got off the airplane, and I took a taxi right away."

7.5   VOCABULARY

Presentation

のりもの	norimono	......	N	transportation facilities; vehicle (see 7.4.1)
まで	made	......	R	as far as; until (see 7.4.2)
キロ	-kiro	......	Nd	short form of *kiromeetoru*—kilometer (see 7.4.3)
マイル	-mairu	......	Nd	mile
むかし	mukashi	......	N	old times
はやい	hayai	......	A	is fast; is rapid; is early
の	no	......	Nd	nominalizer (see 7.4.4)
たいへん	taihen	......	Na	awful; hard; terrible; troublesome
時間	-jikan	......	Nd	hour(s) (see 7.4.19)
しんかん線	Shin'kan'sen	......	N	New Trunk Line (see 7.4.5)
で	de	......	R	within; in (see 7.4.6)

Dialog

ちょっと うかが いますが...	Chotto ukagaimasu ga ...	......	(exp.)	Excuse me, but ... (see 7.4.8)
うかがいます	ukagaimasu	......	V	inquire; hear (normal form of *ukagau*)
新潟	Niigata	......	N	name of a prefecture in northern Honshū
行	-yuki	......	Nd	bound for; for (see 7.4.9)

急行 (きゅうこう)	kyuukoo	......	N	express
さあ	saa	......	SI	well (hesitance) (see 7.4.10)
駅員 (いん)	ekiin	......	N	station employee
聞いて	kiite	......	V	TE form of *kikimasu* ← *kiku*—inquire (see 7.4.12)
あのう	anoo	......	SI	say; well; er-r-r-r (see 7.4.13)
のり	nori	......	V	Stem form of *norimasu* ← *noru*—get on; ride (see 7.4.14)
なん番線 (ばんせん)	nan'ban'sen	......	Ni	what track number? (see 7.4.15)
出ます	demasu	......	V	go out; leave (normal form of *deru*)
どのぐらい (どのくらい)	dono gurai (dono kurai)	......	Ni	how long?; how far?; how much? (see 7.4.17)
かかります	kakarimasu	......	V	require; take (normal form of *kakaru*)
つく	tsuku	......	V	arrive (Dictionary form) (see 7.4.18)
時間	jikan	......	N	time; hour (see 7.4.19)
グリーンけん	guriin'ken	......	N	green ticket for green car (＝first-class car)
中	naka	......	N	inside (see 9.4.2)
のってから	notte kara	......	V＋R	after getting on (see 7.4.20)
しゃしょう	shashoo	......	N	conductor
たまに	tama ni	......	Adv.	occasionally; once in a while
おりる	oriru	......	V	get off (Dictionary form) (see 7.4.22)

Notes

たべもの	tabemono	......	N	food
のみもの	nomimono	......	N	a drink; a beverage
あるきます	arukimasu	......	V	walk (normal form of *aruku*)
はしります	hashirimasu	......	V	run (normal form of *hashiru*)
スージー	Suujii	......	N	Susie
ひきます	hikimasu	......	V	play (the piano, strings, etc.) (normal form of *hiku*)
ニューヨーク	Nyuu Yooku	......	N	New York
サンフランシスコ	San Furan'shisuko	......	N	San Francisco
の	no	......	R	*no* substituting for the subject Relational *ga* (see 7.4.11)
グリーン車 (しゃ)	guriin'sha	......	N	green car (＝first-class car)
番線 (ばんせん)	-ban'sen	......	Nd	track number

せい	sei	......	N	height; stature
メートル	-meetoru	......	Nd	meter
センチ	-sen'chi	......	Nd	centimeter
Drills				
たかい	takai	......	A	is high; is tall
ひくい	hikui	......	A	is low; is short

7.6   KAN'JI

7.6.1 東   (1) TOO   (2) east   (3) classifier 木

(4) 一 厂 亓 万 亘 車 東 東   (5) 東京、東部 [eastern part]

(6) homonym 棟、凍; the sun rising up behind a tree. See 2.6.5 and 4.6.9

7.6.2 京   (1) KYOO   (2) capital   (3) classifier 亠

(4) ` 亠 亠 古 古 亨 亨 京   (5) 東京、京都

7.6.3 間   (1) KAN   (2) space; time; interval   (3) classifier 門 [gate]

(4) l 厂 F P P' 門 門 門 門 閂 閊 間   (5) 時間、九時間

(6) homonym 関、閑、簡; 門 shows the shape of a gate, the sun 日 shining between the gate

7.6.4 外   (1) GAI   (2) foreign; outside   (3) classifier 夕

(4) ノ ク 夕 夗 外   (5) 外国人、外人 [foreigner]

(6) the crescent moon 夕, which means an evening, and the crack of a tortoise shell, together signifying outside or exterior

7.6.5 国   (1) KOKU [-GOKU]   (2) country   (3) classifier 囗 [enclosure]

(4) l 冂 冂 冃 用 国 国 国   (5) 外国、中国

7.6.a 人 [5.6.2]   (1) JIN   (5) 日本人、外国人、アメリカ人

7.6.6 駅   (1) EKI   (2) (train) station   (3) classifier 馬 [horse]

(4) l 厂 Π FF 严 馬 馬 馬 馬 馬 馿 駅 駅

(5) 東京駅、駅員   (6) 馬 is the shape of a horse

7.6.7 聞 (1) *ki*(*kimasu*); *ki*(*ku*) (2) hear; listen; ask; inquire (3) classifier 門 (耳)
(4) 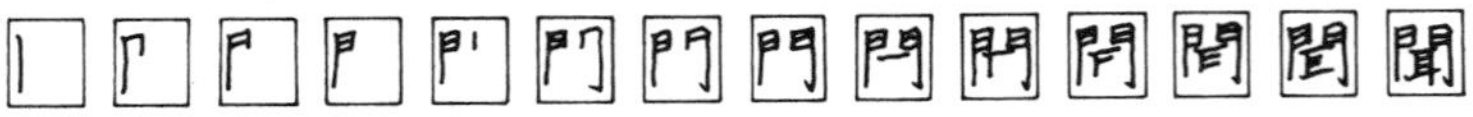
(5) おんがくを聞きます、あの人に聞いてみましょう
(6) an ear 耳 at the gate 門 means "listening" or "asking"

7.6.8 出 (1) *de*(*masu*); *de*(*ru*) (2) go out; come out; start (3) classifier 屮 (凵)
(4)  (5) 出ます、出かけます、出る

7.6.9 中 (1) *naka* (2) inside; within (3) classifier 口 (丨) (4) 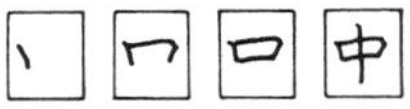
(5) へやの中 (6) a line through the middle of the mouth

7.6.b 行[4.6.3] (1) *yuki* (2) destination (5) 東京行

7.7 DRILLS

7.7.1 Transformation Drill

1.	行きます	⟶	行く	12.	出ます	⟶	出る
2.	きます "wear"	⟶	きる	13.	つきます	⟶	つく
3.	あいます	⟶	あう	14.	かかります	⟶	かかる
4.	べんきょうします	⟶	べんきょうする	15.	はなします	⟶	はなす
5.	のります	⟶	のる	16.	よびます	⟶	よぶ
6.	あるきます	⟶	あるく	17.	さんぽします	⟶	さんぽする
7.	います	⟶	いる	18.	休みます	⟶	休む
8.	聞きます	⟶	聞く	19.	ちがいます	⟶	ちがう
9.	すみます	⟶	すむ	20.	できます	⟶	できる
10.	はしります	⟶	はしる	21.	きます "come"	⟶	くる
11.	おります	⟶	おりる	22.	まちます	⟶	まつ

7.7.2 Transformation Drill

1.	のりません	⟶	のらない	7.	まちません	⟶	またない
2.	ならいません	⟶	ならわない	8.	つきません	⟶	つかない
3.	おりません	⟶	おりない	9.	はしりません	⟶	はしらない
4.	わすれません	⟶	わすれない	10.	知りません	⟶	知らない
5.	かかりません	⟶	かからない	11.	あるきません	⟶	あるかない
6.	出ません	⟶	出ない	12.	聞きません	⟶	聞かない

13.	きません	⟶	こない		
	"do not come"				
14.	りょこうしません	⟶	りょこう しない		

15.	いません	⟶	いない
16.	ありません *Exception	⟶	ない
17.	およぎません	⟶	およがない
18.	よみます	⟶	よまない

7.7.3 Transformation Drill

1.	あそぶ	⟶	あそばない		10.	かかる	⟶	かからない
2.	きく	⟶	きかない		11.	もつ	⟶	もたない
3.	行く	⟶	行かない		12.	のる	⟶	のらない
4.	ちがう	⟶	ちがわない		13.	はしる	⟶	はしらない
5.	おりる	⟶	おりない		14.	つとめる	⟶	つとめない
6.	もらう	⟶	もらわない		15.	できる	⟶	できない
7.	はなす	⟶	はなさない		16.	休む	⟶	休まない
8.	出る	⟶	出ない		17.	くる	⟶	こない
9.	つく	⟶	つかない		18.	およぐ	⟶	およがない

7.7.4 Substitution Drill

A. あれは　あたらしい　でんしゃです。

1. とても　はやい　　　……　あれは　とても　はやい　でんしゃです。

2. たいへん　ふるい　　……　あれは　たいへん　ふるい　でんしゃです。

3. 十時に　出る　　　　……　あれは　十時に　出る　でんしゃです。

4. 大阪（さか）へ　行く　　　……　あれは　大阪（さか）へ　行く　でんしゃです。

5. 東京まで　行かない　……　あれは　東京まで　行かない　でんしゃです。

B. あの　かわいい　子どもは　スージーです。

1. せいが　たかい　　　……　あの　せいが　たかい　子どもは　スージーです。

2. 日本語（ご）が　じょうずな　……　あの　日本語（ご）が　じょうずな　子どもは　スージーです。

3. にわで　あそんでいる　……　あの　にわで　あそんでいる　子どもは　スージーです。

4. おかしを　たべている　……　あの　おかしを　たべている　子どもは　スージーです。

5. でんしゃに　のらない　……　あの　でんしゃに　のらない　子どもは　スージーです。

C. そこは　いい　店（みせ）です。

1. きれいな　　　　　　……　そこは　きれいな　店（みせ）です。

2. レインコートを
　うっている　　　　……　そこは　レインコートを　うっている　店（みせ）です。

3. レコードを
　うっていない　　　　……　そこは　レコードを　うっていない　店（みせ）です。

4. 店員が　あまり　　　……　そこは　店員が　あまり　いない　店です。
　　　　いない

5. 子どもの　くつが　　　……　そこは　子どもの　くつが　ない　店です。
　　　　ない

D. おもしろい　本を　よみたいです。

1. むずかしい　　　　　　……　むずかしい　本を　よみたいです。

2. いろいろな　　　　　　……　いろいろな　本を　よみたいです。

3. みち子さんが　　　　　……　みち子さんが　もっている　本を　よみたいです。
　　　　もっている

4. 図書館に　ある　　　　……　図書館に　ある　本を　よみたいです。

5. みんなが　知らない　……　みんなが　知らない　本を　よみたいです。

E. 急行に　のる　時間を　知っていますか。

1. クラスが　はじまる　……　クラスが　はじまる　時間を　知っていますか。

2. 大阪に　つく　　　　　……　大阪に　つく　時間を　知っていますか。

3. 東京行が　出る　　　　……　東京行が　出る　時間を　知っていますか。

4. スージーさんが　　　　……　スージーさんが　みち子さんに　あう　時間を
　　　　みち子さんに　　　　　　　知っていますか。
　　　　あう

5. この　えいがが　　　　……　この　えいがが　おわる　時間を　知っていますか。
　　　　おわる

F. スージーさんが　たべない　たべものは　なんですか。

1. あなたが　知らない　……　あなたが　知らない　たべものは　なんですか。

2. 日本人が　たべている　……　日本人が　たべている　たべものは　なんですか。

3. あそこで　うっている　……　あそこで　うっている　たべものは　なんですか。

4. あの　子どもが　　　　……　あの　子どもが　もっている　たべものは　なんですか。
　　　　もっている

5. 日本に　ない　　　　　……　日本に　ない　たべものは　なんですか。

7.7.5 Expansion Drill

1. 聞いてください。　　　……　聞いてください。

　　駅員に　　　　　　　　……　駅員に　聞いてください。

　　あそこに　いる　　　　……　あそこに　いる　駅員に　聞いてください。

2. 見せてください。　　　……　見せてください。

　　本を　　　　　　　　　……　本を　見せてください。

よまない	……　よまない　本を　見せてください。
あなたが	……　あなたが　よまない　本を　見せてください。

3.　知っていますか。　　　　　……　知っていますか。

時間を　　　　　　　　　　……　時間を　知っていますか。

つく　　　　　　　　　　　……　つく　時間を　知っていますか。

大阪に　　　　　　　　　　……　大阪に　つく　時間を　知っていますか。

急行が　　　　　　　　　　……　急行が　大阪に　つく　時間を　知っていますか。

4.　います。　　　　　　　　　……　います。

おおぜい　　　　　　　　　……　おおぜい　います。

お客さんが　　　　　　　　……　お客さんが　おおぜい　います。

のらない　　　　　　　　　……　のらない　お客さんが　おおぜい　います。

急行に　　　　　　　　　　……　急行に　のらない　お客さんが　おおぜい　います。

5.　なんですか。　　　　　　　……　なんですか。

花は　　　　　　　　　　　……　花は　なんですか。

さく　　　　　　　　　　　……　さく　花は　なんですか。

四月に　　　　　　　　　　……　四月に　さく　花は　なんですか。

日本で　　　　　　　　　　……　日本で　四月に　さく　花は　なんですか。

7.7.6　Substitution Drill

A.　<u>大阪へ　行く</u>　急行は　どれですか。

　　1.　九時に　出ます　　　　　……　九時に　出る　急行は　どれですか。

　　2.　あなたが　のります　　　……　あなたが　のる　急行は　どれですか。

　　3.　ごご　三時に　つきます　……　ごご　三時に　つく　急行は　どれですか。

　　4.　かとう先生が　のっています　……　かとう先生が　のっている　急行は
　　　　　　　　　　　　　　　　　　　　　どれですか。

　　5.　しょくどうが　あります　……　しょくどうが　ある　急行は　どれですか。

B.　<u>京都へ　行く</u>　学生は　だれですか。

　　1.　くにへ　かえります　　　……　くにへ　かえる　学生は　だれですか。

　　2.　アルバイトを　しません　……　アルバイトを　しない　学生は　だれですか。

　　3.　日本語が　できます　　　……　日本語が　できる　学生は　だれですか。

　　4.　九月に　けっこんします　……　九月に　けっこんする　学生は　だれですか。

　　5.　あそこに　います　　　　……　あそこに　いる　学生は　だれですか。

　　6.　日本語を　ならっていません　……　日本語を　ならっていない　学生は
　　　　　　　　　　　　　　　　　　　　　だれですか。

C.　<u>あした　けんぶつする　所は　どこですか。</u>
　　1.　みずを　のみます　　　　　　　……　みずを　のむ　所は　どこですか。
　　2.　きっぷを　かいます　　　　　　……　きっぷを　かう　所は　どこですか。
　　3.　しんかん線が　つきます　　　　……　しんかん線が　つく　所は　どこですか。
　　4.　大阪行が　出ます　　　　　　　……　大阪行が　出る　所は　どこですか。
　　5.　子どもたちが　あそんでいます　……　子どもたちが　あそんでいる　所は
　　　　　　　　　　　　　　　　　　　　　　　　　　どこですか。
　　6.　今　さくらが　さいています　　……　今　さくらが　さいている　所は　どこですか。
D.　<u>これは　わたしの　もっていない　本です。</u>
　　1.　図書館に　ありません　　　　　……　これは　図書館に　ない　本です。
　　2.　本屋で　うっていません　　　　……　これは　本屋で　うっていない　本です。
　　3.　ぼくは　知りません　　　　　　……　これは　ぼくが　知らない　本です。
　　4.　今　よんでいません　　　　　　……　これは　今　よんでいない　本です。

7.7.7　Substitution Drill

A.　<u>わたしは　はしるのが　好きです。</u>
　　1.　スキーを　します　　……　わたしは　スキーを　するのが　好きです。
　　2.　えいがを　見ます　　……　わたしは　えいがを　見るのが　好きです。
　　3.　ともだちに　あいます　……　わたしは　ともだちに　あうのが　好きです。
　　4.　ラジオを　聞きます　　……　わたしは　ラジオを　聞くのが　好きです。
　　5.　急行に　のります　　……　わたしは　急行に　のるのが　好きです。
　　6.　こうちゃを　のみます　……　わたしは　こうちゃを　のむのが　好きです。
　　7.　かいものを　します　　……　わたしは　かいものを　するのが　好きです。
B.　<u>タクシーで　けんぶつするのは　好きじゃありません。</u>
　　1.　すしを　たべます　　……　すしを　たべるのは　好きじゃありません。
　　2.　でんわを　かけます　……　でんわを　かけるのは　好きじゃありません。
　　3.　花見に　行きます　　……　花見に　行くのは　好きじゃありません。
　　4.　バスに　のります　　……　バスに　のるのは　好きじゃありません。
　　5.　しょくどうで　　　　……　しょくどうで　はたらくのは　好きじゃありません。
　　　　　　はたらきます
　　6.　セーターを　きます　……　セーターを　きるのは　好きじゃありません。
　　7.　クラスを　休みます　……　クラスを　休むのは　好きじゃありません。

C. 日本語を　べんきょうするのは　たいへんです。

1. 日本語の　しんぶんを …… 日本語の　しんぶんを　よむのは　たいへんです。
    よみます

2. 日本語で　はなします …… 日本語で　はなすのは　たいへんです。

3. あそこまで …… あそこまで　あるくのは　たいへんです。
    あるきます

4. 六時に　おきます …… 六時に　おきるのは　たいへんです。

5. 子どもを …… 子どもを　つれて行くのは　たいへんです。
    つれて行きます

6. ふゆ休みに …… ふゆ休みに　アルバイトを　するのは　たいへんです。
    アルバイトします

7. ピアノを　ならいます …… ピアノを　ならうのは　たいへんです。

D. どうぶつ園へ　行くのは　おもしろくありません。

1. えいがを　見ます …… えいがを　見るのは　おもしろくありません。

2. ふねに　のります …… ふねに　のるのは　おもしろくありません。

3. ギターを　ひきます …… ギターを　ひくのは　おもしろくありません。

4. うちに　います …… うちに　いるのは　おもしろくありません。

5. デパートで …… デパートで　はたらくのは　おもしろくありません。
    はたらきます

6. テニスを　します …… テニスを　するのは　おもしろくありません。

7. プールで　およぎます …… プールで　およぐのは　おもしろくありません。

7.7.8　E-J Response Drill

1. どの　学生が　スミスさんですか。

    the student who is over there …… あそこに　いる　学生が　スミスさんです。

2. どの　本を　よみたいですか。

    the book you do not have …… あなたが　もっていない　本を　よみたい
    です。

3. どこを　けんぶつしたいですか。

    the place where there are temples …… おてらが　ある　所を　けんぶつしたいです。

4. だれに　あいましたか。

    a person who is studying at Tōkyō …… 東京大学で　べんきょうしている　人に
    University　　　　　　　　　　　　　　あいました。

5. これは　どこへ　行く　急行ですか。
   the express that goes to Ōsaka   ……　これは　大阪へ　行く　急行です。

6. なにを　聞きましたか。
   the time when a train leaves   ……　でんしゃが　出る　時間を　聞きました。

7. 林さんは　どの　バスで　きますか。
   the bus that arrives at nine   ……　九時に　つく　バスで　きます。

8. なにを　しらべていますか。
   the words that I don't know   ……　知らない　ことばを　しらべています。

7.7.9　Substitution Drill

東京から　大阪まで　十時間半　かかります。

1. 三百マイルぐらい　あります   ……　東京から　大阪まで　三百マイルぐらい
   あります。

2. どのくらい　かかりますか   ……　東京から　大阪まで　どのくらい
   かかりますか。

3. どのくらい　ありますか   ……　東京から　大阪まで　どのくらい
   ありますか。

4. ひこうきで　一時間ぐらいです   ……　東京から　大阪まで　ひこうきで
   一時間ぐらいです。

5. むかしは　たいてい　あるきました   ……　東京から　大阪まで　むかしは　たいてい
   あるきました。

6. しんかん線が　はしっています   ……　東京から　大阪まで　しんかん線が
   はしっています。

7. ひこうきでも　行くことが　できます ……　東京から　大阪まで　ひこうきでも
   行くことが　できます。

7.7.10　E-J Response Drill

1. あなたの　うちから　学校まで　どのくらい　かかりますか。
   fifteen minutes   ……　十五分　かかります。

2. ここから　図書館まで　どのくらい　ありますか。
   about one mile   ……　一マイルぐらい　あります。

3. どのくらい　日本に　いましたか。
   from June to November   ……　六月から　十一月まで　いました。

4. 東京から　京都まで　どのくらい　ありますか。

   about five hundred kilometers 　　　　……　五百キロぐらい　あります。

5. まい日　どのくらい　べんきょうしますか。

   six hours 　　　　　　　　　　　　……　六時間　べんきょうします。

6. 大学から　駅まで　どのくらい　かかりますか。

   thirteen minutes 　　　　　　　　……　十三分　かかります。

7. せいは　どのぐらいですか。

   one meter and seventy-five centimeters ……　一メートル七十五センチです。

7.8　EXERCISES

7.8.1　Using the given Japanese, express the following ideas in Japanese:

1. ヨーロッパへ　行きます。

   Who is the one going to Europe next year?

2. さくらが　さいています。

   Let's go to the park where cherry blossoms are in bloom.

3. 日本の　えいがを　見ます。

   It is interesting to see a Japanese movie.

4. 駅まで　あるきます。

   I like walking up to the station.

5. すしを　たべません。

   A person who does not eat *sushi* is Mr. Hayashi.

6. ドイツ語を　ならいます。

   It is pleasant to learn German.

7.8.2　Answer the following questions in Japanese:

1. 学校から　あなたの　うちまで　どのくらい　かかりますか。
2. ニューヨークから　サンフランシスコまで　ひこうきで　どのくらいですか。
3. あなたは　はしるのが　好きですか。
4. あなたが　学校へ　くる　時間は　なん時ですか。
5. あなたが　よく　ひるごはんを　たべる　しょくどうは　どこですか。
6. なん時間で　ハワイへ　行くことが　できますか。
7. あなたが　おきるのは　なん時ですか。ねるのは　なん時ですか。

7.8.3 Insert an appropriate Relational in each blank:

1. 急行は　二番線（　　）　出ます。

2. この　でんしゃは　なん時（　　）　大阪（　　）　つきますか。

3. たまに　駅（　　）　うち（　　）　タクシー（　　）　のります。

4. しゃしょう（　　）　時間（　　）　聞いてみましょう。

5. ハワイ（　　）　ひこうき（　　）　おりました。そして　すぐ　ふね（　　）　のりました。

6. 東京行（　　）　急行（　　）　つく　時間（　　）　六時ですよ。

7. 日本語（　　）　はなすこと（　　）　できますか。

8. 駅（　　）　ここ（　　）　十五分（　　）　くること（　　）　できますか。

7.8.4 Write the following underlined *hiragana* in *kan'ji*:

1. <u>とうきょう</u>から　ハワイまで　ひこうきで　<u>なんじかん</u>ぐらい　かかりますか。

2. <u>がいこくじん</u>も　<u>にほんじん</u>も　よく　<u>きょう</u>都を　けんぶつします。

3. あの　<u>えき</u>から　急行が　<u>で</u>ますよ。

4. <u>なか</u>で　<u>き</u>いてみてください。

5. ホノルル<u>ゆき</u>の　ひこうきは　なんじに　<u>で</u>ますか。

7.8.5 Write the following in *katakana*:

1. San Furan'shisuko　　3. sen'chi　　5. mairu　　7. guriin

2. Suujii　　4. kiromeetoru　　6. Nyuu Yooku

7.8.6 When you want to make an inquiry to your close friend, you may start by saying:

1.

2.

7.8.7 What would you say under the following circumstances:

1. Asking a stranger where Ueno Park is.

2. Asking your friend where Ueno Park is.

3. Asking someone where Ueno Park is, implying that you hesitate to ask.

7.8.8 Explain the meaning of the following italicized words:

1. Kinoo otaku e *ukagaimashita*.

2. Sore wa moo *ukagaimashita*.

3. Ima sen'sei ni *ukagaimasu* kara, chotto matte kudasai.

4. A: Sen'sei wa ima isogashii n desu ga.

B: Dewa, ashita mata *ukagaimasu*.

7.8.9 Someone asks you about something that you do not know much about. What would you reply, using a word that has a softening effect?

7.9 SITUATIONAL AND APPLICATION CONVERSATION

7.9.1 At the station

A foreigner asks a man where he can catch an express for Tōkyō, the track number, and the time when the train leaves.

The man tells the foreigner to ask either a station employee or a conductor.

7.9.2 At the ticket window

The foreigner wants to know the time when the express leaves, the time required to get to Tōkyō, the arrival time at Tōkyō, and whether there might still be any *guriin* tickets available.

7.9.3 Make a telephone call to the airport and find out about a flight number and other information.

7.9.4 A: Chotto sumimasen ga, kore wa Gin'za-yuki no basu desu ka?

B: Saa.

A: Doomo.

7.9.5 A: Anoo, Katoo kun no otaku wa koko deshoo ka?

B: Katoo san no uchi wa asoko desu yo. Demo, jippun gurai mae* ni dekakemashita kara, ima imasen yo.

*"ago"

7.9.6 A: Anata no otoosan wa eigo ga joozu deshoo?

B: Saa.

7.9.7 A: Otoosan ni aitai n desu ga, raishuu irasshaimasu ka?

B: Saa, ima chichi wa rusu desu kara.

A: Dewa, kon'ban den'wa de ukagatte mimashoo.

B: Hai, sumimasen kedo, soo shite kudasai.

LESSON 8
図書館[1]で

8.1 PRESENTATION

一人の　男の　学生が　図書館の　カードの　所[2]で　本を　さがしています。そこへ　本を
二、三さつ[3]　持った[4]　女の　学生が　来ました。　二人は　前に　おなじ[5]　クラスで　べんきょ
うした　こと[6]が　あります[6]。

8.2 DIALOG

けい子　「ポールさん[7]。」

ポール　「あ、　けい子さん、　べんきょうですか[8]。」

けい子　「ええ。　おととい　かりた　本を　かえしに　来ました。　それに、　ちょっと
　　　　　読みたい　本も　ありますから…[9]。　ポールさんは。」

ポール　「けさの　日本文学の　時間に　わからなかった[10]　もんだいを　しらべたいんですが、
　　　　　てきとうな　本が　見つかりません[11]。」

けい子　「ここの　カードで　しらべてみましたか。」

ポール　「ええ、　しらべてみましたが、　ないんです。」

けい子　「図書館員に　聞いてみましたか。」

ポール　「いいえ、　まだですけど。」

けい子　「私の　読んだ　さんこう書は[12]　せつめいが[12]　とても　くわしかったですよ。
　　　　　だいは〈日本文学〉ですが、　読んだこと[6]が　ありますか。」

ポール　「いいえ、　ありません。　ここで　かりた　本ですか。」

けい子　「いいえ、　古本屋で　買った　本です。　今　うちに　ありますけど、　もう[13]
　　　　　つかっていませんから、　どうぞ[9]。」

ポール　「じゃあ、　かしてください。　あとで　かりに　行きますが、　いいですか[14]。」

けい子　「ええ、　かまいません[15]。　でも、　五時ごろまでに[16]　来てください。　五時半には
　　　　　出かけますから。」

男　持った　女　来ました　前　読みたい
文学　図書館員　私　買った

8.3 PATTERN SENTENCES

8.3.1

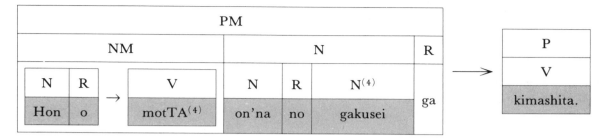

8.3.2

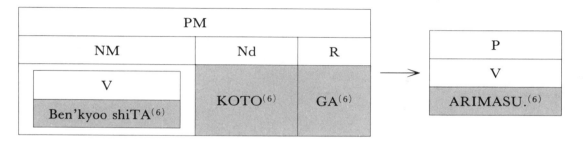

8.3.3

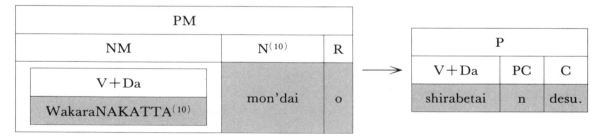

8.3.4

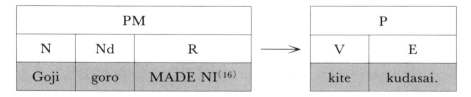

8.4 NOTES

8.4.1 Libraries

The 1981 edition of *Asahi Nen'kan* (Yearbook) listed about four hundred major libraries in Japan. The National Diet library alone holds roughly four million volumes. Japan probably ranks first in the world in literacy.

8.4.2 *Kaado no tokoro* means "where the cards are." In Japanese, a thing or a person usually cannot be followed directly by the Relationals concerning place, for instance *e*, *ni*, *de*, and so on. The Noun *tokoro* is used in cases such as *watakushi no tokoro* "my place," *doa no tokoro* "at the door," *mado no tokoro* "at the window."

Hitori no gakusei ga watakushi no tokoro e kimashita.	"A student came to me."
Sen'sei wa doa no tokoro ni irasshaimashita.	"The teacher was at the door."

8.4.3 *Ni-san'satsu* means "two or three (books)." The numerals in succession may occur immediately before a counter and mean "one or two," "two or three," and so forth. *Ni-san'satsu* is similar in meaning to *nisatsu ka san'satsu*, but *nisatsu ka san'satsu* is said when the numbers referred to are to be more specific. Note that the first numeral to be used in succession is always a regular numeral such as *ichi*, *ni*, *san*, *shi*, and so on.

ichi-nisatsu	san-yon'satsu	go-rokusatsu
ni-san'satsu	shi-gosatsu	etc.

8.4.4 *Motta* in *hon o ni-san'satsu motta on'na no gakusei*, meaning "a girl student who carried two or three books with her" is the TA form or the plain perfect tense form of a Consonant Verb *mochimasu ← motsu*. The TA form of Verbs is formed in the same manner as the TE form is formed. (See Note 1.4.21.)

1. Vowel Verb

age-masu	⟶	age-ru	⟶	age-ta
de-masu	⟶	de-ru	⟶	de-ta
dekake-masu	⟶	dekake-ru	⟶	dekake-ta
deki-masu	⟶	deki-ru	⟶	deki-ta
i-masu	⟶	i-ru	⟶	i-ta
ire-masu	⟶	ire-ru	⟶	ire-ta
kake-masu	⟶	kake-ru	⟶	kake-ta
kari-masu	⟶	kari-ru	⟶	kari-ta
ki-masu "wear"	⟶	ki-ru	⟶	ki-ta
kure-masu	⟶	kure-ru	⟶	kure-ta
mi-masu	⟶	mi-ru	⟶	mi-ta
mise-masu	⟶	mise-ru	⟶	mise-ta
ne-masu	⟶	ne-ru	⟶	ne-ta
oki-masu	⟶	oki-ru	⟶	oki-ta
ori-masu	⟶	ori-ru	⟶	ori-ta
sashiage-masu	⟶	sashiage-ru	⟶	sashiage-ta
shirabe-masu	⟶	shirabe-ru	⟶	shirabe-ta
tabe-masu	⟶	tabe-ru	⟶	tabe-ta
tsure-masu	⟶	tsure-ru	⟶	tsure-ta
tsutome-masu	⟶	tsutome-ru	⟶	tsutome-ta

2. Consonant Verb

arimasu	→ aru	→ atta
furimasu	→ furu	→ futta
hairimasu	→ hairu	→ haitta
hajimarimasu	→ hajimaru	→ hajimatta
hashirimasu	→ hashiru	→ hashitta
kaerimasu	→ kaeru	→ kaetta
kakarimasu	→ kakaru	→ kakatta
mitsukarimasu	→ mitsukaru	→ mitsukatta
norimasu	→ noru	→ notta
owarimasu	→ owaru	→ owatta
shirimasu	→ shiru	→ shitta
torimasu	→ toru	→ totta
urimasu	→ uru	→ utta
wakarimasu	→ wakaru	→ wakatta
yarimasu	→ yaru	→ yatta
aimasu	→ au	→ atta
chigaimasu	→ chigau	→ chigatta
iimasu	→ iu	→ itta
kaimasu	→ kau	→ katta
kayoimasu	→ kayou	→ kayotta
moraimasu	→ morau	→ moratta
naraimasu	→ narau	→ naratta
tsukaimasu	→ tsukau	→ tsukatta
ukagaimasu	→ ukagau	→ ukagatta
machimasu	→ matsu	→ matta
mochimasu	→ motsu	→ motta
arukimasu	→ aruku	→ aruita
hakimasu	→ haku	→ haita
hatarakimasu	→ hataraku	→ hataraita
hikimasu	→ hiku	→ hiita
ikimasu*	→ iku	→ itta *Exception
itadakimasu	→ itadaku	→ itadaita
kakimasu	→ kaku	→ kaita
kikimasu	→ kiku	→ kiita
sakimasu	→ saku	→ saita
tsukimasu	→ tsuku	→ tsuita
hanashimasu	→ hanasu	→ hanashita
kaeshimasu	→ kaesu	→ kaeshita
kashimasu	→ kasu	→ kashita
sagashimasu	→ sagasu	→ sagashita
nomimasu	→ nomu	→ non'da
sumimasu	→ sumu	→ sun'da
yasumimasu	→ yasumu	→ yasun'da
yomimasu	→ yomu	→ yon'da

asobimasu	⟶ asobu	⟶ ason'da	
yobimasu	⟶ yobu	⟶ yon'da	
oyogimasu	⟶ oyogu	⟶ oyoida	

3. Irregular Verb

kimasu	⟶ kuru	⟶ kita	
shimasu	⟶ suru	⟶ shita	

When a Predicate that modifies a Noun is in the perfect tense, the plain TA form should be used. This form may occur in modifying or describing the following Noun in the same structural environment as the Dictionary form occurs.

(Predicate Modifier)+Verb(-ta)+Noun

The subject, if there is one, should be followed by the Relational *ga* or *no* in the Noun Modifier. The Relational *wa* cannot be used after the subject.

ototoi san'koosho o karimashita   ⟶   ototoi karita san'koosho
   "[I] borrowed the reference book the   "the reference book that [I] borrowed
      day before yesterday"   the day before yesterday"

watakushi wa hon o yomimashita   ⟶   watakushi $\begin{Bmatrix} ga \\ no \end{Bmatrix}$ yon'da hon

   "I read the book"   "the book I read"

itta
aruite ita ⎫ hito   "a person who ⎰ went"
kippu o katta ⎭   { was walking"
                                   ⎩ bought tickets"

kaeshita
karita ⎫   ⎰ returned"
moratta ⎬ okane   "the money that [I] ⎨ borrowed"
kashita ⎪   { received"
mitsukatta ⎭   ⎩ lent"
                                      could find"

kono san'koosho o katta ⎫ tokoro   "the place where ⎰ [I] bought this reference book"
boku no sun'de ita ⎭   ⎩ I used to live"

boku ga ben'kyoo shita ⎫
      (no) ⎬ jikan   "the time when ⎰ I studied"
uchi ni ita ⎭   { [he] was home"

Sumisu san wa boku no kaita   "Mr. Smith is reading the report I wrote."
   repooto o yon'de imasu.

Yamada san kara karita san'koosho   "The reference book I borrowed from
   wa totemo ii desu.   Mr. Yamada is very good."

Watashi ga notta kyuukoo wa   "The express I rode was bound for Ōsaka."
   Oosaka yuki deshita.

Shokudoo de anata to hanashite ita   "Who is the lady who was talking with you
   on'na no kata wa donata desu ka?   at the dining hall?"

8.4.5 *Onaji* is a Noun meaning "same," but it is used differently from other Nouns. When used to modify another Noun, it can be placed immediately before that Noun as seen in *onaji kurasu* "the same class." The opposite of *onaji* is the Verb *chigau* "differ."

Onaji and *chigau* are used as shown below:

A wa B to $\left\{ \begin{array}{l} \text{onaji desu} \\ \text{chigaimasu} \end{array} \right.$ "A is $\left\{ \begin{array}{l} \text{the same as} \\ \text{different from} \end{array} \right\}$ B"

A to B wa $\left\{ \begin{array}{l} \text{onaji desu} \\ \text{chigaimasu} \end{array} \right.$ "A and B are $\left\{ \begin{array}{l} \text{the same"} \\ \text{different"} \end{array} \right.$

B to $\left\{ \begin{array}{l} \text{onaji} \\ \text{chigau} \end{array} \right\}$ A "A which is the same as B"
"A which is different from B"

Kore to sore wa onaji desu.	"This and that are the same."
Kore wa sore to chigaimasu yo.	"This is different from that."
Kore to onaji kutsu o kudasai.	"Please give me the same shoes as these."
Chigau hi ni kite mimasu.	"I'll come here some other day."

8.4.6 *Ben'kyoo shita koto ga arimasu* means "I have studied," "I've had an experience of studying," or "There is the fact of having studied." This pattern covers the experience of doing such and such, whereas mere occurrence in the past is covered by the perfect tense form *-mashita,* even though the English equivalents of both would be "have done," and so on.

The Predicate Modifiers such as *ichido* "once," *nido* "twice," *mae* or *mae ni* "before" may be used in this pattern.

(Person+wa)+(Predicate Modifier)+TA form of Verb+*koto ga* + $\left\{ \begin{array}{l} \textit{arimasu} \\ \textit{arimasen} \\ \textit{nai n desu} \end{array} \right.$

yon'da
itta
mita
notta
naratta $\left.\right\}$ koto ga (wa) $\left\{ \begin{array}{l} \text{arimasu} \\ \text{arimasen} \\ \text{nai (n) desu} \end{array} \right.$ "[I] have (once)
"[he] has never $\left\{ \begin{array}{l} \text{read"} \\ \text{been"} \\ \text{seen"} \\ \text{ridden"} \\ \text{learned"} \\ \text{come"} \\ \text{been living"} \\ \text{tried (food)"} \end{array} \right.$
kita
sun'de ita
tabete mita

Sukiyaki o tabeta koto ga arimasu ka?	"Have you ever eaten *sukiyaki*?"
Hai, tabeta koto ga arimasu.	"Yes, I have eaten it (before)."
Keiko san wa hikooki ni notta koto ga arimasu ka?	"Has Keiko ever flown in an airplane?"
Iie, (notta koto wa) arimasen.	"No, she hasn't."
Nikkoo o ken'butsu shita koto ga arimasu ka?	"Have you had the experience of sightseeing in Nikkō?"
Hai, nido arimasu.	"Yes, I have twice."

Katoo sen'sei ni atta koto ga nai n desu ka?	"Haven't you ever met Prof. Katō?"
Ee, nai n desu.	"No, I haven't."

8.4.7 A rather complex set of relationships as well as attitudes among Japanese students toward foreigners is exemplified by this dialog.

1. Paul and Keiko are both students of the same university.
2. Keiko is a Japanese; Paul is a foreigner.
3. Keiko is female; Paul is male.

The levels and styles of speech used in their conversation reflect the above-mentioned relationships. For example, Keiko addresses Paul using his first name plus -*san*. Such a form of address is not as frequently used in for instance, addressing a Japanese male student. Keiko probably uses this form of address to Paul because she is conscious of Paul's foreign status and is aware of foreign customs of address. Normally, the last name is used among Japanese students unless they are intimate.

8.4.8 *Ben'kyoo desu ka?* here is said to ask if one is studying or if one is going to study. *Ben'kyoo shite iru n desu ka?* or *Ben'kyoo suru n desu ka?* is shortened this way.

8.4.9 Clause Omission

As has been described previously, the Japanese tend to omit Predicate Modifiers (i.e., subjects, direct objects, indirect objects, etc.) if they are understood in the context.

There is a similar tendency to omit entire clauses—either final or nonfinal clauses—if that portion is understood, can easily be assumed from the context of the conversation, or the speaker's intent is to make a vague statement. For instance, in this dialog, Keiko's statement *Sore ni, chotto yomitai hon mo arimasu kara . . .* may be translated as "Besides, there are some books I want to read," or "Since there are some books I want to read . . ." It is obvious here that a second clause has been omitted.

There is a similar example of clause omission in the dialog of Lesson 7, when the station employee states, *Tama ni noranai hito ya sugu oriru hito ga imasu kara. . . .* This translates literally as "Since occasionally there are people who might not come or who might get off shortly after. . . ." This implies that you can probably find a seat. Therefore there is no need to state the conclusion of the statement.

A generalization may be made to interpret this language custom in Japan. Due to the long-established homogeneity of Japanese society, especially during the Tokugawa period, such economy of speech could develop because much could be taken for granted and, in a sense, understood by participants in the unified, uniform culture. Thus omission and incomplete statements became frequently used in Japan, both from the point of view of linguistic form and that of communication. Such economy of speech can work, however, only if the societal members share a basic understanding of the society's values. This custom of omitting what can be understood or assumed is also a function of the Japanese attitude of reserve, modesty, and non-self-assertion which has already been described. At the end of the dialog, the one word *doozo* (please) functions similarly in that it serves to imply "I'll lend it to you."

8.4.10 *Wakaranakatta mon'dai* means "the problem that I couldn't solve" or "the question that I didn't understand." As the plain negative imperfect tense form of an adjectival Derivative, *-nai* occurs before a Noun, forming a Noun Modifier (see Note 7.4.21), its plain negative perfect tense form *-nakatta* occurs in the same manner. The *wakaranakatta* is the perfect tense form of *wakaranai*, and the adjectival Derivative *-nai* changes into *-nakatta*.

Pre-Nai form of Verb + -*nai* ⟶ Pre-Nai form of Verb + -*nakatta*

1. Vowel Verb

inai	⟶	inakatta	tabenai	⟶	tabenakatta
minai	⟶	minakatta	dekinai	⟶	dekinakatta
okinai	⟶	okinakatta	karinai	⟶	karinakatta
agenai	⟶	agenakatta	shirabenai	⟶	shirabenakatta

2. Consonant Verb

kasanai	⟶	kasanakatta	nomanai	⟶	nomanakatta
kaesanai	⟶	kaesanakatta	kakanai	⟶	kakanakatta
owaranai	⟶	owaranakatta	tsukawanai	⟶	tsukawanakatta
motanai	⟶	motanakatta	yobanai	⟶	yobanakatta

3. Irregular Verb

konai	⟶	konakatta
shinai	⟶	shinakatta

(Predicate Modifier) + Verb(-*nakatta*) + Noun

orinakatta
kikanakatta   hito   "the person   who   didn't get off"
ben'kyoo shinakatta gakusei   "the student   didn't ask"
soko ni sun'de inakatta   didn't study"
                                                          wasn't living there"

kawanakatta
yomanakatta   san'koosho   "the reference book   that   [I] didn't buy"
tsukatte inakatta jisho   "the dictionary   [I] didn't read"
                                                           [I] wasn't using"

watakushi ga ikanakatta   tokoro   "the place where   I did not go"
sakura no sakanakatta   cherry blossoms did not bloom"

The subject in the Noun Modifier should not be followed by the Relational *wa* but by *ga* or *no*.

Ototoi awanakatta tomodachi ni tegami o kakimasu.	"I'll write a letter to a friend whom I didn't see the day before yesterday."

Kinoo Mori san {ga / no} karinakatta hon wa nan desu ka?	"What is the book that Mr. Mori did not borrow yesterday?"

8.4.11 *Mitsukarimasu* means "something is found." This is an intransitive Verb. The thing one can find is the subject of *mitsukarimasu,* and is followed by the subject Relational *ga.*

Tekitoo na hon ga mitsukarimasen.	"I cannot find any proper books."
Anata no nooto wa mitsukarimashita ka?	"Did you find your notebook?"

8.4.12 (*Watakushi no yon'da*) *san'koosho wa setsumei ga kuwashikatta desu* means "As for the reference book (I read), its explanation was in detail," or "The explanation of the reference book (I read) was in detail." When part of something or someone is described, that is, *A no B wa . . . desu* "B of A is such and such," the same connotation may be expressed by the sentence structure *A wa B ga . . . desu.*

$$\text{Noun 1} + no + \text{Noun 2} + wa + \left\{ \begin{array}{l} \textbf{Adjective} \\ \textbf{adjectival Noun} \end{array} \right\} + desu \longrightarrow$$

$$\text{Noun 1} + wa + \text{Noun 2} + ga + \left\{ \begin{array}{l} \textbf{Adjective} \\ \textbf{adjectival Noun} \end{array} \right\} + desu$$

Kono san'koosho *no* setsumei *wa*
   kuwashii desu.
Kono san'koosho *wa* setsumei *ga*
   kuwashii desu.

"As for this reference book, the explanation is in detail."

Anata *no* me *wa* kirei desu.
Anata *wa* me *ga* kirei desu.

"Your eyes are pretty."

Anata *no* sei *wa* takai desu nee.
Anata *wa* sei *ga* takai desu nee.

"How tall you are!"

Ani *no* te to ashi *wa* ookii desu.
Ani *wa* te to ashi *ga* ookii desu.

"My older brother has big hands and feet."

San'koosho

Although the word *san'koosho* is translated here as "reference book," it sometimes does not have quite the same connotation as the English term. In some respects *san'koosho* resembles the College Outline Series publications. They contain examples of problems, explanations of theories, and, in general, a simplified presentation of course material; in other words, they function as study aids. *San'koosho* have their origin in the very structure of Japanese higher education. In the classroom, there is no interaction between professor and student. The professor merely lectures to classes that often contain several hundred students, where attendance is not mandatory.

8.4.13 When an Adverb *moo* is used with negation, it always means "(not) any more," or "(not) any longer." Note that *moo* in an affirmative sentence has the different meaning of "already."

Moo guriin'ken wa arimasen.

"There are no more first-class (or green) tickets."

Moo ikitaku arimasen.

"I don't want to go there any longer."

Moo Tookyoo ni tsukimashita.

"We have already arrived at Tōkyō."

The Adverb *mada* "still" is often used in the question to ask if something is still so or if it is not so any more.

Otootosan wa mada Okinawa ni
   sun'de imasu ka?

"Is your younger brother still living in Okinawa?"

Iie, moo sun'de imasen.

"No, he is not living there any longer."

8.4.14 *Ii desu ka?* is used here in the meaning of "Is it all right?" asking for permission. Further use of *ii desu* will be introduced in Lesson 9.

8.4.15 *Kamaimasen* means "it does not matter" or "I don't mind," hence it refers to permission, but is more indirect than *Ii desu*. The affirmative form of *kamaimasen* is seldom used in Japanese. When you *do mind*, the pattern "please do not do such and such" may be used instead. See Notes 9.4.5, 9.4.10, and 9.4.11.

8.4.16 *Goji goro made ni* means "by approximately five o'clock." *Made ni* is a double Relational consisting of the time Relational *made* and another time Relational *ni*. When it follows a time Noun, it means "not later than the time given" or "by the time given." While *made* means that an action or state continues until the designated time, *made ni* indicates that an action should be completed by that time.

Itsu made ni keizai no repooto o kakimasu ka?   "By when are you going to write a paper on economics?"

Mokuyoobi made ni kaku tsumori desu.   "I intend to write it by Thursday."

Niji made ni kite kudasai.   "Please come by two o'clock."

8.5 VOCABULARY

Presentation

カード	kaado	......	N	card
持った	motta	......	V	carried (TA form of *mochimasu* ← *motsu*—carry; have; hold) (see 8.4.4)
おなじ	onaji	......	N	same (see 8.4.5)
べんきょうした	ben'kyoo shita	......	V	studied (TA form of *ben'kyoo shimasu* ← *ben'kyoo suru*)
こと	koto	......	Nd	fact (see 8.4.6)

Dialog

けい子	Keiko	......	N	girl's name
ポール	Pooru	......	N	Paul
かりた	karita	......	V	borrowed; rented (TA form of *karimasu* ← *kariru*)
かえし	kaeshi	......	V	Stem form of *kaeshimasu* ← *kaesu*—return; give back
文学	bun'gaku	......	N	literature
わからなかった	wakaranakatta	......	V+Da	did not understand (Pre-Nai form of *wakarimasu* ← *wakaru* plus -*nakatta*) (see 8.4.10)
もんだい	mon'dai	......	N	problem; question
しらべ	shirabe	......	V	Stem form of *shirabemasu* ← *shiraberu*—make researches (on); check up; investigate
てきとう	tekitoo	......	Na	proper; adequate

見つかりません	mitsukarimasen	......	V	is not found; cannot find (negative of *mitsukarimasu* ← *mitsukaru*) (intransitive Verb) (see 8.4.11)
図書館員	toshokan'in	......	N	librarian; library clerk
読んだ	yon'da	......	V	read (TA form of *yomimasu* ← *yomu*)
さんこう書	san'koosho	......	N	reference book
せつめい	setsumei	......	N	explanation
せつめいします	setsumei shimasu	......	V	explain
くわしかった	kuwashikatta	......	A	was in detail (TA form of *kuwashii*)
だい	dai	......	N	title (of books, movies, etc.)
買った	katta	......	V	bought (TA form of *kaimasu* ← *kau*)
もう	moo	......	Adv.	(not) any more; (not) any longer (see 8.4.13)
つかって	tsukatte	......	V	TE form of *tsukaimasu* ← *tsukau*—use
かして	kashite	......	V	TE form of *kashimasu* ← *kasu*—lend; rent
いい	ii	......	A	is all right (see 8.4.14)
かまいません	kamaimasen	......	V	do not mind (see 8.4.15)
までに	made ni	......	R	by (the time) (see 8.4.16)

Notes

ドア	doa	......	N	door
まど	mado	......	N	window
レポート	repooto	......	N	report; paper
なかった	-nakatta	......	Da	TA form of *-nai* (see 8.4.10)
ノート	nooto	......	N	notebook
め	me	......	N	eye
て	te	......	N	hand
あし	ashi	......	N	leg; foot
けいざい	keizai	......	N	economics

8.6   KAN'JI

8.6.1 男 (1) *otoko* (2) man; male (3) classifier 田 [field]; 力 [power]

(4) 丨 冂 冂 吅 田 囲 男 男 (5) 男の学生、男の子

(6) a strong hand bearing down on things and working in the field. See 13.6.5

8.6.2 持 (1) *mo*(*chimasu*); *mo*(*tsu*) (2) have; hold; carry (3) classifier 扌 [hand]

(4) 一 十 扌 扩 扩 扩 拝 持 持

(5) 持っています、本を持った人、持って行く、持ってかえる

(6) 土 means soil and 扌 means measurement, hence 寺 [temple] is the place for judgement

8.6.3 女 (1) *on'na* (2) woman; girl; female (3) forms the classifier 女

(4) 人 女 女 (5) 女の子、女の大学生 (6) a sitting (pregnant) person

8.6.4 来 (1) *ki*(*masu*); *ku*(*ru*); *ko*(*nai*) (2) come (3) classifier 一

(4) 一 ㇐ 㝏 平 平 来 来 (5) 来ます、来てください、来る、来ない人

(6) a barley plant, considered to be a gift from heaven, hence this character's meaning

8.6.5 前 (1) *mae* (2) front; before (3) classifier 丷 (リ)

(4) ` 丷 亠 宀 亍 苮 前 前 前 (5) 駅の前、黒板の前、名前

8.6.6 読 (1) *yo*(*mimasu*); *yo*(*mu*) (2) read (3) classifier 言 [speech]

(4) 一 亠 亖 亖 言 言 訁 計 計 評 詃 読 読

(5) 本を読みました、読み物 [readings]

8.6.7 文 (1) BUN (2) writings; sentence (3) forms the classifier 亠 (文)

(4) ` 亠 ナ 文 (5) 文学、作文 [composition]、文をかきます

8.6.8 員 (1) IN (2) member; personnel (3) classifier 口

(4) 冖 冒 員 員 (5) 駅員、銀行員、店員、事務員

(6) homonym 韻；貝 See 8.6.10

8.6.9 私 (1) *watakushi* (2) I (3) classifier 禾 (4) ` 二 禾 私 私

(5) 私の本

8.6.10 買 (1) *ka*(*imasu*); *ka*(*u*) (2) buy (3) classifier 貝 [shell → money]

(4) ` 冖 ㄇ 冖 ㄇ 尸 買 胃 胃 冒 買 買 (5) 買い物

8.7 DRILLS

8.7.1 Transformation Drill

1. 持ちました	⟶	持った	4. しらべました	⟶	しらべた
2. 行きました	⟶	行った	5. つかいました	⟶	つかった
3. かりました	⟶	かりた	6. かしました	⟶	かした

7. 出ました	⟶ 出た	15. およぎました	⟶ およいだ
8. かえしました	⟶ かえした	16. さがしました	⟶ さがした
9. のりました	⟶ のった	17. のみました	⟶ のんだ
10. 持ちました	⟶ 持った	18. かきました	⟶ かいた
11. 見つかりました	⟶ 見つかった	19. もらいました	⟶ もらった
12. りょこうしました	⟶ りょこうした	20. 読みました	⟶ 読んだ
13. 来ました	⟶ 来た	21. 買いました	⟶ 買った
14. よびました	⟶ よんだ	22. はいりました	⟶ はいった

8.7.2　Transformation Drill

1. わかりませんでした	⟶ わからなかった	8. 聞きませんでした	⟶ 聞かなかった
2. かしませんでした	⟶ かさなかった	9. かえしませんでした	⟶ かえさなかった
3. おりませんでした	⟶ おりなかった	10. はしりませんでした	⟶ はしらなかった
4. さがしませんでした	⟶ さがさなかった	11. かりませんでした	⟶ かりなかった
5. 見つかりませんでした	⟶ 見つから なかった	12. あいませんでした	⟶ あわなかった
		13. 知りませんでした	⟶ 知らなかった
6. しらべませんでした	⟶ しらべなかった	14. 読みませんでした	⟶ 読まなかった
7. つかいませんでした	⟶ つかわなかった		

8.7.3　Transformation Drill

1. 図書館に　かえす　本	⟶ 図書館に　かえした　本
2. 学校で　つかう　さんこう書	⟶ 学校で　つかった　さんこう書
3. けい子さんの　はたらく　じむしょ	⟶ けい子さんの　はたらいた　じむしょ
4. ともだちから　かりる　ノート	⟶ ともだちから　かりた　ノート
5. しょくどうに　いる　時間	⟶ しょくどうに　いた　時間
6. いもうとに　かす　セーター	⟶ いもうとに　かした　セーター
7. 十時に　出る　急行	⟶ 十時に　出た　急行
8. ポールさんが　はなす　日本語	⟶ ポールさんが　はなした　日本語
9. にわで　あそんでいる　子ども	⟶ にわで　あそんでいた　子ども
10. 駅員に　聞いている　外国人	⟶ 駅員に　聞いていた　外国人
11. ピアノを　ひいている　女の子	⟶ ピアノを　ひいていた　女の子
12. 私が　しらべる　もんだい	⟶ 私が　しらべた　もんだい

8.7.4　Transformation Drill

1. わたしが わからない もんだい ⟶ わたしが わからなかった もんだい
2. 先生の せつめいしない ことば ⟶ 先生の せつめいしなかった ことば
3. 学校で ならわない かんじ ⟶ 学校で ならわなかった かんじ
4. くにへ かえらない 人 ⟶ くにへ かえらなかった 人
5. 図書館で 見つからない 本 ⟶ 図書館で 見つからなかった 本
6. ポールさんが 行かない 公園 ⟶ ポールさんが 行かなかった 公園
7. あめが ふっていない 所 ⟶ あめが ふっていなかった 所
8. クラスに 来ない ともだち ⟶ クラスに 来なかった ともだち
9. ひらがなを かくことが できない 人 ⟶ ひらがなを かくことが できなかった 人
10. ぼくの 持っていない さんこう書 ⟶ ぼくの 持っていなかった さんこう書

8.7.5　Transformation Drill

1. 日本文学を 読みました。 ⟶ 日本文学を 読んだことが あります。
2. てんぷらを たべました。 ⟶ てんぷらを たべたことが あります。
3. ぎんこうに つとめました。 ⟶ ぎんこうに つとめたことが あります。
4. 一郎くんに おかねを かしました。 ⟶ 一郎くんに おかねを かしたことが
   あります。
5. あなたの おとうさんに あいました。 ⟶ あなたの おとうさんに あったことが
   あります。
6. その さんこう書を つかいました。 ⟶ その さんこう書を つかったことが
   あります。
7. 学校へ いぬを つれて来ました。 ⟶ 学校へ いぬを つれて来たことが
   あります。
8. しんかん線に のりました。 ⟶ しんかん線に のったことが あります。
9. さけを のみました。 ⟶ さけを のんだことが あります。
10. ハワイへ 一ど 行きました。 ⟶ ハワイへ 一ど 行ったことが あります。

8.7.6　Transformation Drill

1. ドイツ語を べんきょうしませんでした。 ⟶ ドイツ語を べんきょうしたことが
   ありません。
2. なつ休みに アルバイトを
   しませんでした。 ⟶ なつ休みに アルバイトを したことが
   ありません。
3. 辞書を つかいませんでした。 ⟶ 辞書を つかったことが ありません。

4. 日本の　おんがくを　聞きませんでした。　——→　日本の　おんがくを　聞いたことが
　　　　　　　　　　　　　　　　　　　　　　　　　　　　　　　ありません。

5. 林先生に　あいませんでした。　　　——→　林先生に　あったことが　ありません。

6. 日曜日に　うちに　いませんでした。　——→　日曜日に　うちに　いたことが　ありません。

7. しんじゅくで　買い物を　　　　　　——→　しんじゅくで　買い物を　したことが
　　　しませんでした。　　　　　　　　　　　　　　　　　　ありません。

8. ふゆ休みに　くにへ　　　　　　　　——→　ふゆ休みに　くにへ　かえったことが
　　　かえりませんでした。　　　　　　　　　　　　　　　　ありません。

9. ちちは　かいしゃを　休みませんでした。——→　ちちは　かいしゃを　休んだことが
　　　　　　　　　　　　　　　　　　　　　　　　　　　　　ありません。

10. ゴルフを　しませんでした。　　　　——→　ゴルフを　したことが　ありません。

8.7.7　Expansion Drill

1. さんこう書を　かえしに　行きました。

　　かりた　　　　　　　……　かりた　さんこう書を　かえしに　行きました。

　　おととい　　　　　　……　おととい　かりた　さんこう書を　かえしに　行きました。

　　図書館へ　　　　　　……　図書館へ　おととい　かりた　さんこう書を　かえしに
　　　　　　　　　　　　　　　行きました。

2. 駅員が　持っています。

　　今　来た　　　　　　……　今　来た　駅員が　持っています。

　　きっぷは　　　　　　……　きっぷは　今　来た　駅員が　持っています。

3. 本は　むずかしいです。

　　いただいた　　　　　……　いただいた　本は　むずかしいです。

　　けい子さんから　　　……　けい子さんから　いただいた　本は　むずかしいです。

　　月曜日に　　　　　　……　月曜日に　けい子さんから　いただいた　本は　むずかしいです。

4. 学生が　二、三人　いました。

　　来なかった　　　　　……　来なかった　学生が　二、三人　いました。

　　クラスに　　　　　　……　クラスに　来なかった　学生が　二、三人　いました。

　　日本語の　　　　　　……　日本語の　クラスに　来なかった　学生が　二、三人
　　　　　　　　　　　　　　　いました。

5. もんだいを　聞いてください。

　　わからなかった　　　……　わからなかった　もんだいを　聞いてください。

　　よく　　　　　　　　……　よく　わからなかった　もんだいを　聞いてください。

　　あなたが　　　　　　……　あなたが　よく　わからなかった　もんだいを　聞いてください。

8.7.8　Transformation Drill

1. その　本の　せつめいは　　　　　⟶　その　本は　せつめいが
　　よくありませんでした。　　　　　　　　　　　よくありませんでした。

2. あの　外国人の　日本語は　　　　⟶　あの　外国人は　日本語が　じょうずです。
　　じょうずです。

3. ブラウンさんの　めは　とても　　⟶　ブラウンさんは　めが　とても
　　大きいですね。　　　　　　　　　　　　　　大きいですね。

4. きのう　行った　きっさ店の　　　⟶　きのう　行った　きっさ店は　コーヒーが
　　コーヒーは　おいしくありません。　　　　おいしくありません。

5. デパートの　店員の　ことばは　　⟶　デパートの　店員は　ことばが
　　ていねいです。　　　　　　　　　　　　　　ていねいです。

6. 上野の　さくらは　きれいです。　⟶　上野は　さくらが　きれいです。

7. あの　子どもの　せいは　たかいです。⟶　あの　子どもは　せいが　たかいです。

8. あなたの　ては　大きいですね。　⟶　あなたは　てが　大きいですね。

8.7.9　Transformation Drill

1. あにが　のった　でんしゃは　もう　⟶　あにの　のった　でんしゃは　もう　出ました。
　　出ました。

2. わたしが　行かなかった　所は　　⟶　わたしの　行かなかった　所は　にっこうです。
　　にっこうです。

3. みち子さんが　かく　ひらがなは　⟶　みち子さんの　かく　ひらがなは　へたです。
　　へたです。

4. あの　せいが　ひくい　男の　人は　⟶　あの　せいの　ひくい　男の　人は
　　だれですか。　　　　　　　　　　　　　　　だれですか。

5. あなたが　しらべていた　もんだいは　⟶　あなたの　しらべていた　もんだいは
　　どれですか。　　　　　　　　　　　　　　　どれですか。

6. あさって　すきやきが　おいしい　⟶　あさって　すきやきの　おいしい
　　レストランへ　行きます。　　　　　　　　レストランへ　行きます。

7. あなたが　わからなかった　ことばは　⟶　あなたの　わからなかった　ことばは
　　これですか。　　　　　　　　　　　　　　　これですか。

8. ちちが　つとめていた　かいしゃは　⟶　ちちの　つとめていた　かいしゃは　もう
　　もう　ありません。　　　　　　　　　　　ありません。

8.7.10 Response Drill

1. なにを　さがしていますか。
   おととい　買った　さんこう書(しょ)　　　…… 　おとといい　買った　さんこう書(しょ)を
   　　　　　　　　　　　　　　　　　　　　　　さがしています。

2. なにを　しらべていますか。
   わからなかった　もんだい　　　　　…… 　わからなかった　もんだいを　しらべています。

3. なにを　かえしましたか。
   あの　人から　かりた　ノート　　　…… 　あの　人から　かりた　ノートを
   　　　　　　　　　　　　　　　　　　　　　　かえしました。

4. なにが　見つかりませんか。
   けさ　読んでいた　しんぶん　　　　…… 　けさ　読んでいた　しんぶんが
   　　　　　　　　　　　　　　　　　　　　　　見つかりません。

5. どこへ　行きたいですか。
   きょ年　けんぶつしなかった　所　　…… 　きょ年　けんぶつしなかった　所へ
   　　　　　　　　　　　　　　　　　　　　　　行きたいです。

6. だれに　あげましたか。
   にわで　あそんでいた　子ども　　　…… 　にわで　あそんでいた　子どもに　あげました。

7. どの　図書館員(としょかん)に　聞いてみましたか。
   カードの　所に　いた　人　　　　　…… 　カードの　所に　いた　人に　聞いてみました。

8. どんな　本を　かりましたか。
   ポールさんが　前に　読んだ　本　　…… 　ポールさんが　前に　読んだ　本を
   　　　　　　　　　　　　　　　　　　　　　　かりました。

8.7.11 Response Drill

1. 新潟(にいがた)へ　行ったことが　ありますか。
   はい　　　　　　　　　…… 　はい、行ったことが　あります。
   いいえ　　　　　　　　…… 　いいえ、行ったことが　ありません。

2. 日本の　えいがを　見たことが　ありますか。
   はい　　　　　　　　　…… 　はい、見たことが　あります。
   いいえ　　　　　　　　…… 　いいえ、見たことが　ありません。

3. ぎんこうから　おかねを　かりたことが　ありますか。
   はい　　　　　　　　　…… 　はい、かりたことが　あります。
   いいえ　　　　　　　　…… 　いいえ、かりたことが　ありません。

4.　東京に　すんでいたことが　ありますか。

　　はい　　　　　　　……　はい、すんでいたことが　あります。

　　いいえ　　　　　　……　いいえ、すんでいたことが　ありません。

5.　けっこんしたことが　ありますか。

　　はい　　　　　　　……　はい、したことが　あります。

　　いいえ　　　　　　……　いいえ、したことが　ありません。

6.　かんじの　辞書を　つかったことが　ありますか。

　　はい　　　　　　　……　はい、つかったことが　あります。

　　いいえ　　　　　　……　いいえ、つかったことが　ありません。

7.　けいざいを　べんきょうしたことが　ありますか。

　　はい　　　　　　　……　はい、べんきょうしたことが　あります。

　　いいえ　　　　　　……　いいえ、べんきょうしたことが　ありません。

8.　はしで　たべたことが　ありますか。

　　はい　　　　　　　……　はい、たべたことが　あります。

　　いいえ　　　　　　……　いいえ、たべたことが　ありません。

8.7.12 Response Drill

1.　あなたは　まだ　学生ですか。

　　はい　　　　　　　……　はい、まだ　学生です。

　　いいえ　　　　　　……　いいえ、もう　学生ではありません。

2.　山田さんは　まだ　アメリカに　いらっしゃいますか。

　　はい　　　　　　　……　はい、まだ　いらっしゃいます。

　　いいえ　　　　　　……　いいえ、もう　いらっしゃいません。

3.　今　まだ　なつ休みですか。

　　はい　　　　　　　……　はい、まだ　なつ休みです。

　　いいえ　　　　　　……　いいえ、もう　なつ休みではありません。

4.　さんこう書を　まだ　かりたいんですか。

　　はい　　　　　　　……　はい、まだ　かりたいです。

　　いいえ　　　　　　……　いいえ、もう　かりたくありません。

5.　みち子さんは　まだ　おんがくを　聞いていますか。

　　はい　　　　　　　……　はい、まだ　聞いています。

　　いいえ　　　　　　……　いいえ、もう　聞いていません。

6.　かいしゃで　まだ　しごとを　していますか。

　　はい　　　　　　　　……　はい、まだ　しています。

　　いいえ　　　　　　　……　いいえ、もう　していません。

8.7.13　Substitution Drill

<u>五時までに</u>　来てください。

1.　ゆうがた　　　　　　……　ゆうがたまでに　来てください。
2.　金曜日　　　　　　　……　金曜日までに　来てください。
3.　かえるつもりです　……　金曜日までに　かえるつもりです。
4.　ひるごろ　　　　　　……　ひるごろまでに　かえるつもりです。
5.　本を　かえしてください……　ひるごろまでに　本を　かえしてください。
6.　あさって　　　　　　……　あさってまでに　本を　かえしてください。
7.　うかがいたいんですが　……　あさってまでに　うかがいたいんですが。
8.　ごご九時　　　　　　……　ごご九時までに　うかがいたいんですが。

8.7.14　Substitution Drill

A.　<u>おなじ</u>　クラスで　べんきょうしています。

　　1.　<u>ちがう</u>　　　　……　<u>ちがう</u>　クラスで　べんきょうしています。
　　2.　<u>人に　あいました</u>……　ちがう　<u>人に　あいました</u>。
　　3.　おなじ　　　　　……　おなじ　人に　あいました。
　　4.　時間で　　　　　……　おなじ　時間で　いいですか。
　　　　いいですか
　　5.　ちがう　　　　　……　ちがう　時間で　いいですか。

B.　<u>これと　それは　ちがいます</u>。

　　1.　<u>おなじです</u>　……　これと　それは　おなじです。
　　2.　<u>わたし、あなた</u>……　わたしと　あなたは　おなじです。
　　3.　ちがいます　　……　わたしと　あなたは　ちがいます。
　　4.　この　じと　……　この　じと　その　じは　ちがいます。
　　　　その　じ
　　5.　おなじです　……　この　じと　その　じは　おなじです。

8.8 EXERCISES

8.8.1 Make a complete sentence using each of the following expressions as a Noun Modifier.

Example: <u>図書館で</u> <u>かりました</u>。 ⟶ きのう <u>図書館で</u> <u>かりた</u> 本は なん

です か。

1. 私が かえしました。
2. 大学で しらべました。
3. あそこに いました。
4. つかいませんでした。
5. なつ休みに はたらきました。
6. わたしは 読みませんでした。
7. きみは 持っていませんでした。

8.8.2 Insert an appropriate Relational into each of the following blanks:

1. 図書館（　　）てきとうな さんこう書（　　）さがしてみましょう。
2. おととい かりた ざっし（　　）ともだち（　　）所（　　）かえし（　　）
   行きます。
3. 一郎くんは 森さん（　　）外国文学（　　）本（　　）もらいました。
4. この 辞書（　　）せつめい（　　）とても くわしいです。
5. なに（　　）見つかりましたか。
6. あなた（　　）持っている カメラ（　　）わたし（　　）かしてください。
7. かぶき（　　）見たこと（　　）ありますか。
8. 一人（　　）男の子（　　）まど（　　）所（　　）います。
9. 水曜日（　　）レポートを かいてください。
10. これ（　　）おなじ セーターを 買いたいです。

8.8.3 Express the following ideas in Japanese:

1. The movie I saw the day before yesterday was dull.
2. The reference book I bought at Kanda is the same as Yoshiko's.
3. Who is the person you were talking with?
4. I want to ask my teacher about the problem I didn't understand.
5. Please give me the dictionary that you did not use.
6. Have you ever been to Kyōto?

7. I have never met Mr. Brown.

8. Keiko is not taking the Japanese literature class any longer.

9. As I will come home by six, please be waiting (for me).

8.8.4 Write the following underlined *hiragana* in *kan'ji*:

1. <u>おんな</u>の <u>がくせい</u>が <u>もっ</u>ていた <u>ほん</u>の <u>だい</u>は <u>がいこくぶんがく</u>です。

2. <u>しんぶん</u>を <u>よ</u>んでいる <u>おとこ</u>の <u>ひと</u>に <u>き</u>いてみてください。

3. <u>わたくし</u>は <u>まえ</u> <u>えき</u>いんでした。

4. どんな ものを <u>か</u>いに <u>き</u>ましたか。

8.8.5 Write the following in *katakana*:

1. kaado   2. Pooru   3. nooto   4. repooto   5. doa

8.8.6 What generalization can be made to interpret the language custom in Japan of omitting Predicate Modifiers and clauses if understood within the context of the statement?

8.8.7 It is not customary in Japan for people to address each other by their first names, except in special relationships. List as many reasons as you can explaining why both Keiko and Paul address each other by their first names in the dialog.

8.8.8 Complete the following by filling in the blanks:

1. A: Ashita issho ni eiga o mi ni ikimasen ka?

   B: Ashita wa ben'kyoo shimasu kara, _____.

2. A: Ben'kyoo wa doo desu ka?

   B: Doomo _____.

3. A: Okyakusama, ano kata ga Kimura san desu.

   B: Doomo _____.

8.9 SITUATIONAL AND APPLICATION CONVERSATION

8.9.1 At the library

A male college student and a female college student meet in the library.

They ask each other why they are there.

The male student is looking in vain for some reference books.

The female student recommends some good reference books she bought.

She agrees to lend them to the male student.

8.9.2 Carry on a conversation about the books you have read, or about the libraries that you have visited and the reasons why you want to read books, etc.

8.9.3 At a secondhand bookstore

A boy is looking for a certain book and his friend wants to help him.

8.9.4 Child: Kyoo ban'gohan, nani?

Mother: Ten'pura yo.

Child: Mata ten'pura?

8.9.5 Hara: Ueki san, moo kaerimasen ka?

Ueki: Iie, chotto shigoto ga arimasu kara.

8.9.6 Mother: Midori san, omoshiroi terebi ga hajimarimasu yo.

Midori: Atashi ben'kyoo ga aru kara.

8.9.7 Mr. Tōyama: San'po desu ka?

Mr. Fujita: Ee, chotto.

8.9.8 A: Chotto, sumimasen ga, kono hen ni Watanabe san no otaku ga arimasu ka?

B: Asoko desu yo.

A: Doomo.

LESSON 9
日本語の　教室[1]

9.1　　PRESENTATION

　教室の　中[2]に、　先生が　一人、　学生が　八人　います。　先生は　黒板の　前[2]に　たって
います[3]。　学生たちは　いすに　すわっています[3]。　つくえの　上[2]には　本や　ノートや　えん
ぴつなどが　あります。

9.2　　DIALOG

先生　　　「では、　これから　先月　習った　ところ[4]の　しけんを　しましょう。　まず、
　　　　　　紙に　名前を　書いてください。　しつもんが　ありますか。」

学生（一）「先生。」

先生　　　「はい、　なんですか。」

学生（一）「ペンを　わすれました。　えんぴつで　書いても　いい[5]ですか。」

先生　　　「ええ、　いいです。」

学生（二）「辞書を　つかっても　かまいませんか[5]。」

先生　　　「つかっては　いけません[6]。　辞書も　教科書も　つかわないでください[7]。　じゃあ[8]、
　　　　　　はじめましょう。　黒板に　もんだいを　書きますから、　今　わたした　紙に
　　　　　　こたえを　書いてください。」

学生（三）「先生、　こたえだけ[9]　で[10]　いいんですか。」

先生　　　「はい、　かまいません。」

学生（三）「それから、　ローマ字で　こたえても　いいですか。」

先生　　　「いいえ、　かん字と　かなを　つかってください。　おそくて[11]も　かまいませんから[11]。
　　　　　　わかりましたね。[12]」

学生（三）「わかりました。」

日本語　教室　先生　一人　八人　上　先月
習った　紙　名前　書いてください　辞書
教科書　ローマ字

9.3   PATTERN SENTENCES

9.3.1

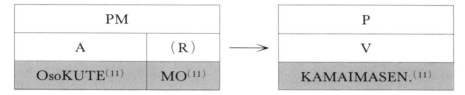

PM				
N	R		V	(R)
En'pitsu	de	→	kaiTE[5]	MO[5]

P		SP
A	C	
II[5]	desu	ka?

9.3.2

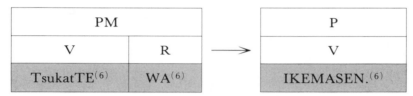

PM	
A	(R)
OsoKUTE[11]	MO[11]

P
V
KAMAIMASEN.[11]

9.3.3

PM	
V	R
TsukatTE[6]	WA[6]

P
V
IKEMASEN.[6]

9.3.4

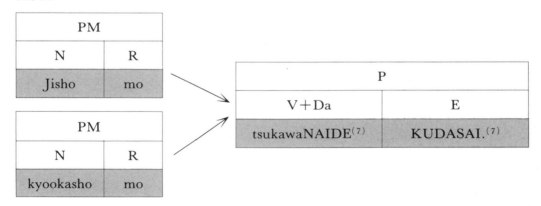

PM	
N	R
Jisho	mo

PM	
N	R
kyookasho	mo

P	
V+Da	E
tsukawaNAIDE[7]	KUDASAI.[7]

9.3.5

PM			
N	R	C	(R)
Kotae	DAKE[9]	DE[10]	MO[10]

P		
A	PC	C
II[10]	n	desu.

9.4 **NOTES**

9.4.1 **The Classroom**

The classroom in a Japanese university is quite different from that of an American university. By comparison, Japanese classrooms are very formal; the wandering around and talking before class so common in American universities is missing in their Japanese counterparts. Japanese students would not think of sitting on the top of a desk or table.

A college teacher's behavior in Japan is also much more formal when compared with that of American teachers. Teachers have a much higher status than students and it is expected that students show them the proper respect. Therefore, a teacher is more formal in dress, behavior, attitude, speech, and so forth than in America. Unlike in American universities, teacher evaluation by students in Japanese universities is practically nonexistent. A student feels totally responsible for any difficulties encountered in his schooling and would blame himself rather than fault the teacher's inadequacy. This traditional attitude is quickly disappearing however.

9.4.2 *Naka* is a Noun meaning "inside." In Japanese, certain Nouns indicate place or location. They will be called "location Nouns." Here are some of them.

naka	中	"inside"	ue	上	"topside; above"
soto	外	"outside"	shita	下	"under; below"
mae	前	"front; before"	soba	そば	"vicinity; near"
ushiro	うしろ	"back; behind"			

These Nouns may be used like other Nouns and followed by Relationals. But they are often preceded by a Noun plus *no*.

$$(\sim no) + \begin{Bmatrix} naka \\ soto \\ mae \\ ushiro \\ ue \\ shita \\ soba \end{Bmatrix} + \begin{Bmatrix} ni \\ de \\ e \\ kara \\ made \\ \text{--------} \\ ga \\ o \\ wa \end{Bmatrix}$$

Kyooshitsu no naka ni gakusei ga oozei imasu.	"There are many students in the classroom."
Soto e ikimashoo.	"Let's go outside."
Naka ni haitte kudasai.	"Please come in."
Gin'koo no mae kara takushii de kimashita.	"I came by taxi from the front of the bank."
Tsukue no ue ga kitanai desu.	"The top of the desk is dirty."
Yamamoto san no ushiro ni suwarimashita.	"I sat behind Mr. Yamamoto."

Kinoo anata no uchi no soba made ikimashita.	"I went as far as the vicinity of your house yesterday."
Ki no shita de inu ga nete imasu.	"A dog is sleeping under the tree."
Yane no ue ni tori ga imasu.	"There is a bird on the roof."

9.4.3 Verbs such as *tachimasu* "stand" and *suwarimasu* "sit" are used normally with the place Relational *ni* to indicate the place in which one gets to stand or on which one gets to sit. The Relational *ni* of existence is used because the result of action *tachimasu* or *suwarimasu* exists or remains in the place. "One sat on a chair" implies "one is on a chair." When it is necessary to mention the place where the action of standing up or of sitting down takes place, *de* may be used.

Kokuban no mae ni tatte imasu.	"He is standing in front of the blackboard."
Gakusei wa isu ni suwarimashita.	"Students sat on their chairs."
Mise de ichinichijuu tatte imashita.	"I was standing all day long in the store."

Likewise, *kakimasu* "write" requires the Relational *ni* to state "on which one writes."

| Kokuban ni ji o kaite kudasai. | "Please write characters on the blackboard." |

9.4.4 *Tokoro* means "place" in *tomodachi no tokoro*. *Tokoro* may mean "a part" as in *naratta tokoro* "the part that [you] studied." Many other meanings of *tokoro* such as "time," "occasion," or "things" will be studied later.

9.4.5 *Kaite mo ii desu ka?* means "May I write it?" or "Will it be all right to write it?" The verbal pattern of permission is formulated by the combination of the TE form of a Verb plus *mo* plus *ii (desu)* "all right," or *kamaimasen* "do not mind." The Relational *mo* in this pattern means "even," but it is optional. The literal translation of the Japanese pattern is "It is all right even if one does such and such," or "I do not mind even if one does such and such."

$$(\textbf{Predicate Modifier}) + \textbf{Verb}(\textit{-te}) + (\textbf{\textit{mo}}) + \begin{cases} \textit{ii desu} \\ \textit{kamaimasen} \end{cases}$$

kashite						[I] lend it"
mite	(mo)	ii desu		"it's all right	(even) if	[you] see it"
suwatte		kamaimasen		"I don't mind		[you] sit"
tsukatte						[he] uses it"

An affirmative response to a question asking for permission can be made by repeating the whole sentence, or the Predicate. Sometimes *hai, doozo* is used as an affirmative answer.

En'pitsu de kaite mo ii desu ka?	"May I write it with pencil?"
Hai, (en'pitsu de kaite mo) ii desu.	"Yes, you may (write it with pencil)."
Hai, doozo.	"Yes, please go ahead."
Jisho o tsukatte mo kamaimasen ka?	"Don't you mind even if I use a dictionary?"
Ee, kamaimasen.	"No, I don't mind it."
Tabako o sutte mo ii desu ka?	"May I smoke?"

| Hai, kamaimasen. | "Yes, you may." |
| Shitsumon shite ii desu ka? | "May I ask a question?" |

-te mo kamaimasen ka?—Heteronomy

The use of -te mo kamaimasen ka? is another example of the Japanese desire to involve the second person. A Verb followed by -te mo kamaimasen ka? actually means "Do you mind if I do something?" and does not simply seek the other's permission. In the situation described in the dialog, it would be more common for an American to simply ask for permission. The Japanese equivalent -te mo ii desu ka? is, however, less formal than the form -te mo kamaimasen ka?, which seeks permission but also involves the other by asking their own feelings on the matter.

9.4.6   *Tsukatte wa ikemasen* means "You must not use it," or "You should not use it." The pattern of prohibition is formulated by the TE form of a Verb plus *wa* plus *ikemasen* "it won't do," or *dame desu* "is no good." The *wa* is mandatory in this pattern. The literal meaning of this pattern is "It is no good if you do such and such." This expression may be used as a strict negative answer to a question asking for permission ~ -te (mo) ii desu ka? The answer may be shortened into *ikemasen* or *dame desu.*

$$(\text{Predicate Modifier}) + \text{Verb}(\text{-}te) + wa + \left\{ \begin{array}{l} \textit{ikemasen} \\ \textit{dame desu} \end{array} \right.$$

$$\left.\begin{array}{l} \text{wasurete} \\ \text{yasun'de} \\ \text{tatte} \\ \text{kaite} \\ \text{motte ite} \end{array}\right\} \text{wa} \left\{\begin{array}{l} \text{ikemasen} \\ \text{dame desu} \end{array}\right. \begin{array}{l} \text{"It won't do"} \\ \text{"it's no good"} \end{array} \text{if you} \left\{\begin{array}{l} \text{forget it"} \\ \text{take leave"} \\ \text{stand up"} \\ \text{write it"} \\ \text{have it"} \end{array}\right.$$

Eigo de kotaete mo ii desu ka?	"May I answer in English?"
Iie, (eigo de kotaete wa) ikemasen.	"No, you may not (answer in English)."
Kyuukoo ni notte wa dame desu yo.	"You must not take an express."
Doa o shimete wa ikemasen ka?	"Do you mind if I close the door?"
Ii desu yo.	"No, I don't mind."

9.4.7   *Tsukawanaide kudasai* means "Please do not use (it)." The polite negative imperative "please do not do such and such" is expressed in Japanese as follows:

Pre-Nai form of Verb + adjectival Derivative (-naide*) + kudasai

$$\left.\begin{array}{l} \text{noranaide} \\ \text{konaide} \\ \text{shinaide} \\ \text{misenaide} \\ \text{wasurenaide} \end{array}\right\} \text{kudasai} \quad \text{"please don't} \left\{\begin{array}{l} \text{get on"} \\ \text{come"} \\ \text{do it"} \\ \text{show it"} \\ \text{forget"} \end{array}\right.$$

*The -naide is another form of -nakute—the TE form of the adjectival Derivative -nai (see Note 9.4.11). This form occurs in some patterns: the polite negative imperative is one of them.

| Jisho mo kyookasho mo tsukawanaide kudasai. | "Please do not use either a dictionary or a textbook." |

Asatte yasumanaide kudasai.	"Please do not be absent the day after tomorrow."
Roomaji de kakanaide kudasai.	"Please do not write it in roman letters."
Shukudai o wasurenaide kudasai.	"Don't forget to bring in homework, please."

The pattern . . . -*naide kudasai* is often used to give a mild negative answer to a question asking for permission.

Mado o akete mo ii desu ka?	"May I open the window?"
Samui (desu) kara, akenaide kudasai.	"Please don't open it, because it's cold."
Doa o shimenaide kudasai.	"Please don't close the door."
Tabako o suwanaide kudasai.	"Please don't smoke."

Note that an English expression "please don't BE such and such" is never applied to this pattern directly. The word that appears before -*naide kudasai* is always a Verb.

The Japanese differentiate the use of prohibition forms according to the other person and the occasion. -*te wa ikemasen* is much more direct than -*naide kudasai*, and therefore speakers always try to avoid its use toward a superior. -*te wa ikemasen* is also far less personal, and therefore is sometimes found in public notices or public admonitions such as "No smoking"; further, it may also signify that the speaker means business, that he strongly objects to the other's doing something, for example, that the speaker is angry and is determined to stop an action.

| Koko de tabako o sutte wa ikemasen. | "Do not smoke here. (It is not permitted here.)" |
| Koko de tabako o suwanaide kudasai. | "Please don't smoke here." |

9.4.8   *Jaa* is the colloquial counterpart of *dewa*. Usually, *jaa* can be used in an informal, colloquial environment and functions to initiate a new topic or action, signifying a change in the situation up to that point.

In Japan, traditionally the classroom situation is far more formal than in America so the teacher uses *dewa* rather than *jaa* to begin his talk. *Dewa* cues the entire situation, making it more formal, serious, and businesslike (relatively speaking). By comparison, though Americans also have degrees of formality, those forms are not used as widely to set the tone of an entire situation.

It should be noted that *jaa* is never used in the formal written style, being largely a conversational form.

9.4.9   *Dake* is a Relational meaning "just," or "only," and functions to limit the reference only to the preceding Noun. The Relational *dake* may take the place of such Relationals as *ga, o, wa,* or it may occur between a Noun and *ga, o,* or *wa.* With other Relationals such as *ni, de, e, kara, to,* and the Relational *dake* may precede or follow another Relational.

$$\textbf{Noun} + \begin{Bmatrix} ga \\ o \\ wa \end{Bmatrix} + \textbf{Predicate} \longrightarrow \textbf{Noun} + dake + \begin{Bmatrix} (ga) \\ (o) \\ (wa) \end{Bmatrix} + \textbf{Predicate}$$

$$\text{Noun} + \begin{Bmatrix} ni \\ de \\ \cdots \\ \cdots \\ e \\ kara \\ to \end{Bmatrix} + \text{Predicate} \longrightarrow \text{Noun} + dake + \begin{Bmatrix} ni \\ de \\ \cdots \\ \cdots \\ e \\ kara \\ to \end{Bmatrix} + \text{Predicate}$$

$$\text{or Noun} + \begin{Bmatrix} ni \\ de \\ \cdots \\ \cdots \\ e \\ kara \\ to \end{Bmatrix} + dake + \text{Predicate}$$

Kotae dake kaite kudasai.	"Please write only the answers."
Nan'nin kimashita ka?	"How many people came?"
San'nin dake kimashita.	"Only three came."
Sen'sei wa`Pooru dake ni shukudai o kaeshimashita.	"The teacher returned the homework only to Paul."

9.4.10 *Kotae dake de ii n desu ka?* means "Is it all right if (I write) only the answer?" *De* of the above sentence is the TE form of the Copula *desu*. The patterns of permission and prohibition that have been explained in Notes 9.4.5 and 9.4.6 are applicable to the copular Predicate.

$$\begin{Bmatrix} \textbf{Noun} \\ \textbf{adjectival Noun} \end{Bmatrix} + de + (mo) + \begin{Bmatrix} ii\ desu \\ kamaimasen \end{Bmatrix}$$

$$\begin{Bmatrix} \textbf{Noun} \\ \textbf{adjectival Noun} \end{Bmatrix} + \begin{matrix} de+wa^{*} \\ (ja) \end{matrix} + \begin{Bmatrix} ikemasen \\ dame\ desu \end{Bmatrix}$$

*As already explained, *de wa* may be shortened to *ja;* ~ *ja ikemasen* or ~ *ja dame desu.*

En'pitsu de mo ii desu ka?	"Is it all right with pencil?"
Heta de mo kamaimasen ka?	"Don't you mind if I am not good at it?"
Nomimono dake de ii desu ka?	"Is it all right with only drinks?"
Nihon'go de wa ikemasen.	"It must not be in Japanese."
Hiragana dake de wa dame desu.	"It's no good with only *hiragana*."

9.4.11 *Osokute mo kamaimasen* means "It is all right if you are slow (in writing)." *Osokute* is the TE form of the Adjective *osoi* meaning "is slow; is late." The TE form of an Adjective is also used in the patterns of permission and prohibition, as explained in Notes 9.4.5, 9.4.6, and 9.4.10.

$$\textbf{TE form of Adjective}\ (\text{-}kute) + (mo) + \begin{Bmatrix} ii\ desu \\ kamaimasen \end{Bmatrix}$$

$$\textbf{TE form of Adjective}\ (\text{-}kute) + wa + \begin{Bmatrix} ikemasen \\ dame\ desu \end{Bmatrix}$$

The TE form of Adjectives is made by changing the final -*i* into -*kute*. Thus:

oso*i*	"is late; is slow"	⟶	oso*kute*
sukuna*i*	"is little; is few"	⟶	sukuna*kute*
oo*i*	"is much; are many"	⟶	oo*kute*
mijika*i*	"is short"	⟶	mijika*kute*
naga*i*	"is long"	⟶	naga*kute*
haya*i*	"is early; is fast"	⟶	haya*kute*
na*i*	"is nonexistent"	⟶	na*kute*

Takakute mo kamaimasen ka?	"Don't you mind if it's expensive?"
Kotae wa mijikakute wa ikemasen.	"Answers must not be short."
Heya no naka wa kitanakute wa dame desu.	"It's no good if the room is dirty."
Setsumei wa nagakute mo ii desu.	"It's all right if the explanation is long."

Note that the TE forms of the plain negative of a Verb, the Copula, and an Adjective are also formulated as an Adjective.

tsukawana*i*	⟶	tsukawana*kute*
tabena*i*	⟶	tabena*kute*
shizuka ja na*i*	⟶	shizuka ja na*kute*
kyuukoo ja na*i*	⟶	kyuukoo ja na*kute*
hayaku na*i*	⟶	hayaku na*kute*
chikaku na*i*	⟶	chikaku na*kute*

Tsukawanakute mo ii desu.	"It is all right if you don't use it." "You don't have to use it."
Tabenakute mo kamaimasen.	"I don't mind if you do not eat it."
Sukoshi yasumanakute wa ikemasen yo.	"You must rest for a while."
Kotae wa hiragana ja nakute mo ii desu.	"Answers do not have to be in *hiragana*."
Koohii wa atsuku nakute wa dame desu.	"It's no good if coffee is not hot."

Kan'ji to kana o tsukatte kudasai and *Osokute mo kamaimasen kara* were two clauses of one sentence inverted into two.

Ikimasu ka? Ashita?	"Do you go tomorrow?"
Tabete kudasai. Oishii desu kara.	"Please eat it. It's delicious."

9.4.12 *Ne* and *Yo* as Emphatic Reminders

As indicated in Note 2.4.14, *ne* and *yo* are attached to a sentence making it a plain expression used mainly toward one's peers or inferiors. In addition, both function as emphatic reminders.

As it is used in this dialog, *Wakarimashita ne*, the Sentence Particle *ne* is employed only by a superior, since the speaker is checking the second person's understanding. In the dialog, *ne* functions to reinforce the statement just made (the sentence to which *ne* is attached). For a person to use this form the second person would have to be someone who needs to be reminded, someone who, without such a reminder, might not understand what is being said. In this situation the use of *ne* is quite appropriate, since the second persons are the teacher's students. The traditional Japanese attitude is that students always need reminding, whereas the teacher—who knows everything—never needs reminding.

9.5   VOCABULARY

Presentation

教室	kyooshitsu	......	N	classroom
黒板	kokuban	......	N	blackboard
前	mae	......	N	front; before (see 9.4.2)
たって	tatte	......	V	TE form of *tachimasu* ← *tatsu*—stand (see 9.4.3)
いす	isu	......	N	chair
すわって	suwatte	......	V	TE form of *suwarimasu* ← *suwaru*—sit (see 9.4.3)
つくえ	tsukue	......	N	desk
上	ue	......	N	top; topside; on; above (see 9.4.2)

Dialog

ところ	tokoro	......	N	part; section (see 9.4.4)
まず	mazu	......	Adv.	first of all; to begin with
しつもん	shitsumon	......	N	question
わすれました	wasuremashita	......	V	forgot (TA form of *wasuremasu* ← *wasureru*)
も	mo	......	R	even (see 9.4.5)
いけません	ikemasen	......	V	it won't do (see 9.4.6)
教科書	kyookasho	......	N	textbook
つかわないで	tsukawanaide	......	V+Da	Pre-Nai form of a Verb+-*naide* (see 9.4.7)
はじめましょう	hajimemashoo	......	V	let's begin (OO form of *hajimemasu* ← *hajimeru*) (transitive Verb) (cf. Vi: *hajimarimasu*)
わたした	watashita	......	V	handed (TA form of *watashimasu* ← *watasu*)
こたえ	kotae	......	N	answer
だけ	dake	......	R	only; just (see 9.4.9)
で	de	......	C	TE form of *desu* (see 9.4.10)
ローマ字	roomaji	......	N	roman letters
こたえて	kotaete	......	V	TE form of *kotaemasu* ← *kotaeru*—answer; respond

かな	kana	......	N	Japanese syllabary
おそくて	osokute	......	A	TE form of *osoi*—is slow; is late (see 9.4.11)

Notes

うしろ	ushiro	......	N	behind; back (see 9.4.2)
下	shita	......	N	under; below (see 9.4.2)
そば	soba	......	N	vicinity; near (see 9.4.2)
木 ki	ki	......	N	tree
やね	yane	......	N	roof
字	ji	......	N	letter; character
たばこ	tabako	......	N	tobacco; cigarette
すって	sutte	......	V	TE form of *suimasu* ← *suu*—smoke; inhale
しつもん（を）します	shitsumon (o) shimasu	......	V	ask a question
しめて	shimete	......	V	TE form of *shimemasu* ← *shimeru*—shut; close
ないで	-naide	......	Da	(see 9.4.7)
しゅくだい	shukudai	......	N	homework
あけて	akete	......	V	TE form of *akemasu* ← *akeru*—open
みじかい	mijikai	......	A	is short
ながい	nagai	......	A	is long
なくて	-nakute	......	Da	TE form of *-nai* (see 9.4.11)

Drills

テーブル	teeburu	......	N	table

9.6   KAN'JI

9.6.1 語　(1) GO　(2) language; word　(3) classifier 言
(4) 丶 丶 亠 三 言 言 言 言 訂 訂 訝 訝 語 語 語
(5) 日本語、外国語、ドイツ語　(6) homonym 五、吾、悟

9.6.2 教　(1) KYOO　(2) teach　(3) classifier 欠
(4) 一 十 土 耂 耂 孝 孝 孝 孝 教 教　(5) 教科書、教室、教育 [education]、キリスト教 [Christianity]

9.6.3 先 (1) SEN (2) previous; ahead (3) classifier 生 (儿)

(4) ノ ⺯ ⺬ 生 先 先 (5) 先生、先月、先週 (6) homonym 洗、銑

9.6.a 人^{5.6.2} (1) NIN (5) 三人、死人 [the dead]

9.6.4 上 (1) *ue* (2) top; above; on (3) classifier 卜 (一) (4) 丨 卜 上

(5) 本の上、つくえの上 (6) a dot above a horizontal line. See 9.6.10

9.6.5 習 (1) *nara(imasu); nara(u)* (2) learn (3) classifier 羽 [feather]

(4) ⁊ ⁊ ⁊ ⁊⁊ ⁊⁊ 羽 羽 習 習

(5) 日本語を習います、習ったところ

9.6.6 紙 (1) *kami* [*-gami*] (2) paper (3) classifier 糸 [thread; string]

(4) く ⺯ ⺯ 糸 糸 糸 紅 紙 紙 紙 (5) しけんの紙、手紙

(6) 糸 is the shape of a silkworm's cocoon

9.6.7 名 (1) *na* (2) name (3) classifier 夕 (口) (4) ノ ク タ 夕 名 名

(5) 名前 (6) open the mouth in the evening—a person cries someone's name in

the dark

9.6.8 書 (1) *ka(kimasu); ka(ku)* (2) write (3) classifier ⺻ (曰)

(4) ⁊ ⁊ ⁊ ⁊ 彐 聿 聿 書 書 書 (5) 書く (6) a hand holding a

brush over a piece of paper

9.6.b 書^{9.6.8} (1) SHO (5) 教科書、辞書、さんこう書、図書館

9.6.9 字 (1) JI (2) letter; character (3) classifier 子

(4) ⸍ ⸍ 宀 字 字 字 (5) ローマ字、かん字

9.6.10 下* (1) *shita* (2) under; beneath; below; bottom (3) classifier 一

(4) 一 丁 下 (5) つくえの下、くつ下 [socks; stockings]、木の下

(6) a dot below a horizontal line as compared to a dot above the horizontal line 上

(See 9.6.4)

9.6.c 外*^{7.6.4} (1) *soto* (2) outside (5) 外へ出ましょう

9.7   DRILLS

9.7.1   Transformation Drill

A.   まどを　あけます。　　　　　　　　⟶　　まどを　あけても　いいです。

  1.　ドアを　しめます。　　　　　　　⟶　　ドアを　しめても　いいです。

  2.　いすに　すわります。　　　　　　⟶　　いすに　すわっても　いいです。

  3.　日本語で　こたえます。　　　　　⟶　　日本語で　こたえても　いいです。

  4.　つぎの　クラスを　休みます。　⟶　　つぎの　クラスを　休んでも　いいです。

  5.　東京駅で　おります。　　　　　　⟶　　東京駅で　おりても　いいです。

  6.　しつもんを　します。　　　　　　⟶　　しつもんを　しても　いいです。

  7.　よるまで　にわで　あそんで　⟶　　よるまで　にわで　あそんでいても
　　　　います。　　　　　　　　　　　　　　　　いいです。

  8.　ともだちから　かりません。　⟶　　ともだちから　かりなくても　いいです。

B.   おてあらいへ　行きます。　　　　⟶　　おてあらいへ　行っても　かまいません。

  1.　しけんを　はじめます。　　　　⟶　　しけんを　はじめても　かまいません。

  2.　カードを　しらべます。　　　　⟶　　カードを　しらべても　かまいません。

  3.　タクシーに　のります。　　　　⟶　　タクシーに　のっても　かまいません。

  4.　けい子さんに　かします。　　　⟶　　けい子さんに　かしても　かまいません。

  5.　たばこを　すいます。　　　　　⟶　　たばこを　すっても　かまいません。

  6.　まどの　そばに　たっています。⟶　　まどの　そばに　たっていても
　　　　　　　　　　　　　　　　　　　　　　　　かまいません。

  7.　先生に　はなしてみます。　　　⟶　　先生に　はなしてみても　かまいません。

  8.　辞書を　つかいません。　　　　⟶　　辞書を　つかわなくても　かまいません。

9.7.2   Transformation Drill

A.   書くのが　おそいです。　　　　　⟶　　書くのが　おそくても　いいです。

  1.　くつは　すこし　きついです。⟶　　くつは　すこし　きつくても　いいです。

  2.　もんだいは　ながいです。　　　⟶　　もんだいは　ながくても　いいです。

  3.　ひるごはんは　おそいです。　⟶　　ひるごはんは　おそくても　いいです。

  4.　しけんは　むずかしいです。　⟶　　しけんは　むずかしくても　いいです。

  5.　ジュースは　つめたくないです。⟶　　ジュースは　つめたくなくても　いいです。

B.   しごとは　いそがしいです。　　⟶　　しごとは　いそがしくても　かまいません。

  1.　レポートは　みじかいです。　⟶　　レポートは　みじかくても　かまいません。

  2.　学校は　とおいです。　　　　　⟶　　学校は　とおくても　かまいません。

  3.　へやは　さむいです。　　　　　⟶　　へやは　さむくても　かまいません。

4. 教科書は　たかいです。	⟶ 教科書は　たかくても　かまいません。
5. 教室は　きたないです。	⟶ 教室は　きたなくても　かまいません。
6. セーターは　大きくないです。	⟶ セーターは　大きくなくても　かまいません。

9.7.3　Transformation Drill

A.　やすい　アルバイトです。	⟶ やすい　アルバイトでも　いいです。
1. 天気が　へんです。	⟶ 天気が　へんでも　いいです。
2. のる　でんしゃは　急行です。	⟶ のる　でんしゃは　急行でも　いいです。
3. こたえは　ローマ字です。	⟶ こたえは　ローマ字でも　いいです。
4. きたない　字です。	⟶ きたない　字でも　いいです。
5. ノートは　四百円です。	⟶ ノートは　四百円でも　いいです。
6. むずかしい　もんだいです。	⟶ むずかしい　もんだいでも　いいです。
7. おたくじゃないです。	⟶ おたくじゃなくても　いいです。
B.　おみやげは　おかしです。	⟶ おみやげは　おかしでも　かまいません。
1. 日本語が　へたです。	⟶ 日本語が　へたでも　かまいません。
2. りょこうが　きらいです。	⟶ りょこうが　きらいでも　かまいません。
3. 大学の　三年生です。	⟶ 大学の　三年生でも　かまいません。
4. すわる　所は　うしろです。	⟶ すわる　所は　うしろでも　かまいません。
5. つまらない　しごとです。	⟶ つまらない　しごとでも　かまいません。
6. しけんは　あさってです。	⟶ しけんは　あさってでも　かまいません。
7. おとうとの　セーターじゃない　です。	⟶ おとうとの　セーターじゃなくても　かまいません。

9.7.4　Transformation Drill

A.　しつもんします。	⟶ しつもんしては　いけません。
1. やねの　上で　あそびます。	⟶ やねの　上で　あそんでは　いけません。
2. まどを　あけます。	⟶ まどを　あけては　いけません。
3. わるい　ことばを　つかいます。	⟶ わるい　ことばを　つかっては　いけません。
4. レポートを　わすれます。	⟶ レポートを　わすれては　いけません。
5. カメラを　買います。	⟶ カメラを　買っては　いけません。
6. えい語で　こたえます。	⟶ えい語で　こたえては　いけません。
7. うちで　ねています。	⟶ うちで　ねていては　いけません。
8. ここに　すわっています。	⟶ ここに　すわっていては　いけません。

B.　学生に　わたします。　　　　　　　⟶　学生に　わたしては　だめです。

  1.　黒板に　書きます。　　　　　　　⟶　黒板に　書いては　だめです。

  2.　教科書を　かります。　　　　　　⟶　教科書を　かりては　だめです。

  3.　バスに　のります。　　　　　　　⟶　バスに　のっては　だめです。

  4.　子どもに　あげます。　　　　　　⟶　子どもに　あげては　だめです。

  5.　えい語で　はなします。　　　　　⟶　えい語で　はなしては　だめです。

  6.　つくえの　上に　すわります。　　⟶　つくえの　上に　すわっては　だめです。

  7.　たばこを　すいます。　　　　　　⟶　たばこを　すっては　だめです。

  8.　そこに　たっています。　　　　　⟶　そこに　たっていては　だめです。

9.7.5　Transformation Drill

A.　へやが　さむいです。　　　　　　　⟶　へやが　さむくては　いけません。

  1.　くつが　大きいです。　　　　　　⟶　くつが　大きくては　いけません。

  2.　せつめいが　みじかいです。　　　⟶　せつめいが　みじかくては　いけません。

  3.　教室は　きたないです。　　　　　⟶　教室は　きたなくては　いけません。

  4.　辞書は　ふるいです。　　　　　　⟶　辞書は　ふるくては　いけません。

  5.　レインコートは　小さいです。　　⟶　レインコートは　小さくては　いけません。

  6.　しけんは　やさしいです。　　　　⟶　しけんは　やさしくては　いけません。

  7.　字が　きたないです。　　　　　　⟶　字が　きたなくては　いけません。

B.　こたえが　みじかいです。　　　　　⟶　こたえが　みじかくては　だめです。

  1.　さんこう書が　むずかしいです。⟶　さんこう書が　むずかしくては　だめです。

  2.　コーヒーが　つめたいです。　　　⟶　コーヒーが　つめたくては　だめです。

  3.　学校は　とおいです。　　　　　　⟶　学校は　とおくては　だめです。

  4.　天気が　わるいです。　　　　　　⟶　天気が　わるくては　だめです。

  5.　おちゃが　あついです。　　　　　⟶　おちゃが　あつくては　だめです。

  6.　男の　人が　おおいです。　　　　⟶　男の　人が　おおくては　だめです。

  7.　しけんは　ながいです。　　　　　⟶　しけんは　ながくては　だめです。

9.7.6　Transformation Drill

A.　えい語の　辞書です。　　　　　　　⟶　えい語の　辞書では（じゃ）　いけません。

  1.　テーブルの　上です。　　　　　　⟶　テーブルの　上では　いけません。

  2.　学生が　一人です。　　　　　　　⟶　学生が　一人では　いけません。

  3.　かん字が　へたです。　　　　　　⟶　かん字が　へたでは　いけません。

  4.　ふるい　さんこう書です。　　　　⟶　ふるい　さんこう書では　いけません。

5.　ながい　せつめいです。　　　⟶　ながい　せつめいでは　いけません。

6.　いすの　下です。　　　⟶　いすの　下では　いけません。

7.　子どもです。　　　⟶　子どもでは　いけません。

B.　べんきょうが　<u>きらいです</u>。　　⟶　べんきょうが　<u>きらいでは　だめです</u>。

1.　教室の　外です。　　　⟶　教室の　外では　だめです。

2.　フランス語の　教科書です。　⟶　フランス語の　教科書では　だめです。

3.　森さんの　うちです。　　⟶　森さんの　うちでは　だめです。

4.　りょこうは　らいしゅうです。　⟶　りょこうは　らいしゅうでは　だめです。

5.　やすい　アルバイトです。　⟶　やすい　アルバイトでは　だめです。

6.　のみものは　おちゃです。　⟶　のみものは　おちゃでは　だめです。

7.　先生が　外国人です。　　⟶　先生が　外国人では　だめです。

9.7.7　Transformation Drill

1.　へやに　<u>はいりません</u>。　　⟶　へやに　<u>はいらないでください</u>。

2.　こたえを　見ません。　　⟶　こたえを　見ないでください。

3.　ドアを　あけません。　　⟶　ドアを　あけないでください。

4.　図書館に　かえしません。　⟶　図書館に　かえさないでください。

5.　しけんを　はじめません。　⟶　しけんを　はじめないでください。

6.　黒板の　前に　たちません。　⟶　黒板の　前に　たたないでください。

7.　さんこう書を　かりません。　⟶　さんこう書を　かりないでください。

8.　えい語を　つかいません。　⟶　えい語を　つかわないでください。

9.　名前を　わすれません。　　⟶　名前を　わすれないでください。

10.　紙を　わたしません。　　⟶　紙を　わたさないでください。

11.　ここに　すわりません。　　⟶　ここに　すわらないでください。

12.　林さんを　よびません。　⟶　林さんを　よばないでください。

9.7.8　Response Drill

1.　えんぴつで　書いても　いいですか。

はい　　　　　……　はい、えんぴつで　<u>書いても　いいです</u>。

いいえ　　　　……　いいえ、えんぴつで　<u>書いては　いけません</u>。

いいえ　　　　……　いいえ、えんぴつで　<u>書かないでください</u>。

2.　まどの　そばに　いても　いいですか。

はい　　　　　……　はい、まどの　そばに　いても　いいです。

```
いいえ          ……  いいえ、まどの　そばに　いては　いけません。
いいえ          ……  いいえ、まどの　そばに　いないでください。
```

3. いすに　すわっても　いいですか。

```
はい            ……  はい、いすに　すわっても　いいです。
いいえ          ……  いいえ、いすに　すわっては　いけません。
いいえ          ……  いいえ、いすに　すわらないでください。
```

4. 学生に　しけんを　わたしても　かまいませんか。

```
はい            ……  はい、学生に　しけんを　わたしても　かまいません。
いいえ          ……  いいえ、学生に　しけんを　わたしては　いけません。
いいえ          ……  いいえ、学生に　しけんを　わたさないでください。
```

5. じむしょの　前に　たっていても　かまいませんか。

```
はい            ……  はい、じむしょの　前に　たっていても　かまいません。
いいえ          ……  いいえ、じむしょの　前に　たっていては　いけません。
いいえ          ……  いいえ、じむしょの　前に　たっていないでください。
```

6. ポールさんから　さんこう書を　かりても　かまいませんか。

```
はい            ……  はい、ポールさんから　さんこう書を　かりても　かまいません。
いいえ          ……  いいえ、ポールさんから　さんこう書を　かりては　いけません。
いいえ          ……  いいえ、ポールさんから　さんこう書を　かりないでください。
```

7. あなたが　買った　本を　読んでも　かまいませんか。

```
はい            ……  はい、わたくしが　買った　本を　読んでも　かまいません。
いいえ          ……  いいえ、わたくしが　買った　本を　読んでは　いけません。
いいえ          ……  いいえ、わたくしが　買った　本を　読まないでください。
```

9.7.9 Response Drill

1. セーターは　きつくても　いいですか。

```
はい            ……  はい、セーターは　きつくても　いいです。
いいえ          ……  いいえ、セーターは　きつくては　いけません。
```

2. もんだいは　ながくても　いいですか。

```
はい            ……  はい、もんだいは　ながくても　いいです。
いいえ          ……  いいえ、もんだいは　ながくては　いけません。
```

3. しごとは　いそがしくても　いいですか。

```
はい            ……  はい、しごとは　いそがしくても　いいです。
いいえ          ……  いいえ、しごとは　いそがしくては　いけません。
```

4. こうちゃは　つめたくても　かまいませんか。

   はい　　　　　　　……　はい、こうちゃは　つめたくても　かまいません。

   いいえ　　　　　　……　いいえ、こうちゃは　つめたくては　いけません。

5. つくえは　小さくても　かまいませんか。

   はい　　　　　　　……　はい、つくえは　小さくても　かまいません。

   いいえ　　　　　　……　いいえ、つくえは　小さくては　いけません。

6. せつめいは　なくても　かまいませんか。

   はい　　　　　　　……　はい、せつめいは　なくても　かまいません。

   いいえ　　　　　　……　いいえ、せつめいは　なくては　いけません。

7. べんきょうする　へやは　うるさくても　かまいませんか。

   はい　　　　　　　……　はい、べんきょうする　へやは　うるさくても　かまいません。

   いいえ　　　　　　……　いいえ、べんきょうする　へやは　うるさくては　いけません。

9.7.10 Response Drill

1. かいわは　<u>へたでも</u>　いいですか。

   はい　　　　　　　……　はい、かいわは　<u>へたでも</u>　いいです。

   いいえ　　　　　　……　いいえ、かいわは　<u>へたでは</u>　いけません。

2. 文学の　本でも　いいですか。

   はい　　　　　　　……　はい、文学の　本でも　いいです。

   いいえ　　　　　　……　いいえ、文学の　本では　いけません。

3. しんかん線は　グリーンでも　いいですか。

   はい　　　　　　　……　はい、しんかん線は　グリーンでも　いいです。

   いいえ　　　　　　……　いいえ、しんかん線は　グリーンでは　いけません。

4. かん字と　ひらがなでも　かまいませんか。

   はい　　　　　　　……　はい、かん字と　ひらがなでも　かまいません。

   いいえ　　　　　　……　いいえ、かん字と　ひらがなでは　いけません。

5. わたしが　持っている　辞書でも　かまいませんか。

   はい　　　　　　　……　はい、あなたが　持っている　辞書でも　かまいません。

   いいえ　　　　　　……　いいえ、あなたが　持っている　辞書では　いけません。

6. せつめいが　みじかい　さんこう書でも　かまいませんか。

   はい　　　　　　　……　はい、せつめいが　みじかい　さんこう書でも　かまいません。

   いいえ　　　　　　……　いいえ、せつめいが　みじかい　さんこう書では　いけません。

9.7.11 Substitution Drill

1. 教室の　中に　ポールさんが　います。

　前　　　　　　　……　教室の　前に　ポールさんが　います。

　そば　　　　　　……　教室の　そばに　ポールさんが　います。

　外　　　　　　　……　教室の　外に　ポールさんが　います。

2. いすの　前に　でんわが　あります。

　上　　　　　　　……　いすの　上に　でんわが　あります。

　うしろ　　　　　……　いすの　うしろに　でんわが　あります。

　下　　　　　　　……　いすの　下に　でんわが　あります。

　そば　　　　　　……　いすの　そばに　でんわが　あります。

3. 図書館の　うしろで　けい子さんに　あいました。

　そば　　　　　　……　図書館の　そばで　けい子さんに　あいました。

　前　　　　　　　……　図書館の　前で　けい子さんに　あいました。

　中　　　　　　　……　図書館の　中で　けい子さんに　あいました。

　外　　　　　　　……　図書館の　外で　けい子さんに　あいました。

4. つくえの　そばが　きたないです。

　上　　　　　　　……　つくえの　上が　きたないです。

　下　　　　　　　……　つくえの　下が　きたないです。

　前　　　　　　　……　つくえの　前が　きたないです。

　中　　　　　　　……　つくえの　中が　きたないです。

9.7.12 Response Drill

1. きっぷは　どこに　ありましたか。

　つくえの　上　　　　　　　……　つくえの　上に　ありました。

2. 子どもたちは　どこに　いましたか。

　公園の　中　　　　　　　　……　公園の　中に　いました。

3. 東京行の　バスは　どこに　つきますか。

　あの　本屋の　そば　　　　……　あの　本屋の　そばに　つきます。

4. どこに　すわりましょうか。

　黒板の　前　　　　　　　　……　黒板の　前に　すわりましょう。

5. ノートは　どこに　ありますか。

　教科書の　下　　　　　　　……　教科書の　下に　あります。

6. どこを　さがしましたか。

　つくえの　うしろ　　　　　……　つくえの　うしろを　さがしました。

7. どこで タクシーに のりましたか。
   きっさ店の そば   …… きっさ店の そばで のりました。
8. どこまで はしりましたか。
   うちの 前から 駅の そばまで   …… うちの 前から 駅の そばまで
                  はしりました。

9.7.13 E-J Transformation Drill

A. まどを あけます。
   1. please don't   …… まどを あけないでください。
   2. may I   …… まどを あけても いいですか。
   3. don't you mind …… まどを あけても かまいませんか。
   4. you may not …… まどを あけては いけません。
   5. I don't mind …… まどを あけても かまいません。
   6. it is all right …… まどを あけても いいです。

B. 黒板の そばに すわります。
   1. please don't   …… 黒板の そばに すわらないでください。
   2. may I   …… 黒板の そばに すわっても いいですか。
   3. don't you mind …… 黒板の そばに すわっても かまいませんか。
   4. you may not …… 黒板の そばに すわっては いけません。
   5. it is no good …… 黒板の そばに すわっては だめです。
   6. it is all right …… 黒板の そばに すわっても いいです。

C. しけんの もんだいが ながいです。
   1. is it all right …… しけんの もんだいが ながくても いいですか。
   2. don't you mind …… しけんの もんだいが ながくても かまいませんか。
   3. it is not all right …… しけんの もんだいが ながくては いけません。
   4. it is no good …… しけんの もんだいが ながくては だめです。

D. 天気が わるいです。
   1. is it all right …… 天気が わるくても いいですか。
   2. don't you mind …… 天気が わるくても かまいませんか。
   3. it is not all right …… 天気が わるくては いけません。
   4. it is no good …… 天気が わるくては だめです。

E.　ローマ字だけです。

    1.　is it all right　　　……　ローマ字だけでも　いいですか。

    2.　don't you mind　……　ローマ字だけでも　かまいませんか。

    3.　it is not all right　……　ローマ字だけでは　いけません。

    4.　it is no good　　　……　ローマ字だけでは　だめです。

    5.　I don't mind　　　……　ローマ字だけでも　かまいません。

F.　日本語が　へたです。

    1.　is it all right　　　……　日本語が　へたでも　いいですか。

    2.　don't you mind　……　日本語が　へたでも　かまいませんか。

    3.　it is not all right　……　日本語が　へたでは　いけません。

    4.　I don't mind　　　……　日本語が　へたでも　かまいません。

    5.　it is all right　　　……　日本語が　へたでも　いいです。

9.7.14　E-J Response Drill

1.　本と　ノートは　どこに　ありますか。

    on the desk　　　　　　　　　　　　……　本と　ノートは　つくえの　上に　あります。

2.　えんぴつは　どこに　ありますか。

    under the chair　　　　　　　　　　　……　えんぴつは　いすの　下に　あります。

3.　先生は　どこに　たっていますか。

    in front of the blackboard　　　　　……　先生は　黒板（こくばん）の　前に　たっています。

4.　スミスさんは　どこに　いますか。

    sitting near Mr. Brown　　　　　　　……　スミスさんは　ブラウンさんの　そばに
    　　　　　　　　　　　　　　　　　　　　　　　すわっています。

5.　ポールさんは　どこに　いますか。

    behind Mr. Smith　　　　　　　　　　……　ポールさんは　スミスさんの　うしろに
    　　　　　　　　　　　　　　　　　　　　　　　います。

6.　ブラウンさんは　なにを　していますか。

    studying Japanese in the classroom　……　ブラウンさんは　教室（しつ）の　中で　日本語を
    　　　　　　　　　　　　　　　　　　　　　　　べんきょうしています。

7.　井上（いのうえ）さんは　どこに　いましたか。

    outside the room　　　　　　　　　　……　井上（いのうえ）さんは　へやの　外に　いました。

9.8 EXERCISES

9.8.1 Answer the following questions according to the pictures below:

Picture A

1. へやの　中に　なにが　ありますか。
2. テレビの　上に　なにが　ありますか。
3. テーブルの　上に　なにが　ありますか。
4. テレビは　どこに　ありますか。
5. 人が　なん人　いますか。
6. どこに　すわっていますか。
7. その　人たちは　なにを　していますか。

Picture B

1. じどうしゃは　どこに　ありますか。
2. 女の　人は　なにを　していますか。
3. 女の　人は　だれと　いっしょですか。
4. 木の　下に　なにが　いますか。
5. とりは　やねの　上に　いますか。

9.8.2 Insert appropriate Relationals into the following blanks:

1. けい子さん（　　）わたして（　　）　いけません。
2. しけんは　ながくて（　　）　いいです。
3. 黒板（　　）　前の　いす（　　）すわっている　人は　だれですか。
4. おそくて（　　）　だめです。
5. さんこう書（　　）　辞書（　　）つかわないでください。
6. 紙（　　）　所（　　）　名前（　　）　書いてください。
7. 図書館（　　）　そば（　　）　ぎんこう（　　）　あるきました。
8. ノート（　　）　ローマ字や　えい語（　　）　書かないでください。
9. かん字（　　）　かな（　　）　書くことができますか。
　　　いいえ、ひらがな（　　）　書くことが　できます。（only ひらがな）

9.8.3 Write the Japanese equivalent:

1. May I go home at nine-thirty?

2. You must not speak English in the classroom.

3. I don't mind even if it is bad weather tomorrow.

4. It is all right for you to smoke in this room.

5. Please don't stand by the blackboard.

6. The examination should not be easy.

7. Please do not open the window because it is very cold outside.

8. You don't have to write the questions. The answers only will do.

9.8.4 Write the following underlined *hiragana* in *kan'ji*:

1. つくえの <u>うえに</u> <u>にほんごの</u> <u>きょう</u>科しょが あります。つくえの <u>した</u>には <u>かみ</u>が あります。

2. へやの <u>なか</u>に <u>がくせい</u>が <u>はちにん</u> います。そして、そとに <u>せんせい</u>が <u>ふたり</u> います。

3. <u>ならった</u> <u>かんじ</u>を <u>か</u>いてください。

4. <u>なまえ</u>を わすれないでください。

9.8.5 Write the following in *katakana*:

1. doa   2. teeburu   3. rooma(ji)

9.8.6 When you want to tell someone superior to you not to enter the room for some reason, you would say:

1. Heya ni haitte wa ikemasen.

2. Heya ni hairanaide kudasai.

9.8.7 Which would you say when you want to tell some children not to play in the garden?

1. Niwa de asobanaide kudasai.

2. Niwa de ason'de wa ikemasen.

9.8.8 Which of the following two expressions sounds more polite?

1. Tatte wa ikemasen.

2. Tatanaide kudasai.

9.8.9 Point out some differences in attitudes between teacher-student relations in Japan and in America.

9.8.10 Transform the following prohibiting expressions into a more polite form:

1. Mado o akete wa ikemasen.

2. Kono heya ni haitte wa ikemasen.

3. Roomaji o tsukatte wa ikemasen.

4. Kono isu ni suwatte wa ikemasen.

5. Kono hen de ason'de wa ikemasen.

9.8.11 Insert the proper form, *dewa, de wa,* or *jaa*:

1. _____, hajimemashoo. (formal)

2. Kotae dake _____ dame desu. (colloquial)

3. Koko _____ tabako o nomanaide kudasai. (formal)

4. _____, shiken o shimashoo. (formal)

5. Watashi _____ ikemasen ka? (colloquial)

9.9 SITUATIONAL AND APPLICATION CONVERSATION

9.9.1 In the classroom

An instructor is about to give a quiz.

A student asks if he can use the textbook and a dictionary.

The instructor gives permission to use a dictionary, but not the textbook.

The student asks if he can write with pencil.

The instructor says that it is all right, but tells him not to forget to bring a pen in the future.

The student asks if he can write the answers in roman letters, but the teacher says no.

9.9.2 In the classroom

A student wants to get his instructor's permission to be absent from his class on the following day.

The instructor asks why.

The student says that he wants to go to his home town since his mother is sick. (sick＝*byooki*)

The instructor gives permission.

9.9.3 Carry on a conversation normally conducted in the Japanese language class.

9.9.4 Talk about "do's and don't's" in the classroom, in the library, etc.

9.9.5 Student: Dewa, sorosoro shitsurei shimasu.

Professor: Soo desu ka? Jaa, mata irasshai.

9.9.6 Mother: Keiko san, mada tabete wa ikemasen yo. Otoosan, ima dekakenaide kudasai. Gohan desu kara.

9.9.7 Police: Minasan, hashiranaide kudasai! Soko no kodomosan, hashitte wa ikemasen yo.

LESSON 10
REVIEW AND APPLICATION

10.1 CONJUGATION
10.1.1 Verbs of plain perfect tense form

a. Vowel Verb

見			見		
見せ			見せ		
いれ			いれ		
つとめ			つとめ		
き			き		
出かけ			出かけ		
くれ			くれ		
わすれ			わすれ		
かり			かり		
おり			おり		
出			出		
ね			ね		
おき	る		おき	た	
しらべ	ない	⟶	しらべ	なかった	
い			い		
でき			でき		
あけ			あけ		
しめ			しめ		
はじめ			はじめ		
かけ			かけ		
こたえ			こたえ		
あげ			あげ		
さしあげ			さしあげ		
たべ			たべ		
つれ			つれ		

b. Consonant Verb

知
はし
かか
の
かえ
見つか
わか
ふ
すわ
はい
はじま
おわ
と
う
や

る
らない

⟶

知
はし
かか
の
かえ
見つか
わか
ふ
すわ
はい
はじま
おわ
と
う
や

った
らなかった

書
聞
はたら
つ
さ
ひ
ある
は
いただ

く
かない

⟶

書
聞
はたら
つ
さ
ひ
ある
は
いただ

いた
かなかった

ま
持
た

つ
たない

⟶

ま
持
た

った
たなかった

あ
つか
買
ち
が

う
わない

⟶

あ
つか
買
ち
が

った
わなかった

い かま かよ もら 習 す うかが	う わない	→	い かま かよ もら 習 す うかが	った わなかった
か かえ さが はな わた	す さない	→	か かえ さが はな わた	した さなかった
す 休 読 の	む まない	→	す 休 読 の	んだ まなかった
あそ よ	ぶ ばない	→	あそ よ	んだ ばなかった
およ	ぐ がない	→	およ	いだ がなかった

c. Irregular Verbs *kuru* and *suru*

来る   →   来た
来ない   →   来なかった

する   →   した
しない   →   しなかった

けんぶつする	しょくじする	しつもんする
けっこんする	アルバイトする	さんぽする
りょこうする	しごとする	でんわする
べんきょうする	せつめいする	しょうかいする

10.2   PATTERNS

10.2.1 Noun Modifier—Verb

a.

| これは | 先生に　かえす
ポールさんに　あげる
私が　かした
学校で　つかわない
スージーさんが　買った
ぼくの　読んでいる | 本です
さんこう書です
ノートです |

あの　店で　うっている	セーターは　　たかいです
図書館で　しらべていた	もんだいは　なんですか
ははが　習いたい	外国語は　日本語です
ジョージさんの　はなしている	ことばは　ていねいです
駅員から　聞いた	名前を　書いてください
スミスさんの　しない	スポーツは　じゅうどうや　からてだけです
あなたの　知らなかった	でんわばんごうは　これですか

b.

| あの　人は
あの　男の　子は | 日本語を　べんきょうしている
ハワイ大学へ　行った
図書館に　いた
まい日　本を　持って来ない | 学生です |

| 今　たっている
クラスに　来なかった
東京駅で　おりた
ぜんぜん　しつもんを　しない
ギターの　できない
しゅくだいを　わすれた | 女の　人は　だれですか
学生は　井上さんです |

c.

| ここは | ともだちが　つとめている
一郎くんが　はたらいている
ぼくの　アルバイトしていた | じむしょです |

198

ここは	前　すんでいた いろいろな　買い物を　した きょ年　花見に　来た	所です
	あした　あそびに　行く 日本語を　べんきょうしている	所は　東京です
	でんわが　ある あなたが　まっていた きのう　コーヒーを　のんだ いつも　パンを　買う	店は　どこですか

d.

それは	この　クラスの　おわる みち子さんが　うちへ　来る おとうとが　学校へ　出かけた ははが　うちに　いなかった	時間です 日です
	図書館で　しらべていた きのう　うちで　べんきょうした	時間は　二時から 五時までです
	東京から　大阪まで　かかる まい日　ぼくが　アルバイトする	時間は　三時間です

10.2.2 Noun Modifier＋*koto*（TA form of a Verb＋*koto* ''experience''）

私 かない あの　学生	は	（前（に））	アルバイトを　した かいしゃを　休んだ しんかん線に　のった 東京に　すんだ 大阪に　いた あの　子どもたちと　あそんだ かぶきを　見た グリーン車で　行った みち子さんに　あった その　さんこう書を　読んだ 先生の　所へ　うかがった	こと	が （は）	あります ありません ない（ん）です

10.2.3 Nominalizer *no* (Dictionary form＋*no*)

ふねで　りょこうする			たのしいです
ギターを　ひく			好きです
おんがくを　聞く			
公園まで　さんぽする			
買い物に　行く			
あさ　五時に　おきる	の	は	たいへんです
あの　人と　いっしょに　はたらく		が	
たばこを　すう			きらいです
日曜日に　うちに　いる			
七時に　出る			むずかしい
日本語の　しんぶんを　読む			やさしいです
えい語で　こたえる			
車を　持つ			

10.2.4 Permission and Prohibition

a. Verb

この　はこを　あけて	（も）	いいです
えい語で　こたえて		かまいません
まどを　しめて		
そこに　すわって		
急行に　のって		
三時間　かかって	は	いけません
黒板の　そばに　たっていて		だめです
辞書を　つかって		
あとで　しつもんして		
この　おかしを　たべてみて		
子どもを　つれて行って		
これを　男の　子に　わたして		

b. Adjective

ざっしは　ふるくて	（も）	いいです
のり物が　なくて		かまいません
しけんは　ながくて		
せつめいが　みじかくて		

書くのが　おそくて			
せいが　ひくくて		いけません	
おきる　時間が　はやくて	は	だめです	
くつが　きつくて			

c.　Copula

先生は　外国人			
いっしょに　行く　人は　ポールさん			
図書館員は　外国人		（も）	いいです
のり物は　タクシー			かまいません
けい子さんの　うしろ	で		
教室の　外			
きっぷは　グリーンけん			
かん字が　へた		は	いけません
しごとが　ひま			だめです
みじかい　しけん			

d.

………………………………		て（も）	いいですか
………………………………		くて（も）	かまいませんか
………………………………		で（も）	
	…………	て（も）	
はい、	…………	くて（も）	いいです
	…………	で（も）	かまいません
	…………	ては	
いいえ、	…………	くては	いけません
	…………	では	だめです
………………………………		ては	
………………………………		くては	いけませんか
………………………………		では	だめですか
	…………	ては	
はい、	…………	くては	いけません
	…………	では	だめです

	…………　て（も）	
いいえ、	…………　くて（も）	いいです
	…………　で（も）	かまいません

10.2.5 Negative Imperative

まどを　あけ		
まだ　しけんを　はじめ		
ローマ字で　こたえ		
ドアを　しめ		
しゅくだいを　わすれ		
そこに　すわら		
急行（きゅうこう）に　のら		
私に　聞か		
たばこを　すわ	ないで	ください
つくえの　上に　たた		
おさけを　のま		
カードを　つかわ		
この　プールで　およが		
日本語で　はなさ		
子どもを　つれて来		
東京へ　行か		
うちへ　かえら		

10.2.6 Location Noun

a.

この		中	が	きたないです
その			（は）	きれいです
あの				
やね		上	に	いました
いす	の	うしろ	を	見ましたか
その　はこ		下		
テーブル		上	で	書いてください
つくえ				

うち へや		中 外	が （は）	うるさいです しずかです
つくえ デパート 木(き)	の	そば 前 うしろ	に	あります います たっています
井上(いのうえ)さん あの 木(き)		そば	へ	来てください
図書館(としょかん)		前 うしろ	まで	あるきましょう はしりました

b.

どうぶつ園(えん) 大学		中 外		店(みせ) しょくどう
駅 デパート	の	そば	の	きっさ店(てん)
おてら ぼくの うち		前 うしろ		本屋(ほんや)
教科書(きょうかしょ) ノート		上 下		えんぴつ 紙

c.

上 下	が （は）	きたないです
そば 中	に	います すわりました
うしろ 外	を	見てください
前 上	で	書いています
中	へ	はいりましょう
そば 前	まで	行ってみます

10.2.7 Relationals *ni* and *kara*

のり物 車	に	のります
急行 しんかん線 ひこうき ふね	から	おります
おたく 東京駅 十八番線 あの　たて物	に	つきます
本屋の　前 うち	から	出ます

10.2.8 Relational *made*

a.　''up to (a place)''

どうぶつ園		行きます
うちの　そば	まで	来ます
東京		かえります
ちか		はしります

b.　''from (a place) to (another)''

しんぶん屋 ともだちの　所 よし子さんの　うち あの　たて物	から	本屋 わたしの　うち 駅 びじゅつ館	まで	行きます 来ます かえります バスに　のります
学校 ちか		しょくどう 三がい		あるきます はしります

あの　たて物 ここ	から	パン屋 学校	まで	一マイル 三キロ 六百メートル	あります
わたしの　うち じむしょ		ぎんこう 駅			です

先生の　おたく		大学		四分ぐらい	かかります
どうぶつ園_{えん}	から	びじゅつ館_{かん}	まで	十分	です
神田_{かんだ}		上野_の			
ハワイ		東京		十一時間半	

↓

…………………	から	…………	まで	どのくらい（どのぐらい）	あります / かかります / です　か

c. "until"

ふゆ休み		います
一九八八年		べんきょうしています
きょ年		はたらきました
三月		すんでいました
先月	まで	うっていました
先しゅう		かかりました
おととい		
火曜日_{よう}		あそびましょう
ごご		まちましょうか
ゆうがた		さがしました
ごぜん　九時		

d. "from (time) to (another)"

むかし		今		おなじです	
ふゆ		なつ		アルバイトします	
一九三十年		一九五十年		大阪_{さか}に　いました	
きょ年	から	ことし	まで	すんでいました	
四月		九月			
月曜日_{よう}		金曜日_{よう}		いそがしくないです	
ごご　二時		七時		かかりました	

10.2.9 ~*wa* ~*ga* instead of ~*no* ~*wa*

（この） （その） （あの）	駅員 しゃしょう 女の　人	の	しごと	は	たいへん おそい はやい いそがしい	です
			せい		たかい ひくい	
			め		大きい かわいい	
	外国人		日本語 かいわ		じょうず へん おもしろい	
	店員		ことば		ていねい しつれい	
	公園		さくら		うつくしい ゆうめい	
	学校		たて物		ふるい あたらしい	
	しょくどう		コーヒー		まずい	
	さんこう書		せつめい		てきとう くわしい	
	男の子		て あし		みじかい ながい	

↓ ↓

（この） （その） （あの）	………………	は	…………	が	…………… です

10.2.10 Relational *de* ''within; in''

一日

四時間

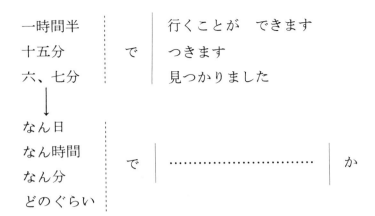

一時間半		行くことが　できます
十五分	で	つきます
六、七分		見つかりました

なん日			
なん時間	で	………………………	か
なん分			
どのぐらい			

10.2.11 Others

a. *dake* ''only; just''

教科書 レポート	だけ（を）	わたしませんでした
森さん 私	だけ（が）	教室に　来ました
一ぱい 三つ	だけ	ください
百メートル		はしりました

b. *dono gurai* ''how long?'' ''how much?'' ''how far?'' etc.

みずを	三ばい		のみました
ネクタイを	二本		買いました
日本語を	四年		習いました
きっぷを	二まい		ください
東京まで	六時間	（ぐらい）	かかります
休みが	十日	（くらい）	あります
ビールを	二、三ばい		のむことが　できます
京都に	五、六時間		いました
みち子さんを	二、三分		まちました
駅まで	四、五マイル		あるきました

↓

....	どのぐらい	....	
....	どのくらい	....	か

10.3   REVIEW DRILLS

10.3.1 Relational Checking Drill (*made ni* and *made*)

1. 三時、来てください　　　　　　　　……　三時までに　来てください。
2. ゆうがた、さんぽしています　　　　……　ゆうがたまで　さんぽしています。
3. 月曜日、先生に　レポートを　　　　……　月曜日までに　先生に　レポートを
     わたすつもりです　　　　　　　　　　　　わたすつもりです。
4. 九月、アルバイトが　おわるはずです　……　九月までに　アルバイトが　おわるはずです。
5. らい年の　二月、日本に　います　　……　らい年の　二月まで　日本に　います。
6. 四時半、まっていてください　　　　……　四時半まで　まっていてください。
7. あさ、大阪に　つきますか　　　　　……　あさまでに　大阪に　つきますか。
8. ごご、時間が　かかりますよ　　　　……　ごごまで　時間が　かかりますよ。

10.3.2 E-J Substitution Drill

A. おみやげは　つくえの　上に　ありますよ。

　　　1. under the table　　　　　　　　……　おみやげは　テーブルの　下に　ありますよ。
　　　2. inside the box　　　　　　　　　……　おみやげは　はこの　中に　ありますよ。
　　　3. in front of the television set　　……　おみやげは　テレビの　前に　ありますよ。
　　　4. near the window　　　　　　　　……　おみやげは　まどの　そばに　ありますよ。
　　　5. outside the room　　　　　　　　……　おみやげは　へやの　外に　ありますよ。

B. でんしゃの　中で　たばこを　すっては　いけません。

　　　1. in the library　　　　　　　　　……　図書館の　中で　たばこを　すっては
　　　　　　　　　　　　　　　　　　　　　　　　いけません。
　　　2. you may not talk　　　　　　　　……　図書館の　中で　はなしては　いけません。
　　　3. in this classroom　　　　　　　　……　教室の　中で　はなしては　いけません。
　　　4. you may not eat　　　　　　　　　……　教室の　中で　たべては　いけません。
　　　5. outside the cafeteria　　　　　　……　しょくどうの　外で　たべては　いけません。

10.3.3 Substitution and Transformation Drill

1. 客　　：　ちょっと　うかがいますが、新宿行の　でんしゃは　どれですか。

　　駅員　：　<u>今　ついた</u>　でんしゃです。いそいでください。（Please hurry.）

　　客　　：　どうも　すみません。

　　　　　　1. 今　来る　　　　　　　　　　2. 一番線から　出る

　　　　　　3. 五番線に　つく　　　　　　　4. 今　二番線に　はいった

2. A：　あそこに　いる　ブラウンさんを　しょうかいしましょうか。

　　B：　どの　かたですか。

　　A：　あの　<u>いすに　すわっている</u>　かたです。

　　B：　あの　かたですか。ぜひ　おねがいします。

　　　　　1. たばこを　すっている　　　　2. せいの　たかい

　　　　　3. ドアの　そばに　たっている　4. 本を　読んでいる

　　　　　5. レインコートを　きている　　6. 手に　カメラを　持った

　　　　　7. 今　すわった

3. A：　わたしは　<u>かん字を　習う</u>のが　大好きです。

　　B：　でも、<u>かん字を　習う</u>のは　たいへんでしょう。

　　A：　あまり　たいへんじゃありませんよ。

　　　　　あなたは　<u>かん字を　習った</u>ことが　ないんですか。

　　B：　ええ、ないんです。

　　　　　1. から手を　する　　　　　　　2. 日本語で　手紙を　書く

　　　　　3. 外国語を　べんきょうする　　4. 日本の　しんぶんを　読む

4. A：　<u>まどを　あけても</u>　かまいませんか。

　　B：　いいえ、<u>あけないで</u>ください。

　　A：　では、<u>ドアを　あけても</u>　いいですか。

　　B：　ええ、<u>あけても</u>　いいです。

　　　　　1. ローマ字で　書く、ひらがなで　書く　2. えい語を　つかう、フランス語を　つかう

　　　　　3. 前に　すわる、うしろに　すわる　4. くだ物を　たべる、おかしを　たべる

5. A：　<u>スキーを　した</u>ことが　ありますか。

　　B：　いいえ、ありません。あなたは？

　　A：　わたしは　<u>スキーを　する</u>のが　好きですから、よく　行きます。こんど　いっしょ
　　　　　に　行きましょう。

　　　　　1. 日本えいがを　見る　　　　　2. 京都へ　行く

　　　　　3. あの　レストランで　たべる　4. お花見を　する

　　　　　5. ぎんざで　買い物する

6. A: <u>あなたを 知っている</u> 人に きのう あいましたよ。

   B: さあ、だれでしょう？

   A: 名前は わすれましたが、<u>ニューヨークから 来た</u> 人です。

   B: ああ、わかりました。ジョージさんでしょう？

   A: そうそう、ジョージさんでした。

       1. おなじ 学校に かよっている、ドイツの 車を 持っている

       2. おたくの そばに すんでいる、日本語が わからない

       3. 日本語の クラスを とっている、かん字を よく 知っている

10.4 REVIEW EXERCISES

10.4.1 Insert a Relational in each blank:

1. 紙（　　）こたえと 名前（　　）書いてください。

2. まい日 しぶや（　　）バス（　　）おります。そして、しぶや駅（　　）
    でんしゃ（　　）のります。

3. 図書館（　　）しらべる（　　）は たいへんでしょう。私の 辞書（　　）
    つかって（　　）かまいませんよ。

4. 私は 先生の 所（　　）本を かえし（　　）行きました。

5. ニューヨーク（　　）サンフランシスコ（　　）車（　　）どのぐらい
    かかりますか。

6. 「かぶきは 五時（　　）はじまります。四時半（　　）来ること（　　）
    できますか。」「ちょっと むずかしいです。でも、四時四十五分（　　）は
    行きます（　　）、まっていてください。」

7. 「まどを しめて（　　）いけませんか。」「しめて（　　）いいですよ。」

8. けいざいの 本（　　）見つかりません。あなたは 見たこと（　　）ありますか。

9. あの せい（　　）たかい 学生（　　）聞いてみましょうか。

10. ドア（　　）所（　　）行ってください。

11. 「東京（　　）どのくらい かかりますか。」「一時間（　　）東京（　　）
    つきますよ。」

12. きっぷは バス（　　）中（　　）は うっていません。

13. この 本は え（　　）たいへん うつくしいですね。私（　　）かしてください。

14. 「男の 人も 女の 人も はしっていましたか。」「いいえ、男の 人（　　）*
    はしっていました。」

15. その 外国人は 日本語の せつめい（　　）わかりませんでした。

    *"only men"

10.4.2 Substitute the underlined part with good Japanese phrases equivalent to the given English:

A. <u>あの　学生</u>を　知っていますか。

    1.   the tall student

    2.   the student who is standing in front of the library

    3.   the student whom I met here yesterday

    4.   the student who comes to this classroom every day

    5.   the student who does not return books

    6.   the student who did not ask any questions

B. <u>その　本</u>を　あとで　かしてください。

    1.   that expensive book

    2.   the book you have (already) read

    3.   the book you borrowed at the library

    4.   the book whose title is long

    5.   the book that you are reading now

    6.   the book that I do not have

    7.   the book that you did not use

C. <u>しけんの　時間</u>は　なん時ですか。

    1.   the time when you got off the airplane

    2.   the time when you started your explanation

    3.   the time when you will not be studying

    4.   the time when you have arrived at the number 5 track

    5.   the time when your husband gets up every day

    6.   the time when the *kabuki* performance starts

10.4.3 Make an appropriate question for each of the following answers:

    1. スキーを　するのが　好きです。

    2. いいえ、したことが　あります。

    3. ええ、ながくても　かまいませんよ。

    4. 四時間　かかりました。

    5. いいえ、つれて来ないでください。

    6. いいえ、おなじでしょう。

    7. 二、三分で　できます。

    8. いいえ、学生だけ　います。

    9. さあ、駅員に　聞いてください。

    10. いいえ、たまに　見に　行きますけど。

10.4.4 Combine each A-group expression with the appropriate B-group expression:

A		B	
1.	まどを　あけても	a.	いけません。
2.	わたしは　スキーも　スケートも　する	b.	人に　聞いてください。
3.	しけんが　はじまる	c.	ことが　ありません。
4.	今　バスから　おりた	d.	かまいません。
5.	へやに　はいっては	e.	のは　たいへんです。
6.	名前を　わすれないで	f.	いいです。
7.	よく　わからない	g.	時間を　知っていますか。
8.	カードを　つかった	h.	ください。
9.	レポートは　みじかくて	i.	ことが　できます。
10.	大阪行の　急行では	j.	もんだいが　一つ　あります。
11.	一時までに　来る	k.	だめです。

10.5　　AURAL COMPREHENSION

10.5.1 A　「手紙を　書きたいけど、持って来た　ボールペンが　見つかりません。」

B　「つくえの　中を　さがしてみましたか。」

A　「ええ、バッグの　中にも　ないんです。」

B　「へんですね。でも、ここに　今　つかっていない　ペンが　ありますから、
つかっても　いいですよ。」

A　「いいですか。すみません。あした　かえしては　いけませんか。」

B　「いいですよ、ごゆっくり。」

10.5.2 学生　「先生、しつもんが　あります。」

先生　「なんですか。」

学生　「あのう、きょう　べんきょうした　ところが　よく　わかりません。ぼくが
持っている　さんこう書は　せつめいが　くわしくないんです。てきとうな
本は　ないでしょうか。」

先生　「ああ、さんこう書ですか。じゃあ、今は　ちょっと　いそがしいから、あとで
聞きに　来てください。」

学生　「はい。二時ごろ　うかがっても　いいでしょうか。」

先生　「ええ、二時半までに　来てください。三時から　クラスが　ありますから。」

学生　「はい、わかりました。」

10.5.3 客　「すみません。しんかん線の　きっぷは　どこで　うっていますか。」

人　「三番で　うっていますよ。」

客　「どうも。」

....

客　「あのう、京都まで　おとな　一まい、子ども　一まい　ください。」

駅員　「いつの　きっぷですか。」

客　「すぐ　のりたいんですけど、ありますか。」

駅員　「ちょっと　まってください。しらべてみますから。十時の　新大阪行の　グリーンが　まだ　ありますけど、グリーンでも　いいですか。」

客　「ええ、いいです。おとな　一まい、子ども　一まい　おねがいします。」

10.5.4 A　「すみません。ここに　すわっても　いいですか。」

B　「どうぞ。」

A　「ちょっと　うかがいますが、成田まで　一時間で　行くことが　できますか。」

B　「さあ、成田まで　行ったことが　ありませんから。でも、たぶん　一時間ぐらいで　つきますよ。」

A　「そうですか。あのう、まどを　しめても　かまいませんか。ちょっと　さむいんです。」

B　「どうぞ、どうぞ。」

A　「すみません。これ、駅で　買った　おかしですが、一つ　どうぞ。」

B　「あ、どうも。いただきます。」

10.5.5　わたしが　行く　図書館は　公園の　そばに　あります。わたしは　その　図書館で　本を　かりたことが　七、八ど　あります。本は　十日　かりることが　できますが、辞書や　ざっしは　うちへ　持って行っては　いけません。

きょう　わたしは　けいざいの　本と　文学の　本を　かりに　行きました。ここの　図書館員は　いつも　しんせつ*です。きょうも　ちょうど　いい　本が　見つかりました。わたしは　こんばん　レポートを　書くつもりです。

*''kind; helpful''

LESSON 11
日本 の 国

11.1 PRESENTATION

日本は 四つの 島と 沖縄（琉球列島）から なる[1] 国です。四つの なかで 一番[2] 大きいの[3]は 本州、 二番目[4]は 北海道、 三番目は 九州、一番 小さいのは 四国です。 日本は 小さいけれども、ほそながい 国ですから、北[5]と 南では ずいぶん 気候が ちがいます。

11.2 DIALOG

青木 「テーラーさん、お国は どちらですか。」

テーラー 「南カリフォルニアです。」

青木 「カリフォルニアは アメリカで 一番 ゆたかな 州でしょう？」

テーラー 「ええ、 まあ[6] そうですね。 それに、 気候が いいから、いろいろな くだ物が 一年じゅう[7] あります。 ほか[8]の 州より[9] スポーツも さかんですね。 青木 さんは 関西[10]でしたね。」

青木 「ええ、 京都です。」

テーラー 「京都と 東京と、どっち[9]が 好きですか。」

青木 「京都と 東京を くらべる[11]のは むずかしいけれど、気候は 東京の ほうが[9] いいですね。 京都は なつ とても むしあついんです。」

テーラー 「でも、けしきは 京都の ほうが きれいでしょう？」

青木 「もちろん、ずっと[12] きれいですよ。 それに、 東京ほど[13] 人口が 多くありません から、おちついています。 やっぱり[14] 歴史の 古い 町は いいですね。」

国 四つ 一番 二番目 北 南 京都 人口
多くありません 古い

11.3 PATTERN SENTENCES

11.3.1

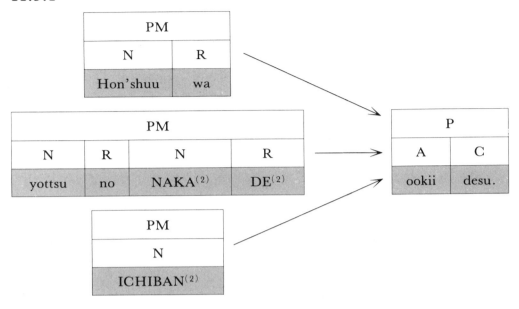

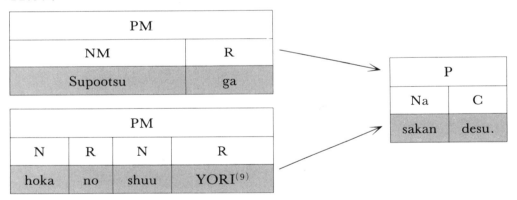

11.3.2

11.3.3

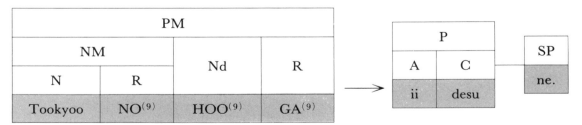

11.3.4

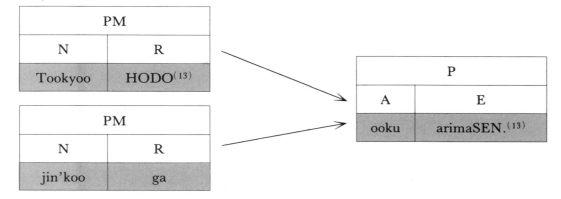

11.4 NOTES

11.4.1 . . . *kara naru kuni* means "country composed of." The Verb *naru* means "become," "turn into," "result in," and so on, when preceded by the Relational *ni*. (See Lesson 12.) When this Verb is preceded by the Relational *kara*, however, it means "from certain sources" or "consisting of."

Nihon wa takusan no shima kara naru kuni desu.	"Japan is a country consisting of many islands."
Amerika wa gojuu no shuu kara narimasu.	"The United States of America is composed of fifty states."

11.4.2 Unlike in English, an Adjective in Japanese does not have the superlative degree and the comparative degree as do "best," "better," and the like. Instead, the superlative degree of an Adjective or of an adjectival Noun is shown by using the Noun *ichiban*, which literally means "number one." To indicate items or persons, one of which the superlative description is true, phrases (*gakusei*) *no naka de, sono naka de, kono naka de*, and the like may be used. The *naka* here means "within a scope." The Relational *de* is also used to show a scope or an area to which the superlative description is applied.

$$\left.\begin{array}{l}\sim \textit{no naka}\\ \textit{sono naka}\\ \text{-----------}\\ \textbf{scope or area}\end{array}\right\} + \textit{de} + \textit{ichiban} + \left\{\begin{array}{l}\textbf{Adjective}\\ \textbf{adjectival Noun}\end{array}\right\} + \textit{desu}$$

The subject of the sentence or what is superlative may precede (~*no*) *naka de* or may occur between ~(*no*) *naka de* and *ichiban*, followed by the emphatic subject Relational *ga* or the topic Relational *wa*, depending upon the emphasis. The superlative expressions of adjectival Nouns and Adjectives may be used as Noun Modifiers.

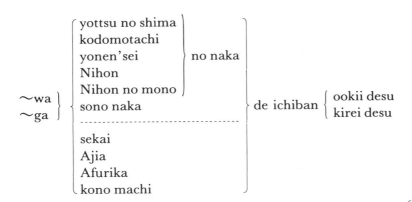

$\left.\begin{array}{c}\sim wa \\ \sim ga\end{array}\right\}$ $\left\{\begin{array}{l}\left.\begin{array}{l}\text{yottsu no shima} \\ \text{kodomotachi} \\ \text{yonen'sei} \\ \text{Nihon} \\ \text{Nihon no mono} \\ \text{sono naka}\end{array}\right\} \text{no naka} \\ \text{sekai} \\ \text{Ajia} \\ \text{Afurika} \\ \text{kono machi}\end{array}\right\}$ de ichiban $\left\{\begin{array}{l}\text{ookii desu} \\ \text{kirei desu}\end{array}\right.$

"$\sim$ is the biggest $\left.\right\}$
"$\sim$ is the prettiest $\left.\right\}$ $\left\{\begin{array}{l}\text{of the four islands''} \\ \text{among the children''} \\ \text{of the seniors''} \\ \text{of the Japanese people''} \\ \text{of the Japanese things''} \\ \text{among them''} \\ \text{in the world''} \\ \text{in Asia''} \\ \text{in Africa''} \\ \text{in this town''}\end{array}\right.$

Norimono no naka de, hikooki ga ichiban hayai desu.	"Among transportation facilities, the airplane is the fastest."
Tookyoo wa sekai de ichiban hito ga ooi desu ka?	"Does Tōkyō have the greatest population in the world?"
Gakusei no naka de, watakushi wa ichiban sei ga hikui desu.	"I am the shortest of the students."
Ichiban ookii okashi o kudasai.	"Please give me the biggest piece of candy."

When several items are given for choice, a question is formulated as follows:

Noun 1 *to* **Noun 2** *to* . . . **Noun N** (*to*) *de* (*wa*),

   dore ga ichiban $\left\{\begin{array}{l}\textbf{Adjective} \\ \textbf{adjectival Noun}\end{array}\right\}$ *desu ka?*

The interrogative Noun *dore* may be replaced by other interrogative Nouns such as *nani, dare, doko, itsu,* or by *dono* plus Noun, depending upon the items being compared in the sentence. The answer to the above question is $\sim$ *ga ichiban* $\sim$ *desu.*

Suujii san to Pooru san to Jooji san to de wa, dare ga ichiban nihon'go ga joozu desu ka?	"Among Susie, Paul, and George, who is the most proficient in Japanese?"
Pooru san ga ichiban joozu desu.	"Paul is the most proficient."
Kyoo no shiken no naka de, dore ga ichiban muzukashikatta desu ka?	"Which was the most difficult among the exams today?"

Nihon no kisetsu no naka de, itsu
  ga ichiban suki desu ka?

"Of the Japanese seasons, which do you
  like the best?"

Ajia to Afurika to Kita Amerika de wa,
  doko ga ichiban hiroi desu ka?

"Of Asia, Africa, and North America,
  which is the largest?"

11.4.3 *Ichiban ookii no* means "the biggest one." The Noun that is modified by an Adjective, an adjectival Noun + *na,* or a Verb may be replaced by the dependent Noun *no* "one(s)," when the Noun is understood by both the speaker and the listener. The *no* may be followed by any Relational.

$$
\left.\begin{array}{l}\textbf{Adjective}\\\textbf{adjectival Noun}+\textit{na}\\\textbf{Verb}\end{array}\right\} +\textbf{Noun} \longrightarrow \left.\begin{array}{l}\textbf{Adjective}\\\textbf{adjectival Noun}+\textit{na}\\\textbf{Verb}\end{array}\right\} +\textit{no}
$$

ookii shima	"big islands"	⟶	ookii no	"the big ones"
yutaka na shuu	"the rich state"	⟶	yutaka na no	"the rich one"
soko ni aru isu	"the chair that is there"	⟶	soko ni aru no	"the one that is there"
kinoo katta hon	"the books I bought yesterday"	⟶	kinoo katta no	"the ones I bought yesterday"

Amerika no shuu no naka de
  ichiban ookii no wa Arasuka desu.

"Of the states in the U.S.A., the largest
  one is Alaska."

Ichiban atarashii no o kudasai.

"Please give me the newest one."

Haha ga kureta no wa kore desu.

"This is the one my mother gave me."

Suki na no o totte kudasai.

"Please take the one you like."

When an object is already under discussion and one wants to mention the kind of object, the object may be followed by the topic Relational *wa* and a Noun Modifier plus *no* may then follow *wa.*

$$
\textbf{Noun}+\textit{wa}+ \left\{\begin{array}{l}\textbf{Adjective}\\\textbf{adjectival Noun}+\textit{na}\\\textbf{Verb}\end{array}\right\} +\textit{no}+ \left\{\begin{array}{l}\textit{ga}\ldots\\\textit{o}\ldots\end{array}\right.
$$

    "as for a Noun, (the) ∼ one . . ."

Koohii wa atsui no ga hoshii n
  desu ga . . .

"As for coffee, I would like to have it hot."

Nekutai wa takai no o kaimashita.

"As for a tie, I bought an expensive one."

Kotae wa ichiban tekitoo na no o
  kaite kudasai.

"As for the answer, please write the most
  appropriate one."

11.4.4 *Niban'me* and *futatsume* both mean "the second." The dependent Noun -*me* is attached to a number to show a sequence.

hitotsume	"the first (object)"	yon'haime	"the fourth cup (of ∼)"
ninen'me	"the second year"	goban'me	"the fifth (object)"
san'nin'me	"the third person"		

Futatsume no mise wa tabakoya desu.	"The second store is a cigarette stand."
Koko kara yonin'me no gakusei wa Tanaka san desu.	"The fourth student from here is Mr. Tanaka."
Daigaku no ninen'me ni Nihon e kimashita.	"I came to Japan in my second year of college."
Goban'me no mon'dai wa totemo muzukashii desu.	"The fifth question is very difficult."

11.4.5 *Kita* is "north." Here are other words of direction:

higashi	東	"east"	minami	南	"south"
nishi	西	"west"	kita	北	"north"

Higashi Yooroppa	"East Europe"	Minami Amerika	"South America"
Nishi Nihon	"the western part of Japan"	Kita Afurika	"North Africa"

11.4.6 Vagueness

The expression *Maa, soo desu* is another typical example of the vagueness of Japanese expression. Its use shows that, while you are not in agreement with the other person, you do not wish to say so outright. Its English equivalents are "Well, more or less, it is so." The Japanese *maa*—similar to *saa* and *doomo*—is a convenient device to avoid offending others and is used more often than English equivalents in America.

11.4.7 *Ichinen'juu* means "all year long" and is the combination of *ichinen* "one year" and a dependent Noun *-juu* that means "throughout."

Kyonen wa ichinen'juu ason'de imashita.	"Last year I was not doing anything all year long."

11.4.8 The Noun *hoka* is translated "other," "another," "different," "else," and so forth. The meaning of *hoka* is "(one or ones) excluding the particular one(s) that has been mentioned or is understood."

Hoka e ikimashoo.	"Let's go somewhere else."
Hoka no tokoro de shokuji o shimashita.	"I had a meal somewhere else."
Hoka no mono o misete kudasai.	"Please show me other things."
Hoka no hito ni kikimashoo.	"I'll ask someone else."
Hoka ni shitsumon ga arimasu ka?	"Are there any other questions?"

11.4.9 *Yori* is a Relational meaning "(more) than." The comparative degree is expressed as follows when a sentence is a statement.

$$\textbf{Noun 1} + wa + \textbf{Noun 2} + yori + \left\{ \begin{array}{l} \textbf{Adjective} \\ \textbf{adjectival Noun} \end{array} \right\} + desu$$

"N1 is more . . . than N2"

Nihon wa Kariforunia yori chiisai desu.	"Japan is smaller than California."
Koko no ten'in wa ano mise no ten'in yori kotoba ga teinei desu.	"The salesclerk here speaks more politely than the salesclerk in that store."

A question of comparative degree is formulated as follows:

$$\textbf{Noun 1} + to + \textbf{Noun 2} + to + \left\{ \begin{array}{l} (de), \\ (de\ wa), \end{array} \right.$$

$$\left\{ \begin{array}{l} dochira\,(no\ hoo) \\ dotchi\,(no\ hoo) \end{array} \right\} + ga + \left\{ \begin{array}{l} \textbf{Adjective} \\ \textbf{adjectival Noun} \end{array} \right\} desu\ ka?$$

"which is more . . . , N1 or N2?"

When the two items to be compared are understood, Noun 1 *to* Noun 2 *to* (*de wa*) may be omitted. Note that the interrogative Noun *dochira* or an informal alternative *dotchi* meaning "which one of the two?" should be used in comparison of two items. The ∼ *no hoo* may be attached to *dotchi* or *dochira*. *Hoo* is a dependent Noun meaning "alternative," "side," and so forth. The interrogative Noun *dore* cannot be used in the above pattern as it means "which one of the three or more items?" *Dore* is used in the pattern of superlative degree.

Kono san'koosho to sono san'koosho to, dotchi ga yasui desu ka?	"Which is cheaper, this reference book or that reference book?"
Sukiyaki to ten'pura to de wa, dochira no hoo ga suki desu ka?	"Which do you like better, *sukiyaki* or *tempura?*"

A reply to the above question is made in one of the following ways:

∼ *no hoo ga . . . desu*

∼ *no hoo ga* ∼ *yori . . . desu* or ∼ *yori* ∼ *(no hoo) ga . . . desu*

∼ *ga . . . desu*

San Furan'shisuko to Hawai to de wa, dotchi ga atatakai desu ka?	"Which is warmer, San Francisco or Hawaii?"
Hawai no hoo ga atatakai desu.	"Hawaii is warmer."
Anata no uchi to Yoshiko san no uchi to de wa, dotchi ga tooi desu ka?	"Which is farther, your house or Yoshiko's?"
Watakushi no hoo ga tooi desu.	"Mine is farther (than Yoshiko's)."
Kinoo mita eiga to kyoo no to de wa, dotchi ga omoshirokatta desu ka?	"Which movie was more interesting, the one you saw yesterday or the one you saw today?"
Kyoo no hoo ga omoshirokatta desu.	"Today's was more interesting (than yesterday's)."

11.4.10 *Kantō* and *Kansai*

In Japan, the main island of Honshū is divided into many districts. The Tōkyō area is called the Kantō and the Kyōto, Ōsaka, and Nara vicinity is called the Kansai. These two terms have their historical origin in feudal Japan. *Kan* itself refers to the barricades created by feudal lords which functioned as checkpoints against any undesirable movements at strategic places like Hakone Mountain. The Kantō area is located to the east of the Hakone barricade, and the Kansai to the west.

Even today, the Kantō and Kansai demonstrate great differences in language, custom, behavior, personality, and culture. For example, the Japanese words for rain and for candy have the same two syllables, *a* and *me*. In Tōkyō rain is pronounced *a͞me*, with the accent dropping after *a*, and candy is pronounced *a͞me* with the accent rising after the *a*. In Kyōto, however, the pronunciations are just the opposite: rain $=$ *a͞me*, and candy $=$ *a͞me*.

11.4.11

Kuraberu is a transitive Verb meaning "compare." Some Verbs or Predicates whose function is equally related to two items or two persons occur in the following patterns:

Noun 1 *to* Noun 2
o kurabemasu	"compare N1 and (with) N2"
ga kekkon shimasu	"N1 and N2 will get married"
wa chigaimasu	"N1 and N2 are different"
wa onaji desu	"N1 and N2 are the same"

or

Noun 1 $\begin{Bmatrix} o \\ --- \\ ga \\ wa \end{Bmatrix}$ Noun 2 *to*
kurabemasu	"compare N1 with N2"
kekkon shimasu	"N1 will marry N2"
chigaimasu	"N1 is different from N2"
onaji desu	"N1 is the same as N2"

Boku no katta san'koosho to anata
no o kurabete mimashita.

Boku no katta san'koosho o anata
no to kurabete mimashita.

"I compared a reference book I bought with yours."

To answer the question N1 *to* N2 *to dotchi ga* $\begin{Bmatrix} \text{Na} \\ \text{A} \end{Bmatrix}$ *desu ka?,* (N1 *to* N2 *o*) *kuraberu no wa muzukashii desu* or, *onaji desu* or N1 (or N2) *no hoo ga* $\begin{Bmatrix} \text{Na} \\ \text{A} \end{Bmatrix}$ *desu* may be said.

11.4.12

An Adverb *zutto* "by far" may occur in the comparison to mean "far (better)," "much (more)," and so on.

Nyuu Yooku wa Kariforunia yori
zutto samui desu.

"New York is much colder than California."

Pooru san no hoo ga zutto atama
ga ii desu yo.

"Paul is much smarter."

Kono heya yori watashi no heya
no hoo ga zutto semai desu.

"My room is much smaller than this room."

11.4.13 *Tookyoo hodo jin'koo ga ooku arimasen* means a negative comparison "(Kyōto) does not have as large a population as Tōkyō." The *hodo* is a Relational meaning "as much as," and when it is used with a negative Predicate it carries the meaning of negative comparison "is not as . . . as," or "someone does not do so . . . as someone else does," and so on.

Noun 1 + *wa* + Noun 2 + *hodo* + negative Predicate

Hawai		Kariforunia		hiroku		
nihon'jin		amerikajin		sei ga takaku		
kamera	wa	rajio	hodo	hoshiku		arimasen nai desu
sukiyaki		ten'pura		suki de wa		
boku		kimi		gen'ki de wa		

Kyuushuu wa Okinawa hodo atsuku
arimasen.
"Kyūshū is not as hot as Okinawa."

Basu wa takushii hodo hayaku
arimasen.
"A bus is not as fast as a taxi."

Kono tatemono wa ano depaato
hodo furuku arimasen.
"This building is not as old as that department store."

Koko wa asoko hodo kirei ja
arimasen.
"This place is not as clean as that place."

Watashi wa Pooru san hodo
nihon'go ga joozu de wa
arimasen yo.
"I am not as good as Paul is at Japanese."

11.4.14 *Yappari* means "as expected," "as everyone agrees," "as understood (by all)," or "as I first thought." Surprisingly, it is used quite often by the Japanese, because in Japan, traditionally people would try to avoid disagreeing with others openly. *Yappari* is the colloquial equivalent of *yahari* and occurs more frequently in spoken language.

11.5   VOCABULARY

Presentation

島	shima	......	N	island
沖縄	Okinawa	......	N	name of a prefecture
琉球列島	Ryuukyuu rettoo	......	N	Ryūkyū Islands
から	kara	......	R	(consist; is composed) of (see 11.4.1)
なる	naru	......	V	consist; is composed (of) (see 11.4.1)
なか	naka	......	N	among (them) (see 11.4.2)
で	de	......	R	(see 11.4.2)
一番	ichiban	......	N	the most (see 11.4.2)

の	no	......	Nd	one(s) (see 11.4.3)
本州	Hon'shuu	......	N	the main island of Japan
二番目	niban'me	......	N	the second (see 11.4.4)
九州	Kyuushuu	......	N	Kyūshū Island
四国	Shikoku	......	N	Shikoku Island
けれども	keredomo	......	Rc	although (full-length equivalent of *kedo*)
ほそながい	hosonagai	......	A	is long and narrow
北	kita	......	N	north (see 11.4.5)
南	minami	......	N	south
気候	kikoo	......	N	climate

Dialog

青木	Aoki	......	N	family name
テーラー	Teeraa	......	N	Taylor
カリフォルニア	Kariforunia	......	N	California
ゆたか	yutaka	......	Na	rich; abundant
州	shuu	......	N	state
まあ	maa	......	SI	you might say; roughly; well, I think (showing some hesitation) (see 11.4.6)
一年じゅう	ichinen'juu	......	N	all year round; throughout the year (see 11.4.7)
ほか	hoka	......	N	other; another; different; else (see 11.4.8)
より	yori	......	R	(more) than (see 11.4.9)
さかん	sakan	......	Na	flourishing; prosperous; popular
関西	Kan'sai	......	N	a district including Ōsaka, Kyōto, Kōbe, etc. (see 11.4.10)
くらべる	kuraberu	......	V	compare (Dictionary form) (see 11.4.11)
けれど	keredo	......	Rc	although (shortened form of *keredomo*)
ほう	hoo	......	Nd	alternative (see 11.4.9)
けしき	keshiki	......	N	scenery
もちろん	mochiron	......	SI	of course; certainly
ずっと	zutto	......	Adv.	by far; much (more) (see 11.4.12)
ほど	hodo	......	R	as much as (see 11.4.13)
人口	jin'koo	......	N	population
おちついて	ochitsuite	......	V	TE form of *ochitsukimasu* ← *ochitsuku*—become calm

やっぱり	yappari	......	Adv.	as I thought; as I expected; as it is said (see 11.4.14)
歴史	rekishi	......	N	history
町	machi	......	N	town; city

Notes

物	mono	......	N	thing (tangible)
せかい	sekai	......	N	world
アジア	Ajia	......	N	Asia
アフリカ	Afurika	......	N	Africa
ひろい	hiroi	......	A	is large; is wide; is spacious
アラスカ	Arasuka	......	N	Alaska
目	-me	......	Nd	(see 11.4.4)
東	higashi	......	N	east
西	nishi	......	N	west
じゅう	-juu	......	Nd	throughout (see 11.4.7)
どちら	dochira	......	Ni	which (of the two)? (see 11.4.9)
関東	Kan'too	......	N	a district including Tōkyō, Yokohama, Chiba, etc. (see 11.4.10)
あたま	atama	......	N	head
せまい	semai	......	A	is small; is narrow; is limited (in space)
やはり	yahari	......	Adv.	formal equivalent of *yappari* (see 11.4.14)

Drills

りんご	rin'go	......	N	apple

11.6 KAN'JI

11.6.a 国 [7.6.5]　(1) *kuni*　(5) ぼくの国はドイツです

11.6.1 番　(1) BAN　(2) number; order　(3) classifier 釆 (田)

(4) ⌐ ⌐ ⌐ ⎞ ⎞ ⎞ ⎞ ⎞ ⎞ ⎞ 番

(5) 一番、八番、三番線

11.6.2 目　(1) *me*　(2) eye; ordinal suffix　(3) forms the classifier 目

(4) │ ⎢ ⎢ ⎢ 目　(5) 目が大きい、三番目、五つ目

(6) shape of an eye

11.6.3 北　(1) *kita*　(2) north　(3) classifier 北 (匕)　(4) ⌐ ⎢ ⎢ ⎢ 北

(5) 北アメリカ、北九州、北アジア、北日本　(6) two men seated back to back

11.6.4 南　(1) *minami*　(2) south　(3) classifier 十
(4) 一 十 十 冇 芇 苬 商 商 南　(5) 南アメリカ、南日本、東京の南
(6) get warm in a tent, hence south

11.6.5 都　(1) TO　(2) capital city　(3) classifier 阝・邑 [village]
(4) 一 土 耂 者 者 都　(5) 京都、東京都　(6) 阝 is placed at the right
side of *kan'ji*

11.6.6 多　(1) *oo(i)*　(2) abundant; many　(3) classifier 夕
(4) ノ ク 夕 夛 多 多　(5) 本が多いです、人口が多い

11.6.7 古　(1) *furu(i)*　(2) old; antique; ancient　(3) classifier 十（口）
(4) 一 十 十 古 古　(5) 古い 町、古しんぶん
(6) ten generations of people. See 1.6.10 and 13.6.1

11.6.8 新　(1) *atara(shii)*　(2) new　(3) classifier 立（斤）
(4) ` 亠 亠 产 立 立 辛 辛 亲 亲 新 新 新　(5) 新しい国
(6) 斤 means an ax; 亲 is the phonetic sign of SHIN; 薪、親 are homonyms

11.6.b 東^7.6.1　(1) *higashi*　(5) 東ヨーロッパ、東ドイツ、東日本

11.6.9 西　(1) *nishi*　(2) west　(3) forms the classifier 西
(4) 一 亅 襾 襾 西 西　(5) 西アジア、駅の西、西日本

11.6.10 少　(1) *suku(nai)*　(2) few; scarce　(3) classifier 小　(4) ノ 小 小 少
(5) 少ない　(6) four little points, hence few

11.7　DRILLS

11.7.1 Substitution Drill

A. 東京は 京都より 新しいです。

1. ひろい …… 東京は 京都より ひろいです。
2. アメリカ、日本 …… アメリカは 日本より ひろいです。
3. ゆたかな 国 …… アメリカは 日本より ゆたかな 国です。
4. 人口が 多い …… アメリカは 日本より 人口が 多いです。
5. ニューヨーク、サンフランシスコ …… ニューヨークは サンフランシスコより 人口が 多いです。
6. 大きい 町 …… ニューヨークは サンフランシスコより 大きい 町です。

    7.　とおい　　　　　　　　　　　……　ニューヨークは　サンフランシスコより
　　　　　　　　　　　　　　　　　　　　　　　　とおいです。

    8.　おもしろい　所　　　　　　　……　ニューヨークは　サンフランシスコより
　　　　　　　　　　　　　　　　　　　　　　　　おもしろい　所です。

B.　テーラーさんは　わたしより　せいが　たかいです。

    1.　日本語が　じょうず　　　　　……　テーラーさんは　わたしより　日本語が
　　　　　　　　　　　　　　　　　　　　　　　　じょうずです。

    2.　あの　人、ブラウンさん　　　……　あの　人は　ブラウンさんより　日本語が
　　　　　　　　　　　　　　　　　　　　　　　　じょうずです。

    3.　あたまが　いい　　　　　　　……　あの　人は　ブラウンさんより　あたまが
　　　　　　　　　　　　　　　　　　　　　　　　いいです。

    4.　げん気　　　　　　　　　　　……　あの　人は　ブラウンさんより　げん気です。

    5.　ことばが　ていねい　　　　　……　あの　人は　ブラウンさんより　ことばが
　　　　　　　　　　　　　　　　　　　　　　　　ていねいです。

    6.　青木さん、林さん　　　　　　……　青木さんは　林さんより　ことばが
　　　　　　　　　　　　　　　　　　　　　　　　ていねいです。

    7.　せいが　ひくい　　　　　　　……　青木さんは　林さんより　せいが　ひくい
　　　　　　　　　　　　　　　　　　　　　　　　です。

    8.　私、あなた　　　　　　　　　……　私は　あなたより　せいが　ひくいです。

C.　これは　それより　ずっと　たかいです。

    1.　あなたの　くつ、わたしの　くつ……　あなたの　くつは　わたしの　くつより
　　　　　　　　　　　　　　　　　　　　　　　　ずっと　たかいです。

    2.　きれい　　　　　　　　　　　……　あなたの　くつは　わたしの　くつより
　　　　　　　　　　　　　　　　　　　　　　　　ずっと　きれいです。

    3.　いい　　　　　　　　　　　　……　あなたの　くつは　わたしの　くつより
　　　　　　　　　　　　　　　　　　　　　　　　ずっと　いいです。

    4.　コーヒー、こうちゃ　　　　　……　コーヒーは　こうちゃより　ずっと
　　　　　　　　　　　　　　　　　　　　　　　　いいです。

    5.　好き　　　　　　　　　　　　……　コーヒーは　こうちゃより　ずっと　好き
　　　　　　　　　　　　　　　　　　　　　　　　です。

    6.　京都、東京　　　　　　　　　……　京都は　東京より　ずっと　好きです。

    7.　歴史が　古い　　　　　　　　……　京都は　東京より　ずっと　歴史が
　　　　　　　　　　　　　　　　　　　　　　　　古いです。

    8.　けしきが　いい　　　　　　　……　京都は　東京より　ずっと　けしきが　いいです。

11.7.2 Substitution Drill

ひこうきと　ふねと、どちらが　たかいですか。

1. でんしゃ、バス　　　……　でんしゃと　バスと、どちらが　たかいですか。
2. おそい　　　　　　　……　でんしゃと　バスと、どちらが　おそいですか。
3. 好き　　　　　　　　……　でんしゃと　バスと、どちらが　好きですか。
4. みち子さん、　　　　……　みち子さんと　よし子さんと、どちらが　好きですか。
   よし子さん
5. すきやき、てんぷら　……　すきやきと　てんぷらと、どちらが　好きですか。
6. 東日本、西日本　　　……　東日本と　西日本と、どちらが　好きですか。
7. いい　気候　　　　　……　東日本と　西日本と、どちらが　いい　気候ですか。
8. あたたかい　　　　　……　東日本と　西日本と、どちらが　あたたかいですか。

11.7.3 Expansion Drill

1. しずかです。　　　　……　しずかです。

   ずっと　　　　　　　……　ずっと　しずかです。

   ここの　ほうが　　　……　ここの　ほうが　ずっと　しずかです。

   あの　店より　　　　……　あの　店より　ここの　ほうが　ずっと　しずかです。
2. ゆたかです。　　　　……　ゆたかです。

   南日本の　ほうが　　……　南日本の　ほうが　ゆたかです。

   北日本より　　　　　……　北日本より　南日本の　ほうが　ゆたかです。

   くだ物は　　　　　　……　くだ物は　北日本より　南日本の　ほうが　ゆたかです。
3. さかんでした。　　　……　さかんでした。

   ずっと　　　　　　　……　ずっと　さかんでした。

   むかしの　ほうが　　……　むかしの　ほうが　ずっと　さかんでした。

   今より　　　　　　　……　今より　むかしの　ほうが　ずっと　さかんでした。

   かぶきは　　　　　　……　かぶきは　今より　むかしの　ほうが　ずっと　さかんでした。
4. 好きですか。　　　　……　好きですか。

   どちらが　　　　　　……　どちらが　好きですか。

   あついのと　　　　　……　あついのと　つめたいのでは、どちらが　好きですか。
   　つめたいのでは

   こうちゃは　　　　　……　こうちゃは　あついのと　つめたいのでは、どちらが
   　　　　　　　　　　　　　　　好きですか。

5. あたたかいです。　　……　あたたかいです。

　　ことしの　ほうが　　……　ことしの　ほうが　あたたかいです。

　　きょ年の　ふゆより……　きょ年の　ふゆより　ことしの　ほうが　あたたかいです。

　　東京は　　　　　　　……　東京は　きょ年の　ふゆより　ことしの　ほうが

　　　　　　　　　　　　　　　　あたたかいです。

11.7.4 Substitution Drill

のり物の　なかで、なにが　一番　好きですか。

1. くだ物　　　　　　　……　くだ物の　なかで、なにが　一番　好きですか。
2. たべ物　　　　　　　……　たべ物の　なかで、なにが　一番　好きですか。
3. のみ物　　　　　　　……　のみ物の　なかで、なにが　一番　好きですか。
4. ほしい　　　　　　　……　のみ物の　なかで、なにが　一番　ほしいですか。
5. 日本の　物　　　　　……　日本の　物の　なかで、なにが　一番　ほしいですか。
6. ゆうめい　　　　　　……　日本の　物の　なかで、なにが　一番　ゆうめいですか。
7. 日本の　スポーツ　　……　日本の　スポーツの　なかで、なにが　一番　ゆうめいですか。
8. さかん　　　　　　　……　日本の　スポーツの　なかで、なにが　一番　さかんですか。

11.7.5 Expansion Drill

1. むしあついです。　　……　むしあついです。

　　一番　　　　　　　　……　一番　むしあついです。

　　一年じゅうで　　　　……　一年じゅうで　一番　むしあついです。

　　七月が　　　　　　　……　七月が　一年じゅうで　一番　むしあついです。

2. くわしいです。　　　……　くわしいです。

　　一番　　　　　　　　……　一番　くわしいです。

　　さんこう書の　　　　……　さんこう書の　せつめいが　一番　くわしいです。

　　　せつめいが

　　よし子さんの　　　　……　よし子さんの　持っている　さんこう書の　せつめいが　一番

　　　持っている　　　　　　　くわしいです。

　　この　なかで　　　　……　この　なかで　よし子さんの　持っている　さんこう書の

　　　　　　　　　　　　　　　　せつめいが　一番　くわしいです。

3. さかんですか。　　　……　さかんですか。

　　一番　　　　　　　　……　一番　さかんですか。

　　どの　スポーツが　　……　どの　スポーツが　一番　さかんですか。

　　この　大学では　　　……　この　大学では　どの　スポーツが　一番　さかんですか。

228

4. どこですか。　　　　　……　どこですか。

州は　　　　　……　州は　どこですか。

大きい　　　　　……　大きい　州は　どこですか。

一番　　　　　……　一番　大きい　州は　どこですか。

アメリカで　　　　　……　アメリカで　一番　大きい　州は　どこですか。

5. 青木さんです。　　　　　……　青木さんです。

学生は　　　　　……　学生は　青木さんです。

フランス語の　　　　　……　フランス語の　じょうずな　学生は　青木さんです。
　じょうずな

一番　　　　　……　一番　フランス語の　じょうずな　学生は　青木さんです。

四年生の　なかで　……　四年生の　なかで、一番　フランス語の　じょうずな　学生は
　　　　　　青木さんです。

11.7.6　Transformation Drill

1. 一番　ほそながい　島は　本州です。⟶　一番　ほそながいのは　本州です。

2. 一番　ひまな　人は　だれですか。　⟶　一番　ひまなのは　だれですか。

3. くだ物が　ゆたかな　州は　　　　⟶　くだ物が　ゆたかなのは
　　カリフォルニアです。　　　　　　　　カリフォルニアです。

4. あそこに　いる　男の　子は　ぼくの　⟶　あそこに　いるのは　ぼくの
　　おとうとです。　　　　　　　　　　　おとうとです。

5. きみが　習った　外国語は　　　　⟶　きみが　習ったのは　日本語ですか。
　　日本語ですか。

6. 青木さんが　読みたい　本は　ここで　⟶　青木さんが　読みたいのは　ここで
　　うっています。　　　　　　　　　　うっています。

7. きのう　来なかった　学生は　　　⟶　きのう　来なかったのは
　　テーラーさんです。　　　　　　　　テーラーさんです。

8. 人口が　一番　少ない　所は　どこ　⟶　人口が　一番　少ないのは　どこですか。
　　ですか。

11.7.7　Substitution Drill

A.　この　なかで　むずかしいのは　どれですか。

　　1.　てきとうな　……　この　なかで　てきとうなのは　どれですか。

　　2.　ほしい　……　この　なかで　ほしいのは　どれですか。

　　3.　たかかった　……　この　なかで　たかかったのは　どれですか。

4. つまらなかった …… この　なかで　つまらなかったのは　どれですか。

5. 読みたかった …… この　なかで　読みたかったのは　どれですか。

6. 読んだ …… この　なかで　読んだのは　どれですか。

B. スポーツの　なかで　<u>好きなの</u>は　なんですか。

1. むずかしい …… スポーツの　なかで　むずかしいのは　なんですか。

2. さかんな …… スポーツの　なかで　さかんなのは　なんですか。

3. 新しい …… スポーツの　なかで　新しいのは　なんですか。

4. じょうずな …… スポーツの　なかで　じょうずなのは　なんですか。

5. 大好きな …… スポーツの　なかで　大好きなのは　なんですか。

6. きらいな …… スポーツの　なかで　きらいなのは　なんですか。

C. あなたの　ともだちの　なかで　<u>すわっているの</u>は　だれですか。

1. 来なかった …… あなたの　ともだちの　なかで　来なかったのは　だれですか。

2. 休んだ …… あなたの　ともだちの　なかで　休んだのは　だれですか。

3. アルバイト …… あなたの　ともだちの　なかで　アルバイトしているのは
   している 　　　　　　　だれですか。

4. ぎんこうに …… あなたの　ともだちの　なかで　ぎんこうに
   つとめている 　　　　　　　つとめているのは　だれですか。

5. 日本文学を …… あなたの　ともだちの　なかで　日本文学を　習ったのは
   習った 　　　　　　　だれですか。

6. たばこを …… あなたの　ともだちの　なかで　たばこを　すわないのは
   すわない 　　　　　　　だれですか。

D. この　なかで　一番　<u>ちかいの</u>は　どこですか。

1. すずしい …… この　なかで　一番　すずしいのは　どこですか。

2. ゆうめいな …… この　なかで　一番　ゆうめいなのは　どこですか。

3. おもしろかった …… この　なかで　一番　おもしろかったのは　どこですか。

4. 行きたい …… この　なかで　一番　行きたいのは　どこですか。

5. せまい …… この　なかで　一番　せまいのは　どこですか。

6. けんぶつしたい …… この　なかで　一番　けんぶつしたいのは　どこですか。

11.7.8 Response Drill

1. 一年生の　なかで、だれが　一番　せいが　たかいですか。
   青木一郎さん（あおきいちろう） …… 青木一郎さん（あおきいちろう）が　一番　せいが　たかいです。

2. はると　なつと　あきと　ふゆで、どの　気候（こう）が　一番　よかったですか。
   あき …… あきが　一番　よかったです。

3. スミスさんは　フランス語と　ドイツ語と　日本語とでは、どれが　一番

　　じょうずですか。

　　日本語　　　　　　　……　日本語が　一番　じょうずです。

4. 日本の　物(もの)で　なにが　一番　ほしいですか。

　　カメラ　　　　　　　……　カメラが　一番　ほしいです。

5. ともだちの　なかで　だれの　カメラが　一番　新しいですか。

　　スミスさんの　　　　……　スミスさんのが　一番　新しいです。

6. この　なかで　どれが　一番　やすいですか。

　　これ　　　　　　　　……　これが　一番　やすいです。

11.7.9 E-J Substitution Drill

あの　店(みせ)より　この　店(みせ)の　ほうが　きれいです。

1. more quiet　　　　……　あの　店(みせ)より　この　店(みせ)の　ほうが　しずかです。
2. farther　　　　　　……　あの　店(みせ)より　この　店(みせ)の　ほうが　とおいです。
3. noisier　　　　　　……　あの　店(みせ)より　この　店(みせ)の　ほうが　うるさいです。
4. cooler　　　　　　……　あの　店(みせ)より　この　店(みせ)の　ほうが　すずしいです。
5. more expensive　……　あの　店(みせ)より　この　店(みせ)の　ほうが　たかいです。
6. smaller　　　　　　……　あの　店(みせ)より　この　店(みせ)の　ほうが　小さいです。
7. more famous　　　……　あの　店(みせ)より　この　店(みせ)の　ほうが　ゆうめいです。
8. more spacious　　……　あの　店(みせ)より　この　店(みせ)の　ほうが　ひろいです。

11.7.10 Transformation Drill

1. 沖縄(おきなわ)は　九州(きゅうしゅう)より　むしあついです。──→　九州(きゅうしゅう)は　沖縄(おきなわ)ほど　むしあつくありません。

2. タクシーは　バスより　はやいです。──→　バスは　タクシーほど　はやくありません。

3. 北海道(ほっかいどう)は　ハワイより　大きいです。──→　ハワイは　北海道(ほっかいどう)ほど　大きくありません。

4. あなたは　青木(あおき)さんより　せいが　──→　青木(あおき)さんは　あなたほど　せいが　たかく

　　たかいです。　　　　　　　　　　　　　　ありません。

5. カリフォルニアは　この　州(しゅう)より　──→　この　州(しゅう)は　カリフォルニアほど　くだ物(もの)が

　　くだ物(もの)が　多いです。　　　　　　　　多くありません。

6. ポールさんは　ぼくより　日本語が　──→　ぼくは　ポールさんほど　日本語が

　　じょうずです。　　　　　　　　　　　　じょうずじゃありません。

7. てんぷらは　すきやきより　好きです。──→　すきやきは　てんぷらほど　好きじゃ

　　　　　　　　　　　　　　　　　　　　　ありません。

8. じゅうどうは　から手(て)より　さかんです。──→　から手(て)は　じゅうどうほど　さかんじゃ

　　　　　　　　　　　　　　　　　　　　　　ありません。

11.7.11 E-J Response Drill

1. 京都と　東京では、どちらが　歴史が　古いですか。

   Kyōto　　　　　　……　（東京より）京都の　ほうが　歴史が　古いです。

2. この　本と　その　本と、どっちが　てきとうですか。

   this book　　　　……　（その　本より）この　本の　ほうが　てきとうです。

3. のり物は　ひこうきと　ふねと、どっちの　ほうが　好きですか。

   airplane　　　　　……　（ふねより）ひこうきの　ほうが　好きです。

4. タイプライターと　ラジオと、どっちが　ほしいですか。

   radio　　　　　　……　（タイプライターより）ラジオの　ほうが　ほしいです。

5. ニューヨークと　サンフランシスコとでは、どちらの　ほうが　古いですか。

   New York　　　　……　（サンフランシスコより）ニューヨークの　ほうが　古いです。

6. きみと　ぼくとでは、どっちの　せいが　たかいですか。

   you　　　　　　　……　（ぼくより）きみの　ほうが　（せいが）たかいです。

7. 日本では　ゴルフと　テニスと、どちらが　さかんですか。

   golf　　　　　　　……　（テニスより）ゴルフの　ほうが　さかんです。

8. 四国と　九州では、どっちが　ひろいですか。

   Kyūshū　　　　　……　（四国より）九州の　ほうが　ひろいです。

11.7.12 E-J Response Drill

1. 習った　外国語の　なかで、どれが　一番　やさしかったですか。

   French　　　　　　……　フランス語が　一番　やさしかったです。

2. 日本の　四つの　島の　なかで、どの　島が　一番　ひろいですか。

   Honshū　　　　　……　本州が　一番　ひろいです。

3. はると　なつと　あきでは、どの　きせつが　一番　好きですか。

   autumn　　　　　……　あきが　一番　好きです。

4. あなたが　買った　本の　なかで、どれが　一番　新しいですか。

   this one　　　　　……　これが　一番　新しいです。

5. この　なかで、どの　さんこう書の　せつめいが　一番　くわしいですか。

   this big one　　　　……　この　大きいのが　一番　くわしいです。

6. バスと　タクシーと　でんしゃとでは、どれが　一番　おそいですか。

   bus　　　　　　　……　バスが　一番　おそいです。

7. 歴史と　文学と　けいざいでは、どれが　一番　おもしろいですか。

   economics　　　　……　けいざいが　一番　おもしろいです。

8. せかいで　どこの　人口が　一番　多いですか。

   China　　　　　　……　中国の　人口が　一番　多いです。

232

11.8 EXERCISES

11.8.1 Answer the following in Japanese:

1. きょ年 見た えいがの なかで、 なにが 一番 おもしろかったですか。

2. せかいで どこへ 一番 行ってみたいですか。

3. この 教室の なかで、 一番 せいが たかい 人は だれですか。

4. イギリスと ドイツでは、 どっちが ひろいですか。

5. スポーツの なかで、 なにが 好きですか。

6. あなたが 今 一番 ほしい 物は なんですか。

7. 花の なかで、 なにが 一番 いいですか。

8. ひらがなと かたかなでは、 どっちが やさしいですか。

11.8.2 Insert an appropriate Relational in each blank:

1. よし子さんは ほか（　　）女の人（　　）せい（　　）たかいです。

2. ドイツは フランス（　　）大きくないでしょう？

3. 南（　　）北（　　）、 南（　　）ほう（　　）好きです。

4. 日本は 小さい（　　）、 人口（　　）多い 国です。

5. アメリカは 五十（　　）州（　　）なる 大きい 国です。

6. 日本（　　）一番 たかい 山を 知っていますね。

11.8.3 Make an appropriate question that fits each of the following answers:

1. いいえ、 ハワイほど けしきが よくありません。

2. これが 一番 みじかいです。

3. 青木さんが 一番 たかいです。

4. いいえ、 東京は 北海道より ずっと むしあついです。

5. こっちの ほうが 古いでしょう。

6. いいえ、 わたしの こたえは あなたの こたえほど よくありません。

11.8.4 Choose any two or three countries, states, districts, or cities and compare as to the following features:

1. climate
2. population
3. scenery
4. history
5. location

11.8.5 Write the underlined *hiragana* in *kan'ji*:

1. <u>きた</u>アメリカと <u>みなみ</u>アメリカとでは どちらの ほうが <u>おおきい</u>ですか。

2. ときどき あの 店へ <u>かい</u>物に <u>い</u>きますけど、 いつも 客が <u>すくない</u> です。

3. <u>にし</u>にほんと <u>ひがし</u>にほんを くらべてください。

4. ぼくは いろいろな スポーツを しますが、 スキーを するのが <u>いちばん</u> すきです。 <u>にばんめ</u>が スケートです。 そして、 <u>さんばんめ</u>が テニス です。

5. <u>きょうと</u>は <u>ふるい</u> 町ですか、 <u>あたらしい</u> 町ですか。

6. ここは <u>いちねんじゅう</u> あめが <u>おおい</u>です。

7. <u>お</u>くには どちらですか。

11.8.6 Write the following in *katakana*:

1. Kariforunia   3. Afurika   5. Teeraa

2. Ajia   4. Arasuka   6. supootsu

11.8.7 Explain the origin of the following city names: Tōkyō and Kyōto.

11.9   SITUATIONAL AND APPLICATION CONVERSATION

11.9.1 Home town

A Japanese man asks an American where he is from.

The American says he is from Hawaii.

The Japanese man says he knows little about Hawaii. But he understands that Hawaii is the warmest state in the States with lots of fruit throughout the year.

The American asks where the Japanese man's home is.

The Japanese answers he is from Okinawa, but presently living in Ōsaka. He prefers Okinawa because Okinawa is a much quieter place than Ōsaka, although it is much hotter during the summer months.

11.9.2 Compare your home town with your friend's in terms of size, climate, scenery, and so on.

11.9.3 Make comparisons concerning Japan and your country.

Example: Amerika wa Nihon yori zutto hiroi desu.

11.9.4 Compare two or three objects in the classroom. Make questions and then answer these questions.

11.9.5 A: Sekai de ichiban hito ga ooi machi wa Tookyoo deshoo?

B: Maa, soo deshoo ne.

A: Jaa, Nyuu Yooku wa doo desu ka?

B: Saa.

11.9.6 Mr. Fujita: Kan'too to Kan'sai to dotchi ga ookii desu ka?

Mr. Kimura: Saa, wakarimasen.

11.9.7 Mr. Hayata: Den'sha no naka de wa shin'kan'sen ga yappari ichiban hayai n deshoo?

Mr. Kubota: Soo desu yo.

Mr. Hayata: Asa shichiji ni Tookyoo kara deru shin'kan'sen wa nan'ji ni Okayama ni tsukimasu ka?

Mr. Kubota: Saa. . . .

Mr. Hayata: Tookyoo kara Oosaka made wa san'jikan gurai deshoo?

Mr. Kubota: Soo desu kedo. . . . Demo, Oosaka kara Okayama made ga chotto. . . .

Mr. Hayata: Wakarimasen ka?

Mr. Kubota: Ee.

LESSON 12
料理[1]
りょうり り

12.1   PRESENTATION

日本料理は、あじも いいですが、 いろや かたちの ひじょうに 美しい 料理です。
年取った 人は 日本料理が 好きですが、 わかい 人は だいたい 日本料理を 食べるより[2]
西洋料理や 中国料理を 食べる ほう[2]が 好きです。

12.2   DIALOG

大川 「あ、 もう 六時に なりました[3]ね。 おそくなります[4]から、 そろそろ しつれい
　　　 します[5]。」

中山 「もう そんな 時間ですか[6]。 いっしょに 食事しませんか。」

大川 「そうですね。 どこへ 食事に 行きましょうか。」

中山 「ごちそうは できないけど[7]、 ぼくが 作りますよ。」

大川 「でも、 作るのは たいへんでしょう[8]?」

中山 「いえ、 すぐ できます[9]よ。 待っていてください。 大川さんが おもうほど[10]
　　　 たいへんじゃありませんよ。」

大川 「中山さんは まい日 自分で 料理を?」

中山 「ええ、 この へんの 食べ物屋は まずいから、 自分で 料理した ほう[11]が
　　　 ずっと おいしいんです。」

大川 「そうですか。 じゃあ、 ぼくも 手つだいます[8]。中山さんは 何を 作るの[12]が
　　　 一番[12] とくいですか[13]。」

中山 「カレーライスや とんかつですね。 にくと やさいが ありますから、 きょうは
　　　 カレーを 作りましょうか。」

大川 「いいですね。 ぼくは カレー が 大好きです。」

中山 「じゃあ、 カレーに しましょう[14]。」

美しい	年取った	食べる	中国	大川	食事
作ります	待っていてください	自分で			
食べ物屋	何				

12.3 PATTERN SENTENCES

12.3.1

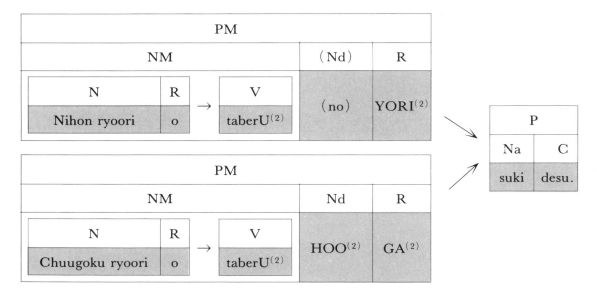

12.3.2

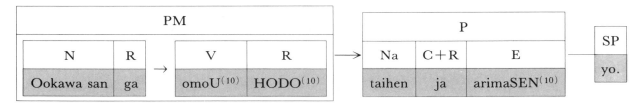

12.3.3

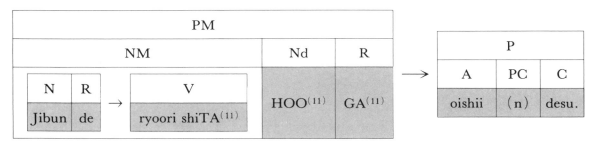

12.3.4

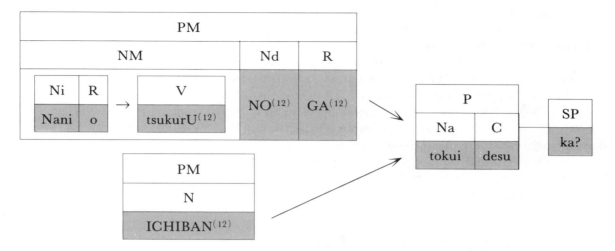

12.3.5

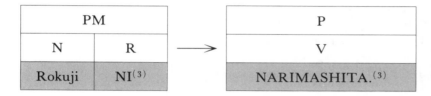

12.4 NOTES

12.4.1 Japanese Food

Japanese food is known not only for its taste, but also for its overall appearance. In preparing food, the Japanese endeavor to retain the original shape, color, and flavor of the ingredients. The various ingredients are combined from the point of view of the overall harmonization of color, shape, and taste. In addition, the utensils, the dishes, platters, bowls, and so on are considered an integral part of the total appearance of the food. Japanese food is unique in this respect and in the importance placed on the selection of serving ware.

In Japan, the most sincere and wholehearted welcome is shown by providing the other person with refreshments. The American way of expressing welcome is far simpler by comparison. Consequently, the American treatment of others may be regarded as insufficient by the Japanese, while, to Americans, the Japanese may seem too extravagant and overwhelming in their hospitality. The Japanese quite frequently invite friends to eat out, although in present-day Japan cocktail parties have become popular.

Eclecticism and Cultural Pluralism

Just as in clothing, various types of cooking—Western, Chinese, and Japanese—exist side by side in ordinary Japanese life. For example, the ordinary Japanese may eat Western-style bacon and eggs and toast for breakfast, Chinese noodles for lunch, and Japanese food for dinner. Such practices demonstrate an important feature of Japanese culture, namely, cultural pluralism. While the Japanese retain their own focus in all areas, still varieties of things coexist and have been integrated and incorporated into everyday life. This cultural pluralism also extends to the political, economic, and other social spheres. This indicates the eclecticism which is another important feature of the Japanese approach to culture.

The cultural pluralism of Japan is strongly evidenced in the sheer variety of foods which are popular there. For instance, a large number of restaurants specializing in the food of almost any country in the world may be found in Japanese cities, and such restaurants are frequented with far more regularity by the general public than in most other countries. This in no way indicates, however, that the Japanese prefer foreign foods to their own native cuisine. Rather, foreign dishes have been accepted for what they are, and are allowed a reasonable place in the culture. As such they are simply enjoyed by the Japanese people without prejudice as to place of origin. Especially popular in recent times are items such as pizza, hamburgers, and fried chicken.

Some foreign dishes have grown so popular in Japan that they have almost become Japanese, and as such exemplify the Japanese talent for incorporating foreign elements and thereby creating a new cultural synthesis. *Kareeraisu* (curry and rice), *ton'katsu* (pork cutlet), *korokke* (croquette), and *han'baagu* (hamburger steak) are some of the Japanized foods of foreign origin which are very popular.

12.4.2 *Nihon ryoori o taberu yori seiyoo ryoori ya Chuugoku ryoori o taberu hoo ga suki desu* means "They like eating Western and Chinese dishes better than eating Japanese dishes." The comparative patterns introduced in Note 11.4.9 can be applied to a comparison of two actions instead of two items. The Verbs stating actions to be compared are in the Dictionary form of those Verbs, and, depending upon the Relational following them, the dependent Noun *no* that has been introduced in Lesson 7 may occur after the Dictionary form. Thus:

$$\begin{matrix} \textbf{Verb 1} \\ \textbf{(Dictionary form)} \end{matrix} (no) + yori + \begin{matrix} \textbf{Verb 2} \\ \textbf{(Dictionary form)} \end{matrix} + hoo\ ga + \left\{ \begin{matrix} \textbf{Adjective} \\ \textbf{adjectival Noun} \end{matrix} \right\} desu$$

$$\begin{matrix} \textbf{Verb 2} \\ \textbf{(Dictionary form)} \end{matrix} + no\ wa + \begin{matrix} \textbf{Verb 1} \\ \textbf{(Dictionary form)} \end{matrix} + (no)\ yori + \left\{ \begin{matrix} \textbf{Adjective} \\ \textbf{adjectival Noun} \end{matrix} \right\} desu$$

sakana o taberu
jibun de tsukuru } yori { niku o taberu
tetsudau } hoo ga ii desu
tenisu o suru oyogu

niku o taberu
tetsudau } no wa { sakana o taberu
jibun de tsukuru } (no) yori ii desu
oyogu tenisu o suru

"it is better to { eat meat / help / swim } than to { eat fish" / make by oneself" / play tennis" }

Koyama san wa doitsugo o hanasu yori furan'sugo o hanasu hoo ga joozu desu.	"Mr. Koyama can speak French better than German."
Roomaji de kaku yori hiragana de kaku hoo ga zutto muzukashii desu.	"Writing in *hiragana* is far more difficult (to me) than writing in *rōmaji*."
Biiru o nomu yori osake o nomu hoo ga ii desu.	"I prefer drinking *sake* to drinking beer."

A comparative question is formulated as follows:

Verb 1
(Dictionary form) + *no to* + **Verb 2**
(Dictionary form) + *no to* { (*de*),
{ (*de wa*),

dochira (*no hoo*)
dotchi (*no hoo*) } *ga* + { **Adjective**
adjectival Noun } *desu ka?*

A reply to the above question is made in one of the following ways:

Verb 1 (Dictionary form) + *hoo ga* . . . *desu*

Verb 1 (Dictionary form) + *hoo ga* + **Verb 2 (Dictionary form)** + *yori* . . . *desu*
   or **Verb 2 (Dictionary form)** + *yori* + **Verb 1 (Dictionary form)** + *hoo ga* . . . *desu*

Verb 1 (Dictionary form) + *no ga* . . . *desu*

Kabuki o miru no to Nihon no eiga o miru no to de wa, dotchi ga ii desu ka?	"Which do you like better, to see *kabuki* or a Japanese movie?"
Kabuki o miru hoo ga (Nihon no eiga o miru yori) ii desu.	"I prefer seeing *kabuki* (to seeing a Japanese movie)."
Kyooto o ken'butsu suru no to Nikkoo o ken'butsu suru no to, dochira ga omoshiroi desu ka?	"Which is more interesting, to see Kyōto or to see Nikkō?"
Mochiron Kyooto o ken'butsu suru hoo ga omoshiroi desu.	"It is certainly more interesting to see Kyōto."
Kareeraisu o tsukuru no to ton'katsu o tsukuru no to, dotchi ga hayai desu ka?	"Which is faster, to make curry and rice or pork cutlet?"
Ton'katsu o tsukuru no ga hayai desu.	"It is faster to make pork cutlet."

12.4.3 *Rokuji ni narimashita* means "It got to be six o'clock." *Narimasu* is an intransitive Verb meaning "become," "get to be," "come to be," and so on. In the structure "Noun 1 becomes Noun 2," Noun 2 is always followed by the goal Relational *ni*. This is also true of an adjectival Noun.

Noun 1 + { *wa*
{ *ga* } + { **Noun 2**
{ **adjectival Noun** } + *ni* + *narimasu*

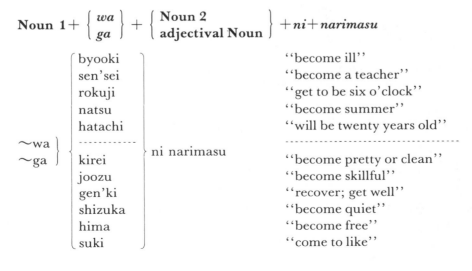

~wa ~ga	byooki	"become ill"
	sen'sei	"become a teacher"
	rokuji	"get to be six o'clock"
	natsu	"become summer"
	hatachi	"will be twenty years old"
	kirei	"become pretty or clean"
	joozu	"become skillful"
	gen'ki	"recover; get well"
	shizuka	"become quiet"
	hima	"become free"
	suki	"come to like"

(ni narimasu)

Rainen boku wa hatachi ni narimasu may be translated as "I will be twenty years old next year." When a change is referred to, the future form of English "will be" may be expressed by using *narimasu*. Note that *narimasu* is not always equivalent to English "become."

Watakushi wa rainen nihon'go no sen'sei ni narimasu.	"I will become a Japanese language teacher next year."
Ashita wa hima ni narimasu.	"I will be free tomorrow."
Koko wa mae kissaten deshita ga, hon'ya ni narimashita.	"This place was a coffee shop before, but it became [changed to] a bookstore."
Kodomo wa byooki deshita keredo, gen'ki ni narimashita.	"The child was sick, but he got well."
Osashimi wa mae suki ja arimasen deshita ga, suki ni narimashita.	"I did not like raw fish before, but I came to like it."
Watakushi wa rainen Meriiran'do Daigaku no gakusei ni narimasu.	"I'll be a student at the University of Maryland next year."
Musuko wa isha ni narimasen deshita.	"My son didn't become a physician."

12.4.4 *Osoku narimasu* means "It is getting late" or "It will become late." When an Adjective precedes *narimasu*, the Adjective is always in the KU form and the combination means "become such and such," "get to be such and such," "come to be such and such," and so forth. Note that a Noun or an adjectival Noun is always followed by the Relational *ni* before *narimasu* while an Adjective is in the KU form before *narimasu*.

$$\textbf{Noun} + \begin{Bmatrix} \textbf{\textit{wa}} \\ \textbf{\textit{ga}} \end{Bmatrix} + \textbf{Adjective (\textit{-ku})} + \textbf{\textit{narimasu}}$$

atsuku		"become hot"
yasuku		"become inexpensive"
furuku		"(things) get old"
ookiku	narimasu	"will be larger"
hayaku		"become faster or earlier"
hoshiku		"come to want"
yoku		"become well; improve"

Natsu kono heya wa totemo atsuku narimasu.	"This room gets very hot in summer."
Ten'ki ga yoku narimasen deshita kara, ohanami ni ikimasen deshita.	"The weather didn't get better, so I didn't go flower viewing."
Nihon'go no ben'kyoo ga omoshiroku narimashita.	"I have come to find more interest in studying Japanese."
Kono koohii wa tsumetaku narimashita kara, atsui no o kudasai.	"This coffee has become cold, so please give me a hotter one."

| Sen'shuu seetaa o kaimashita ga, mata atarashii no ga hoshiku narimashita. | "I bought a sweater last week, but I got to wanting a new one again." |

12.4.5 Approximation

Sorosoro in *Sorosoro shitsurei shimasu* functions as a signal to soften the tone of what might be an abrupt statement, and in this way is not unlike "Well . . . I'm going to leave." However, it has gradually lost its original meaning, and now is used only as a softener to avoid abruptness. This reveals the characteristically vague and indirect manner of the Japanese. Similarly *Gojihan goro matte imasu yo* in Lesson 2 and *gogo yoji juugofun goro, nan'ji goro* in Lesson 4 reveal this tendency of offering approximation, thus being less explicit in Japanese.

12.4.6 *Moo son'na jikan desu ka?* is often used as an expression equivalent to "Is it so late now?" or "Is the time up already?" This expression shows a surprise about time's rapid passing. *Kon'na jikan* may also occur in the expression.

Ohirugohan desu yo.	"It's lunch."
Moo son'na jikan desu ka?	"Is it already time for lunch?"
Hachiji desu kara, isoide kudasai.	"It's eight o'clock, so please hurry."
E! Moo son'na jikan desu ka?	"My! Is it so late now?"

12.4.7 Modesty

Nakayama's use of *Gochisoo wa dekinai kedo* provides another typical example of Japanese self-deprecation and modesty. In America a statement such as "Although I cannot feed you good food" might be regarded as somewhat strange. Nakayama's later statement *Ōkawa san ga omou hodo taihen ja arimasen yo* is another example of such polite modesty. These statements should not be taken as a true indication of Nakayama's cooking ability. It is simply another example of the habitual Japanese refusal to appear self-asserting, self-congratulatory, or self-assuming.

12.4.8 Heteronomy

Ōkawa's two statements "It's very troublesome to cook at home, isn't it?" and "I would also like to help you" both indicate the preferred Japanese norm of behavior, which is to show your understanding of the hardships and difficulties of the other side, and give him your help. To be considerate is always a recommended virtue in Japan.

12.4.9 *Sugu dekimasu yo* here means "It will be ready soon." The Verb *dekimasu* has the meanings "is ready," "is done," "is made," "is able to."

Gohan wa nan'ji ni dekimasu ka?	"What time will the meal be ready?"
Watashi no rein'kooto wa dekite imasu ka? (said to a laundry man)	"Is my raincoat ready?"
Shukudai wa moo dekimashita.	"The homework has been completed already."

12.4.10 *Ookawa san ga omou hodo taihen ja arimasen* means "It is not so troublesome as Mr. Ōkawa may think." The negative comparison introduced in Note 11.4.13 may be applied to comparing two actions.

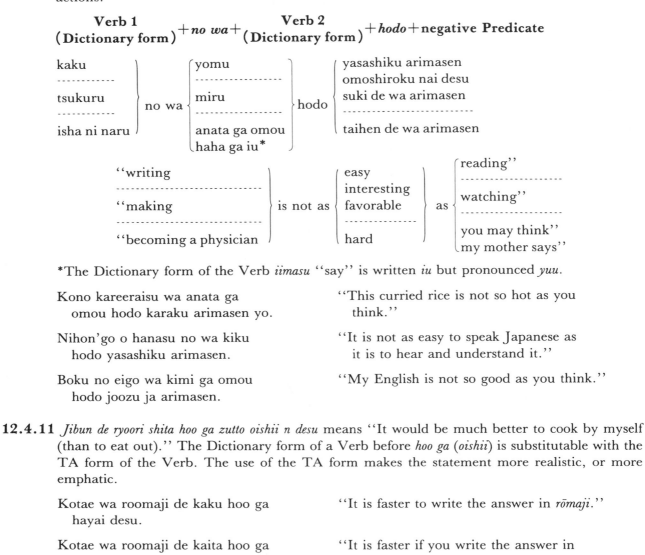

Verb 1
(Dictionary form) *+no wa+* **Verb 2**
(Dictionary form) *+hodo+*negative Predicate

kaku

tsukuru } no wa { yomu

miru

anata ga omou

haha ga iu* } hodo { yasashiku arimasen

omoshiroku nai desu

suki de wa arimasen

taihen de wa arimasen

isha ni naru

"writing

"making } is not as { easy

interesting

favorable

hard } as { reading"

watching"

you may think"

my mother says"

"becoming a physician

*The Dictionary form of the Verb *iimasu* "say" is written *iu* but pronounced *yuu*.

Kono kareeraisu wa anata ga omou hodo karaku arimasen yo.	"This curried rice is not so hot as you think."
Nihon'go o hanasu no wa kiku hodo yasashiku arimasen.	"It is not as easy to speak Japanese as it is to hear and understand it."
Boku no eigo wa kimi ga omou hodo joozu ja arimasen.	"My English is not so good as you think."

12.4.11 *Jibun de ryoori shita hoo ga zutto oishii n desu* means "It would be much better to cook by myself (than to eat out)." The Dictionary form of a Verb before *hoo ga* (*oishii*) is substitutable with the TA form of the Verb. The use of the TA form makes the statement more realistic, or more emphatic.

Kotae wa roomaji de kaku hoo ga hayai desu.	"It is faster to write the answer in *rōmaji*."
Kotae wa roomaji de kaita hoo ga hayai desu.	"It is faster if you write the answer in *rōmaji*."

When the TA form of a Verb precedes *hoo ga ii*, and the statement is addressed to the hearer, the statement is normally that of advice or suggestion to the hearer and corresponds to "you'd better do such and such."

Verb(-*ta*)+ *hoo ga ii* (*desu*) (*yo*)

Uchi e kaetta hoo ga ii desu yo.	"You'd better go home."
Koohii yori gyuunyuu o non'da hoo ga ii desu.	"You'd better drink milk rather than coffee."
Koyama san, isoida hoo ga ii desu yo.	"Mr. Koyama, you'd better hurry."
Sugu osara o aratta hoo ga ii desu ne.	"It would be better to wash dishes right away."

12.4.12 The superlative pattern has been introduced in Lesson 11. When three or more actions instead of items are to be compared, the Dictionary form of a Verb followed by the dependent Noun *no* will take the place of Nouns representing items to be compared.

Dictionary form of Verb + *no* + $\left\{ \begin{array}{c} wa \\ ga \end{array} \right\}$ + *ichiban* + $\left\{ \begin{array}{c} \textbf{Adjective} \\ \textbf{adjectival Noun} \end{array} \right\}$ *desu*

$\left. \begin{array}{l} \text{gitaa o hiku} \\ \text{tenisu o suru} \\ \text{kodomo to hanasu} \end{array} \right\}$ no $\left\{ \begin{array}{c} \text{wa} \\ \text{ga} \end{array} \right\}$ ichiban $\left\{ \begin{array}{l} \text{tanoshii desu} \\ \text{omoshiroi desu} \\ \text{suki desu} \end{array} \right.$

$\left. \begin{array}{l} \text{``playing a guitar} \\ \text{``playing tennis} \\ \text{``talking with children} \end{array} \right\}$ is the most $\left\{ \begin{array}{l} \text{enjoyable''} \\ \text{interesting''} \\ \text{favorable''} \end{array} \right.$

Seiyoo ryoori o tsukuru no wa   "To cook Western food is the most difficult."
ichiban muzukashii desu.

Watakushi wa yuumei na niwa o   "It is my favorite pastime to visit famous
ken'butsu suru no ga ichiban suki desu.   gardens."

When several actions are given for choice, a question is formulated as follows:

Verb 1 + *no to* + **Verb 2** + *no to* + . . . **Verb N** *no* (*to*) *de* (*wa*), *dore ga ichiban* . . . *ka?*

"of Verb 1, Verb 2, . . . Verb N, which is the most . . . ?"

In the above pattern, Verb 1, Verb 2, . . . Verb N are all in the Dictionary form.

Nihon'go o kaku no to yomu no to kiku no to, dore ga ichiban $\left\{ \begin{array}{l} \text{yasashii desu} \\ \text{joozu desu} \\ \text{suki desu} \end{array} \right\}$ ka?

"of writing, reading, and understanding Japanese, which $\left\{ \begin{array}{l} \text{is the easiest?''} \\ \text{are you the best at?''} \\ \text{do you like best?''} \end{array} \right.$

Gitaa o hiku no to baiorin o hiku   "Which are you the most proficient in,
no to piano o hiku no to de wa,   playing a guitar, a violin, or a piano?"
dore ga ichiban joozu desu ka?

Juudoo o suru no to karate o   "Which is the most difficult, practicing *jūdō*,
suru no to tenisu o suru no   *karate*, or tennis?"
to de, dore ga ichiban muzukashii
desu ka?

Nikkoo e iku no to Kyooto o ken'butsu   "Of going to Nikkō, visiting Kyōto, and
suru no to kabuki o miru no to, dore   seeing *kabuki*, which is the best?"
ga ichiban ii desu ka?

12.4.13 Indirectness

From this dialog we can tell that Ōkawa and Koyama are single men, possibly students. From the forms of address used (both men use last names plus -*san*), it is obvious that they are not very close. Ōkawa's question "What do you cook best?" might be similar to the American expression of "What do you like to cook?" or "What are we going to have?" The latter two American expressions, however, would be considered too direct in the Japanese context. The curious

Japanese guest must ask the indirect (and inoffensive) question of "What do you cook best?" to find out in a roundabout fashion exactly what will be prepared. To ask "What would you like to cook for me?" or "What are you going to cook for me?" would be seeking a clarification of someone else's intentions, and the Japanese avoid pursuing such a matter. Koyama is doing a favor for Ōkawa, and it would be impolite for him to ask what favor Koyama is going to give him.

On the other hand, straightforward, frank expressions can be used if the two parties are really close to each other. In such circumstances one could say he is good at cooking such and such, implying that he is offering the other person his best. Such directness is, it must be stressed, limited to very close, intimate relationships, or to social discourse among young people.

12.4.14 *Karee ni shimashoo* means here "Let's make it curry and rice" or "Let's decide on curry and rice." The *ni* is the Relational of goal and is followed by the transitive Verb *shimasu* "make." In the complete pattern of "make Noun 1 into Noun 2," Noun 1 is followed by the Relational *o* and Noun 2 is followed by the goal Relational *ni*. Noun 2 may be an adjectival Noun.

Noun 1 + o + Noun 2 + ni + shimasu

Noun 1		Noun 2		
musume		isha		"make my daughter a doctor"
musuko		sen'sei		"make my son a teacher"
heya	o	kirei	ni shimasu	"clean the room"
nooto		dame		"damage the notebook"
supootsu		sakan		"make sport popular"

Musuko o gun'jin ni shimashita.	"I made my son a career soldier."
Musume o isha ni shimasu.	"I will make my daughter a doctor."
Kyooshitsu o kirei ni shimashoo.	"Let's clean the classroom."

In the meaning of "making a choice" (e.g., in deciding on what dish you are going to order in a restaurant or setting the date of a meeting, etc.), *o* seldom occurs and *ni shimasu* will be usually equivalent to "I'll have (beefsteak)" or "We'll make it (Tuesday)."

Nani o tabemashoo ka?	"What shall we eat?"
Boku wa yappari osashimi ni shimasu.	"I will have *sashimi* as I first thought."
Kitanakatta kara, heya o kirei ni shimashita.	"I cleaned my room because it was dirty."
Urusai desu nee. Shizuka ni shite kudasai.	"It is noisy. Please be quiet. [lit. Please make yourself quiet.]"

Note that the pattern N1 *o* N2 *ni shimasu* and the pattern N1 *wa* N2 *ni narimasu* form a contrast.

Compare the following:

Watakushi wa musuko o isha ni shimashita.	"I made my son a physician."

Musuko wa isha ni narimashita.	"My son became a physician."
Minoru wa heya o kirei ni shimashita.	"Minoru cleaned up the room."
Heya wa kirei ni narimashita.	"The room became clean."
Isha wa kodomo o gen'ki ni shimasu.	"A medical doctor makes a child get healthy."
Kodomo wa gen'ki ni narimasu.	"The child will get well."
Hayashi sen'sei wa kono daigaku o yuumei ni shimashita.	"Professor Hayashi made this college famous."
Kono daigaku wa yuumei ni narimashita.	"This college became famous."

When an Adjective precedes the Verb *shimasu* "make," the Adjective is in the KU form and the thing or person that is made in a certain state is followed by the Relational *o*.

Noun + *o* + Adjective(*-ku*) + *shimasu*

amaku		sweet"
suppaku		sour"
oishiku		tasty"
atsuku	*shimasu* "make (something)	hot" "heat"
nagaku		long" "lengthen"
osoku		slow; late" "slow down"
yasashiku		easy"
atarashiku		new"

Compare the following:

Ryoori o oishiku shimasu.	"I will make the food tasty."
Ryoori ga oishiku narimasu.	"The food will be made tasty."
Oyu o atsuku shimashoo.	"I'll make the (warm) water hotter."
Oyu ga atsuku narimashita.	"The (warm) water got hotter."
Shiken o muzukashiku shimashita.	"They made the exam difficult."
Shiken ga muzukashiku narimashita.	"The exam became difficult."
Sono tatemono o ookiku shimasu.	"They'll enlarge that building."
Sono tatemono wa ookiku narimashita yo.	"That building became larger."

12.5   VOCABULARY

Presentation

料理	ryoori	......	N	cooking; dish; food
あじ	aji	......	N	taste; flavor
いろ	iro	......	N	color
かたち	katachi	......	N	shape; form; appearance

ひじょうに	hijoo ni	......	Adv.	extremely
年取った	toshitotta	......	V	aged (person)
わかい	wakai	......	A	is young
西洋	seiyoo	......	N	Western (countries); the Occident (cf. *tooyoo* ''Eastern (countries); the Orient'')

Dialog

大川	Ookawa	......	N	family name
に	ni	......	R	goal Relational (see 12.4.3)
なりました	narimashita	......	V	became (TA form of *narimasu ← naru*) (see 12.4.3 and 12.4.4)
なります	narimasu	......	V	become (after KU form of A) (see 12.4.4)
中山	Nakayama	......	N	family name
ごちそう	gochisoo	......	N	feast; treat
ごちそうします	gochisoo shimasu	......	V	treat (one to something to eat or drink) (normal form of *gochisoo (o) suru*)
作ります	tsukurimasu	......	V	make; create; prepare; cook (normal form of *tsukuru*)
できます	dekimasu	......	V	is ready; is done; is made (normal form of *dekiru*) (see 12.4.9)
おもう	omou	......	V	think (Dictionary form)
自分で	jibun de	......	Adv.	by oneself; for oneself
食べ物屋	tabemonoya	......	N	eating place
料理した	ryoori shita	......	V	cooked (TA form of *ryoori suru*)
手つだいます	tetsudaimasu	......	V	help; assist (a person to do something) (normal form of *tetsudau*)
とくい	tokui	......	Na	proud, favorite, or strong point
カレーライス	kareeraisu	......	N	curry and rice
とんかつ	ton'katsu	......	N	pork cutlet
にく	niku	......	N	meat
やさい	yasai	......	N	vegetables
しましょう	shimashoo	......	V	let's make; let's decide on (OO form of *shimasu ← suru*) (see 12.4.14)

Notes

| さかな | sakana | ...... | N | fish |
| びょう気 | byooki | ...... | N | illness; sickness |

むすこ	musuko	......	N	son
いしゃ	isha	......	N	medical doctor; physician
からく	karaku	......	A	KU form of *karai*—is salty; is spicy
いそいだ	isoida	......	V	TA form of *isogimasu* ← *isogu*—hurry
（お）さら	(o)sara	......	N	dish; plate
あらう	arau	......	V	wash (Dictionary form)
バイオリン	baiorin	......	N	violin
むすめ	musume	......	N	daughter; girl
ぐん人	gun'jin	......	N	military personnel; career soldier
（お）さしみ	(o)sashimi	......	N	raw fish
あまい	amai	......	A	is sweet
すっぱい	suppai	......	A	is sour
おゆ	oyu	......	N	hot or warm boiled water

12.6   KAN'JI

12.6.1 美   (1) *utsuku(shii)*   (2) beauty   (3) classifier 羊 [sheep]
(4) ［ ］ ［ ］ ［ ］ ［ ］ ［ ］ ［ ］ ［ ］ ［ ］ ［ ］   (5) 美しい人、美しいことば
(6) a big sheep, hence beautiful

12.6.a 年[2.6.4]   (1) *toshi*   (2) age; year   (5) 年はいくつですか、年取った人

12.6.2 食   (1) *ta(bemasu)*; *ta(beru)*   (2) eat   (3) forms the classifier 食 [eat]
(4) ［ ］ ［ ］ ［ ］ ［ ］ ［ ］ ［ ］ ［ ］ ［ ］ ［ ］   (5) なにを食べますか
(6) a roof ⌒ and some rice 白 over a fire 火 for cooking

12.6.b 食[12.6.2]   (1) SHOKU   (5) 食堂、食事

12.6.c 中[7.6.9]   (1) CHUU   (5) 中国、中年 [middle age]   (6) homonym 仲、虫、忠

12.6.3 川   (1) *kawa*   (2) river   (3) forms the classifier 川   (4) ［ ］ ［ ］ ［ ］
(5) 山と川、ながい川、石川さん   (6) a flowing river

12.6.4 事   (1) JI   (2) thing; matter   (3) classifier 一 （｜）
(4) ［ ］ ［ ］ ［ ］ ［ ］ ［ ］ ［ ］ ［ ］ ［ ］   (5) 事務所、事故   [accident]
(6) a hand holding a stick with a flag, which means work

12.6.5 作 （1） *tsuku(rimasu)*; *tsuku(ru)* （2） make （3） classifier イ [man]

（4） ノ イ 亻 竹 竹 作 作 （5） 料理を作ります、文を作る [make a sentence]

12.6.6 待 （1） *ma(chimasu)*; *ma(tsu)* （2） await （3） classifier 彳

（4） ノ ク 彳 行 行 社 待 待 待

（5） ポールさんを待っています （6） the crossroad 行 also means to go and 寺 means temple—go to the temple for waiting. See 8.6.2

12.6.7 自 （1） JI （2） self （3） forms the classifier ' （自）

（4） ノ 亻 𠃊 白 自 自 （5） 自由 [freedom]、自分、自動車

（6） a nose, hence oneself

12.6.8 物 （1） *mono* （2） thing; article （3） classifier 牜 [animal]

（4） ノ 𠂉 牛 牛 牜 物 物 物

（5） のみ物、くだ物、のり物、食べ物、いろいろな物、買い物

（6） 牜 is a cow and 勿 is the phonetic sign

12.6.9 屋 （1） *ya* （2） shop （3） classifier 尸

（4） 一 コ 尸 尸 居 居 屋 屋 屋 （5） パン屋、屋根、さかな屋、花屋

12.6.10 何 （1） *nani* [*nan-*] （2） what?; how many? （3） classifier イ

（4） 亻 仃 何 何 （5） 何時、何しんぶん、何いろ、何人

12.7 DRILLS

12.7.1 Transformation Drill

西洋料理を　食べるより　中国料理を　食べる　ほうが　好きです。

1. ピアノを　ひきます、ギターを　　　　⟶　ピアノを　ひくより　ギターを　ひく
   ひきます　　　　　　　　　　　　　　　　　　ほうが　好きです。

2. ふねに　のります、ひこうきに　のります ⟶　ふねに　のるより　ひこうきに　のる
   　　　　　　　　　　　　　　　　　　　　　　　ほうが　好きです。

3. 日本料理を　作ります、西洋料理を　⟶　日本料理を　作るより　西洋料理を　作る
   作ります　　　　　　　　　　　　　　　　　ほうが　好きです。

4. 東京に　すみます、京都に　すみます ⟶　東京に　すむより　京都に　すむ　ほうが
   　　　　　　　　　　　　　　　　　　　　　好きです。

5. えいがを　見ます、かぶきを　見ます ⟶　えいがを　見るより　かぶきを　見る
   　　　　　　　　　　　　　　　　　　　　　ほうが　好きです。

6. 図書館へ　行きます、うちに　います　──→　図書館へ　行くより　うちに　いる　ほうが
　　　　　　　　　　　　　　　　　　　　　　　　好きです。

7. スポーツを　します、さんぽします　──→　スポーツを　するより　さんぽする　ほうが
　　　　　　　　　　　　　　　　　　　　　　　　好きです。

8. おさらを　あらいます、料理します　──→　おさらを　あらうより　料理する　ほうが
　　　　　　　　　　　　　　　　　　　　　　　　好きです。

12.7.2 Transformation Drill

<u>ビールを　のむのは　てんぷらを　食べるより　いいです。</u>

1. 日本語を　はなします、日本語を　──→　日本語を　はなすのは　日本語を　書くより
　　書きます　　　　　　　　　　　　　　　　いいです。

2. 東京へ　行きます、京都を　けんぶつ　──→　東京へ　行くのは　京都を　けんぶつする
　　します　　　　　　　　　　　　　　　　　より　いいです。

3. 料理を　作ります、外で　食べます　──→　料理を　作るのは　外で　食べるより
　　　　　　　　　　　　　　　　　　　　　　いいです。

4. ぎんこうに　つとめます、デパートで　──→　ぎんこうに　つとめるのは　デパートで
　　はたらきます　　　　　　　　　　　　　　はたらくより　いいです。

5. 本を　読みます、おんがくを　聞きます　──→　本を　読むのは　おんがくを　聞くより
　　　　　　　　　　　　　　　　　　　　　　いいです。

6. バスに　のります、あるきます　──→　バスに　のるのは　あるくより　いいです。

7. 自分で　作ります、手つだいます　──→　自分で　作るのは　手つだうより　いいです。

8. すっぱい　物を　食べます、あまい　──→　すっぱい　物を　食べるのは　あまい　物を
　　物を　食べます　　　　　　　　　　　　　食べるより　いいです。

12.7.3 Transformation Drill

わたしは　<u>カレーライスを　作るのが</u>　一番　とくいです。

1. ピアノを　ひきます　──→　わたしは　ピアノを　ひくのが　一番　とくいです。

2. 日本語で　はなします　──→　わたしは　日本語で　はなすのが　一番　とくいです。

3. かん字を　書きます　──→　わたしは　かん字を　書くのが　一番　とくいです。

4. テニスを　します　──→　わたしは　テニスを　するのが　一番　とくいです。

5. から手を　します　──→　わたしは　から手を　するのが　一番　とくいです。

6. フランス語を　読みます　──→　わたしは　フランス語を　読むのが　一番　とくいです。

7. 中国料理を　作ります　──→　わたしは　中国料理を　作るのが　一番　とくいです。

8. 料理します　──→　わたしは　料理するのが　一番　とくいです。

12.7.4 Transformation Drill

1. 手つだいます、自分で 作ります ⟶ <u>手つだうのは 自分で 作る</u>ほど
   たいへんじゃありません。

2. フランス語を 習います、日本語を ⟶ フランス語を 習うのは 日本語を 習う
   習います　　　　　　　　　　　　　　　ほど　たいへんじゃありません。

3. ひらがなで 書きます、かん字で ⟶ ひらがなで 書くのは かん字で 書くほど
   書きます　　　　　　　　　　　　　　　たいへんじゃありません。

4. ここから うちまで はしります、⟶ ここから うちまで はしるのは あなたが
   あなたが おもいます　　　　　　　　　おもうほど たいへんじゃありません。

5. 日本の しんぶんを 読みます、⟶ 日本の しんぶんを 読むのは 中山さんが
   中山さんが いいます　　　　　　　　　いうほど たいへんじゃありません。

6. 学校の 先生に なります、いしゃに ⟶ 学校の 先生に なるのは いしゃに
   なります　　　　　　　　　　　　　　　なるほど たいへんじゃありません。

7. ひらがなで 書きます、かたかなで ⟶ ひらがなで 書くのは かたかなで
   書きます　　　　　　　　　　　　　　　書くほど たいへんじゃありません。

8. アルバイトを します、みんなが ⟶ アルバイトを するのは みんなが
   いいます　　　　　　　　　　　　　　　いうほど たいへんじゃありません。

12.7.5 Expansion Drill

1. 好きです。　　　　　　　…… 好きです。
   ふねに のる ほうが　　　…… ふねに のる ほうが 好きです。
   ひこうきに のるより　　　…… ひこうきに のるより ふねに のる ほうが 好きです。
   いもうとは　　　　　　　　…… いもうとは ひこうきに のるより ふねに のる
   　　　　　　　　　　　　　　　　ほうが 好きです。

2. ずっと はやいです。　　　…… ずっと はやいです。
   ははが 作った ほうが　　…… ははが 作った ほうが ずっと はやいです。
   わたしが 作るより　　　　…… わたしが 作るより ははが 作った ほうが ずっと
   　　　　　　　　　　　　　　　　はやいです。
   料理は　　　　　　　　　　…… 料理は わたしが 作るより ははが 作った ほうが
   　　　　　　　　　　　　　　　　ずっと はやいです。

3. 一番 じょうずです。　　　…… 一番 じょうずです。
   日本語を はなすのが　　　…… 日本語を はなすのが 一番 じょうずです。
   外国語の なかで　　　　　…… 外国語の なかで 日本語を はなすのが 一番
   　　　　　　　　　　　　　　　　じょうずです。

スミスさんは　　　　　　……　スミスさんは　外国語の　なかで　日本語を
　　　　　　　　　　　　　　　　はなすのが　一番　じょうずです。

4.　一番　おそかったです。　……　一番　おそかったです。

クラスに　来るのが　　　　……　クラスに　来るのが　一番　おそかったです。

学生の　なかで　　　　　　……　学生の　なかで　クラスに　来るのが　一番
　　　　　　　　　　　　　　　　おそかったです。

青木さんは　　　　　　　　……　青木さんは　学生の　なかで　クラスに　来るのが　一番
　　　　　　　　　　　　　　　　おそかったです。

5.　やさしくありません。　……　やさしくありません。

森さんが　いうほど　　　　……　森さんが　いうほど　やさしくありません。

学校の　先生に　なるのは……　学校の　先生に　なるのは　森さんが　いうほど
　　　　　　　　　　　　　　　　やさしくありません。

12.7.6 Response Drill

1.　おんがくを　聞くのと　本を　読むのと、どっちが　好きですか。

　おんがくを　聞く　　　　……　おんがくを　聞く　ほうが　好きです。

2.　ひらがなを　書くのと　読むのと、どっちの　ほうが　やさしいですか。

　ひらがなを　読む　　　　……　ひらがなを　読む　ほうが　やさしいです。

3.　日曜日に　行くのと　土曜日に　行くのと、どっちの　ほうが　つごうが　いいですか。

　土曜日に　行く　　　　　……　土曜日に　行く　ほうが　つごうが　いいです。

4.　中国料理を　作るのと　西洋料理を　作るのと　日本料理を　作るのとで、どれが　一番
　　たいへんですか。

　日本料理を　作る　　　　……　日本料理を　作るのが　一番　たいへんです。

5.　えい語を　はなすのと　フランス語を　はなすのと　ドイツ語を　はなすのとでは、
　　どれが　一番　じょうずですか。

　えい語を　はなす　　　　……　えい語を　はなすのが　一番　じょうずです。

6.　バスで　来るのと　タクシーで　来るのと　でんしゃで　来るのとでは、どれが　一番
　　はやいですか。

　でんしゃで　来る　　　　……　でんしゃで　来るのが　一番　はやいです。

12.7.7 E-J Substitution Drill

自分で　作った　ほうが　いいですよ。

1.　go to the doctor　　　　　　……　いしゃへ　行った　ほうが　いいですよ。

2.　take an express　　　　　　……　急行に　のった　ほうが　いいですよ。

3. return the books to the library ⋯⋯ 図書館に　本を　かえした　ほうが
　　　　　　　　　　　　　　　　　　　　　　いいですよ。

4. buy them because they are inexpensive ⋯⋯ やすいから、買った　ほうが　いいですよ。

5. marry Susie ⋯⋯ スージーと　けっこんした　ほうが
　　　　　　　　　　　　　　　　いいですよ。

6. speak in English with Michiko ⋯⋯ みち子さんと　えい語で　はなした　ほうが
　　　　　　　　　　　　　　　　　　いいですよ。

7. use the *kan'ji* you have learned ⋯⋯ 習った　かん字を　つかった　ほうが
　　　　　　　　　　　　　　　　　　いいですよ。

8. stay home because it is raining ⋯⋯ あめが　ふっていますから、うちに　いた
　　　　　　　　　　　　　　　　　　ほうが　いいですよ。

12.7.8 Transformation Drill

1. もう　六時です。 ⟶ もう　六時に　なりました。
2. とても　げん気です。 ⟶ とても　げん気に　なりました。
3. 外国でも　じゅうどうが ⟶ 外国でも　じゅうどうが　さかんに
　　さかんです。 　　　なりました。
4. 林さんは　先生です。 ⟶ 林さんは　先生に　なりました。
5. むすめは　きれいです。 ⟶ むすめは　きれいに　なりました。
6. 井上先生は　ゆうめいです。 ⟶ 井上先生は　ゆうめいに　なりました。
7. おとうとは　ぐん人です。 ⟶ おとうとは　ぐん人に　なりました。
8. すきやきが　大好きです。 ⟶ すきやきが　大好きに　なりました。
9. ともだちは　いしゃです。 ⟶ ともだちは　いしゃに　なりました。
10. 教室は　しずかです。 ⟶ 教室は　しずかに　なりました。

12.7.9 Transformation Drill

1. きょうは　天気が　わるいです。 ⟶ きょうは　天気が　わるくなりました。
2. 一郎くんは　せいが　たかいです。 ⟶ 一郎くんは　せいが　たかくなりました。
3. みち子さんは　美しいです。 ⟶ みち子さんは　美しくなりました。
4. とても　むしあついですね。 ⟶ とても　むしあつくなりましたね。
5. 子どもたちは　かわいいです。 ⟶ 子どもたちは　かわいくなりました。
6. この　辞書は　やすいです。 ⟶ この　辞書は　やすくなりました。
7. こんしゅうは　いそがしいです。 ⟶ こんしゅうは　いそがしくなりました。

8. しけんが　むずかしいです。　　　　⟶　しけんが　むずかしくなりました。

9. 日本語の　べんきょうが　　　　　　⟶　日本語の　べんきょうが　おもしろく
　　おもしろいです。　　　　　　　　　　　　　　　　なりました。

10. えんぴつが　みじかいです。　　　　⟶　えんぴつが　みじかくなりました。

12.7.10 Mixed Transformation Drill

1. 日本語が　じょうずです。　　　　　⟶　日本語が　じょうずに　なりました。

2. しごとが　いそがしいです。　　　　⟶　しごとが　いそがしくなりました。

3. 教科書が　新しいです。　　　　　　⟶　教科書が　新しくなりました。

4. 森さんは　大学の　先生です。　　　⟶　森さんは　大学の　先生に　なりました。

5. デパートが　きれいです。　　　　　⟶　デパートが　きれいに　なりました。

6. わたしの　ともだちは　いしゃです。⟶　わたしの　ともだちは　いしゃに　なりました。

7. あたまが　へんです。　　　　　　　⟶　あたまが　へんに　なりました。

8. ごご　天気が　いいです。　　　　　⟶　ごご　天気が　よくなりました。

9. むすこは　ぐん人です。　　　　　　⟶　むすこは　ぐん人に　なりました。

10. くだ物が　あまいです。　　　　　　⟶　くだ物が　あまくなりました。

12.7.11 Transformation Drill

1. しけんは　やさしいです。　　　　　⟶　しけんを　やさしくします。

2. 教室は　きれいです。　　　　　　　⟶　教室を　きれいに　します。

3. せつめいは　くわしいです。　　　　⟶　せつめいを　くわしくします。

4. しゅくだいは　多いです。　　　　　⟶　しゅくだいを　多くします。

5. 子どもの　へやは　ひろいです。　　⟶　子どもの　へやを　ひろくします。

6. おゆは　あついです。　　　　　　　⟶　おゆを　あつくします。

7. こたえは　ながいです。　　　　　　⟶　こたえを　ながくします。

12.7.12 Response Drill

1. ばんごはんは　何に　しましたか。

　　ビフテキ　　　　　　　　　……　ばんごはんは　ビフテキに　しました。

　　さかな　　　　　　　　　　……　ばんごはんは　さかなに　しました。

　　中国料理　　　　　　　　　……　ばんごはんは　中国料理に　しました。

　　あたたかい　料理　　　　　……　ばんごはんは　あたたかい　料理に　しました。

　　あなたが　好きな　食べ物……　ばんごはんは　あなたが　好きな　食べ物に　しました。

254

2. りょこうに 行くのは いつに しますか。

らいしゅうの 木曜日 …… りょこうに 行くのは らいしゅうの 木曜日に します。

四月 …… りょこうに 行くのは 四月に します。

らい年の あき …… りょこうに 行くのは らい年の あきに します。

あしたの ごご 三時 …… りょこうに 行くのは あしたの ごご 三時に します。

3. けんぶつする 所は どこに しましょうか。

京都 …… けんぶつする 所は 京都に しましょう。

おてら …… けんぶつする 所は おてらに しましょう。

しずかな 町 …… けんぶつする 所は しずかな 町に しましょう。

ちかい 所 …… けんぶつする 所は ちかい 所に しましょう。

12.7.13 E-J Substitution Drill

いもうとは 先生に なりました。

1. a college student …… いもうとは 大学生に なりました。

2. big …… いもうとは 大きくなりました。

3. sick …… いもうとは びょう気に なりました。

4. healthy …… いもうとは げん気に なりました。

5. a junior student …… いもうとは 三年生に なりました。

6. famous …… いもうとは ゆうめいに なりました。

7. a librarian …… いもうとは 図書館員に なりました。

8. busy …… いもうとは いそがしくなりました。

12.7.14 E-J Substitution Drill

へやを あたたかくしました。

1. wide …… へやを ひろくしました。

2. small (narrow) …… へやを せまくしました。

3. cool …… へやを すずしくしました。

4. clean …… へやを きれいに しました。

5. dirty …… へやを きたなくしました。

6. a dining room …… へやを 食堂に しました。

7. new …… へやを 新しくしました。

8. beautiful …… へやを 美しくしました。

12.8 EXERCISES

12.8.1 Answer the following in Japanese:

1. ここから　図書館へ　行くのと　食堂へ　行くのと、どっちの　ほうが　とおい
   ですか。

2. あなたは　何に　なりたいですか。

3. きのうの　ひるごはんは　何に　しましたか。

4. おんがくを　聞くのと　本を　読むのとでは、どっちが　好きですか。

5. らいしゅうの　日曜日に　えいがへ　行くのと　町へ　食事に　行くのと　うちに
   いるのとでは、どれが　一番　いいですか。

6. 自分の　へやを　いつ　きれいに　しますか。

7. あなたの　すんでいる　所では　何月ごろ　さむくなりますか。

12.8.2 Insert an appropriate word in each blank using one of the given words:

<u>こと</u>、<u>ほど</u>、<u>より</u>、<u>の</u>　なかで、<u>物</u>、<u>に</u>、<u>の</u>

1. 日本の　大学では　から手を　する（　　）　テニスを　する　ほうが　さかん
   です。

2. 日本語を　習う（　　）は　ポールさんが　おもう（　　）　やさしくありません。

3. むすこを　ぐん人（　　）　したかったんですが、むすこは　いしゃ（　　）
   なりました。

4. 一年生（　　）　だれが　一番　はしる（　　）が　はやいですか。

5. 日本で　どんな（　　）を　買いたいですか。

6. 日本で　どんな（　　）を　したいですか。

12.8.3 Make a comparative question and an answer for it using the given words:

1. あるく、バスに　のる

2. あるく、バスに　のる、はしる

3. 買い物する、さんぽに　行く

4. 買い物する、さんぽに　行く、うちに　いる

12.8.4 Carry on the following conversation in Japanese:

———At a restaurant———

Yamada:　　I'll treat you today.

Katō:　　　Thank you.

Yamada:　　What shall we have（order）?

Katō: Let's see . . . I'll have pork cutlet and (boiled) rice.

Yamada: I'll have fish today. I didn't care for fish before, but I've come to like it.

Katō: Will the dishes be ready soon?

Yamada: Are you in a hurry?

Katō: Yes, I am.

Yamada: (To the waitress) Pardon me, please bring one pork cutlet and this dish (pointing at a menu).

Waitress: Yes, sir.

Yamada: Please hurry.

Waitress: Yes. Shall I bring coffee now?

Yamada: Yes, please.

Katō: Please bring mine later.

12.8.5 Express the following ideas in Japanese:

1. I prefer drinking black tea to drinking coffee.

2. I wanted to be (become) a school teacher, but I could not become a teacher.

3. My father wanted to make me a career soldier, but I did not become one.

4. My Japanese is not as good as you may think.

5. You'd better hurry, as it is going to be late.

6. Mr. Smith speaks Japanese better than any other language.

7. As it has become cold, you'd better put on your pullover.

12.8.6 Write the following underlined *hiragana* in *kan'ji*:

1. <u>しょくじ</u>に　うちへ　<u>かえ</u>ります。

2. <u>じぶん</u>で　<u>つく</u>る　ほうが　<u>はや</u>いです。

3. <u>うつく</u>しい　いろの　<u>の</u>み<u>もの</u>

4. <u>とし取</u>った　<u>ちゅうごくじん</u>

5. <u>なに</u>を　<u>た</u>べたいですか。

6. <u>おおかわ</u>さんを　<u>はなや</u>の　<u>まえ</u>で　<u>ま</u>ちましょう。

12.8.7 When you offer a guest some delicious melon, you may say either one of the following two expressions. What would make you decide to use one of them?

1. Kono meron oishii n desu yo. Hitotsu doozo.

2. Kono meron amari oishiku arimasen ga, hitotsu doozo.

12.8.8 Which of the following expressions would be more traditional in Japan under non-intimate circumstances (i.e., among acquaintances):

    1. A: This is delicious, please eat it.

        B: Although this is not delicious, please eat it.

    2. A: I would like to offer you a good thing.

        B: Although this is not good at all, I would like to offer it to you.

12.8.9 Give examples of Japan's cultural pluralism.

12.8.10 Which of the following underlined words are softeners?

    1. <u>Jaa</u>, mata ne.

    2. <u>Sorosoro</u> dekakemashoo ka?

    3. <u>Chotto</u> sumimasen ga.

    4. <u>Doomo</u> sumimasen.

    5. <u>Maa</u>, soo desu ne.

    6. <u>Chotto</u> jikan ga arimasu.

    7. <u>Saa</u>, yoku wakarimasen.

    8. <u>Amari</u> muzukashiku arimasen.

    9. <u>Doomo</u> yoku arimasen.

    10. <u>Yappari</u> soo deshita ka?

12.8.11 Under the following circumstances what would a Japanese say? Explain.

    1. Giving a present to a friend on his birthday.

    2. Offering a guest something to eat.

    3. Just before beginning to sing in front of guests.

12.9   SITUATIONAL AND APPLICATION CONVERSATION

12.9.1 Dinner

Three friends are discussing what they will have for dinner.

A asks where they should eat: at home, at a restaurant, or at a cafeteria nearby.

B wants to eat at the cafeteria nearby.

C invites A and B to his home. He would like to know what the other two want to eat.

A says he would like to eat *sukiyaki*.

B wants to eat *ten'pura*.

C decides to cook *sukiyaki,* which can be cooked faster than *ten'pura*.

12.9.2 Father and daughter

A girl wants to become a music instructor.

Her father recommends that she becomes a physician.

The daughter says that she would like to be a music instructor because to become a physician is more difficult than to become a music instructor, and, in addition, it takes more time.

The father then tells the daughter that she'd better take piano lessons.

12.9.3 Develop conversations at the dinner table.

12.9.4 Suppose that you and your friends are in a restaurant and talk about what to order.

12.9.5 A: Yoku ben'kyoo shimasu nee.

B: Iie, zen'zen.

12.9.6 Prof.: Yamada kun, kimi no shiken o mimashita yo. Totemo yoku dekimashita nee.

Yamada: Soo desu ka! Okagesama de.

LESSON 13
東京[1]の　交通[2]

13.1　PRESENTATION

　東京は　人口が　ひじょうに　多い　町です。　電車や　バスや　地下鉄は　いつも　こんでいます[3]。　自動車、　タクシー、　トラック、　オートバイなど　たくさんの　のり物が　せまい　みちを[4]　はしっています。

13.2　DIALOG

木村　「じつは、　これから　フランス大使館へ　行かなければなりません[5]。　田中さん、　ばしょを　ごぞんじですか。」

田中　「フランス大使館なら[6]、　よく　知っていますよ。」

木村　「そうですか。　どう　行けば　いい[7]んですか。　みちを　教えてください。」

田中　「きょうは　車です[8]か。」

木村　「いいえ。　でも、　ちかければ[9]、　あるいて行く[10]つもりですけど。」

田中　「ちょっと　とおいですよ。　十五番の　バスで　行けば[11]、　大使館の　すぐ　そばに　とまります[12]から、　バスに　した　ほうが　いいでしょう。　三つ目で　おりれば、　すぐ　わかりますよ。」

木村　「十五番の　バスですね？　バス停は　どこですか。」

田中　「この　とおりの　二番目の　かどを[4]　左へ　まがります。　ほら[13]、　今　あかい[14]　自転車が　はしって　来ますね。　あの　かどです。」

木村　「ええ、　わかります。」

田中　「それから、　まっすぐ　五十メートルぐらい　あるいて行きます。　すると、　右に　しろい　たて物が　あります。　バス停は　その　たて物の　入口の　前です。」

木村　「よく　わかりました。　どうも　ありがとう。」

人口　町　電車　自動車　田中
教えてください　左　自転車　右　入口

13.3 PATTERN SENTENCES

13.3.1

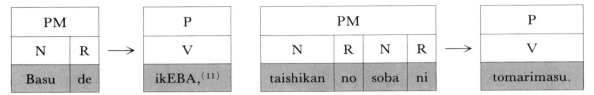

13.3.2

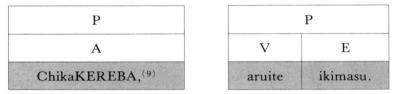

13.3.3

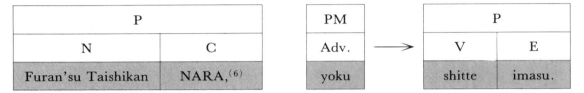

13.3.4

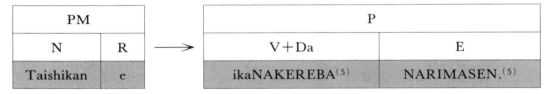

13.3.5

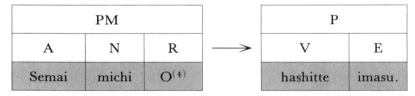

13.4 NOTES

13.4.1 Tōkyō

Tōkyō is a unique administrative unit in that it is both the national capital as well as a province and is administered by a governor-mayor combination. As a result of its special position, Tōkyō is treated differently from other Japanese cities. In addition, it is the largest city in the world; with a population exceeding ten million people, Tōkyō comprises 10 percent of the Japanese population.

Another unusual feature of the city originates in the Edo period when Tōkyō was the capital of the Shogunate. During this time the roads in Tōkyō were deliberately constructed in a complicated and confounding pattern as the city's best defense. Roads were narrow and winding, and streets and houses were numbered in a deliberately irrational and bewildering fashion. During World War II, Tōkyō was leveled, yet the Occupation did not bring about any fundamental changes in city planning or in the arrangement of roads.

13.4.2 Tōkyō Transportation

The transportation system in Tōkyō is often so congested as to reach a standstill. Millions of people commute every morning from the outskirts of the city and return home after work. Transportation in Tōkyō includes buses, subways, electric trains, taxis, private cars, trucks, and cargo trains for material goods. The subway system is the fastest and cheapest transportation in Tōkyō. All but one of the streetcar lines has been eliminated in Tōkyō, and people today rely mainly on subways, buses, trains, and automobiles as their mode of transportation.

13.4.3 *Kon'de imasu* means "is crowded," and *suite imasu* means "is less crowded."

Den'sha ga kon'de imasu.	"The train is crowded."
Kon'de iru basu ni wa noritaku nai desu.	"I don't want to ride in a crowded bus."
Guriin'sha wa totemo suite imasu.	"There is plenty of room in the first-class car."
Onaka ga suite imasu.	"I am hungry."

13.4.4 *Semai michi o hashitte imasu* means "They are running along the narrow streets." The Relational *o* is used after a place Noun when a motion takes place through the place. It is often translated as "through (the place)," "along (the street)," "at (the corner)," and so on. Note that the Verb following this Relational *o* is not a transitive Verb but a Verb of motion to cover a certain distance or space, such as *arukimasu* "walk," *ikimasu* "go," *magarimasu* "turn."

Gin'za michi		arukimasu hashirimasu san'po shimasu	"walk "run "stroll		the Ginza" the street"
eki no mae	o	ikimasu kimasu	"go "come	along through	the front of the station"
kado		magarimasu	"turn	(at)	the corner"

Hiroi michi o hashitte imasu.	"It is running on the wide street."
Ichiroo kun ga deguchi no soba o aruite imashita.	"Ichirō was walking near the exit."
Ano kado o magarimashoo.	"Let's turn at that corner."
Kooen o san'po suru tsumori desu.	"I intend to take a walk in the park."
Kan'sai o ryokoo shita koto ga arimasu ka?	"Have you traveled in the Kansai?"

13.4.5 *Ikanakereba narimasen* means "I have to go." *Ikanakereba* is the BA form of the plain negative of *iku,* namely *ikanai,* and is followed by the Extender *narimasen* "it won't do" to form the pattern meaning "obligation" or "necessity." The BA form of the plain negative Adjective and the BA form of the plain negative Copula may also occur before the Extender *narimasen.* The plain negative form of Adjectives and plain negative form of the Copula are formed by replacing the Extender *arimasen* with *nai.* See Note 13.4.11 for the BA form of Verbs.

kaimasen = kawan*ai*   ⟶   kawan*akereba*

ookiku arimasen = ookiku na*i*   ⟶   ookiku na*kereba*

∼ ja arimasen = ∼ ja na*i*   ⟶   ∼ ja na*kereba*

∼ de wa arimasen = ∼ de wa na*i*   ⟶   ∼ de* na*kereba*

BA form of $\begin{Bmatrix} \textbf{plain negative of Verb} \\ \textbf{plain negative of Adjective} \\ \textbf{plain negative of Copula} \end{Bmatrix}$ + $\begin{Bmatrix} \textit{narimasen} \\ (\textit{ikemasen}) \end{Bmatrix}$

Ikemasen "it won't do" is substitutable for *narimasen* in the above pattern and in the pattern of *-te wa ikemasen,* although the combinations of *-nakereba narimasen* and *-te wa ikemasen* are more commonly used than other combinations.

$\left.\begin{array}{l} \text{ikanakereba} \\ \text{kakanakereba} \\ \text{minakereba} \\ \text{------------} \\ \text{atsuku nakereba} \\ \text{omoshiroku nakereba} \\ \text{yoku nakereba} \\ \text{------------} \\ \sim \text{ja nakereba} \\ \sim \text{de* nakereba} \end{array}\right\}$ narimasen $\begin{array}{l} \text{"(one)"} \\ \text{"(it)"} \end{array}$ has to $\left\{\begin{array}{l} \text{go''} \\ \text{write''} \\ \text{see''} \\ \text{------------} \\ \text{be hot''} \\ \text{be interesting''} \\ \text{be good''} \\ \text{------------} \\ \text{be such and such''} \end{array}\right.$

*Wa never occurs here.

The negative answer to a question *-nakereba narimasen ka?* "Do I have to (do)...?" is expressed by an expression of permission: "it is all right if you don't (do it)" or "you don't have to (do it)" (*shi*)*nakute mo ii desu.*

Asa goji ni okinakereba narimasen ka?	"Do I have to get up at five in the morning?"
Hai, goji ni okinakereba narimasen.	"Yes, you have to get up at five."
Iie, goji ni okinakute mo ii desu.	"No, you don't have to get up at five."
Kinoshita san ni hi o shirasenakute mo ii desu ka?	"Is it unnecessary to inform Mr. Kinoshita of the date?"
Iie, shirasenakereba narimasen yo.	"No, you have to inform him."

13.4.6 *Furan'su Taishikan nara, yoku shitte imasu* means "If it is the French Embassy, I know it well." *Nara* is the provisional of the Copula *desu* ← *da.* The original form of *nara* is *naraba* and it is called the BA form of the Copula *da. Nara* occurs before a comma as a provisional clause, and the clause is equivalent to "if it is the case that or of..." or "provided that it is true..." *Nara* may occur after a Verb or an Adjective as well as a Noun, but only the case of a Noun preceding *nara* will be dealt with in this lesson. When the subject occurs in the provisional clause, the subject should be followed by the emphatic subject Relational *ga*. (In a dependent clause, the subject is always followed by *ga*.) When the subject of the dependent clause is at the same time the subject of the final clause, the subject may be followed by the Relational *wa*.

$$(moshi) + (Noun + ga) + \left\{ \begin{array}{l} \textbf{Noun} \\ \textbf{adjectival Noun} \end{array} \right\} + nara, \dots$$

aoi no			it is the blue one, . . . ''
asatte			it is the day after tomorrow, . . . ''
anata ga kirai	*nara*, . . .	''if	you don't like it, . . . ''
setsumei ga tekitoo			the explanation is adequate, . . . ''

In the provisional clause, the Adverb *moshi* may occur as a signal of a supposition, and it functions to emphasize the provisional or suppositional meaning of the clause.

Doyoobi nara, tsugoo ga ii n desu ga.	''I'll be available if it is Saturday.''
Moshi hima nara, issho ni ikimasen ka?	''If you are free, won't you go with us?''
Nihon'go no kurasu nara, moo owarimashita yo.	''If you are talking about the Japanese language class, it is already finished.''
Kono kuroi kutsu ga gosen'en nara, totemo yasui desu yo.	''If these black shoes cost five thousand yen, they are very cheap.''

The negative provisional expression of a copular Predicate is formed by transforming the plain negative form of the Copula. The plain negative of the Copula is formed replacing *arimasen* in *ja arimasen* with the Extender *nai*. When these are transformed into the BA form, the Relational *wa* in *de wa nai* should always be deleted.

~ ja arimasen	$\longrightarrow$	~ ja nai	$\longrightarrow$	~ ja nakereba
~ de wa arimasen	$\longrightarrow$	~ de (wa) nai	$\longrightarrow$	~ de nakereba

aki de nakereba	''if it is not fall''
tekitoo na hon ja nakereba	''if it is not an adequate book''
Byooki de nakereba, zehi kite kudasai.	''If you are not sick, please come by all means.''

13.4.7 The BA, or provisional, form of a Verb will be explained in Note 13.4.11. When the BA form of a Verb is followed by *ii desu, ii n desu, ii desu ka?* or *ii n desu ka?* the expression means if the action expressed by the Verb is taken, then it will do. It could be an indirect command or granting of permission. When *doo* precedes this expression such as in *Doo ikeba ii n desu ka?*, then it carries the meaning of ''How shall I do or act in order to be proper, appropriate, or permissible?''

Doo sureba ii desu ka?	''What shall I do?''
Itsu kureba ii deshoo?	''When will be the best time to come?''

13.4.8 *Desu* can be used in many cases to replace a lengthy statement.

Kyoo wa sashimi desu. (=sashimi ni shimasu.)	''I have decided to eat *sashimi* today.''
Kyoo wa kuruma desu ka? (=kuruma de kimashita ka?)	''Do you have your car with you today?''

13.4.9 *Chikakereba, aruite iku tsumori desu* means "If it is near, I intend to walk." *Chikakereba* is the BA form or the provisional form of the Adjective *chikai*. The BA form of an Adjective is formed regularly by replacing -*i* with -*kereba*.

Adjective(-*i*) ⟶ Adjective(-*kereba*)

chika*i*	chika*kereba*
hiro*i*	hiro*kereba*
sema*i*	sema*kereba*
yo*i*	yo*kereba*

Like the provisional clause of the Copula explained in Note 13.4.6, the subject in the clause is followed by the Relational *ga*, and the Adverb *moshi* may occur.

(moshi) + (Noun + *ga*) + Adjective(-*kereba*), . . .

ten'ki ga yokereba, . . .	"if the weather is good, . . . "
eiga ga nagakereba, . . .	"if the movie is long, . . . "
uchi ga furukereba, . . .	"if the house is old, . . . "
heya ga semakereba, . . .	"if the room is small, . . . "
ryoori ga amakereba, . . .	"if the food is sweet, . . . "

Saizu ga chiisakereba, ookii no o sashiagemasu.	"If the size is small, I'll give you a big(ger) one."
Moshi ten'ki ga warukereba, aruku yori kuruma ni notta hoo ga ii desu ne.	"Provided that the weather is bad, we'd better ride in a car than walk."
Atsukereba, nomimono wa tsumetai mono no hoo ga ii deshoo.	"If it is hot, cold drinks may be preferable."

The negative provisional form of an Adjective "if something is not so" is formed by transforming the plain negative form of an Adjective, which is the combination of the KU form of an Adjective plus the Extender *nai*. The Extender *nai* is the plain equivalent of the Extender *arimasen*. The BA form of the Extender *nai* is formed in the same way as that of Adjectives.

Adjective(-*ku*) + *nai* ⟶ Adjective(-*ku*) + *nakereba*

shiroku nai	⟶	shiroku nakereba	"if it is not white"
hikuku nai	⟶	hikuku nakereba	"if someone is not short"
nagaku nai	⟶	nagaku nakereba	"if it is not long"

Amari furuku nakereba, kaitai n desu ga.	"If it is not too old, I would like to buy it."
Koohii ga hoshiku nakereba, ocha wa doo desu ka?	"If you don't want coffee, how about tea?"

Likewise, the BA form -*takereba* of an adjectival Derivative -*tai* can follow a Verb with the meaning "if one wants to [do something]."

(moshi) + Verb + adjectival Derivative(-*ta kereba*), . . .

ikitakereba, . . .	"if one wants to go, . . . "
takushii ni noritakereba, . . .	"if one wants to take a taxi, . . . "
Kaeritakereba, kaette mo ii desu yo.	"If you want to go home, you can do so."

Kareeraisu o tsukuritakereba,   "If you want to cook curried rice,
  niku ya yasai o kai ni   you must go to buy meat,
  ikanakereba narimasen yo.   vegetables and the like."

13.4.10 *Aruite iku tsumori desu* means "I intend to walk (to the place)." The TE form of Verbs such as *norimasu* "ride," *arukimasu* "walk," *hashirimasu* "run" may be followed by the Extender *ikimasu, kimasu,* or *kaerimasu,* and the combinations mean how one goes, comes, goes back, or comes back, and so on. They may be translated into various English expressions.

notte		ikimasu	"go			riding"
aruite		kimasu	"come			walking"
hashitte		kaerimasu	"go (come) back			running"

Chikatetsu ni notte ikimasen ka?   "Won't you go by subway?"

Shin'juku Eki kara aruite kimashita.   "I walked here from Shinjuku Station."

Mainichi uchi made hashitte kaerimasu.   "I run home every day."

Hikooki ni notte ikitakatta desu.   "I wanted to go by airplane."

13.4.11 *Basu de ikeba, taishikan no sugu soba ni tomarimasu* means "If you go by bus, the bus will stop right near the embassy." *Ikeba* is the BA form, or the provisional form, of the Verb *iku* and occurs as a nonfinal Predicate of the provisional clause meaning "if one does such and such, . . ."

The BA form of Verbs is constructed in the following ways:

   1. Vowel Verb . . . Stem form plus *-reba*

ake-masu	⟶	ake-ru	⟶	ake-reba
deki-masu	⟶	deki-ru	⟶	deki-reba
de-masu	⟶	de-ru	⟶	de-reba
i-masu	⟶	i-ru	⟶	i-reba
kurabe-masu	⟶	kurabe-ru	⟶	kurabe-reba
oki-masu	⟶	oki-ru	⟶	oki-reba
oshie-masu	⟶	oshie-ru	⟶	oshie-reba
shime-masu	⟶	shime-ru	⟶	shime-reba

   2. Consonant Verb . . . Base form plus *-eba*

fur-imasu	⟶	fur-u	⟶	fur-eba
hashir-imasu	⟶	hashir-u	⟶	hashir-eba
magar-imasu	⟶	magar-u	⟶	magar-eba
nor-imasu	⟶	nor-u	⟶	nor-eba
suwar-imasu	⟶	suwar-u	⟶	suwar-eba
tomar-imasu	⟶	tomar-u	⟶	tomar-eba
tsukur-imasu	⟶	tsukur-u	⟶	tsukur-eba
wakar-imasu	⟶	wakar-u	⟶	wakar-eba
ara-imasu	⟶	ara-u	⟶	ara-eba
i-imasu	⟶	i-u	⟶	i-eba
nara-imasu	⟶	nara-u	⟶	nara-eba
tetsuda-imasu	⟶	tetsuda-u	⟶	tetsuda-eba
tsuka-imasu	⟶	tsuka-u	⟶	tsuka-eba

ma/t/-imasu	$\longrightarrow$	ma/t/-u	$\longrightarrow$	mat-eba
ta/t/-imasu	$\longrightarrow$	ta/t/-u	$\longrightarrow$	tat-eba
aruk-imasu	$\longrightarrow$	aruk-u	$\longrightarrow$	aruk-eba
ik-imasu	$\longrightarrow$	ik-u	$\longrightarrow$	ik-eba
suk-imasu	$\longrightarrow$	suk-u	$\longrightarrow$	suk-eba
tsuk-imasu	$\longrightarrow$	tsuk-u	$\longrightarrow$	tsuk-eba
hana/s/-imasu	$\longrightarrow$	hanas-u	$\longrightarrow$	hanas-eba
wata/s/-imasu	$\longrightarrow$	watas-u	$\longrightarrow$	watas-eba
kom-imasu	$\longrightarrow$	kom-u	$\longrightarrow$	kom-eba
nom-imasu	$\longrightarrow$	nom-u	$\longrightarrow$	nom-eba
yasum-imasu	$\longrightarrow$	yasum-u	$\longrightarrow$	yasum-eba
asob-imasu	$\longrightarrow$	asob-u	$\longrightarrow$	asob-eba
yob-imasu	$\longrightarrow$	yob-u	$\longrightarrow$	yob-eba
isog-imasu	$\longrightarrow$	isog-u	$\longrightarrow$	isog-eba
oyog-imasu	$\longrightarrow$	oyog-u	$\longrightarrow$	oyog-eba

3. Irregular Verb

shimasu	$\longrightarrow$	sur-u	$\longrightarrow$	sur-eba
kimasu	$\longrightarrow$	kur-u	$\longrightarrow$	kur-eba

$$(moshi)+(Noun+ga)+ \begin{cases} \textbf{Verb}(\textit{-reba}), \ldots \\ \quad \text{or} \\ \textbf{Verb}(\textit{-eba}), \ldots \end{cases}$$

(moshi) dekireba, . . .	"if possible, . . . "
(moshi) isogeba, . . .	"if you hurry, . . . "
(moshi) michi ga komeba, . . .	"if the streets are crowded, . . . "

Dekireba, gin'koo no mae ni tomatte kudasai. — "If possible, please stop in front of the bank."

Aruite ikeba, san'jippun kakaru hazu desu yo. — "If you go by walking, it should take thirty minutes."

Nihon'go ga wakareba, Nihon o yoku shiru koto ga dekimasu. — "If you understand the Japanese language, you will be able to know Japan better."

Sono kado o magareba, sugu eki desu yo. — "If you turn that corner, the station is right there."

Moshi ame ga fureba, tenisu wa shimasen. — "If it should rain, we are not going to play tennis."

The negative provisional form of Verbs "if one does not do such and such" is made by transforming the plain negative form of the Verb into the BA form of the adjectival Derivative -*nai*.

Pre-Nai form of Verb+ -*nai* $\longrightarrow$ **Pre-Nai form of Verb+ -*nakereba***

ikanai	$\longrightarrow$	ikanakereba	"if I don't go"
komanai	$\longrightarrow$	komanakereba	"if it doesn't get crowded"

tomaranai	⟶	tomaranakereba	"if it doesn't stop"
shinai	⟶	shinakereba	"if it doesn't do"
oshienai	⟶	oshienakereba	"if you don't teach"

Chikatetsu de iku koto ga dekinakereba, takushii ni notte ikimashoo.	"If we cannot go by subway, let's go by taxi."
Ame ga furanakereba, ashita no hoo ga ii desu.	"Tomorrow will be better if it doesn't rain."

13.4.12 *Sugu soba ni tomarimasu* is "It stops right near (the embassy)." The Verb *tomarimasu* is an intransitive Verb meaning "stop" or "come to a halt." The place Noun indicating the place where something stops may be followed by the Relational *ni* or *de*. As explained in Note 9.4.3, *ni* is used when the location is stressed, while *de* is used to emphasize the action. Therefore, when a train or a bus stops at a station or a bus stop, the Relational *ni* will be used.

Koko de tomatte kudasai.	"Please stop here."
Kyuukoo wa kono eki ni tomarimasu ka?	"Does an express stop at this station?"
Basu wa juuji gofun ni kono basutei ni tomarimasu.	"The bus will stop at this bus stop at ten-o-five."

13.4.13 *Hora* means "Look!" "Here!" or "Hey!" and is used to catch the attention of others. Not unlike the American use of "Hey!" this term has limited usage, and would not be used toward a superior.

13.4.14 *Akai* is an Adjective meaning "is red." Here are some Adjectives of color:

akai	"is red"	aoi	"is blue"
shiroi	"is white"	kiiroi*	"is yellow"
kuroi	"is black"	chairoi*	"is brown"

*These Adjectives are derived from the Nouns *kiiro* and *chairo*. Therefore, "is yellow" and "is brown" may be expressed using their adjectival forms *kiiroi* (*desu*) and *chairoi* (*desu*) or Nouns of color *kiiro* and *chairo* plus *desu*.

Akai jidoosha ga hoshii desu.	"I want a red car."
Kutsu wa chairokute mo ii desu ka?	"Is it all right if the shoes are brown?"

When the names of color are expressed, *aka*, *shiro*, *kuro*, *ao*, *kiiro*, and *chairo* stand as Nouns describing colors.

Aka ga suki desu.	"I like red (color)."
Kinoo katta seetaa no iro wa kiiro desu.	"The color of the sweater I bought yesterday is yellow."

The Noun for "color" is iro, and *don'na iro* or *nani iro* are used to ask "what kind of color?" or "what color?"

Anata no kuruma wa nani iro desu ka?   "What color is your car?"

Don'na iro no kaado deshita ka?   "What color was the card?"

13.5   VOCABULARY

Presentation

交通	kootsuu	......	N	traffic
地下鉄	chikatetsu	......	N	subway (lit. underground railway)
こんで	kon'de	......	V	TE form of *komimasu* ← *komu*—get crowded (see 13.4.3)
自動車	jidoosha	......	N	automobile
トラック	torakku	......	N	truck
オートバイ	ootobai	......	N	motorcycle
みち	michi	......	N	street; road; way
を	o	......	R	through; along; at; in; on (see 13.4.4)

Dialog

木村	Kimura	......	N	family name
大使館	taishikan	......	N	embassy (cf. *taishi* "ambassador")
行かなければ	ikanakereba	......	V	BA form of *ikanai*—do not go (see 13.4.5)
なりません	narimasen	......	E	it won't do (see 13.4.5)
田中	Tanaka	......	N	family name
ばしょ	basho	......	N	location
なら	nara	......	C	if it is a ∼ (BA form of *desu* ← *da*) (see 13.4.6)
行けば	ikeba	......	V	if one goes (BA form of *iku*) (see 13.4.7)
教えて	oshiete	......	V	TE form of *oshiemasu* ← *oshieru*—teach; instruct; tell; show
ちかければ	chikakereba	......	A	if it is near (BA form of *chikai*) (see 13.4.9)
すぐ（そば）	sugu (soba)	......	Adv.	right (near); immediately
とまります	tomarimasu	......	V	stop (normal form of *tomaru*) (intransitive Verb) (see 13.4.12)
おりれば	orireba	......	V	if one gets off (BA form of *oriru*)
わかります	wakarimasu	......	V	find (normal form of *wakaru*)

バス停	basutei	. . . . . .	N	bus stop
とおり	toori	. . . . . .	N	avenue; street
かど	kado	. . . . . .	N	corner; turn
左	hidari	. . . . . .	N	left
まがります	magarimasu	. . . . . .	V	turn (normal form of *magaru*) (see 13.4.4)
ほら	hora	. . . . . .	SI	look!; there! (see 13.4.13)
あかい	akai	. . . . . .	A	is red (see 13.4.14)
自転車	jiten'sha	. . . . . .	N	bicycle
まっすぐ	massugu	. . . . . .	Adv.	straight
すると	suruto	. . . . . .	SI	thereupon; and just then
右	migi	. . . . . .	N	right
しろい	shiroi	. . . . . .	A	is white
入口	iriguchi	. . . . . .	N	entrance

Notes

すく	suku	. . . . . .	V	get scarce (see 13.4.3)
出口	deguchi	. . . . . .	N	exit
なければ	-nakereba	. . . . . .	Da	BA form of -*nai* (see 13.4.5)
なければ	nakereba	. . . . . .	E	BA form of *nai* (see 13.4.5)
なくて	-nakute	. . . . . .	Da	TE form of -*nai* (see 13.4.5)
あおい	aoi	. . . . . .	A	is blue
もし	moshi	. . . . . .	Adv.	if; provided (see 13.4.9)
ならば	naraba	. . . . . .	C	(see 13.4.6)
くろい	kuroi	. . . . . .	A	is black
たければ	-takereba	. . . . . .	Da	if one wants to (do) (BA form of -*tai*) (see 13.4.9)
きいろい	kiiroi	. . . . . .	A	is yellow (see 13.4.14)
ちゃいろい	chairoi	. . . . . .	A	is brown
あか	aka	. . . . . .	N	red
しろ	shiro	. . . . . .	N	white
くろ	kuro	. . . . . .	N	black
あお	ao	. . . . . .	N	blue
きいろ	kiiro	. . . . . .	N	yellow
ちゃいろ	chairo	. . . . . .	N	brown

13.6　KAN'JI

13.6.1　口　(1)　KOO　(2)　mouth; gate　(3)　forms the classifier 口
(4)　丨 冂 口　(5)　人口　(6)　shape of the mouth

13.6.2　町　(1)　*machi*　(2)　town; city　(3)　classifier 田 [rice paddy]
(4)　丨 口 冂 田 町 町　(5)　町へ行く、町の東、町中 [throughout the town]

13.6.3　電　(1)　DEN　(2)　lightning; electricity　(3)　classifier 雨 (あめ)
(4)　一 丆 戸 両 雨 雨 雨 雪 雪 雷 雷 電
(5)　電車、電気 [electricity]、電話 (わ)　(6)　falling rain 雨 with a streak of lightning

13.6.a　車 2.6.9　(1)　SHA　(2)　wheel; vehicle　(3)　forms the classifier 車
(4)　一 丆 冂 百 盲 車 車　(5)　自動車、電車、自転車

13.6.4　動　(1)　DOO　(2)　move　(3)　classifier ノ (力) (ちから) [power]
(4)　丿 二 千 千 甹 盲 車 重 重 動 動
(5)　動物園 (ぶつえん)、自動的 (てき) [automatic]、運動 (うん)　(6)　homonym 働; a standing man with a heavy thing on his back is the shape of 重; when power 力 is applied, then it moves

13.6.5　田　(1)　*ta* [*-da*]　(2)　rice field　(3)　forms the classifier 田
(4)　丨 口 冂 田 田　(5)　田中、山田　(6)　the shape of rice paddies

13.6.b　教 9.6.2　(1)　*oshi*(*emasu*); *oshi*(*eru*)　(2)　teach; instruct; inform; tell
(5)　日本語を教えます、みちを教えてください

13.6.6　左　(1)　*hidari*　(2)　left　(3)　classifier ナ (エ)　(4)　一 ナ 七 左 左
(5)　左手 (て) [left hand]　(6)　use a measure エ in the left hand

13.6.7　右　(1)　*migi*　(2)　right　(3)　classifier ナ (口)　(4)　丿 ナ 七 右 右
(5)　右手 (て) [right hand]　(6)　eat food 口 with the right hand ナ

13.6.8　入　(1)　*i*(*ru*); *i*(*reru*)　(2)　enter; insert　(3)　forms the classifier 入
(4)　丿 入　(5)　入(り)口

13.6.c　口 13.6.1　(1)　*kuchi* [*-guchi*]　(5)　入口 (いり)、出口、まど口、西口、東口、南口、北口

13.7   DRILLS

13.7.1 Transformation Drill

1. 京都は　きれいです。 —— 京都が　きれいなら、いっしょに　行って
　　　　　　　　　　　　　　　　　　みましょう。

2. その　店は　しずかです。 —— その　店が　しずかなら、いっしょに
　　　　　　　　　　　　　　　　　　行ってみましょう。

3. あなたは　ひまです。 —— あなたが　ひまなら、いっしょに　行って
　　　　　　　　　　　　　　　　　　みましょう。

4. いい　おてらです。 —— いい　おてらなら、いっしょに　行って
　　　　　　　　　　　　　　　　　　みましょう。

5. おもしろい　えいがです。 —— おもしろい　えいがなら、いっしょに
　　　　　　　　　　　　　　　　　　行ってみましょう。

6. にわが　ゆうめいです。 —— にわが　ゆうめいなら、いっしょに　行って
　　　　　　　　　　　　　　　　　　みましょう。

7. きれいな　公園です。 —— きれいな　公園なら、いっしょに　行って
　　　　　　　　　　　　　　　　　　みましょう。

8. にっこうは　大好きです。 —— にっこうが　大好きなら、いっしょに
　　　　　　　　　　　　　　　　　　行ってみましょう。

13.7.2 Transformation Drill

1. 大使館は　とおいです。 —— 大使館が　とおければ、行きたくありません。

2. その　えいがは　つまらないです。 —— その　えいがが　つまらなければ、行きたく
　　　　　　　　　　　　　　　　　　ありません。

3. 天気は　わるいです。 —— 天気が　わるければ、行きたくありません。

4. きっさ店は　うるさいです。 —— きっさ店が　うるさければ、行きたく
　　　　　　　　　　　　　　　　　　ありません。

5. みちが　せまいです。 —— みちが　せまければ、行きたくありません。

6. 時間が　おそいです。 —— 時間が　おそければ、行きたくありません。

7. 自転車が　ないです。 —— 自転車が　なければ、行きたくありません。

8. えいがは　古いです。 —— えいがが　古ければ、行きたくありません。

13.7.3 Transformation Drill

1. 十五番の　バスに　のります。 —— 十五番の　バスに　のれば、すぐ　わかります。

2. 大使館に　行きます。 —— 大使館に　行けば、すぐ　わかります。

3. しゃしょうに　聞きます。　　　　　　⟶　しゃしょうに　聞けば、すぐ　わかります。

4. この　本を　読みます。　　　　　　　⟶　この　本を　読めば、すぐ　わかります。

5. うちへ　かえります。　　　　　　　　⟶　うちへ　かえれば、すぐ　わかります。

6. 図書館で　しらべます。　　　　　　　⟶　図書館で　しらべれば、すぐ　わかります。

7. 井上さんに　あいます。　　　　　　　⟶　井上さんに　あえば、すぐ　わかります。

8. 四つ目の　バス停で　おります。　　　⟶　四つ目の　バス停で　おりれば、すぐ

　　　　　　　　　　　　　　　　　　　　　　わかります。

9. ぼくの　うちへ　来ます。　　　　　　⟶　ぼくの　うちへ　来れば、すぐ　わかります。

10. 田中さんに　電話します。　　　　　　⟶　田中さんに　電話すれば、すぐ　わかります。

13.7.4 Transformation Drill

1. カレーライスは　好きじゃありません。⟶　カレーライスが　好きじゃなければ、
　　作りません。　　　　　　　　　　　　　　作りません。

2. びょう気ではありません。　　　　　⟶　びょう気でなければ、りょこうに
　　りょこうに　行きます。　　　　　　　　行きます。

3. セーターは　きいろではありません。⟶　セーターが　きいろでなければ、ほしく
　　ほしくありません。　　　　　　　　　　ありません。

4. わかくありません。　　　　　　　　⟶　わかくなければ、から手を　習うことは
　　から手を　習うことは　できません。　　　できません。

5. おそくありません。　　　　　　　　⟶　おそくなければ、あるいて行きましょう。
　　あるいて行きましょう。

6. 地下鉄は　はやくありません。　　　⟶　地下鉄が　はやくなければ、タクシーで
　　タクシーで　行きましょう。　　　　　　行きましょう。

13.7.5 Response Drill

1. うちへ　かえりたいんですが。　　　……　かえりたければ、かえっても　いいですよ。

2. わたしも　コーヒーを　　　　　　　……　のみたければ、のんでも　いいですよ。
　　のみたいんですが。

3. こんばん　出かけたいんですけど。　……　出かけたければ、出かけても　いいですよ。

4. あした　しごとを　休みたいんですが。……　休みたければ、休んでも　いいですよ。

5. この　にわで　あそびたいんですけど。……　あそびたければ、あそんでも　いいですよ。

6. もう三さつ　本を　かりたいんですが。……　かりたければ、かりても　いいですよ。

13.7.6 Transformation Drill

1. バスは　こみません。
   バスに　のって行きましょう。 ⟶ <u>バスが　こまなければ</u>、バスに　のって
   　　行きましょう。

2. いそぎません。
   おそくなりますよ。 ⟶ いそがなければ、おそくなりますよ。

3. まい日　日本語を　べんきょうしません。
   じょうずに　なりません。 ⟶ まい日　日本語を　べんきょうしなければ、
   　　じょうずに　なりません。

4. てきとうな　本が　見つかりません。
   図書館員に　聞いてください。 ⟶ てきとうな　本が　見つからなければ、
   　　図書館員に　聞いてください。

5. あした　うちに　いません。
   たぶん　大学に　います。 ⟶ あした　うちに　いなければ、たぶん
   　　大学に　います。

6. しゅくだいは　ありません。
   自分で　べんきょうしてください。 ⟶ しゅくだいが　なければ、自分で
   　　べんきょうしてください。

7. 林さんは　手つだいません。
   だれが　手つだいますか。 ⟶ 林さんが　手つだわなければ、　だれが
   　　手つだいますか。

8. 日本語が　できません。
   えい語で　はなしても　いいです。 ⟶ 日本語が　できなければ、えい語で
   　　はなしても　いいです。

9. よく　わかりません。
   先生に　うかがった　ほうが　いいです。 ⟶ よく　わからなければ、先生に
   　　うかがった　ほうが　いいです。

10. あめが　ふりません。
    出かけるつもりです。 ⟶ あめが　ふらなければ、
    　　出かけるつもりです。

13.7.7 Mixed Combination Drill

1. <u>学校の　入口です。</u>
   あの　かどに　あります。 ⟶ <u>学校の　入口なら</u>、あの　かどに
   　　あります。

2. 日本語です。
   テーラーさんが　一番　じょうずです。 ⟶ 日本語なら、テーラーさんが　一番
   　　じょうずです。

3. あの　店は　しずかです。
   あそこで　休みましょう。 ⟶ あの　店が　しずかなら、あそこで
   　　休みましょう。

4. 天気が　わるいです。
   うみへ　行きたくありません。 ⟶ 天気が　わるければ、うみへ　行きたく
   　　ありません。

5. 急行の　ほうが　はやいです。
   急行に　のって行きましょう。 ⟶ 急行の　ほうが　はやければ、急行に
   　　のって　行きましょう。

6. ここから　あるいて行きます。 ⎫→ ここから　あるいて行けば、十分ぐらい
　　十分ぐらい　かかります。 ⎭　　　　かかります。

7. その　かどを　まがります。 ⎫→ その　かどを　まがれば、すぐ
　　すぐ　わかりますよ。 ⎭　　　　わかりますよ。

8. 電車が　こんでいます。 ⎫→ 電車が　こんでいれば、グリーン車に
　　グリーン車に　しましょう。 ⎭　　　　しましょう。

9. ハワイと　カリフォルニアを ⎫→ ハワイと　カリフォルニアを　くらべれば、
　　　くらべます。 ⎭　　　ハワイの　ほうが　あついでしょう。
　　ハワイの　ほうが　あついでしょう。

10. まい日　日本語を　べんきょうします。 ⎫→ まい日　日本語を　べんきょうすれば、
　　じょうずに　なります。 ⎭　　　じょうずに　なります。

13.7.8 E-J Substitution Drill

A. <u>コーヒーなら</u>、ほしいです。

   1. if it is a red car　　　　　…… あかい　車なら、ほしいです。

   2. if it is a movie ticket　　　…… えいがの　きっぷなら、ほしいです。

   3. if it is a good thing　　　　…… いい　物なら、ほしいです。

   4. if it is curry and rice　　　…… カレーライスなら、ほしいです。

   5. if it is pretty　　　　　　　…… きれいなら、ほしいです。

   6. if that book is famous　　　…… その　本が　ゆうめいなら、ほしいです。

B. <u>ちかければ</u>、タクシーに　のって行きます。

   1. if it is cold　　　　　　　　…… さむければ、タクシーに　のって行きます。

   2. if it is inexpensive　　　　…… やすければ、タクシーに　のって行きます。

   3. if it is late　　　　　　　　…… おそければ、タクシーに　のって行きます。

   4. if it is all right　　　　　…… よければ、タクシーに　のって行きます。

   5. if the weather is bad　　　…… 天気が　わるければ、タクシーに
　　　　　　　　　　　　　　　　　　　　　のって行きます。

   6. if the office is far　　　　…… 事務所（むしょ）が　とおければ、タクシーに
　　　　　　　　　　　　　　　　　　　　　のって行きます。

C. <u>この　とおりを　まがれば</u>、すぐ　わかります。

   1. if you walk about three minutes　…… 三分ぐらい　あるけば、すぐ　わかります。

   2. if you speak in Japanese　…… 日本語で　はなせば、すぐ　わかります。

   3. if you ask a train conductor　…… しゃしょうに　聞けば、すぐ　わかります。

   4. if you read a newspaper　…… しんぶんを　読めば、すぐ　わかります。

5. if you check it at the library ...... 図書館で　しらべれば、すぐ　わかります。

6. if you get off at the third stop ...... 三つ目の　バス停で　おりれば、すぐ
　　　　わかります。

13.7.9 Transformation Drill

A. 1. フランス大使館へ　行きます。 ⟶ フランス大使館へ　行かなければ
　　　　なりません。

2. へやを　きれいに　します。 ⟶ へやを　きれいに　しなければなりません。

3. すぐ　いしゃを　よびます。 ⟶ すぐ　いしゃを　よばなければなりません。

4. 十分ぐらい　あるきます。 ⟶ 十分ぐらい　あるかなければなりません。

5. おさらを　たくさん　あらいます。⟶ おさらを　たくさん　あらわなければ
　　　　なりません。

6. あしたまでに　本を　かえします。⟶ あしたまでに　本を　かえさなければ
　　　　なりません。

7. 駅で　ともだちに　あいます。 ⟶ 駅で　ともだちに　あわなければ
　　　　なりません。

8. おみやげを　持って来ます。 ⟶ おみやげを　持って来なければなりません。

B. 1. 辞書は　新しいです。 ⟶ 辞書は　新しくなければなりません。

2. コーヒーは　あついです。 ⟶ コーヒーは　あつくなければなりません。

3. 子どもが　かよう　学校は
　　ちかいです。 ⟶ 子どもが　かよう　学校は
　　　　ちかくなければ　なりません。

4. レポートは　もうすこし
　　ながいです。 ⟶ レポートは　もうすこし　ながくなければ
　　　　なりません。

5. しけんの　紙は　しろいです。 ⟶ しけんの　紙は　しろくなければ
　　　　なりません。

6. スポーツを　する
　　ばしょは　ひろいです。 ⟶ スポーツを　する　ばしょは
　　　　ひろくなければなりません。

7. くつずみは　くろいです。 ⟶ くつずみは　くろくなければ　なりません。

8. せつめいは　くわしいです。 ⟶ せつめいは　くわしくなければなりません。

C. 1. のり物は　自動車です。 ⟶ のり物は　自動車でなければなりません。

2. のるのは　十五番の　バスです。⟶ のるのは　十五番の　バスでなければ
　　　　なりません。

3. 店員の　ことばは　ていねいです。⟶ 店員の　ことばは　ていねいで　なければ
　　　　なりません。

4. ペンは　あかいのです。 ⟶ ペンは　あかいのでなければ　なりません。

5. 先生は　中国人です。　　　　　—→　先生は　中国人でなければ　なりません。

6. アルバイトを　するのは　　　　—→　アルバイトを　するのは　なつ休み
　　なつ休みです。　　　　　　　　　　でなければ　なりません。

7. 買う　きっぷは　大阪行です。　—→　買う　きっぷは　大阪行でなければ
　　　　　　　　　　　　　　　　　　　　なりません。

8. あさごはんは　パンと　コーヒー —→　あさごはんは　パンと　コーヒーで
　　です。　　　　　　　　　　　　　　　なければ　なりません。

13.7.10 Response Drill

1. 大使館へ　行かなければ　　　　……　いいえ、行かなくても　いいです。
　　なりませんか。

2. 先生は　中国人でなければ　　　……　いいえ、中国人でなくても　いいです。
　　なりませんか。

3. せつめいは　ながくなければ　　……　いいえ、ながくなくても　いいです。
　　なりませんか。

4. グリーン車じゃなければ　　　　……　いいえ、グリーン車じゃなくても　いいです。
　　なりませんか。

5. あしたまでに　おかねを　　　　……　いいえ、かえさなくても　いいです。
　　かえさなければなりませんか。

6. カレーライスは　　　　　　　　……　いいえ、からくなくても　いいです。
　　からくなければなりませんか。

7. かいしゃに　電話を　　　　　　……　いいえ、かけなくても　いいです。
　　かけなければなりませんか。

8. 自転車の　いろは　　　　　　　……　いいえ、あかでなくても　いいです。
　　あかでなければなりませんか。

13.7.11 Transformation Drill

A.　1. 自転車に　のりましょう。　　　—→　自転車に　のって行きましょう。

　　2. 出口まで　あるきました。　　　—→　出口まで　あるいて行きました。

　　3. 大学の　前まで　はしりました。—→　大学の　前まで　はしって行きました。

　　4. 事務所まで　タクシーに　　　　—→　事務所まで　タクシーに
　　　　のりませんか。　　　　　　　　　のって行きませんか。

　　5. バス停まで　はしりましょう。　—→　バス停まで　はしって行きましょう。

B.　1.　天気が　いいから、あるきます。　──→　天気が　いいから、あるいてかえります。

　　2.　まい日　バスに　のります。　──→　まい日　バスに　のってかえります。

　　3.　うちの　前まで　車に　　　　　──→　うちの　前まで　車に　のってかえりました。
　　　　のりました。

　　4.　公園の　中を　あるきましょう。　──→　公園の　中を　あるいてかえりましょう。

　　5.　大使館の　そばを　はしりました。──→　大使館の　そばを　はしってかえりました。

C.　1.　あの　かどまで　はしりました。　──→　あの　かどまで　はしって来ました。

　　2.　ひこうきに　のります。　──→　ひこうきに　のって来ます。

　　3.　三つ目の　かどまで　　　　　　──→　三つ目の　かどまで　あるいて来ましたか。
　　　　あるきましたか。

　　4.　その　とおりを　二十メートル　──→　その　とおりを　二十メートルぐらい
　　　　ぐらい　はしりました。　　　　　　　　はしって来ました。

　　5.　タクシーに　のってください。　──→　タクシーに　のって来てください。

13.7.12 Substitution Drill

あの　みちを　あるいて行きます。

　1.　この　とおり　　　　　　　……　この　とおりを　あるいて行きます。

　2.　あの　たて物の　うしろ　……　あの　たて物の　うしろを　あるいて行きます。

　3.　その　自動車の　前　　　……　その　自動車の　前を　あるいて行きます。

　4.　はしって来ました　　　　……　その　自動車の　前を　はしって来ました。

　5.　公園の　中　　　　　　　……　公園の　中を　はしって来ました。

　6.　あの　せまい　みち　　　……　あの　せまい　みちを　はしって来ました。

　7.　まがってください　　　　……　あの　せまい　みちを　まがってください。

　8.　三つ目の　かど　　　　　……　三つ目の　かどを　まがってください。

13.7.13 Expansion Drill

　1.　あるいて行きます。　　　……　あるいて行きます。

　　　五十メートルぐらい　　　……　五十メートルぐらい　あるいて行きます。

　　　バス停まで　　　　　　　……　バス停まで　五十メートルぐらい　あるいて行きます。

　　　大学の　そばから　　　　……　大学の　そばから　バス停まで　五十メートルぐらい
　　　　　　　　　　　　　　　　　　あるいて行きます。

　2.　はしってかえりました。　……　はしってかえりました。

　　　まっすぐ　　　　　　　　……　まっすぐ　はしってかえりました。

　　　うちまで　　　　　　　　……　うちまで　まっすぐ　はしってかえりました。

	あの　かどから	……　あの　かどから　うちまで　まっすぐ　はしって 　　　　かえりました。
3.	とまりますか。	……　とまりますか。
	前に	……　前に　とまりますか。
	大使館の	……　大使館の　前に　とまりますか。
	十五番の　バスは	……　十五番の　バスは　大使館の　前に　とまりますか。
4.	休みましょう。	……　休みましょう。
	あそこで	……　あそこで　休みましょう。
	しずかなら	……　しずかなら、あそこで　休みましょう。
	あの　きっさ店が	……　あの　きっさ店が　しずかなら、あそこで　休みましょう。
5.	買いたいです。	……　買いたいです。
	その　さんこう書を	……　その　さんこう書を　買いたいです。
	くわしければ	……　くわしければ、その　さんこう書を　買いたいです。
	せつめいが	……　せつめいが　くわしければ、その　さんこう書を 　　　　買いたいです。
6.	あります。	……　あります。
	左に	……　左に　あります。
	その　店は	……　その　店は　左に　あります。
	あるいて行けば	……　あるいて行けば、その　店は　左に　あります。
	この　とおりを	……　この　とおりを　あるいて行けば、その　店は　左に 　　　　あります。

13.7.14 E-J Response Drill

1. どんな　いろの　自動車に　のって来ましたか。
   in a red car　　　　　　　　　　　　　……　あかい　自動車に　のって来ました。
2. 東京行の　バスは　どこに　とまりますか。
   near that white building　　　　　　　……　あの　しろい　たて物の　そばに
   　　　　　　　　　　　　　　　　　　　　　　とまります。
3. あおい　車は　どこへ　行きましたか。
   turned to the left at the second corner　……　二つ目の　かどを　左へ　まがりました。
4. 十五番の　バスの　バス停は　どこですか。
   in front of the entrance of the department　……　デパートの　入口の　前です。
   　　store

5.　あした　うみへ　行きましょうか。

　　yes, if the weather is good　　　　　……　ええ、天気が　よければ、
　　　　　　　　　　　　　　　　　　　　　　　行きましょう。

6.　火曜日に　出かけることが　できますか。

　　no, if it is Tuesday　　　　　　　　……　いいえ、火曜日なら、出かけることが
　　　　　　　　　　　　　　　　　　　　　　　できません。

7.　タクシーに　のって行きますか。

　　yes, if the train is crowded　　　　……　はい、電車が　こんでいれば、タクシーに
　　　　　　　　　　　　　　　　　　　　　　　のって行きます。

8.　あした　かまくらへ　行きませんか。

　　yes, if you want to go　　　　　　　……　ええ、あなたが　行きたければ、行きましょう。

13.7.15 Substitution Drill（Review）

大使館へ　行く　みちを　教えてください。

1.　木村さんが　駅に　つく　時間　　　……　木村さんが　駅に　つく　時間を　教えて
　　　　　　　　　　　　　　　　　　　　　　　ください。

2.　電車が　こんでいない　時間　　　　……　電車が　こんでいない　時間を　教えて
　　　　　　　　　　　　　　　　　　　　　　　ください。

3.　この　急行が　とまる　駅　　　　　……　この　急行が　とまる　駅を　教えて
　　　　　　　　　　　　　　　　　　　　　　　ください。

4.　大阪行が　出る　所　　　　　　　　……　大阪行が　出る　所を　教えてください。

5.　田中先生が　教えている　大学の　　……　田中先生が　教えている　大学の　ばしょを
　　　ばしょ　　　　　　　　　　　　　　　　　教えてください。

6.　あなたが　行った　びじゅつ館の　名前　……　あなたが　行った　びじゅつ館の　名前を
　　　　　　　　　　　　　　　　　　　　　　　教えてください。

7.　かずおさんの　しらべた　もんだい　……　かずおさんの　しらべた　もんだいを
　　　　　　　　　　　　　　　　　　　　　　　教えてください。

8.　さんこう書を　買った　本屋の　名前　……　さんこう書を　買った　本屋の　名前を
　　　　　　　　　　　　　　　　　　　　　　　教えてください。

13.8　EXERCISES

13.8.1 Insert an appropriate Relational in each blank:

　　1.　あかい　自動車（　　）　大使館（　　）　前（　　）　とまりました。

　　2.　せまい　みち（　　）　はしらないでください。

3. 田中さん（　　）　あの　ちゃいろい　たて物（　　）　そば（　　）　たって
   いる　人です。

4. 三つ目（　　）　かど（　　）　右（　　）　まがりましょう。

5. バス（　　）　地下鉄（　　）　のって来ます。

6. この　とおり（　　）　タクシー（　　）　行けば、二十分ぐらいです。

13.8.2 Express the following ideas in Japanese:

1. Please turn to the right at the fourth corner.

2. If you go riding on that bus, the embassy is in front of the next stop.

3. If it rains, I won't come.

4. If the coffee is cold, I'll make it hotter.

5. Mr. Tanaka does not come walking down that street. He comes riding a bicycle.

6. Please walk straight about two hundred meters down this street.

7. Please tell me the way to the station.

8. I have to arrive at the embassy by two o'clock.

13.8.3 Direct the way to your home or dormitory from where you are now.

13.8.4 Using the illustration below, tell the way to:

    a. coffee shop b. Tanaka residence c. post office d. bookstore e. bus stop

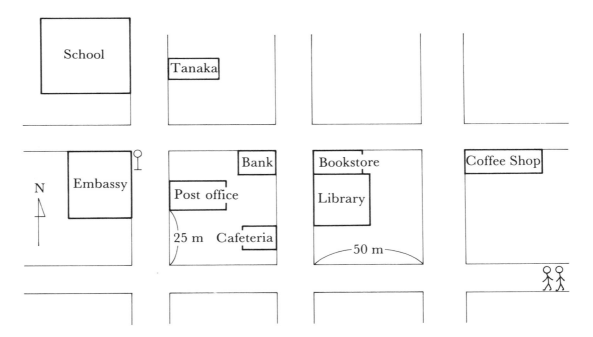

13.8.5 Complete the following sentences:

1. はやい　しんかん線なら、＿＿＿＿＿＿＿＿＿＿＿。
2. おそくなれば、＿＿＿＿＿＿＿＿＿＿＿。
3. あの　かどを　まがれば、＿＿＿＿＿＿＿＿＿＿。
4. 電車が　すいていれば、＿＿＿＿＿＿＿＿＿＿。
5. 沖縄へ　行きたければ、＿＿＿＿＿＿＿＿＿＿。
6. きっぷが　ほしければ、＿＿＿＿＿＿＿＿＿＿。
7. ＿＿＿＿＿＿＿＿＿＿ば、二時間で　行くことが　できます。
8. ＿＿＿＿＿＿＿＿＿＿ければ、車に　のって行くつもりですけど。
9. ＿＿＿＿＿＿＿＿＿＿なら、よく　知っていますよ。
10. ＿＿＿＿＿＿＿＿＿＿なければなりません。

13.8.6 Write the following underlined *hiragana* in *kan'ji*:

1. でんしゃや　じどうしゃが　たてものの　まえを　はしっています。
2. みぎにも　ひだりにも　くるまが　とまっています。
3. とうきょうは　じんこうが　おおいです。
4. いりぐちか　でぐちを　おしえてください。
5. たなかさんの　すんでいる　まちは　どちらですか。

13.8.7 Write the following in *katakana*:

1. torakku　2. ootobai　3. basu　4. takushii

13.8.8 When can you use: (1) *hora*, (2) *chotto*, or (3) *sumimasen* in calling for someone's attention? Use concrete examples involving no. 1, no. 2, or no. 3.

13.9 SITUATIONAL AND APPLICATION CONVERSATION

13.9.1 Direction to the U.S. Embassy

A stranger and an employee at a store talk about the way to the U.S. Embassy. The stranger does not know the direction.

The employee at the bakery gives the directions to the stranger.

The stranger would like to know how long it takes to get there by taxi.

The employee answers that if the stranger goes by taxi, it will take about seven minutes, but it will take twenty minutes by bus.

13.9.2 In a taxi

A taxi driver asks where his passenger wants to go.

The passenger says he wants to go to Shinjuku.

Arriving at the Shinjuku district, the passenger directs the driver: turn to the left at the next corner and go straight for three hundred meters.

The driver says he cannot turn to the left at that corner.

Then the passenger asks the driver to stop in front of a tobacco store near the corner.

13.9.3 Carry on a conversation acting as a taxi driver and his passenger going to a particular destination.

13.9.4 Direct the way to your house for someone who is going to visit you.

13.9.5 An'doo: Baba san, anata no iu tabakoya wa eki no soba no desu ka?

Baba: Chigaimasu yo. Hora, itsumo Hayashi san ga kau tabakoya ga aru deshoo?

An'doo: Aa, wakarimashita.

13.9.6 Masao: Totemo hayai hikooki desu nee.

Hiroko: Doko desu ka?

Masao: Hora, asoko desu yo. Hora!

13.9.7 Small child: Okaasan, kono mise ni wa nai yo.

Mother: Iie, arimasu yo. Hora, asoko ni aru deshoo.

Small child: Doko?

Mother: Hora, mado no ue!

LESSON 14
INTRODUCTION TO CORRESPONDENCE

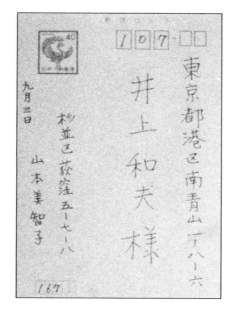

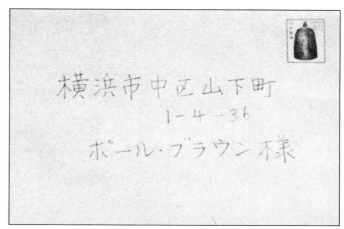

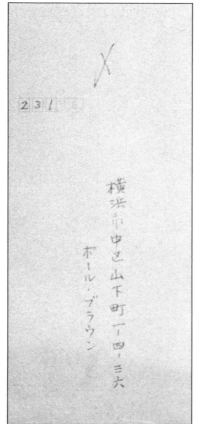

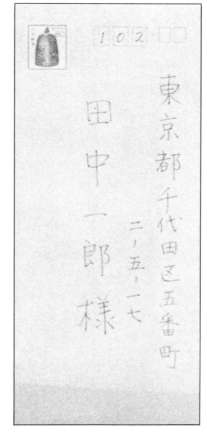

手紙[1]

14.1　PRESENTATION

あつくなりましたが、お元気ですか。

さっそくですが[2]、来月の　一日と　二日、富士山に

のぼるつもりです。　パターソンさんも　いらっしゃい

ませんか。　ぼくの　ほかに　山田さんと　石井さんも

行くはずです。

電車の　きっぷを　買わなければなりませんから、今月の

二十八日までに　電話で　返事を　くだされば、つごうが

いいんですが[3]。

ぼくの　電話番号は　四五一一五八九二です。

では、よい　返事を　待っています。

　　　　　　　　　　　　　さようなら

　　　　　　　　　　　　　　木下

七月二十四日

パターソン様

14.2　DIALOG

木下　　　「木下です。」

パターソン　「もしもし、パターソンですが₃、手紙を　ありがとうございました。」

木下　　　「あ、パターソンさん、　待っていました。　いっしょに　行きますか。」

パターソン　「ええ、ぜひ　つれて行ってください₄。」

木下　　　「それは　よかった₄。くわしい　ことは　二十九日に　なれば、わかるはず
　　　　　　ですから。」

パターソン　「じゃあ、あう　時間や　場所は　あとで　知らせてください。」

木下　　　「ええ、知らせます。　山の　上は　かなり　さむいから、ぼくは　ウインド
　　　　　　ブレーカー₅や　セーターを　持って行くつもりです。　パターソンさんも
　　　　　　セーターや　ジャンパーを　持って行って行った　ほうが　いいですよ。」

パターソン　「おべんとうは？」

木下　　　「出かける　日の　よるの　べんとうは　持って行かなければなりませんね。
　　　　　　おかしや　くだ物は　いっしょに　買いますから、　持って来なくても　いい
　　　　　　ですけど…₃。」

パターソン　「わかりました。」

14.3　Pattern of Letters

1（Opening）＋2（Preamble）＋3（Main Text—3a the start＋3b main body＋3c the ending）
＋4（Ending）＋5（Date）＋6（Sender's Name）＋7（Addressee）＋8（Postscript）

1.　　*Ogen'ki desu ka?*
　　　Otegami arigatoo gozaimashita.
　　　Tegami arigatoo.

2.　　Reference to season or weather
　　　Reference to the addressee's and his/her family members' health
　　　Reference to the sender's own current or recent state
　　　Apology for his/her negligence in corresponding with the addressee

3a.　*Sassoku desu ga,*　　　　''I will come to the point at once.''
　　　Jitsu wa,　　　　　　　''In reality,'' ''The fact is . . .''
　　　Tsukimashite wa,　　　　''On (that matter),'' ''On (this subject),'' ''As a matter of fact''
　　　Sate,　　　　　　　　　''Now,'' ''Well,'' ''And''

3b.　Reference to the main content

3c.   *Dewa, yoi hen'ji o matte imasu.*

Pray for the addressee's and his/her family's health, message, etc.

4.   *Keigu*   "Sincerely yours," "Yours respectfully"
        Soosoo   "In haste"
        Kashiko   "Your obedient servant" (limited to female)
        Sayoonara   "Good-bye"
        Ogen'ki de   "Wishes for your health"

5.   *hizuke*   "date"

6.   *jibun no shimei*   "sender's name"

7.   *atena*   "addressee"

8.   *tsuishin*   "PS"

14.4   NOTES

14.4.1   Format for Letter Writing

In writing letters in Japanese, pairs of expressions are used, one at the beginning and one at the end, which convey certain meanings. Two such pairs are *Zen'ryaku* and *Soosoo*, *Haikei* and *Keigu*.

In the first pair, *Zen'ryaku* indicates "I omit preliminaries," and *Soosoo*, "I have done it in haste." Together they show that the letter was more rushed than the writer preferred, for whatever reasons. The second pair is more formal and polite. *Haikei* means "speak respectfully," and *Keigu*, "respectfully submitted by."

Dewa, ogen'ki de or *Sayoonara* may also be placed at the end of the letter meaning "please be spirited (in good health)" and "good-bye" respectively. The use of these two expressions is more informal, casual, and colloquial.

Sometime after the beginning of the letter, the writer moves into talk about the weather and greetings, for instance, *Samui mainichi desu ga, ogen'ki desu ka?* meaning "Every day has been cold, but are you doing well?" and *Gobusata shite imasu ga, sono go ikaga desu ka?* meaning "I have not been in correspondence with you for some time, but how have you been?"

Toriisogi yooken nomi de shitsurei shimasu is a more formal counterpart of *Soosoo*, but still implies the writer hasn't done justice to his letter writing. It literally means "I lost my etiquette by limiting myself to important business in such a rush."

14.4.2   *Sassoku desu ga, . . .* "I'll come to the point at once" is often used in telephone conversation or in correspondence. This expression is used frequently in Japanese because many Japanese think it is a lack of courtesy to start talking about the subject without giving sufficient (to the Japanese mind) preliminary remarks, such as comments on weather, health, and the like.

Nonabruptness

In Japanese there are various ways of introducing a main theme in conversation without being abrupt. This is done by means of various expressions which serve as a bridge between what is being said and what is being introduced. Some of them, like *Eeto* and *Anoo*, are used only in daily conversations.

1. *Sassoku desu ga* is used when the various greetings and preliminaries in conversation are being eliminated and the speaker is jumping right into his main business.

2. *Jitsu wa*, which has been discussed previously, means "as a matter of fact" and is used as a preamble to some explanation.

3. *Tokoro de* means "well," "now," "by the way" and is used to change the topic or shift gear into a related matter.

4. *Sate*—"now, well, so, and, however, but"—is used when the speaker is ready to cover the main theme.

5. *Eeto* shows that one is thinking, after which he will break the silence.

6. *Anoo*—"well"—also indicates thinking prior to introducing the main topic.

7. *Hanashi wa chigaimasu ga* means that the speaker is changing the topic of conversation. This expression may be rendered as "May I be allowed to change the topic?" *Hanashi* means "talk" and *chigaimasu* means "different." This expression has a very different meaning from *hanashi ga chigaimasu ga* which means either "the story is different" or "that's not what you said," "that's not what you promised me."

14.4.3 Softening

Ga appears several times in this lesson. In the phrase *Kudasareba, tsugoo ga ii n desu ga*, it functions in the way which has been described in previous lessons, stressing indirectness and softening a request: "It would be good, but, however...," with the content of the *ga* ending rather meaningless.

A different use of *ga* is seen in the phrase *Sassoku desu ga* which begins Kinoshita's letter to Patterson. Here *ga* has no meaning whatsoever and functions as a kind of bridge to the next clause, which is omitted; the other, then, is still allowed to finish the meaning.

Ga appears again in the first line of the telephone conversation, when Patterson introduces himself. *Kedo*—used in the last line of Kinoshita's utterance—functions in the same way as *ga*. It means "although," and also softens the air of command which accompanies a request.

Indirectness

When an American reads an answer by a certain date, he would feel quite comfortable expressing himself or herself with "Please let me know (or, I need to know) by the twenty-eighth." The Japanese traditionally would indicate it less directly. In this dialog, for example, the request is rendered as, "If you could give me an answer by telephone by the twenty-eighth of this month, it would be convenient." This could certainly be said in English without sounding strange, but conversely, the directness of the English alternatives above would be considered too direct in Japanese.

14.4.4 Hierarchical Expressions

It is apparent from this conversation that Kinoshita is a little bit superior to Patterson or a peer. For example Kinoshita used *ikimasu ka?* instead of *irasshaimasu ka?* and the plain form *yokatta*, which is used only toward an intimate friend, an inferior, or a close in-group associate. Likewise, Patterson used a more polite form than Kinoshita used, and Patterson is soon asking Kinoshita to take him along—*Ee, zehi tsurete itte kudasai*—whereas a superior speaking to an inferior could have said very simply "I'll go with you." The superior-inferior relationship, however, could be only psychologically relative to favor-giving and favor-receiving situations.

14.4.5 *Gairaigo* or Loan Words

Originally, Japan had only a limited vocabulary for abstract concepts, and such concepts have mainly come to be covered by Chinese compounds. Checking the Chinese character dictionary, we find that over 30 percent of such vocabulary items are Chinese compounds. However, such compounds have been thoroughly integrated into the Japanese language system and, from the Japanese point of view, are not regarded as foreign loan words anymore.

Today, it is words from the Portuguese, Spanish, Dutch, English, and sometimes German and French—that is, words from the West—which are normally considered to be foreign loan words. Such loan words are called *gairaigo* and are normally written in *katakana*. The Japanese phonetic system is used to adjust the foreign sounds, making, for instance, Taylor into Teeraa.

At the present time, foreign loan words are flooding Japan, and have even extended their jurisdiction over possessive forms, no longer being limited to nouns. For example, the English "my home" has become one word. *Maihoomushugi* refers to the principle of owning one's own home and devoting oneself to one's family and oneself (derived from "my home + ism"); *maihoomuzoku* refers to that group of people who advocate *maihoomushugi*. *Mooretsushugi*, hard working without paying attention to its consequence, is just the opposite in meaning of *maihoomushugi*. Similarly, *maikaazoku* refers to those who wish to, or in fact do, own their own automobiles.

14.5   VOCABULARY

Presentation

さっそく	sassoku	......	immediately (see 14.4.2)
のぼる	noboru	......	climb; go up
パターソン	Pataason	......	Patterson
いらっしゃいません	irasshaimasen	......	do not come; do not go (*irasshaimasu* is polite equivalent of *kimasu* or *ikimasu*)
返事	hen'ji	......	reply; response
木下	Kinoshita	......	family name

Dialog

こと	koto	......	matter; thing (intangible)
知らせて	shirasete	......	inform; let one know (TE form of *shiraseru*)
かなり	kanari	......	quite
ウインドブレーカー	uin'dobareekaa	......	windbreaker (jacket)
ジャンパー	jan'paa	......	casual jacket; jumper
べんとう	ben'too	......	packed lunch; meal to take out

14.6 EXERCISES

14.6.1 Read the following letter:

お手紙 ありがとうございました。 じつは、八月の はじめから 九州の ともだちの 所へ あそびに 行きます。 富士山には のぼったことが ありませんから、ぜひ 行きたいのですが、ざんねん*¹です。できれば、来年 のぼりたいです。

山田さんたちに よろしく*²。

では また—

七月二十六日　　　　　　　　　　　　　　　　　　　　　　　　　　　　　　　パターソン

木下様

　　　　*¹"pity; sorry"　　　*²"give my best regards to . . ."

14.6.2 Write the following letter in Japanese:

July 6

Dear Mr. Ishii:

How are you? It is hot and humid every day, isn't it?

If the weather is nice, Mr. Yamada and I are planning to go to the seaside on July 18. Won't you go with us? I cannot swim well, but Mr. Yamada can swim very well. How about you?

If it rains on the eighteenth, Mr. Yamada is supposed to come to my house. Please let me know by letter whether this is convenient.

So long,

Ikuo Watanabe

14.6.3 Write a letter in a Japanese way, answering the letter above:

Dear Mr. Watanabe: July 9, 1984

   Thank you very much for (your) letter. I love swimming, so I'd like to join you. Do I have to bring my packed lunch with me? What time and where are we going to meet? I'd like to know more about your plan. Is it all right if I call you up on the twelfth?

                                                            Yours,
                                                            Ishii

14.6.4 Write a letter inviting your friend to dinner, a movie, or *kabuki*.

14.6.5 Write a letter to your friend inquiring if you can visit him during the vacation.

14.6.6 Send a letter to your Japanese friend about your plans for next summer.

14.6.7 Write a letter to your Japanese friend asking her to join you for a mountain climbing trip.

   1.   You ask your friend if she has ever climbed mountains.

   2.   Tell her that if the weather is nice next Sunday, you intend to go to Mt. Fuji, and two friends of yours are supposed to go with you. One of them is Ms. Smith and the other is Mr. Yamada.

   3.   You are planning to take a jacket or a pullover since it is cold on the mountain and advise her to bring a meal for the departure night, should she decide to join you.

14.6.8 Japanese telephone numbers are often the object of word play, in the sense that the spoken sound of the collection of numbers carries a meaning. For example, the telephone number 141-4414 reads *iyoiyoyoiyo* which means "better and better." 874-5960 reads *hanashi gokuroo* meaning "Thank you for your talking." Take your own phone number and see if you can figure out something meaningful, reading from its Japanese translation. (1=*hi, i*; 2=*ni, fu*; 3=*sa, mi*; 4=*shi, yon, yo*; 5=*go*; 6=*ro, mu*; 7=*na, nana*; 8=*ya, ha*; 9=*ku, kyuu*; 10=*too*)

14.6.9 Explain the functions or meanings of the following italicized words and expressions:

   1.   *Sorosoro* shitsurei shimasu.

   2.   *Jitsu wa,* watashi wa . . .

   3.   *Chotto* shitsurei shimasu.

   4.   *Sassoku* desu ga, Katoo san . . .

   5.   *Eeto,* watashi wa . . .

   6.   *Anoo,* watashi wa . . .

   7.   *Hanashi wa chigaimasu ga,* . . .

14.6.10 Describe the customs you should follow when writing a letter in Japanese. Then, write a short letter following these customs.

LESSON 15
REVIEW AND APPLICATION

15.1   PATTERNS

15.1.1 Obligation ''have to''

   a. Verb

あしたは　しごとを　休ま		
四時に　ともだちに　あわ		
いろいろな　物を　買わ		
この　本を　いもうとに　わたさ		
いしゃを　よば		
かりた　教科書を　すぐ　かえさ	なければ	なりません
かないを　つれて行か		（いけません）
しゅくだいを　持って来		
はしを　つかわ		
まいばん　べんきょうし		
料理を　手つだわ		

   b. Adjective

学生が　多いから　教室は　ひろく		
カレーライスは　からく		
にくや　さかなは　新しく	なければ	なりません
子どもに　やる　本は　やさしく		（いけません）
せつめいは　くわしく		

   c. Noun＋Copula

ことばは　ていねい			
べんきょうする　へやは　しずか	で		なりません
花見に　行くのは　ゆうがた	じゃ	なければ	（いけません）
およぐのは　七月			
あう　所は　駅			

15.1.2 ''do not have to''

a.

いそが		
辞書を　持って来		
よし子さんに　電話し		
いそがしければ、手つだわ		
えい語で　はなさ		
タクシーを　よば		
まどを　あけ		

自動車は　あおく		いいです
へやは　大きく	なくても	かまいません
おみやげは　多く		
バス停が　ちかく		
のり物は　はやく		

店員は　女で		
作る　食べ物は　日本料理で		
のる　バスは　十五番で		
手紙は　あまり　ていねいで		
日本語が　とくいじゃ		

b.

…………………………………	なくても	いいです / かまいません	か
はい、…………………………	なくても	いいです / かまいません	
いいえ、…………………………	なければ	なりません（いけません）	

…………………………………	なければ	なりません（いけません）	か
はい、…………………………	なければ	なりません（いけません）	
いいえ、…………………………	なくても	いいです / かまいません	

15.1.3 Provisional Clause ''if''

a. Verb

あの　かどを　左へ　まがれば、	バス停は　右に　あります
地下鉄に　のって行けば、	十分ぐらいで　つきます
（もし）この　もんだいが　わかれば、	つぎの　もんだいは　やさしくなります
北海道と　九州を　くらべれば、	北海道の　ほうが　ひろいです
一時に　はじまれば、	五時までに　おわります
電車が　こまなければ、	電車で　来た　ほうが　いいですよ
（もし）およぐことが　できなければ、	山に　しましょうか
先生が　行かなければ、	あなたも　行っては　いけません
よし子さんは　図書館に　いなければ、	うちに　いるはずです
（もし）知らなければ、	こたえなくても　かまいません

b. Adjective

（もし）天気が　よければ、	さんぽに　行きましょう
辞書が　古ければ、	新しいのを　買った　ほうが　いいです
（もし）気分が　わるければ、	ここで　休んでください
たかければ、	そんな　物は　買わないでください
へやが　きたなければ、	きれいに　してください
（もし）しゅくだいが　なければ、	えいがを　見に　行きたいです
こうちゃが　ほしくなければ、	何が　ほしいですか
ちかくなければ、	タクシーに　のらなければなりません
（もし）せつめいが　くわしくなければ、	ほかの　さんこう書を　かりなければ　なりません
うるさくなければ、	あの　へやを　つかいましょう

c. Noun＋Copula

しごとが　たいへんなら、	手つだいましょうか
とんかつが　好きなら、	ごちそうしますよ
テニスなら、	よし子さんが　とくに　じょうずです
青木くんの　電話番号なら、	ぼくが　知っています
来月の　七日なら、	ひじょうに　つごうが　いいです
ゆうめいじゃなければ、	あまり　見たくありません
そこが　しずかじゃなければ、	しずかな　所を　さがしましょう
日曜日じゃなければ、	ぼくは　行くことが　できません
はやい　のり物でなければ、	一時までに　つきませんね
木村さんでなければ、	あの　人は　たぶん　小山さんでしょう

15.1.4 Superlative Expression

a. Noun

これ		教科書の		新しいです おもしろかったです
一郎くん		学生の この	なかで	せいが　ひくいです あたまが　いいです
これ この料理	は （が）	この 中国料理の		おいしいです たかいでしょう
アメリカ		せかい	一番	ゆたかな　国ですか
その　たて物		この　町 東京	で	大きいです ゆうめいです
七月		一年じゅう		むしあついです

$$(\ldots\ldots\ldots で)\ \left|\begin{array}{l}どれ\\だれ\\どの\ \sim\\何\\どこ\\いつ\end{array}\right|\ が\ \left|一番\right|\ \left|\begin{array}{l}\ldots\ldots\ldots\ldots\\\ldots\ldots\ldots\ldots\end{array}\right|\ か$$

日本料理（りょうり）		中国料理（りょうり）		西洋料理（せいようりょうり）	
これ		それ		あれ	
にっこう	と	京都	と	新潟（にいがた）	の　なかで、
みち子さん		よし子さん		けい子さん	（と）では、
日曜日（よう）		火曜日（よう）		木曜日（よう）	

$$\left|\begin{array}{l}日本料理（りょうり）\\それ\\京都\\よし子さん\\火曜日（よう）\end{array}\right|\ が\ \left|一番\right|\ \left|\begin{array}{l}好きです\\おもしろいです\\ゆうめいです\\せいが　たかいです\\つごうが　いいです\end{array}\right|$$

↓

………… …………	と	………… …………	と	………… …………	の　なかで、（と）では、

$$\left|\begin{array}{l}何\\どれ\\どこ\\だれ\\いつ\end{array}\right|\ が\ \left|一番\right|\ \left|\begin{array}{l}\ldots\ldots\ldots\ldots\ldots\\\ldots\ldots\ldots\ldots\ldots\end{array}\right|\ か$$

b. **Adjective**

この　なか			古い	本		これです
日本の　物			ほしい	物		カメラです
日本料理			作るのが やさしい	の		すきやきです
のり物の なか			はやい	の		ひこうきです
ぼくの 大学	で	一番	さかんな	スポーツ	は	じゅうどうです
この　島			しずかな	所		ここです
一年			あつい	きせつ		なつです
一日じゅう			いそがしい	時間		二時から 三時までです
学生の なか			よく べんきょうする	人		テーラーさんです
ともだちの なか			わかい	の		一郎くんです

↓

…………… …………	で	一番	………… …………	……… ………	は	どれです 何です どこです いつです だれです	か

c. **Verb**

おんがくを 聞く		スポーツを する		本を 読む	
中国料理を 作る	の　と	日本料理を 作る	の　と	西洋料理を 作る	の　（と）では、
先生に なる		いしゃに なる		店員に なる	

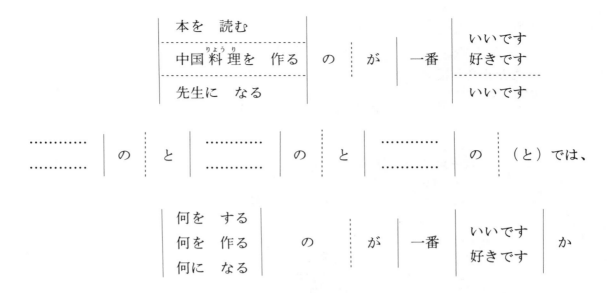

本を　読む				いいです
中国料理を　作る	の	が	一番	好きです
先生に　なる				いいです

……… | の | と | ……… | の | と | ……… | の | （と）では、

何を　する				いいです	
何を　作る	の	が	一番	好きです	か
何に　なる					

15.1.5 Comparative Expression

a. Noun

	より		の　ほうが	（ずっと）	
中国料理		西洋料理			おいしいです
あじ		かたち			いいです
さかな		にく			たかいです
ふね		ひこうき			はやいです
はる	より	あき	の　ほうが	（ずっと）	ひまです／いそがしいです
日曜日		土曜日			
どうぶつ園		びじゅつ館			好きです／ちかいです
山		うみ			
森さん		林さん			せいが　ひくいです／あたまが　いいです

↓

	と		と、／で(は)、／とで(は)、	どっち（の　ほう）が／どちら（の　ほう）が		か
………	と	………			………	か

b. Verb

	より		ほうが（ずっと）	
ローマ字で　こたえを　書く		ひらがなで　こたえを　書く		むずかしいです
フォークを　つかう		はしを　つかう		たいへんです
まどを　あける		ドアを　あける		すずしいです
いしゃに　なる		大学の　先生に　なる		いいです
東京に　すむ		京都に　すむ		たのしいです
ぎんこうで　はたらく	より	図書館で　はたらく	ほうが（ずっと）	
うちで　待つ		大学で　待つ		つごうが　いいです
北海道へ　行く		九州へ　行く		好きです
バスで　行く		タクシーに　のった		はやいです
たっている		いすに　すわった		いいです
ほかの　人が　料理する		あなたが　料理した		じょうずです

↓

……… ………	の	と	……… ………	の	と、 では、 とでは、	どっち（の　ほう）が どちら（の　ほう）が	……… ………	か

c. "had better"

	ほうが	いいです（よ）
いそいだ すぐ　うちへ　かえった ぐん人に　なった まどを　しめた しけんを　はじめた 三時に　また　来た		

大学で　しらべた		
東京駅で　おりた	ほうが	いいです（よ）
あの　先生に　あった		
自分で　作った		

15.1.6 Negative Comparison

a. Noun

	は		ほど	
カリフォルニア州		ニューヨーク州		さむくありません
この　本は		あなたの　本		おもしろくないです
ぼくの　うち		井上さんの　うち		大きくありません
うちの　いぬ		この　いぬ		小さくありません
大川さん	は	青木さん	ほど	美しくないです / わかくありません
この　公園		上野公園		ゆうめいじゃありません
わたしの　ことば		林さんの　ことば		ていねいではありません
ここの　コーヒー		きっさ店の　コーヒー		おいしくないんです
ラジオ		カメラ		ほしくありません
すきやき		てんぷら		好きじゃありません
日本料理		中国料理		とくいじゃありません

b. Verb

		は		ほど	
西洋料理					やさしくありません
かん字			あなたが　おもう		むずかしくないです
ジョージさんの　日本語		は	みんなが　いう	ほど	じょうずではありません
わたしの　かいわ			ポールさんが　おもう		おもしろくありません
東京を　けんぶつする	の		京都を　けんぶつする		たのしくないです
ピアノを　ひく			ギターを　ひく		とくいではありません

テニスを する		スケートを する		好きではありません
えいがを 見る		テレビを 見る		きらいではありません
しんぶんを 読む	の は	ざっしを 読む	ほど	むずかしくありません
はしを つかう		フォークを つかう		たいへんではないです
日本文学を しらべる		アメリカ文学を しらべる		

15.1.7 ''become,'' ''get,'' etc.

私		図書館員（としょかんいん）		
むすめ		いしゃ		
むすこ		ぐん人		
おとうと		ゆうめい	に	
へやの 中		きれい		
べんきょう		好き		
中国語	は（が）	じょうず		なります
せつめい		くわしく		
セーター		たかく		
ぼくの うち		新しく		
天気		よく		
かえる 時間		おそく		
しごと		いそがしく		

↓

⋯⋯⋯⋯	は（が）	何に	なりますか
⋯⋯⋯⋯		どう	

15.1.8 "make"

むすこ		ぐん人	
むすめ		いしゃ	
子ども		大学の　先生	に
あの　人	を	ともだち	
へや	（は）	しずか	
うち		るす	
国		ゆたか	に　　します
スポーツ		さかん	
教室（しつ）		ひろく	
サイズ		大きく	
コーヒー		あつく	
とんかつ		おいしく	

↓

………………	を（は）	何に	しますか
………………		どう	

15.2　OTHERS

15.2.1　Relational *o* with motion Verb

あの　かど		まがってください
		右へ　まがった　ほうが　いいですよ
この　とおり		二十メートルぐらい　行けば、すぐ　見つかります
図書館（としょかん）の　そば		はしっている　バスが　しんじゅく行です
町の　中	を	
あの　たばこ屋の　前		まっすぐ　あるいて行けば、パン屋は　右に　あります
大学の　中		あるいて来ました
公園（こうえん）		さんぽしましょう
この　みち		まっすぐ　行ってください

15.2.2 Relational *keredomo* "although"

この　へやは　むしあつい（です）		まどを　あけないでください
しけんは　みじかい（です）		あなたが　おもうほど　やさしくありません
ぼくの　うちは　新しくない（です）		とても　いい　うちです
えいがを　見たかった（です）		おかねが　ありませんでした
あの　店は　きれいです	けれども、けれど、けど、	この　店の　ほうが　しずかです
これは　おとうとの　本です		つかっても　かまいません
一郎くんの　うちへ　行きました		一郎くんは　るすでした
バスは　タクシーほど　はやくありません		バスに　のった　ほうが　いいですよ
辞書を　見ても　いい（です）		さんこう書を　見ては　だめです
これは　この　なかで　一番　たかかった（です）		あまり　よくないんです

15.3　REVIEW DRILLS

15.3.1 Transformation Drill

A.　<u>天気が　よければ、ぜひ　行きたいです。</u>

　1.　つごうが　よい　　　　……　つごうが　よければ、ぜひ　行きたいです。
　2.　きっぷが　やすい　　　……　きっぷが　やすければ、ぜひ　行きたいです。
　3.　あなたが　かまわない　……　あなたが　かまわなければ、ぜひ　行きたいです。
　4.　天気が　わるくない　　……　天気が　わるくなければ、ぜひ　行きたいです。
　5.　いそがしくない　　　　……　いそがしくなければ、ぜひ　行きたいです。
　6.　あめが　ふらない　　　……　あめが　ふらなければ、ぜひ　行きたいです。
　7.　びょう気じゃない　　　……　びょう気じゃなければ、ぜひ　行きたいです。
　8.　日曜日でない　　　　　……　日曜日でなければ、ぜひ　行きたいです。

B.　<u>右に　まがれば、すぐですよ。</u>

　1.　まっすぐ　行く　　　　……　まっすぐ　行けば、すぐですよ。

2.　タイプライターを　　……　タイプライターを　つかえば、すぐですよ。
　　つかう

3.　みんなで　手つだう　　……　みんなで　手つだえば、すぐですよ。

4.　四つ目で　おりる　　　……　四つ目で　おりれば、すぐですよ。

5.　ちかてつに　のる　　　……　ちかてつに　のれば、すぐですよ。

6.　百メートルぐらい　　　……　百メートルぐらい　あるけば、すぐですよ。
　　あるく

C.　大使館なら、よく　知っています。

1.　電話番号です　　　　　……　電話番号なら、よく　知っています。

2.　あかい　自動車です　　……　あかい　自動車なら、よく　知っています。

3.　やさしい　かん字です　……　やさしい　かん字なら、よく　知っています。

4.　田中さんに　あう　　　……　田中さんに　あう　時間なら、よく　知っています。
　　時間です

5.　スージーさんが　　　　……　スージーさんが　けっこんした　人なら、よく
　　けっこんした　人です　　　　　知っています。

6.　かどの　本屋です　　　……　かどの　本屋なら、よく　知っています。

15.3.2 Transformation Drill

A.　あそびに　行きたければ、行っても　いいです。

1.　ねる　　　　　　　　　……　ねたければ、ねても　いいです。

2.　タクシーに　のる　　　……　タクシーに　のりたければ、のっても　いいです。

3.　えい語を　つかう　　　……　えい語を　つかいたければ、つかっても　いいです。

4.　バイオリンを　ひく　　……　バイオリンを　ひきたければ、ひいても　いいです。

5.　しつもんする　　　　　……　しつもんしたければ、しても　いいです。

6.　しゅうまつに　あそぶ　……　しゅうまつに　あそびたければ、あそんでも
　　　　　　　　　　　　　　　　　いいです。

7.　のみ物を　持って来る　……　のみ物を　持って来たければ、持って来ても
　　　　　　　　　　　　　　　　　いいです。

8.　すこし　休む　　　　　……　すこし　休みたければ、休んでも　いいです。

B.　行きたくなければ、行かなくても　いいです。

1.　日本語で　はなす　　　……　日本語で　はなしたくなければ、はなさなくても
　　　　　　　　　　　　　　　　　いいです。

2.　みんなに　教える　　　……　みんなに　教えたくなければ、教えなくても
　　　　　　　　　　　　　　　　　いいです。

3. 手つだう　　　　　　　……　手つだいたくなければ、手つだわなくても　いいです。

4. 前に　すわる　　　　　……　前に　すわりたくなければ、すわらなくても
　　　　　　　　　　　　　　　　　いいです。

5. おかねを　かす　　　　……　おかねを　かしたくなければ、かさなくても
　　　　　　　　　　　　　　　　　いいです。

6. 料理する　　　　　　　……　料理したくなければ、しなくても　いいです。

7. あの　客に　あう　　　……　あの　客に　あいたくなければ、あわなくても
　　　　　　　　　　　　　　　　　いいです。

8. 私たちに　見せる　　　……　私たちに　見せたくなければ、見せなくても
　　　　　　　　　　　　　　　　　いいです。

15.3.3 Substitution and Transformation Drill

1. A：　おかしを　食べなければなりませんか。

　B：　いいえ、おかしじゃなくても　いいですよ。

　A：　じゃあ、わたしは　くだ物に　します。

　　1. カレーライスを　食べる、とんかつ　　2. コーヒーを　のむ、こうちゃ

　　3. この　本を　読む、その　本　　　　　4. あした　出かける、あさって

　　5. 食べ物を　買う、おさけ　　　　　　　6. こんしゅう　かえす、らいしゅう

2. A：　右と　左と、どっちが　いいですか。

　B：　左の　ほうが　もちろん　いいです。

　　1. みず、ビール、ほしいです　　　　　　2. あかい　車、しろい　車、たかいです

　　3. えんぴつ、ペン、いいです　　　　　　4. ギター、ピアノ、とくいです

　　5. フランス語、ドイツ語、じょうずです　6. じゅうどう、テニス、さかんです

15.4　REVIEW EXERCISES

15.4.1 Insert an appropriate Relational:

　　1. 山田さんの　くつは　わたし（　　）（　　）　大きいでしょう。

　　2. 料理の　なか（　　）、何（　　）作るの（　　）　一番　じょうずですか。

　　3. 図書館（　　）前（　　）左（　　）　まがってください。

　　4. 十番線（　　）出る　電車（　　）のって行けば、すぐ　わかりますよ。

　　5. 山（　　）行く（　　）うみ（　　）行った　ほう（　　）　おもしろいです。

　　6. いしゃ（　　）なる（　　）ぐん人（　　）　なりたかったんです。

　　7. あの　しろい　たて物（　　）前（　　）たっていて（　　）　いいですか。

8. 東京は　あなた（　　）　おもう（　　）　さむくありません。

9. 自分（　　）　作りたい（　　）、にくも　さかなも　やさいも　ないんです。

10. すきやき（　　）　てんぷら（　　）、どっち（　　）　いいですか。

11. てんぷら（　　）　ほう（　　）　いいです。

12. せかい（　　）　一番　小さい　国（　　）　どこですか。

13. 北（　　）　南（　　）　くらべるのは　むずかしいです。

14. 紙の　上（　　）　あるかないでください。

15. アメリカは　五十（　　）　州（　　）　なる　ひろい　国です。

16. 自転車は　この　みち（　　）　はしっては　いけません。

17. 私は　前は　日本料理（　　）　中国料理（　　）　ほう（　　）　好きでした（　　）、
　　　今は　日本料理（　　）　ほう（　　）　好き（　　）　なりました。

18. 「おひるは　何を　食べましょうか。」「わたしは　カレー（　　）　します。」

15.4.2 Connect each of the A-group expressions with appropriate B-group expressions and give the English equivalent. There will be one or more choices.

A	B
1. カレーが　好きなら、	a. 電車に　のって行きましょう。
2. もし　からければ、	b. 作ってください。
3. どう　すれば、	c. 買いたいです。
4. 三つ目の　かどを　まがれば、	d. いいでしょうか。
5. あまり　たかくなければ、	e. 食べなくても　いいです。
6. おそくなれば、	f. みずを　すこし　入れてください。
7. みちが　こんでいれば、	g. 古本屋は　すぐ　そばです。
8. 中国料理が　とくいなら、	h. ごちそうしますよ。
9. いっしょに　来たければ、	i. 電話してください。
10. 食べたくなければ、	j. タクシーで　かえります。

15.4.3 Make appropriate questions that will lead to the following answers:

1. この　本が　一番　新しいです。
2. いいえ、あらわなくても　いいですよ。
3. ドイツ大使館なら、よく　知っていますけど、フランス大使館は　知りません。
4. まっすぐ　一キロぐらい　行けば、右に　あります。
5. あかい　自動車を　持っています。

6. ははが　いうほど　たいへんじゃありませんでした。

7. 作る　ほうが　好きです。

8. いいえ、スポーツを　するのが　一番　たのしいです。

15.4.4 Transform the code sentence according to the given English sentences:

A. 日本語を　教えます。

   1. I had to teach Japanese.

   2. I'll go to teach Japanese.

   3. I can't teach Japanese.

   4. I have taught Japanese once.

   5. I'm planning to teach Japanese next week.

   6. The man who is teaching me Japanese is Mr. Itō.

   7. If Mr. Itō teaches Japanese, I would like to learn (from him).

   8. You had better teach Japanese to your children.

   9. If you don't teach Japanese, what are you going to do?

  10. Teaching Japanese to foreigners is the most interesting.

B. しんかん線に　のります。

   1. Minoru has never ridden on a *shin'kan'sen* train.

   2. Minoru, please don't take a *shin'kan'sen* train.

   3. I prefer riding on a *shin'kan'sen* train to going by airplane.

   4. If you take a *shin'kan'sen* train, it will be faster.

   5. Minoru has to take a *shin'kan'sen* train.

   6. If I don't take a *shin'kan'sen* train, I won't be able to arrive there by noon.

C. 天気が　いいです。

   1. If the weather is good, please come to play.

   2. The weather will become better tomorrow.

   3. If the weather is not good, I prefer to stay at home.

D. そこが　しずかです。

   1. If that place is quiet, let's have a talk there.

   2. If that place is not quiet, let's try to find (some) other place.

   3. Please make yourself quiet.

   4. It was very noisy in the afternoon, but it has become quiet in the evening.

15.4.5 Compose sentences in Japanese by using the words or phrases given below, and state your original ideas in English:

Example: ずっと …… 京都の　ほうが　ずっと　あついです。

1. もちろん
2. やっぱり
3. 〜ことは　ありませんか
4. ひじょうに
5. 自分で
6. ほど
7. 〜なら
8. 〜なければなりません
9. 〜ければ
10. 〜より　〜の　ほうが
11. ずっと
12. 一番
13. 〜に　なりました
14. 〜に　しましょう
15. 〜く　なりました

15.4.6 Read the following *kan'ji*:

1. 木、水、本、来
2. 山、出
3. 西、四
4. 見、目、自、百
5. 田、町、男
6. 聞、間
7. 字、学
8. 少ない、小さい
9. 読む、語
10. 待つ、持つ
11. 持、時、待
12. 行、待
13. 入口、人口
14. 多い、外
15. 員、買
16. 何、作る、休む
17. 左、右
18. 天、大、火
19. 分、今
20. 土、上

15.4.7 Read the following *kan'ji*:

1. 教える、教科書
2. 山、富士山
3. 東、東京
4. 口、入口
5. 人、人口、六人
6. 車、自動車
7. 九つ、九時
8. 書く、辞書
9. 食べる、食事
10. 国、中国、外国
11. 中、中国
12. 大きい、大学生
13. 本、一本、二本、三本
14. こん月、四月
15. 日、日本、たんじょう日、日曜日
16. 五分、十分、気分

308

15.4.8 Replace the underlined *hiragana* with *kan'ji*:

1. <u>ひがし</u>、　<u>にし</u>、　<u>みなみ</u>、　<u>きた</u>
2. <u>うえ</u>、　<u>した</u>、　<u>みぎ</u>、　<u>ひだり</u>、　<u>なか</u>、　<u>そと</u>、　<u>まえ</u>
3. <u>げつ</u>曜、　<u>か</u>曜、　<u>すい</u>曜、　<u>もく</u>曜、　<u>きん</u>曜、　<u>ど</u>曜、　<u>にち</u>曜
4. <u>たなかせんせい</u>は　<u>だいがく</u>で　<u>にほんぶんがく</u>を　<u>おしえています</u>。ぼくは<u>がいこくご</u>を　<u>ならっています</u>。
5. この　<u>きょう</u>室に　<u>おとこ</u>が　<u>じゅうはちにん</u>、<u>おんな</u>が　<u>きゅうにん</u>　います。<u>おとこ</u>の　<u>ほう</u>が　<u>おおい</u>です。
6. <u>らいげつ</u>の　<u>ようか</u>に　<u>じどうしゃ</u>で　<u>やま</u>へ　<u>いく</u>つもりです。
7. <u>えき</u>の　<u>そば</u>の　<u>しょく</u>堂で　<u>しょくじ</u>を　しました。
8. <u>いま</u>　<u>よじ</u>　<u>にじっぷん</u>です。<u>すこし</u>　<u>やすみ</u>ましょう。
9. あなたの　<u>すき</u>な　<u>おんがく</u>を　<u>きき</u>ましょう。
10. <u>かみ</u>に　<u>じぶん</u>で　<u>なまえ</u>を　<u>かいて</u>ください。
11. <u>せんきゅうひゃくろくじゅうよねん</u>に　この　<u>まち</u>へ　<u>きました</u>。
12. <u>とうきょう</u>の　<u>じんこう</u>は　<u>せんひゃくまんにん</u>ぐらいです。
13. <u>きょうと</u>ゆきの　<u>でんしゃ</u>は　<u>なんばん</u>線から　<u>で</u>ますか。
14. あの　<u>ちいさい</u>　<u>きっさ</u>店で　<u>まって</u>います。
15. <u>おもしろい</u>　<u>もの</u>を　<u>もって</u>いますね。<u>みせて</u>ください。
16. この　<u>かんじ</u>を　<u>よむ</u>ことが　できますか。
17. <u>てんき</u>が　<u>よければ</u>、<u>はなみ</u>に　<u>いき</u>ましょう。
18. <u>くつ</u>が　<u>ふるく</u>なりましたから、<u>あたらしい</u>のを　<u>かい</u>ました。
19. <u>けしき</u>の　<u>うつくしい</u>　<u>ところ</u>は　<u>すくない</u>ですね。
20. そこまで　<u>でんしゃ</u>で　<u>いちじかんはん</u>　かかります。
21. <u>わたくし</u>の　<u>つくる</u>　カレーライスは　カレーライス<u>や</u>さんのより　おいしいですよ。
22. あの　<u>め</u>の　<u>おおきい</u>　<u>こども</u>は　スージーです。
23. 店<u>いん</u>は　<u>いりぐち</u>の　<u>そば</u>に　<u>たって</u>います。

15.5　AURAL COMPREHENSION

15.5.1 人㈠　「ちょっと　うかがいますが、駅へ　行く　みちを　教えてください。」

　　　　人㈡　「この　みちを　まっすぐ　二百メートルぐらい　行きます。」

　　　　人㈠　「はい、はい。」

　　　　人㈡　「すると、右の　かどに　ゆうびんきょくが　ありますから、そこを　右へ　まがります。」

人(一)　「右ですね。」

人(二)　「そう。その　みちを　五、六分　あるいて行けば、駅ですから。」

人(一)　「わかりました。どうも　ありがとうございました。」

15.5.2　ともだち　「井上さん、ちょっと　聞きたいんですけど、ぎんざまで　どのくらい
　　　　　　　　　　　　かかりますか。」

　　　　井上　　「車ですか、地下鉄ですか。」

　　　　ともだち　「どっちが　はやいでしょう？」

　　　　井上　　「今の　時間なら、地下鉄の　ほうが　はやいでしょうね。みちが　こんで
　　　　　　　　　いますから。地下鉄で　行けば、二十分ぐらいでしょうね。」

　　　　ともだち　「そうですか。どうも　ありがとう。」

15.5.3　けい子　「買い物ですか。」

　　　　みち子　「ええ、こんばん　お客さんが　来ますから、　これから　ごちそうを
　　　　　　　　　作らなければなりません。それに、へやも　きれいに　しなければ*¹。」

　　　　けい子　「たいへんですね。どんな　物を　作るつもりですか。」

　　　　みち子　「お客さんは　外国人ですから、みんなが　食べることが　できる　物に
　　　　　　　　　したいんです。」

　　　　けい子　「てんぷらは？」

　　　　みち子　「ええ、ちょうど　いい　おさかなが　あれば、てんぷらに　するつもりです。
　　　　　　　　　なければ、いろいろな　料理を　作ってみます。」

　　　　けい子　「手つだいましょうか。わたしは　料理を　するのが　大好きですから。」

　　　　みち子　「それは　ありがとう。二人で　作る　ほうが　ずっと　はやいわ*²。」

　　　　　　　　　　*¹なりません　deleted　　*²women's speech

15.5.4　学生　「先生、日本文学の　レポートの　しゅくだいですが、きょうじゅうでなければ
　　　　　　　　　なりませんか。」

　　　　先生　「あ、あの　レポートなら　あしたでも　いいですよ。」

　　　　学生　「すみません。それから、先生の　水曜日の　日本語クラス、　ぜひ
　　　　　　　　　ちょうこう*したいんですが、いいでしょうか。」

　　　　先生　「とりたければ、とっても　いいですけど、やさしい　クラスですよ。あの
　　　　　　　　　クラスの　学生は　あなたほど　日本語が　できませんから。」

　　　　学生　「ぼくは　まだ　はなすより　聞くほうが　むずかしいです。」

　　　　先生　「聞くのが　むずかしければ、テープを　つかうのが　一番　いいですよ。
　　　　　　　　　テープが　ほしければ、図書館に　たくさん　新しいのが　ありますから。」

学生　「わかりました。あとで、ちょうど　いい　テープを　さがしてみます。」
　　　　*"audit"

15.5.5　　ずいぶん　さむくなりました。お元気ですか。ぼくも　かぞくも　みんな　元気です。
こちらは　まい日　ゆきが　ふっています。ことしは　いつもより　ゆきが　多いです。
今、ゆきは　五十センチぐらいです。

　ところで、こん月の　二十六日ごろから　三十日ごろまで、こちらへ　スキーに
来ませんか。いもうとは　らいしゅうから　学校が　ふゆ休みに　なるはずですから、
みんなで　一日じゅう　スキーを　しましょう。もし、スキーを　したことが
なければ、習うことも　できます。ポールさんなら、すぐ　じょうずに　なりますよ。
スキーも　かりたければ、こちらに　あります。

　つごうが　よければ、電話か　手紙を　ください。待っています。

　　　　　　　　　　　　　　　　　　　　　　　　　では、さようなら

十二月十五日

　　　　　　　　　　　　　　　　　　　　　　　　　　　　　　　鈴木

ポール様

APPENDIX I
ABBREVIATIONS

A	· · · · · ·	Adjective	*furui, kuwashii, hirokute*
Adv.	· · · · · ·	Adverb	*zutto, taihen*
B	· · · · · ·	Base	*mitsukar(imasu), tabe(ru), atarashi(i)*
C	· · · · · ·	Copula	*desu, de, na, nara*
D	· · · · · ·	Derivative	
Da	· · · · · ·	adjectival Derivative	*-nai, -tai*
Dv	· · · · · ·	verbal Derivative	*-masu, -mashoo*
E	· · · · · ·	Predicate Extender	*(-te) imasu, (-te) kudasai, (de wa) nai*
I	· · · · · ·	Inflection	*(mitsukar)i(masu), (atarashi)i*
N	· · · · · ·	Noun	
Na	· · · · · ·	adjectival Noun	*taihen, teinei*
Nd	· · · · · ·	dependent Noun	*koto, no, tsumori, hazu, -doru, -ban*
Ni	· · · · · ·	interrogative Noun	*dochira, dotchi, dore, ikura*
N	· · · · · ·	ordinary Noun	*kudamono, ototoi, tsuitachi*
NM	· · · · · ·	Noun Modifier	*kirei na (hana), tsugi no eki de oriru (hito)*
P	· · · · · ·	Predicate	
PC	· · · · · ·	Pre-Copula	*n (desu)*
PM	· · · · · ·	Predicate Modifier	(Adverb, time Noun, N+R, number)
PN	· · · · · ·	Pre-Noun	*don'na, son'na*
R	· · · · · ·	Relational	
Rc	· · · · · ·	clause Relational	*kara, keredomo*
Rp	· · · · · ·	phrase Relational	*yori, made ni, ni*
S	· · · · · ·	Sentence	
SI	· · · · · ·	Sentence Interjective	*anoo, eeto*
SP	· · · · · ·	Sentence Particle	*ka, yo, ne, nee*
V	· · · · · ·	Verb	*iku, arukeba, yasun'da*

APPENDIX II
SENTENCE STRUCTURE
PHRASE STRUCTURE

$$S=SI+PM\left\{\begin{array}{l}(NM)^{*1}\left\{\begin{array}{l}PN\\N+(R)^{*2}\\Adv.^{*3}\\P^{*4}\end{array}\right\}^{*5}+N+(R)\\(Adv.)+Adv.+(R)\\P^{*6}+(R)\end{array}\right\}//P\left\{\begin{array}{l}\left\{\begin{array}{l}V\{B+I+D\}\\A\{B+I+D\}\\(NM)+N+(R)+C\end{array}\right\}+(R)+(E)^{*7}+(PC)^{*8}+(C)^{*9}\end{array}\right\}+SP$$

*1 (NM)=NM optional

*2 (R)=R optional

*3 Adv. is only followed by Na such as *kirei*, adverbially used N such as *san'nin*, *kyoo*, or place N such as *ushiro*, *ue*.

*4 limited to final-clause Predicate such as *iku*, *itta*.

*5 { }=specification or limitation

*6 limited to TE, KU, TARI, Stem forms. R is obligatory for TARI, Stem forms, but optional for TE, KU forms.

*7 (E)=E optional

*8 (PC)=PC optional

*9 (C)=C optional

APPENDIX III
RELATIONALS

Relational		Lesson	Functions	Example Sentences
dake	Rp	9	limitation [only; just; no more than]	*Kotae dake kaite kudasai.* *Kono kudamono wa Kariforunia ni dake arimasu.*
de	Rp	1	totalizing	*Mittsu de hyakuen desu.* *Zen'bu de ikura desu ka?*
	Rp	7	limiting the length of time [within; in]	*Ichijikan de kaku koto ga dekimasu ka?* *Nan'pun de tsukurimashita ka?*
	Rp	11	designation of scope [among; of]	*Sono naka de ichiban ookii desu.* *Amerika de ichiban yuumei na hito wa dare desu ka?*
hodo	Rp	11, 12	[as much as]	*Watakushi wa anata hodo joozu ja arimasen.* *Anata ga omou hodo oishiku nai desu.*
kara	Rc	5	reason [because; since]	*Sugu kimasu kara, matte ite kudasai.* *Yasui (desu) kara, kau tsumori desu.*
(kedo) *keredo* *keredomo*	Rc	11	reversal [but; although; however]	*Takai keredo, sore ni shimasu.*
made	Rp	7	time or place of goal [until; as far as]	*Eki made arukimashoo.* *Asa goji made ben'kyoo shimashita.*
made ni	Rp	8	[by (the time given); not later than]	*Tooka made ni den'wa o kudasai.*
mo	Rp	9	[even]	*Itte mo ii desu ka?*
ni	Rp	1	[into]	*Hako ni iremashoo.*
	Rp	2	target time [at; in; on]	*Yoji ni dekakemashoo.*
	Rp	4	direction [to]	*Uchi ni kaeritai desu.*
	Rp	5	purpose (of going) [for; to]	*San'po ni ikimasen ka?* *Gohan o tabe ni kaerimashita.*
	Rp	12	(to become) goal (to make) (to choose)	*Sen'sei ni naritai n desu.* *Kirei ni shimashoo.* *Ban'gohan wa bifuteki ni shimasu.*
no	Rp	7	follows the subject in a Noun Modifier	*Kyuukoo no tsuku jikan o shitte imasu ka?* *Sei no takai hito wa dare desu ka?*
o	Rp	13	place through which action has taken place [through; along; in, etc.]	*Kono toori o tsugi no kado made arukimasu.* *Kooen o san'po shimashita.*
yori	Rp	11	comparison [than]	*Kyooto yori Tookyoo no hoo ga ookii desu.* *Soto de taberu yori uchi de tsukuru hoo ga ii desu.*

APPENDIX IV
CONJUGATION TABLE
FORM

1. Verb

a. Vowel Verb

ageru	I, 13	ireru	II, 1	kuraberu	II, 11	oriru	II, 7	tsureru	II, 4
akeru	II, 9	iru	I, 5	kureru	I, 13	oshieru	II, 13	tsutomeru	II, 2
dekakeru	I, 4	kakeru	II, 4	miru	I, 4	sashiageru	II, 1	wasureru	II, 9
dekiru	II, 5, 12	kariru	I, 9	miseru	II, 1	shimeru	II, 9		
deru	II, 7	kiru	II, 1	neru	II, 4	shiraberu	II, 8		
hajimeru	II, 9	kotaeru	II, 9	okiru	II, 4	taberu	I, 3		

a.1 Conjugation

	Neutral Form				Plain Style	
Stem Form	Base Form	TE Form	BA Form	Pre-Nai Form	Dictionary Form	TA Form
tabe(masu)	tabe	tabete	tabereba	tabe(nai)	taberu	tabeta
mi(masu)	mi	mite	mireba	mi(nai)	miru	mita

a.2 Tense & Negation

Normal Style				Plain Style				Neutral Form	
Imperfect		Perfect		Imperfect		Perfect		Provisional	
Affirmative	Negative	Affirmative	Negative	Affirmative	Negative	Affirmative	Negative	Affirmative	Negative
tabemasu	tabemasen	tabe-mashita	tabemasen deshita	taberu	tabenai	tabeta	tabe-nakatta	tabereba	tabe-nakereba
mimasu	mimasen	mimashita	mimasen deshita	miru	minai	mita	minakatta	mireba	mi-nakereba

b. Consonant Verb

Group 1 /r/ group

aru	I, 4	irassharu	II, 4	mitsukaru	II, 8	suwaru	II, 9	wakaru	II, 4, 13
furu	I, 11	kaeru	I, 3	naru	II, 11, 12	tomaru	II, 13	yaru	I, 13
hairu	I, 8	kakaru	II, 7	noru	II, 7	toru	II, 4		
hajimaru	II, 4	kudasaru	II, 1	owaru	II, 4	tsukuru	II, 12		
hashiru	II, 7	magaru	II, 13	shiru	II, 2	uru	II, 1		

Group 2 /w/ group

arau	II, 12	iu	I, 11	kayou	II, 2	omou	II, 12	tsukau	II, 8
au	II, 4	kamau	II, 8	morau	I, 13	suu	II, 9	ukagau	II, 2, 7
chigau	II, 4	kau	I, 3	narau	I, 7	tetsudau	II, 12		

Group 3 /t/ group

matsu	I, 13	motsu	II, 2	tatsu	II, 9

Group 4 /k/ group

aruku	II, 7	hiku	II, 7	kaku	I, 4	saku	II, 5
haku	II, 1	iku	I, 3	kiku	I, 4; II, 7	suku	II, 13
hataraku	II, 2	itadaku	II, 1	ochitsuku	II, 11	tsuku	II, 7

Group 5 /s/ group
| hanasu | I, 7 | kaesu | II, 8 | kasu | II, 8 | sagasu | I, 9 | watasu | II, 9 |

Group 6 /m/ group
| komu | II, 13 | nomu | I, 3 | sumu | II, 2 | yasumu | II, 4 | yomu | I, 9 |

Group 7 /b/ group
| asobu | II, 5 | yobu | I, 5 |

Group 8 /g/ group
| isogu | II, 12 | oyogu | I, 11 |

Group 9 /n/ group
| shinu | — |

b.1 Conjugation

Group	Neutral Form					Plain Style	
	Stem Form	Base Form	TE Form	BA Form	Pre-Nai Form	Dictionary Form	TA Form
1	furi(masu)	fur	futte	fureba	fura(nai)	furu	futta
2	ai(masu)	a(w)	atte	aeba	awa(nai)	au	atta
3	machi(masu)	mat	matte	mateba	mata(nai)	matsu	matta
4	aruki(masu)	aruk	aruite	arukeba	aruka(nai)	aruku	aruita
5	hanashi(masu)	hanas	hanashite	hanaseba	hanasa(nai)	hanasu	hanashita
6	komi(masu)	kom	kon'de	komeba	koma(nai)	komu	kon'da
7	asobi(masu)	asob	ason'de	asobeba	asoba(nai)	asobu	ason'da
8	isogi(masu)	isog	isoide	isogeba	isoga(nai)	isogu	isoida
9	shini(masu)	shin	shin'de	shineba	shina(nai)	shinu	shin'da

b.2 Tense & Negation

Group	Normal Style				Plain Style				Neutral Form	
	Imperfect		Perfect		Imperfect		Perfect		Provisional	
	Affirmative	Negative	Affirmative	Negative	Affirmative	Negative	Affirmative	Negative	Affirmative	Negative
1	furimasu	furimasen	furi-mashita	furimasen deshita	furu	furanai	futta	furanakatta	fureba	fura-nakereba
2	aimasu	aimasen	aimashita	aimasen deshita	au	awanai	atta	awanakatta	aeba	awa-nakereba
3	machimasu	machi-masen	machi-mashita	machi-masen deshita	matsu	matanai	matta	mata-nakatta	mateba	mata-nakereba
4	arukimasu	aruki-masen	aruki-mashita	arukimasen deshita	aruku	arukanai	aruita	aruka-nakatta	arukeba	aruka-nakereba
5	hanashi-masu	hanashi-masen	hanashi-mashita	hanashi-masen deshita	hanasu	hanasanai	hanashita	hanasa-nakatta	hanaseba	hanasa-nakereba
6	komimasu	komimasen	komi-mashita	komimasen deshita	komu	komanai	kon'da	koma-nakatta	komeba	koma-nakereba
7	asobimasu	asobi-masen	asobi-mashita	asobimasen deshita	asobu	asobanai	ason'da	asoba-nakatta	asobeba	asoba-nakereba
8	isogimasu	isogi-masen	isogi-mashita	isogimasen deshita	isogu	isoganai	isoida	isoga-nakatta	isogeba	isoga-nakereba
9	shinimasu	shini-masen	shini-mashita	shinimasen deshita	shinu	shinanai	shin'da	shina-nakatta	shineba	shina-nakereba

c. Irregular Verb

kuru	I, 3	den'wa suru	I, 12	ken'butsu suru	I, 12	setsumei suru	II, 8
suru	I, 3; II, 12	gochisoo suru	II, 12	ryokoo suru	I, 12	shigoto suru	II, 2
arubaito suru	II, 2	kaimono suru	I, 4	ryoori suru	II, 12	shitsumon suru	II, 9
ben'kyoo suru	I, 4	kekkon suru	II, 2	san'po suru	II, 5	shokuji suru	I, 4

shookai suru I, 7

c.1 Conjugation

Neutral Form					Plain Style	
Stem Form	Base Form	TE Form	BA Form	Pre-Nai Form	Dictionary Form	TA Form
ki(masu)	k	kite	kureba	ko(nai)	kuru	kita
shi(masu)	s	shite	sureba	shi(nai)	suru	shita

c.2 Tense & Negation

Normal Style				Plain Style				Neutral Form	
Imperfect		Perfect		Imperfect		Perfect		Provisional	
Affirmative	Negative	Affirmative	Negative	Affirmative	Negative	Affirmative	Negative	Affirmative	Negative
kimasu	kimasen	kimashita	kimasen deshita	kuru	konai	kita	konakatta	kureba	konakereba
shimasu	shimasen	shimashita	shimasen deshita	suru	shinai	shita	shinakatta	sureba	shi-nakereba

2. Adjective

akai	II, 13	hikui	II, 7	kuroi	II, 13	ookii	I, 8	tooi	I, 8
amai	II, 12	hiroi	II, 11	kuwashii	II, 8	osoi	I, 13; II, 9	tsumaranai	I, 9
aoi	II, 13	hoshii	II, 1	mazui	I, 8	samui	I, 11	tsumetai	I, 11
atarashii	II, 5	hosonagai	II, 11	mijikai	II, 9	semai	II, 11	urusai	I, 8
atatakai	I, 11	ii	I, 8; II, 8	mushiatsui	I, 11	shiroi	II, 13	utsukushii	II, 5
atsui	I, 11	isogashii	I, 8	muzukashii	I, 9	subarashii	I, 12	wakai	II, 12
chairoi	II, 13	karai	II, 12	nagai	II, 9	sukunai	II, 5	warui	I, 8
chiisai	I, 8	kawaii	II, 5	nai	I, 9	suppai	II, 12	yasashii	I, 9
chikai	I, 8	kiiroi	II, 13	oishii	I, 8	suzushii	I, 11	yasui	I, 9
furui	II, 5	kitanai	I, 8	omoshiroi	I, 9	takai	I, 9; II, 7	yoi	I, 8
hayai	I, 13; II, 7	kitsui	II, 1	ooi	II, 5	tanoshii	I, 12		

1. Conjugation

Plain Style		Neutral Form			
Dictionary Form	TA Form	TE Form	KU Form	BA Form	Base Form
akai	akakatta	akakute	akaku	akakereba	aka

2. Tense & Negation

Normal Style				Plain Style				Neutral Form	
Imperfect		Perfect		Imperfect		Perfect		Provisional	
Affirmative	Negative	Affirmative	Negative	Affirmative	Negative	Affirmative	Negative	Affirmative	Negative
akai desu	akaku arimasen	akakatta desu	akaku arimasen deshita	akai	akaku nai	akakatta	akaku nakatta	akakereba	akaku nakereba

3. Adjectival Derivative

Plain Style		Neutral Form			
Dictionary Form	TA Form	TE Form	KU Form	BA Form	Base Form
-nai	-nakatta	-nakute	-naku	-nakereba	-na
-tai	-takatta	-takute	-taku	-takereba	-ta

4. Copula

Normal Style			Neutral Form		
Dictionary Form	TA Form	OO Form	TE Form	NA* Form	BA Form
desu	deshita	deshoo	de	na	nara(ba)

*NA Form is used only with adjectival Nouns such as:

daijoobu	II, 4	hen	II, 5	kirai	I, 8	shitsurei	II, 5	tekitoo	II, 8
daikirai	I, 8	heta	I, 7	kirei	I, 7	shizuka	I, 7	tokui	II, 12
daisuki	I, 8	hima	I, 5	nigiyaka	I, 7	suki	I, 8	yutaka	II, 11
dame	I, 8	iroiro	II, 5	rippa	I, 9	taihen	II, 7	yuumei	II, 5
gen'ki	I, 8	joozu	I, 7	sakan	II, 11	teinei	II, 1		

APPENDIX V
KAN'JI ANALYSIS

As stated in Volume I, Lesson 2, there were no writing symbols in Japan before the introduction of *kan'-ji*. After *kan'ji* were introduced, however, the Japanese started to use them to write their language. Some of their forms are based on (1) visual shapes (such as 木、人、月、日、etc.), (2) some on abstract indications (such as 上、本、中、etc.), and (3) some combine a meaningful part and a phonetic part (such as 語、時、etc.). Still others are formed by combining two simpler *kan'ji* to show a combined meaning (such as 多、見、東、分、etc.). More than 50,000 *kan'ji* were formulated in China throughout her thousands of years of history. As early as A.D. 98, Chinese characters numbering 9,353 were explained in a book in China. A few *kan'ji*, however, were created in Japan.

SOME ORIGINS OF KAN'JI

(1) Visual shapes

1. → → 日 "sun"
2. → → → 水 "water"
3. → 山 "mountain"
4. → → → 月 "moon"
5. → 川 "river"
6. → → 火 "fire"
7. → → → 目 "eye"
8. → → 耳 "ear"
9. → 口 "mouth"
10. → → → 手 "hand"
11. → → → 人 "man"
12. → → 毛 "hair; feather; fur"
13. → → → 女 "woman"
14. → → → 母 "mother"
15. → → → 子 "child"

16. → → 羊 "sheep"
17. → → → 馬 "horse"
18. → → → 鳥 "bird"
19. → → → 燕 "swallow"
20. → → → 魚 "fish"
21. → → → 爪 "nail"
22. → 田 "field"
23. → → 木 "tree"
24. → → 艹 "grass"
25. → → → 禾 "grain"
26. → 井 "well"
27. → → 冊 "book"
28. → → → 果 "fruit"
29. → → → 門 "gate"
30. → 戸 "door"

(2) Abstract indicators

1. → → 上 "above"
2. → → 下 "below"
3. → → 本 "base"
4. → → 末 "end"
5. → → 天 "heaven; sky; above"
6. → → 出 "step out"
7. △+廿 → 合 → 合　△ "to close" □ "mouth" = "to get together"

8. 桑 ⟶ 雧 ⟶ 集   "assemble"

9. 𣏦 ⟶ 森   "multiple trees" = "woods"

10. 品 ⟶ 品   "things"

11. 𠨗 ⟶ 𠨗 ⟶ 交   "crossing"

12. 㐅 ⟶ 五   "crossing in counting ten" → "five"

（3）　Semantic Combinations and Semantic-Phonetic Combinations

	(a) Semantic Part	(b) Second Semantic or Phonetic Part	(c) Result	(d) Pronun- ciation	(e) Meaning
1.	氵 [water]	青	清	sei	"clear water"
2.	日 [day]	青	晴	sei	"clear sky"
3.	米 [rice]	青	精	sei	"refined rice"
4.	言 [word]	吾	語	go	"word"
5.	忄 [mind]	吾	悟	go	"realization"
6.	木 [tree]	同	桐	too	"paulownia"
7.	月 [body]	同	胴	doo	"body trunk"
8.	氵 [water]	同	洞	doo	"hole"
9.	竹 [bamboo]	同	筒	too	"tube; pipe"
10.	金 [metal]	同	銅	doo	"copper"
11.	土 [soil]	反	坂	han	"slope"
12.	木 [tree]	反	板	han	"wooden board"
13.	食 [eating]	反	飯	han	"meal"
14.	貝 [money]	反	販	han	"to sell"
15.	衣 [cloth]	甫	補	ho	"to mend"
16.	氵 [water]	甫	浦	ho	"bay, creek"
17.	扌 [hand]	甫	捕	ho	"to capture"
18.	舍 [house]	甫	舖	ho	"shop"
19.	石 [stone]	包	砲	hoo	"cannon"
20.	扌 [hand]	包	抱	hoo	"to hug"
21.	月 [body]	包	胞	hoo	"compatriot"
22.	食 [eating]	包	飽	hoo	"feel full after eating"
23.	日 [sun]	生	星	sei	"star"
24.	忄 [heart]	生	性	sei	"temperament"
25.	女 [woman]	生	姓	sei	"family name"
26.	牜 [animal]	生	牲	sei	"sacrifice"
27.	言 [word]	寺	詩	shi	"poetry"
28.	日 [sun]	寺	時	ji	"time"
29.	扌 [hand]	寺	持	ji	"to hold"
30.	イ [man]	寺	侍	ji	"to attend on"
31.	食 [eating]	官	館	kan	"inn"
32.	竹 [bamboo]	官	管	kan	"pipe; conduct"
33.	木 [tree]	官	棺	kan	"coffin"

KAN'JI CLASSIFIERS

Kan'ji characters are frequently arranged according to classifiers. Most dictionaries list about 220 classifiers. You will learn them gradually. Some classifiers carry meaning, some indicate the kind, and some suggest grouping. The following listed classifiers, which are in frequent use in traditional dictionaries, may be helpful to you as a possible clue to your understanding of *kan'ji*.

Classifier	Meaning	Examples
イ	[person]	人（ひと）、作（つく）る、休（やす）む
氵	[water]	泳（およ）ぐ、海（うみ）、洗（あら）う
扌	[hand]	持（も）つ、指（ゆび）[finger]、打（う）つ[beat]
艹	[grass]	花（はな）、草（くさ）[grass]
口	[mouth]	口（くち）、右（みぎ）、名（な）
木	[tree]	木（き）、林（はやし）[forest]、森（もり）[woods]
日	[day; sun]	時（じ）、明（あか）るい[bright]
目	[eye]	目（め）、眠（ねむ）い[sleepy]
田	[field]	田（た）、男（おとこ）、町（まち）
糸	[string]	糸（いと）、紙（かみ）、線（せん）[line]
言	[speech]	言（い）う、話（はな）す、語（ご）、読（よ）む
車	[vehicle]	車（くるま）、軍（ぐん）[military]、輪（わ）[ring]
雨	[rain]	雨（あめ）、電（でん）、雪（ゆき）
門	[gate]	門（もん）、問（もん）、開（ひら）く[open]
金	[gold; metal]	金（きん）、銀（ぎん）[silver]、鉄（てつ）[iron]
食	[eating]	食（た）べる、飲（の）む、ご飯（はん）、館（かん）

POSTWAR KAN'JI REFORMS

Since there were so many *kan'ji* and so many readings for each *kan'ji,* efforts to limit the number of *kan'ji* and their readings have been made from time to time. Major reform measures adopted after the Second World War by the Japanese government were as follows:

1. On November 16, 1946, the Japanese government promulgated a restricted list of 1,850 *kan'ji* called *Tooyoo Kan'ji* for general use, and, at the same time, reformed the *kana* spelling system.

2. On February 16, 1948, the Japanese government decided to limit the readings of each *Tooyoo Kan'ji* to the minimum, thus reducing the total number of readings to 3,122; also it selected, out of 1,850 *kan'ji*, 881 called *Kyooiku Kan'ji.* These are deemed the most essential *kan'ji* for compulsory educational purpose, and are taught during the first six years of elementary school throughout Japan.

3. On May 25, 1951, the Japanese government added 92 *kan'ji* to be used for personal names and surnames.

4. On December 12, 1958, a guide to the reading and writing of place names was published by the Ministry of Education.

5. On July 11, 1959, the Japanese government decided to adopt a *kan'ji-kana* combination system.

6. In July 1968, the government added 115 more *kan'ji* to the *Kyooiku Kan'ji* list, making the total of 996 *kan'ji* compulsory for mandatory education.

7. In June 1973, the original list limiting the *Tooyoo Kan'ji* reading of 3,122 was expanded to 3,938 plus 106 phonetic equivalent characters called *ateji.* At the same time the 1959 *kan'ji-kana* combination system was revised.

8. In July 1976, the government added 28 more *kan'ji* for personal and surname use.

9. Starting in October 1981, the recommended *Jooyoo Kan'ji* containing 1,945 *kan'ji* replaced *Tooyoo Kan'ji*; and 54 more *kan'ji* were added to *kan'ji* for personal and surname use, making 2,111 *kan'ji* available for such a purpose. Altogether 996 *kan'ji* are taught to school children under the mandatory education system.

APPENDIX VI
PRESENTATION AND DIALOG
ROMANIZATION AND ENGLISH EQUIVALENT

1.1 ——Kaimono——

Nihon no depaato nado no ten'in no kotoba wa taihen teinei desu. Tsugi wa ten'in to kyaku no kaiwa desu.

——Shopping——

The clerks at department stores and the like in Japan are very polite in their speech. The following is a conversation between a clerk and a customer.

1.2

Ten'in:	Irasshaimase. Nani o sashiagemashoo ka
On'na no kyaku:	Buutsu ga hoshii n desu ga.
Ten'in:	Buutsu wa kochira desu. Doozo.
On'na no kyaku:	Sore o misete kudasai.
Ten'in:	Kore wa nijuu yon desu ga, okyakusama no saizu wa
On'na no kyaku:	Nijuu san-han desu. Ichiman gosen'en gurai no o kaitai n desu ga, sore wa oikura desu ka
Ten'in:	Kore wa ichiman san'zen roppyakuen desu. Doozo haite mite kudasai.
On'na no kyaku:	Sukoshi kitsui desu ne.
Ten'in:	De wa, kore wa ikaga desu ka ... Choodo ii desu ne
On'na no kyaku:	Ee. Jaa, kore o itadakimasu. Sore kara, kutsuzumi o hitotsu kudasai.
Ten'in:	Arigatoo gozaimasu. Buutsu wa hako ni iremashoo ka
On'na no kyaku:	Ee, soo shite kudasai. Sore kara, rein'kooto wa nan'gai desu ka
Ten'in:	Yon'kai de utte imasu.
On'na no kyaku:	Jaa, ato de itte mimashoo. Zen'bu de ikura desu ka
Ten'in:	Ichiman san'zen kyuuhyakuen desu. Doomo arigatoo gozaimashita.

Clerk:	Welcome. What shall I give to you? [What are you looking for?]
Lady customer:	I want boots.
Clerk:	Boots are here. Please (come and have a look).
Lady customer:	Please show me those.
Clerk:	These are twenty-four in size, but what is your size?
Lady customer:	Twenty-three and half. I would like to buy those of about fifteen thousand yen, but how much are those?

Clerk: These cost thirteen thousand and six hundred yen. Please try these on.
Lady customer: These are a little tight.
Clerk: Then, how about these? . . . Just right, are they?
Lady customer: Yes. Well, I will take these. And, please give me a shoe polisher.
Clerk: Thank you very much. Shall I put (these) boots in a box?
Lady customer: Yes, please do so. And, on what floor are there raincoats?
Clerk: We sell them on the fourth floor.
Lady customer: Fine, I will go and see later. How much is the total?
Clerk: 13,900 yen, madam. Thank you very much.

2.1 ——Daigakusei——

Ichiroo wa daigaku no yonen'sei desu. Kyooiku-gaku o ben'kyoo shite imasu.

Nihon no daigakusei wa natsuyasumi ni yoku arubaito o shimasu. Daigaku no natsuyasumi wa shichigatsu to hachigatsu desu. Ichiroo wa shichigatsu ni depaato de hatarakimashita.

——College Students——

Ichirō is a senior student of a college. He is studying education.

Japanese college students often work for money during the summer vacation. The summer vacation of colleges is during July and August. Ichirō worked at a department store during July.

2.2

Hayashi: Ichiroo kun, shibaraku.

Ichiroo: A, sen'pai, shibaraku desu.

Hayashi: Kimi wa mada gakusei deshoo /

Ichiroo: Ee, yonen desu. Hayashi san wa ima nan no shigoto o shite imasu ka /

Hayashi: Kaisha ni tsutomete imasu.

Ichiroo: Soo desu ka. Kaisha e wa kuruma de kayotte imasu ka /

Hayashi: Iie, kuruma wa motte imasen. Basu de kayotte imasu. Ichiroo kun, ashita no ban uchi e kimasen ka /Yukkuri hanashimashoo.

Ichiroo: Ee, zehi ukagaimasu.

Hayashi: Boku no tokoro wa shitte imasu ne /Ima mo mae no apaato ni sun'de imasu.

Ichiroo: Eeto . . . Shibuya deshita ne /Nan'ji ni ukagaimashoo ka /

Hayashi: Gojihan wa doo desu ka /

Ichiroo: Ee, ii desu.

Hayashi: Dewa, gojihan goro matte imasu yo /

Ichiroo: Ee. Tanoshimi ni shite imasu.

Mr. Hayashi: Ichirō, I haven't seen you for a long time.
Ichirō: Oh, sen'pai, it's been a long time since I last saw you.
Mr. Hayashi: You are still a student, aren't you?

Ichirō:	Yes, I am a senior. Mr. Hayashi, what work are you doing now?
Mr. Hayashi:	I am working for a company.
Ichiro:	Oh, you are? Are you commuting to your company by car?
Mr. Hayashi:	No, I don't have a car. I am commuting by bus. Ichirō, won't you come to my house tomorrow night? Let's talk leisurely at home.
Ichiro:	Yes, I'll visit you, by all means.
Mr. Hayashi:	You know my place, don't you? I am now still living in the apartment where I used to live.
Ichiro:	Let me see . . . It was in Shibuya, wasn't it? What time shall I come?
Mr. Hayashi:	How about five-thirty?
Ichiro:	All right, that's fine with me.
Mr. Hayashi:	Then I'll be waiting for you at about five-thirty.
Ichiro:	Yes. I will be looking forward (to seeing you tomorrow).

4.1 ——Den'wa——

Inoue san wa suiyoobi no kurasu o totte imasu. Yoshiko san mo sono kurasu ni kuru hazu deshita ga, kimasen deshita. Sore de, tsugi no hi ni, Inoue san wa Yoshiko san no uchi ni den'wa o kakemashita. Yoshiko san no uchi no den'wa ban'goo wa zerosan no yon'goo ichi no goonana kyuunii desu.

——The Telephone——

Inoue is taking a Wednesday class. Yoshiko was also supposed to come to that class, but she did not. Therefore, next day Inoue made a phone call to Yoshiko's house. Yoshiko's home telephone number is 03-451-5792.

4.2

Inoue:	Moshi moshi, Mori san no otaku desu ka /
Yoshiko:	Hai, soo desu.
Inoue:	Yoshiko san, irasshaimasu ka /
Yoshiko:	Watakushi desu ga . . .
Inoue:	A, boku, Inoue desu.
Yoshiko:	Ara, kon'nichi wa
Inoue:	Kinoo aitakatta n desu kedo, gakkoo ni kimasen deshita ne /
Yoshiko:	Ee, ikimasen deshita. Chotto kibun ga warukatta n desu ga, moo daijoobu desu. Ashita wa yasumanai tsumori desu.
Inoue:	Soo desu ka. Jitsu wa, doyoobi ni imooto o kabuki ni tsurete iku tsumori desu kedo, Yoshiko san mo mitaku arimasen ka /
Yoshiko:	Ee, mitai desu. Zehi tsurete itte kudasai.
Inoue:	Jaa, gogo yoji juugofun goro Kabukiza de aimashoo.
Yoshiko:	Wakarimashita. Doomo arigatoo. Soosoo, kabuki wa nan'ji goro owarimasu ka /
Inoue:	Kujihan goro owaru hazu desu kedo.

Yoshiko:	Soo desu ka. Dewa, doyoobi ni.
Inoue:	Jaa, mata

Mr. Inoue:	Hello, is this the Mori home?
Yoshiko:	Yes, it is.
Mr. Inoue:	Is Yoshiko there?
Yoshiko:	This is she speaking.
Mr. Inoue:	Oh, this is Inoue.
Yoshiko:	Oh, hello.
Mr. Inoue:	I wanted to see you yesterday, but you didn't come to school, did you?
Yoshiko:	No, I didn't. I didn't feel well, but I am all right now. I am not going to be absent from school tomorrow.
Mr. Inoue:	I see. The fact is (the reason why I've called you is), I am planning to take my younger sister to *kabuki* plays on Saturday. Wouldn't you like to see them too, Yoshiko?
Yoshiko:	Yes, I'd like to. Please let me join you by all means.
Mr. Inoue:	Then let's meet at the Kabuki Theater at about four-fifteen in the afternoon.
Yoshiko:	All right. Thank you very much. Oh, yes, about what time will the *kabuki* performance be over?
Mr. Inoue:	It is supposed to be over at about nine-thirty.
Yoshiko:	Is it? Then I'll see you on Saturday.
Mr. Inoue:	Well, see you again.

5.1 ——Hanami——

Sakura wa yuumei na Nihon no hana desu. Tookyoo de wa daitai shigatsu no hajime ni sakimasu. Nihon no hitotachi wa yoku iroiro na hana o mi ni ikimasu ga, toku ni sakura ga suki desu.

——Cherry Blossom Viewing——

Cherry blossoms are famous Japanese flowers. Roughly speaking, they bloom in early April in Tōkyō. Japanese people often go to view various flowers, but they particularly like cherry blossoms.

5.2

Michiko:	Kyoo wa ii oten'ki desu ne /
Jooji:	Hon'to ni subarashii hi desu ne. Michiko san wa kyoo nani o suru tsumori desu ka /
Michiko:	Betsu ni . . . Demo, dooshite /
Jooji:	Gogo san'po ni ikimasen ka /
Michiko:	Ii desu ne. Ikimashoo.
Jooji:	Ii tokoro o shitte imasu ka /
Michiko:	Ueno wa doo desu ka / Choodo ima sakura ga saite imasu kara, ohanami ni ikimashoo ka.
Jooji:	Aa, hanami desu ne / Sakura wa daisuki na hana desu kara, mi ni ikitai desu. Demo, soko wa don'na tokoro desu ka /
Michiko:	Soo desu nee . . . Totemo ookii kooen desu. Bijutsukan ya doobutsuen nado ga arimasu

kara, otona mo chiisai kodomo mo oozei asobi ni ikimasu. Ueno no yama wa sakura de yuumei desu yo /

Jooji: Jaa, ima wa hanami no kisetsu desu kara, hito ga ooi deshoo ne /

Michiko: Ee. Jaa, Jooji san, koo shimashoo. Hajime ni, doobutsuen e ikimasen ka /Soshite, yuugata ohanami o shimashoo.

Jooji: Sore ga ii desu ne /Yuugata wa hito ga sukunai deshoo kara, tabun yukkuri ohanami o suru koto ga dekimasu ne /

Michiko: It's a nice day [weather] today, isn't it?
George: It's really a wonderful day! What are you going to do today, Michiko?
Michiko: Nothing particular . . . But, why (are you asking)?
George: Won't you go for a walk in the afternoon?
Michiko: That's nice. Let's go.
George: Do you know any good place (to go)?
Michiko: How about Ueno? Cherry blossoms are in bloom right now, so shall we go cherry blossom viewing?
George: Oh, cherry blossom viewing! Cherry blossoms are my favorite flowers, so I would like to go to see them. But, what sort of place is that?
Michiko: Let me see. . . . It is a very big park. As there are art museums, a zoo, and the like, many adults as well as many little children go there to have a good time. The Ueno Hill is famous for cherry trees, you know.
George: Well, then, as it is the cherry blossom viewing season now, there will be many people, won't there?
Michiko: Yes. Now, George, let's do it this way. At first, wouldn't you like to go to the zoo? Then let's view cherry blossoms early in the evening.
George: That's a good idea. People will (probably) be scarce toward evening, so we will probably be able to see cherry blossoms without hurrying.

7.1 ——Norimono——

Tookyoo kara Oosaka made gohyaku gojuurokkiro (san'byaku yon'juu rokumairu) arimasu ga, mukashi wa hayai norimono ga arimasen deshita kara, ryokoo suru no wa taihen deshita. Ima wa hikooki de wa ichijikan, shin'kan'sen de wa san'jikan de iku koto ga dekimasu.

——Transportation——

It is 556 kilometers (346 miles) from Tōkyō to Ōsaka, and in the past, it was very hard to travel because there were no fast transportation facilities. Now we can go in one hour by airplane and in three hours by the New Tōkaidō Line.

7.2

Gaikokujin: Chotto ukagaimasu ga, Niigata-yuki no kyuukoo wa dore deshoo ka /

Nihon'jin: Saa, yoku wakarimasen. Asoko ni iru ekiin ni kiite mite kudasai.

Gaikokujin: Hai, doomo.

. . . .

Gaikokujin: Anoo, Niigata-yuki no kyuukoo ni noritai n desu ga, nan'ban'sen kara demasu ka

Ekiin: Nijuu san'ji nijippun ni deru kyuukoo desu ka /Nanaban'sen kara desu.

Gaikokujin: Niigata made dono gurai kakarimasu ka

Ekiin: Kyuukoo ga Niigata ni tsuku jikan wa ashita no gozen goji juugofun desu kara, gojikan go-juu gofun kakarimasu.

Gaikokujin: Soo desu ka. Guriin'ken o naka de kau koto ga dekimasu ka

Ekiin: Saa, wakarimasen ne. Notte kara, shashoo ni kiite mite kudasai. Tama ni noranai hito ya sugu oriru hito ga imasu kara.

Gaikokujin: Jaa, soo shimasu. Doomo arigatoo.

Foreigner: Excuse me, but which will be an express bound for Nīgata?
Japanese: Well. . . . I don't know exactly. Please ask the station employee over there and find out.
Foreigner: All right. Thank you.

. . . .

Foreigner: Say, I want to take an express bound for Nīgata. From what track does it leave?
Employee: Is it an express that leaves at 2320 hours? It leaves from track number 7.
Foreigner: How long does it take to Nīgata?
Employee: The time when the express arrives at Nīgata is five-fifteen tomorrow morning, so it takes five hours and fifty-five minutes.
Foreigner: I see. Can I buy a green ticket on the train?
Employee: Well . . . I don't know. After getting on the train, please ask a conductor. (He may have some) because, once in a while, there are some persons who do not take train (after buying tickets) or some who get off a train soon (making a vacant seat).
Foreigner: Then, I'll do so. Thank you.

8.1 ——Toshokan de——

Hitori no otoko no gakusei ga toshokan no kaado no tokoro de hon o sagashite imasu. Soko e hon o nisan'satsu motta on'na no gakusei ga kimashita. Futari wa mae ni onaji kurasu de ben'kyoo shita koto ga arimasu.

——At the Library——

A male student is looking for a book where the cards of the library are. There a female student arrives carrying two or three books with her. The two have studied in the same class once.

8.2

Keiko: Pooru san.

Pooru: A, Keiko san, ben'kyoo desu ka /

Keiko: Ee. Ototoi karita hon o kaeshi ni kimashita. Sore ni, chotto yomitai hon mo arimasu kara . . . Pooru san wa /

Pooru: Kesa no Nihon bun'gaku no jikan ni wakaranakatta mon'dai o shirabetai n desu ga, tekitoo na hon ga mitsukarimasen.

Keiko: Koko no kaado de shirabete mimashita ka

Pooru: Ee, shirabete mimashita ga, nai n desu.

Keiko: Toshokan'in ni kiite mimashita ka

Pooru: Iie, mada desu kedo.

Keiko: Watakushi no yon'da san'koosho wa setsumei ga totemo kuwashikatta desu yo / Dai wa *Nihon Bun'gaku* desu ga, yon'da koto ga arimasu ka

Pooru: Iie, arimasen. Koko de karita hon desu ka

Keiko: Iie, furuhon'ya de katta hon desu. Ima uchi ni arimasu kedo, moo tsukatte imasen kara, doozo.

Pooru: Jaa, kashite kudasai. Ato de kari ni ikimasu ga, ii desu ka

Keiko: Ee, kamaimasen. Demo, goji goro made ni kite kudasai. Gojihan ni wa dekakemasu kara.

Keiko: Paul!
Paul: Oh, Keiko, are you studying here?
Keiko: Yes. I came (here) to return the book I borrowed the day before yesterday. Besides, there are some books I want to read. How about you?
Paul: I want to check on a matter that I could not understand in the Japanese literature class this morning, but I can't find the proper books.
Keiko: Did you check these cards?
Paul: Yes, I checked but I can't find anything.
Keiko: Did you ask the librarian?
Paul: No, not yet.
Keiko: The reference book I read had a detailed explanation. The title is *Japanese Literature*. Have you ever read it?
Paul: No, I haven't. Is it the book you borrowed here?
Keiko: No, it's the book I bought at a secondhand bookstore. It's at my house now, but I am not using it any more. So please (use it).
Paul: Then please lend it to me. Is it all right if I come to get it [go to borrow it] later?
Keiko: Yes, it's all right. But please come by about five o'clock, as I will be leaving home at five-thirty.

9.1 ——Nihon'go no Kyooshitsu——

Kyooshitsu no naka ni, sen'sei ga hitori, gakusei ga hachinin imasu. Sen'sei wa kokuban no mae ni tatte imasu. Gakuseitachi wa isu ni suwatte imasu. Tsukue no ue ni wa hon ya nooto ya en'pitsu nado ga arimasu.

——The Japanese Classroom——

In the classroom, there are a teacher and eight students. The teacher is standing in front of the blackboard. The students are seated on the chairs. On their desks there are books, notebooks, pencils, etc.

9.2

Sen'sei: Dewa, kore kara sen'getsu naratta tokoro no shiken o shimashoo. Mazu, kami ni namae o kaite kudasai. Shitsumon ga arimasu ka

Gakusei (1):   Sen'sei.

Sen'sei: Hai, nan desu ka

Gakusei (1):   Pen o wasuremashita. En'pitsu de kaite mo ii desu ka

Sen'sei: Ee, ii desu.

Gakusei (2):   Jisho o tsukatte mo kamaimasen ka

Sen'sei: Tsukatte wa ikemasen. Jisho mo kyookasho mo tsukawanaide kudasai. Jaa, hajimemashoo. Kokuban ni mon'dai o kakimasu kara, ima watashita kami ni kotae o
kaite kudasai.

Gakusei (3):   Sen'sei, kotae dake de ii n desu ka

Sen'sei: Hai, kamaimasen.

Gakusei (3):   Sore kara, roomaji de kotaete mo ii desu ka

Sen'sei: Iie, kan'ji to kana o tsukatte kudasai. Osokute mo kamaimasen kara. Wakarimashita
ne

Gakusei (3):   Wakarimashita.

Teacher: Well, now, let's have an examination on the part we learned last month. First of all,
please write your name on the paper.

Student (1):   Sir.

Teacher: Yes, what is it?

Student (1):   I forgot (to bring) a pen. May I write with a pencil?

Teacher: Yes, you may.

Student (2):   Don't you mind if we use dictionaries?

Teacher: It isn't all right (for you) to use them. Don't use either a dictionary or the textbook,
please. Now, let's start. I will write the questions on the blackboard, so please write the
answers on the paper I just handed to you.

Student (3):   Sir, only answers will be all right?

Teacher: Yes, it's all right.

Student (3):   And may I answer them in *rōmaji*?

Teacher: No, please use *kan'ji* and *kana*. I don't mind it even if it takes time. Is that clear?

Student (3):   Yes.

11.1   ——Nihon no Kuni——

Nihon wa yottsu no shima to Okinawa (Ryuukyuu rettoo) kara naru kuni desu. Yottsu no naka de
ichiban ookii no wa Hon'shuu, niban'me wa Hokkaidoo, san'ban'me wa Kyuushuu, ichiban chiisai no
wa Shikoku desu. Nihon wa chiisai keredomo, hosonagai kuni desu kara, kita to minami de wa zuibun
kikoo ga chigaimasu.

——The Country of Japan——

Japan is a country consisting of four islands and Okinawa (the Ryūkyū Islands). Among the four
the biggest one is Honshū, the second is Hokkaidō, the third is Kyūshū, and the smallest is Shikoku.
Japan is a small but long and narrow country, so the climate differs a great deal between the northern
and the southern parts (of Japan).

11.2

Aoki: Teeraa san, okuni wa dochira desu ka

Teeraa: Minami Kariforunia desu.

Aoki: Kariforunia wa Amerika de ichiban yutaka na shuu deshoo

Teeraa: Ee, maa soo desu ne Sore ni, kikoo ga ii kara, iroiro na kudamono ga ichinen'juu arimasu. Hoka no shuu yori supootsu mo sakan desu ne Aoki san wa Kan'sai deshita ne

Aoki: Ee, Kyooto desu.

Teeraa: Kyooto to Tookyoo to, dotchi ga suki desu ka

Aoki: Kyooto to Tookyoo o kuraberu no wa muzukashii keredo, kikoo wa Tookyoo no hoo ga ii desu ne Kyooto wa natsu totemo mushiatsui n desu.

Teeraa: Demo, keshiki wa Kyooto no hoo ga kirei deshoo

Aoki: Mochiron, zutto kirei desu yo. Sore ni, Tookyoo hodo jin'koo ga ooku arimasen kara, ochi-tsuite imasu. Yappari rekishi no furui machi wa ii desu ne.

Aoki: Mr. Taylor, where is your hometown?
Taylor: It's in southern California.
Aoki: California is the richest state in the States, isn't it?
Taylor: Yes, something like that. Moreover, because of the nice climate there are various kinds of fruit throughout the year. Sports also are more popular than in other states. You are from the Kan-sai area, aren't you?
Aoki: Yes, I'm from Kyōto.
Taylor: Which do you like better, Kyōto or Tōkyō?
Aoki: It is difficult to compare Kyōto with Tōkyō, but Tōkyō is better in climate. Kyōto is very hot and humid in summer, you know.
Taylor: But as to scenery, Kyōto is prettier, isn't it?
Aoki: Of course. It's much prettier. Besides, Kyōto does not have as large a population as Tōkyō does, so it is calm. After all, I like towns which are historically old.

12.1 ——Ryoori——

Nihon ryoori wa, aji mo ii desu ga, iro ya katachi no hijoo ni utsukushii ryoori desu. Toshitotta hito wa Nihon ryoori ga suki desu ga, wakai hito wa daitai Nihon ryoori o taberu yori seiyoo ryoori ya Chuugoku ryoori o taberu hoo ga suki desu.

——Cooking——

Japanese food is the food whose colors and shapes are extremely beautiful as well as being tasty. Old folks are fond of Japanese food; however, young people generally prefer eating Western or Chinese food to eating Japanese food.

12.2

Ookawa: A, moo rokuji ni narimashita ne. Osoku narimasu kara, sorosoro shitsurei shimasu.

Nakayama: Moo son'na jikan desu ka Issho ni shokuji shimasen ka

Ookawa: Soo desu ne. Doko e shokuji ni ikimashoo ka.

Nakayama: Gochisoo wa dekinai kedo, boku ga tsukurimasu yo.

Ookawa: Demo, tsukuru no wa taihen deshoo /

Nakayama: Iie, sugu dekimasu yo. Matte ite kudasai. Ookawa san ga omou hodo taihen ja arimasen yo /

Ookawa: Nakayama san wa mainichi jibun de ryoori o /

Nakayama: Ee, kono hen no tabemonoya wa mazui kara, jibun de ryoori shita hoo ga zutto oishii n desu.

Ookawa: Soo desu ka. Jaa, boku mo tetsudaimasu. Nakayama san wa nani o tsukuru no ga ichiban tokui desu ka /

Nakayama: Kareeraisu ya ton'katsu desu ne. Niku to yasai ga arimasu kara, kyoo wa karee o tsukurimashoo ka.

Ookawa: Ii desu ne. Boku wa karee ga daisuki desu.

Nakayama: Jaa, karee ni shimashoo.

Mr. Ōkawa: Oh, it's already six o'clock. It's getting late, so I'd better be leaving.

Mr. Nakayama: Is it so late already? Won't you have supper with me?

Mr. Ōkawa: All right. Where shall we go to eat?

Mr. Nakayama: I'll cook something, though I can't give you very good food.

Mr. Ōkawa: But it is much trouble to cook, isn't it?

Mr. Nakayama: No, the meal will be ready soon. Please be waiting. It is not so much trouble (to cook) as you may think, Mr. Ōkawa.

Mr. Ōkawa: Do you cook yourself every day?

Mr. Nakayama: Yes. Food at eating places in this area is not good, so it would be much better if I cooked it myself (than if we were to eat out).

Mr. Ōkawa: I see. Then I'll help you. What do you cook best?

Mr. Nakayama: Curry and rice, pork cutlet, and the like. Since I have meat and vegetables, shall we cook curry and rice today?

Mr. Ōkawa: That's fine. I like curry and rice very much.

Mr. Nakayama: Well, then, let's (decide to) have curry and rice.

13.1   ——Tookyoo no Kootsuu——

Tookyoo wa jin'koo ga hijoo ni ooi machi desu. Den'sha ya basu ya chikatetsu wa itsumo kon'de imasu. Jidoosha, takushii, torakku, ootobai nado takusan no norimono ga semai michi o hashitte imasu.

——Transportation in Tōkyō——

Tōkyō is a city that has an extremely great population. The trains, buses, and subways are always crowded. A lot of vehicles, such as automobiles, taxis, trucks, motorcycles, etc., are running on narrow streets.

13.2

Kimura: Jitsu wa, kore kara Furan'su Taishikan e ikanakereba narimasen. Tanaka san, basho o gozon'ji desu ka /

Tanaka: Furan'su Taishikan nara, yoku shitte imasu yo.

Kimura: Soo desu ka. Doo ikeba ii n desu ka /Michi o oshiete kudasai.

Tanaka: Kyoo wa kuruma desu ka /

Kimura: Iie. Demo, chikakereba, aruite iku tsumori desu kedo.

Tanaka: Chotto tooi desu yo. Juugoban no basu de ikeba, taishikan no sugu soba ni tomarimasu kara, basu ni shita hoo ga ii deshoo. Mittsume de orireba, sugu wakarimasu yo /

Kimura: Juugoban no basu desu ne /Basutei wa doko desu ka /

Tanaka: Kono toori no niban'me no kado o hidari e magarimasu. Hora, ima akai jiten'sha ga hashitte kimasu ne /Ano kado desu.

Kimura: Ee, wakarimasu.

Tanaka: Sore kara, massugu gojuumeetoru gurai aruite ikimasu. Suruto, migi ni shiroi tatemono ga arimasu. Basutei wa sono shiroi tatemono no iriguchi no mae desu.

Kimura: Yoku wakarimashita. Doomo arigatoo.

Mr. Kimura: The fact is, I must go to the French Embassy. Do you know where it is?

Mr. Tanaka: If it is the French Embassy, I know it very well.

Mr. Kimura: Do you? How should I go? Please tell me the way.

Mr. Tanaka: Are you riding in a car today?

Mr. Kimura: No. But if it is near (from here), I will go by walking.

Mr. Tanaka: It is a little far. If you go by the number 15 bus, it'll stop right by the embassy, so you'd better (decide to) take a bus. If you get off at the third stop, you'll find the embassy right away.

Mr. Kimura: Number 15 bus? Where is the bus stop?

Mr. Tanaka: You turn to the left at the second corner on this street. Look, there is a red bicycle coming through now, isn't there? It's that corner.

Mr. Kimura: Yes, I see.

Mr. Tanaka: And you walk down straight about fifty meters. Then there is a white building on the right. The bus stop is in front of the entrance to that building.

Mr. Kimura: I got it well. Thank you very much.

APPENDIX VII
GLOSSARY

Numbers refer to lessons in this volume in which the words first occur.

（A）

aa	ああ	SI	5	oh; ah
Afurika	アフリカ	N	11	Africa
aimasu	あいます	V	4	meet (normal form of *au*) (see 4.4.13)
aji	あじ	N	12	taste; flavor
Ajia	アジア	N	11	Asia
aka	あか	N	13	red (see 13.4.14)
akai	あかい	A	13	is red (see 13.4.14)
akemasu	あけます	V	9	open (normal form of *akeru*) (transitive Verb)
amai	あまい	A	12	is sweet
an'na	あんな	PN	5	that sort of (see 5.4.9)
anoo	あのう	SI	7	say; well; er-r-r-r (see 7.4.13)
ao	あお	N	13	blue
aoi	あおい	A	13	is blue
Aoki	青木	N	11	family name
apaato	アパート	N	2	apartment
ara	あら	SI	4	oh; ah (used only by women) (see 4.4.12)
araimasu	あらいます	V	12	wash (normal form of *arau*)
Arasuka	アラスカ	N	11	Alaska
arubaito	アルバイト	N	2	(student's) work (for money)
arubaito shimasu	アルバイトします	V	2	do a side-job (see 2.4.4)
arukimasu	あるきます	V	7	walk (normal form of *aruku*)
ashi	あし	N	8	leg; foot
asobimasu	あそびます	V	5	play (normal form of *asobu*) (see 5.4.12)
atama	あたま	N	11	head
atarashii	新しい	A	5	is new; is fresh
ato de	あとで	Adv.	1	later

（B）

baiorin	バイオリン	N	12	violin
-ban	番	Nd	4	counter for naming numbers in succession
ban'goo	番号	N	4	(sequential) number
-ban'sen	番線	Nd	7	track number ～ (see 7.4.15)
basho	ばしょ	N	13	location
basutei	バス停	N	13	bus stop
bijutsukan	びじゅつ館	N	5	art museum
bun'gaku	文学	N	8	literature
buutsu	ブーツ	N	1	boots
byooki	びょう気	N	12	illness; sickness

(C)

chigaimasu	ちがいます	V	4	differ; is different (normal form of *chigau*) (see 4.4.8 and 8.4.5)
chairo	ちゃいろ	N	13	brown
chairoi	ちゃいろい	A	13	is brown
chika	地下	N	1	basement (lit. underground)
chikatetsu	地下鉄	N	13	subway (lit. underground railway)
choodo	ちょうど	Adv.	1	just; exactly
Chotto ukagaimasu ga...	ちょっと うかがいますが…	(exp.)	7	Excuse me for asking you a question, but... (see 7.4.8)

(D)

-daasu	ダース	Nd	1	dozen
dai	だい	N	8	title
daigakusei	大学生	N	2	college student
daijoobu	だいじょうぶ	Na	4	all right; safe (this word is used to allay fear or doubt)
daitai	だいたい	Adv.	5	roughly speaking; mostly; approximately
dake	だけ	R	9	only; just (see 9.4.9)
de	で	R	1	totalizing (see 1.4.19)
de	で	R	5	(famous) for (see 5.4.13)
de	で	R	7	within; in (see 7.4.6)
de	で	C	9	TE form of *desu* (see 9.4.10)
de	で	R	11	of; among (see 11.4.2)
deguchi	出口	N	13	exit
dekimasu	できます	V	5,7	is able to; can (do); is possible (normal form of *dekiru*) (see 5.4.15 and 7.4.7)
dekimasu	できます	V	12	is ready; is done; is made (normal form of *dekiru*) (see 12.4.9)
demasu	出ます	V	7	go out; leave (normal form of *deru*)
doa	ドア	N	8	door
dochira	どちら	Ni	11	which (of the two)? (see 11.4.9)
don'na	どんな	PN	5	what sort of? (see 5.4.9)
dono gurai (dono kurai)	どのぐらい (どのくらい)	Ni	7	how long?; how far?; how much? (see 7.4.17)
doobutsuen	どうぶつ園	N	5	zoo
Doomo arigatoo gozaimashita.	どうも ありがとう ございました。	(exp.)	1	Thank you very much for what you have done for me. (see 1.4.20)
-doru	ドル	Nd	1	dollar(s) (see 1.4.10)
doyoobi	土曜日	N	4	Saturday

(E)

eeto	ええと	SI	2	let me see; well
ekiin	駅員	N	7	station employee
-en	円	Nd	1	unit for Japanese currency (see 1.4.10)

(F)

Fujisan	ふじ山	N	5	Mt. Fuji
-fun	分	Nd	4	minute (see 4.4.23)
furui	古い	A	5	is old (thing)

| futsuka | 二日 | N | 2 | the second day of the month; two days |

(G)

getsuyoobi	月曜日	N	4	Monday (see 4.4.2)
gitaa	ギター	N	5	guitar
gochisoo	ごちそう	N	12	treat; feast
gochisoo shimasu	ごちそうします	V	12	treat (one to something to eat or drink) (normal form of *gochisoo suru*)
gogatsu	五月	N	2	May
gogo	ごご	N	4	P.M.; in the afternoon (see 4.4.22)
-goro	ごろ	Nd	2	about (time); approximately (see 2.4.13)
gorufu	ゴルフ	N	5	golf
gozen	ごぜん	N	4	A.M.
gun'jin	ぐん人	N	12	military personnel; career soldier
-gurai	ぐらい	Nd	1	about; approximately (see 1.4.11)
guriin'ken	グリーンけん	N	7	green ticket for green car (＝first-class car)
guriin'sha	グリーン車	N	7	green car (＝first-class car)

(H)

hachigatsu	八月	N	2	August
-hai	はい	Nd	1	counter for cupfuls or glassfuls (see 1.4.17)
hajimarimasu	はじまります	V	4	begin (intransitive Verb) (normal form of *hajimaru*)
hajime	はじめ	N	5	beginning
hajimemasu	はじめます	V	9	begin (transitive Verb) (normal form of *hajimeru*)
hakimasu	はきます	V	1	put on (shoes, pants, a skirt, socks, etc.) (normal form of *haku*)
hako	はこ	N	1	box; case
-han	半	Nd	1	half (see 1.4.9)
hana	花	N	5	flower; blossom
hanami	花見	N	5	flower viewing (usually cherry blossom viewing) (see 5.4.1)
han'kachi	ハンカチ	N	1	handkerchief
hashirimasu	はしります	V	7	run (normal form of *hashiru*)
hatarakimasu	はたらきます	V	2	work; labor (normal form of *hataraku*) (see 2.4.4)
hatsuka	二十日	N	2	the twentieth day of the month; twenty days
hayai	はやい	A	7	is fast; is rapid; is early
Hayashi	林	N	2	family name
hazu	はず	Nd	4	expected to (do); supposed to (do) (see 4.4.3)
hen	へん	Na	5	strange; unusual; funny
hi	日	N	4	day
hidari	左	N	13	left
higashi	東	N	11	east
hijoo ni	ひじょうに	Adv.	12	extremely
hikimasu	ひきます	V	7	play (the piano, strings, etc.) (normal form of *hiku*)
hikui	ひくい	A	7	is low; is short (stature)
hiragana	ひらがな	N	1	the cursive Japanese syllabary

hiroi	ひろい	A	11	is large; is wide; is spacious
hodo	ほど	R	11	as much as (see 11.4.13 and 12.4.10)
hoka	ほか	N	11	other; another; different; else (see 11.4.8)
-hon	本	Nd	1	counter for long and thin objects (see 1.4.17)
Hon'shuu	本州	N	11	the main island of Japan
hon'to ni	ほんとに	Adv.	5	really; truly
hoo	ほう	Nd	11	alternative (see 11.4.9, 12.4.2, and 12.4.11)
hora	ほら	SI	13	look!; there!
hoshii	ほしい	A	1	want; is desirous (see 1.4.6)
hosonagai	ほそながい	A	11	is long and narrow; is slim

(I)

ichiban	一番	N	11	the most (see 11.4.2 and 12.4.12)
ichigatsu	一月	N	2	January (see 2.4.5)
ichinen'juu	一年じゅう	N	11	all year round; throughout the year (see 11.4.7)
ichinichi	一日	N	2	a day
Ichiroo	一郎	N	2	boy's first name
ii	いい	A	8	is all right (see 8.4.14 and 9.4.5)
ikemasen	いけません	V	9	it won't do (see 9.4.6)
ikimasu	行きます	E	4	(see 4.4.20)
ikura	いくら	Ni	1	how much? (see 1.4.12)
imasu	います	E	1,2	normal form of *iru* (see 2.4.2)
Inoue	井上	N	4	family name
irasshaimasu	いらっしゃいます	V	4	exist; is (normal form of *irassharu*; polite equivalent of *imasu*) (see 4.4.10)
Irasshaimase.	いらっしゃいませ。	(exp.)	1	Welcome. (see 1.4.3)
iremasu	入れます	V	1	put it in (normal form of *ireru*)
iriguchi	入口	N	13	entrance
iro	いろ	N	12	color
iroiro	いろいろ	Na	5	various
isha	いしゃ	N	12	medical doctor; physician
isogimasu	いそぎます	V	12	hurry (normal form of *isogu*)
isu	いす	N	9	chair
itadakimasu	いただきます	V	1	get; receive (normal form of *itadaku*) (polite equivalent of *moraimasu*) (see 1.4.14)
itsuka	五日	N	2	the fifth day of the month; five days

(J)

ji	字	N	9	letter; character
jibun de	自分で	Adv.	12	by oneself; for oneself
jidoosha	自動車	N	13	automobile
jikan	時間	N	7	time; hour (see 7.4.19)
-jikan	時間	Nd	7	hour(s) (see 7.4.19)
jin'koo	人口	N	11	population
jiten'sha	自転車	N	13	bicycle
Jooji	ジョージ	N	5	George
-juu	じゅう	Nd	11	throughout (see 11.4.7)

juudoo	じゅうどう	N	5	*judō*; a Japanese art of self-defense
juugatsu	十月	N	2	October
juuichigatsu	十一月	N	2	November
juunigatsu	十二月	N	2	December
juu yokka	十四日	N	2	the fourteenth day of the month; fourteen days

（K）

kaado	カード	N	8	card
kabuki	かぶき	N	4	*kabuki* performance（see 4.4.19）
Kabukiza	かぶきざ	N	4	*Kabuki* Theater near the Ginza
kado	かど	N	13	corner; turn
kaerimasu	かえります	E	4	（see 4.4.20）
kaeshimasu	かえします	V	8	return; give back（normal form of *kaesu*）
-kai	かい	Nd	1	counter for floor; stories（see 1.4.17）
kaisha	かいしゃ	N	2	company
kaiwa	かいわ	N	1	dialog; conversation
kakarimasu	かかります	V	7	require; take（normal form of *kakaru*）
kakemasu	かけます	V	4	turn on; dial（normal form of *kakeru*）
kamaimasen	かまいません	V	8	do not mind（see 8.4.15 and 9.4.5）
kana	かな	N	9	Japanese syllabary
kan'ji	かん字	N	1	Chinese character
Kan'sai	関西	N	11	a district including Ōsaka, Kyōto, Kōbe, etc.（see 11.4.10）
Kan'too	関東	N	11	a district including Tōkyō, Yokohama, Chiba, etc.
kara	から	Rc	5	because; since（see 5.4.8）
kara	から	R	11	（consist; is composed）of（see 11.4.1）
karai	からい	A	12	is salty; is spicy
karate	から手	N	5	*karate*; an art of self-defense originated in the Ryūkyū Islands
kareeraisu	カレーライス	N	12	curry and rice
Kariforunia	カリフォルニア	N	11	California
kashimasu	かします	V	8	lend; rent（normal form of *kasu*）
katachi	かたち	N	12	shape; form; appearance
katakana	かたかな	N	1	the square Japanese syllabary
kawaii	かわいい	A	5	is cute
kayoimasu	かよいます	V	2	commute; go to and from（normal form of *kayou*）（see 2.4.7）
kayoobi	火曜日	N	4	Tuesday
Keiko	けい子	N	8	girl's name
keizai	けいざい	N	8	economics
kekkon	けっこん	N	2	marriage
kekkon shimasu	けっこんします	V	2	marry（normal form of *kekkon suru*）
keredo(mo)	けれど（も）	Rc	11	although（informally *kedo*）
keshiki	けしき	N	11	scenery
ki	木	N	9	tree
kibun	気分	N	4	feeling（cf. feel sick, feel fine）
kiiro	きいろ	N	13	yellow
kiiroi	きいろい	A	13	is yellow
kikimasu	聞きます	V	7	inquire（normal form of *kiku*）（see 7.4.12）

kikoo	気候	N	11	climate
kimasu	きます	V	1	wear (normal form of *kiru*)
kimasu	来ます	E	4	(see 4.4.20)
Kimura	木村	N	13	family name
kin'yoobi	金曜日	N	4	Friday
-kiro	キロ	Nd	7	short form of *kiromeetoru*—kilometer (see 7.4.3)
kisetsu	きせつ	N	5	season
kita	北	N	11	north (see 11.4.5)
kitsui	きつい	A	1	is tight
ko	子	N	11	child (usually preceded by a modifier, e.g., *otoko no ko* ''boy'')
kokonoka	九日	N	2	the ninth day of the month; nine days
kokuban	黒板	N	9	blackboard
komimasu	こみます	V	13	get crowded (normal form of *komu*) (see 13.4.3)
kon'na	こんな	PN	5	this sort of
koocha	こうちゃ	N	5	English tea
kooen	公園	N	5	park; public garden
koohai	こうはい	N	2	junior member of school, etc.
kootsuu	交通	N	13	traffic
kotae	こたえ	N	9	answer
kotaemasu	こたえます	V	9	answer; respond (normal form of *kotaeru*)
koto	こと	Nd	5,7,8	act; fact (see 5.4.15, 7.4.7, and 8.4.6)
kotoba	ことば	N	1	speech; word; language
kudasai	ください	E	1	please (do) (see 1.4.7)
kudasai	ください	V	1	please give me (see 1.4.15)
kudasaimasu	くださいます	V	1	give me (or us) (polite equivalent of *kuremasu*) (normal form of *kudasaru*) (see 1.4.15)
kugatsu	九月	N	2	September
kurabemasu	くらべます	V	11	compare (normal form of *kuraberu*) (see 11.4.11)
-kurai	くらい	Nd	1	about; approximately (see 1.4.11)
kuro	くろ	N	13	black
kuroi	くろい	A	13	is black
kutsu	くつ	N	1	shoes
kutsuzumi	くつずみ	N	1	shoe polisher
kuwashii	くわしい	A	8	is in detail
kyaku	客	N	1	customer; guest; visitor
kyooiku-gaku	教育学	N	2	study of education; pedagogy
kyookasho	教科書	N	9	textbook
kyooshitsu	教室	N	9	classroom
kyuukoo	急行	N	7	express
Kyuushuu	九州	N	11	Kyūshū Island

(M)

| maa | まあ | SI | 11 | you might say; roughly; well, I think (showing some hesitation) (see 11.4.6) |

machi	町	N	11	town; city
mada	まだ	Adv.	2	still
made	まで	R	7	as far as; until (see 7.4.2)
made ni	までに	R	8	by (the time) (see 8.4.16)
mado	まど	N	8	window
mae	前	N	9	front; before (see 9.4.2)
magarimasu	まがります	V	13	turn (normal form of *magaru*)
-mairu	マイル	Nd	7	mile
massugu	まっすぐ	Adv.	13	straight
mazu	まず	Adv.	9	first of all; to begin with
me	目	N	8	eye
-me	目	Nd	11	(see 11.4.4)
-meetoru	メートル	Nd	7	meter
michi	みち	N	13	street; road; way
Michiko	みち子	N	5	girl's first name
migi	右	N	13	right
mijikai	みじかい	A	9	is short
mikka	三日	N	2	the third day of the month; three days
mimasu	みます	E	1	try; (do and) see (after TE form) (normal form of *miru*) (see 1.4.13)
minami	南	N	11	south (see 11.4.5)
misemasu	見せます	V	1	show (normal form of *miseru*)
mitsukarimasu	見つかります	V	8	is found; can find (intransitive Verb) (normal form of *mitsukaru*) (see 8.4.11)
(o)miyage	(お)みやげ	N	4	souvenir; gift
mo	も	R	9	even (see 9.4.5)
mochimasu	持ちます	V	2	have; hold; possess (normal form of *motsu*) (see 2.4.8)
mochiron	もちろん	SI	11	of course; certainly
mokuyoobi	木曜日	N	4	Thursday
mon'dai	もんだい	N	8	problem; question
mono	物	N	11	thing (tangible)
moo	もう	Adv.	8	(not) any more; (not) any longer (see 8.4.13)
Mori	森	N	4	family name
moshi	もし	Adv.	13	if; provided (see 13.4.6, 13.4.9, and 13.4.11)
moshi moshi	もしもし	SI	4	hello (regularly used in telephone conversation)
muika	六日	N	2	the sixth day of the month; six days
mukashi	むかし	N	7	old times
musuko	むすこ	N	12	son
musume	むすめ	N	12	daughter; girl

(N)

na	な	C	5	NA form of the Copula (see 5.4.2)
-nado	など	Nd	1	etc.; and the like
nagai	ながい	A	9	is long
-nai	ない	Da	4	negative Derivative (see 4.4.3)
-naide	ないで	Da	9	(see 9.4.7)

naka	中	N	7	inside (see 9.4.2)
naka	なか	N	11	among (them) (see 11.4.2)
Nakayama	中山	N	12	family name
nan'ban'sen	何番線	Ni	7	what track number? (see 7.4.15)
nan'gai	何がい	Ni	1	what floor? (see 1.4.17)
nan'gatsu	何月	Ni	2	what month? (see 2.4.5)
nanoka	七日	N	2	the seventh day of the month; seven days
nan'yoobi	何曜日	Ni	4	what day of the week? (see 4.4.2)
nara(ba)	なら(ば)	C	13	if it is a ～ (BA form of *desu* ← *da*) (see 13.4.6)
narimasen	なりません	E	13	it won't do (see 13.4.5)
narimasu	なります	V	11	consist (of); is composed (of) (normal form of *naru*) (see 11.4.1)
narimasu	なります	V	12	become (normal form of *naru*) (see 12.4.3 and 12.4.4)
nekutai	ネクタイ	N	1	necktie
nemasu	ねます	V	4	go to bed; sleep (normal form of *neru*)
-nen'sei	年生	Nd	2	(～th)-year student (see 2.4.1)
ni	に	R	1	into (see 1.4.16)
ni	に	R	2	at; in; on (time Relational) (see 2.4.3)
ni	に	R	4	to (a place) (see 4.4.14)
ni	に	R	5	Relational of purpose (see 5.4.3)
ni	に	R	12	goal Relational (see 12.4.3)
-nichi	日	Nd	2	counter for days (see 2.4.5)
nichiyoobi	日曜日	N	4	Sunday
nigatsu	二月	N	2	February
Niigata	新潟	N	7	name of a prefecture in northern Honshū
nijuu yokka	二十四日	N	2	the twenty-fourth day; twenty-four days
niku	にく	N	12	meat
nishi	西	N	11	west
no	の	R	7	*no* substituting *ga* (see 7.4.11)
no	の	Nd	7	nominalizer (see 7.4.4)
no	の	Nd	11	one(s) (see 11.4.3)
nomimono	のみ物	N	7	a drink; a beverage
nooto	ノート	N	8	notebook
norimasu	のります	V	7	get on; ride (normal form of *noru*) (see 7.4.14)
norimono	のり物	N	7	transportation facilities; vehicle (see 7.4.1)
notte kara	のってから	V+R	7	after getting on (see 7.4.20)
Nyuu Yooku	ニューヨーク	N	7	New York

(O)

o	を	R	13	through; along; at; in; on (see 13.4.4)
ochitsukimasu	おちつきます	V	11	become calm (normal form of *ochitsuku*)
okimasu	おきます	V	4	get up (intransitive Verb) (normal form of *okiru*)
Okinawa	沖縄	N	11	name of a prefecture in the Ryūkyū Islands
omoimasu	おもいます	V	12	think (normal form of *omou*)
onaji	おなじ	N	8	same (see 8.4.5)
on'na	女	N	1	female (see 1.4.5)

ooi	多い	A	5	are many; is much (see 5.4.14)
Ookawa	大川	N	12	family name
Oosaka	大阪	N	2	the biggest city in western Japan
ootobai	オートバイ	N	13	motorcycle
orimasu	おります	V	7	get off (normal form of *oriru*) (see 7.4.22)
oshiemasu	教えます	V	13	teach; instruct; tell; show (normal form of *oshieru*)
osoi	おそい	A	9	is slow; is late
otaku	おたく	N	4	someone else's house; home (polite equivalent of *uchi*) (see 4.4.7)
otoko	男	N	1	male (see 1.4.5)
otona	おとな	N	5	adult; grown-ups
owarimasu	おわります	V	4	end; finish (intransitive Verb) (normal form of *owaru*)
oyu	おゆ	N	12	warm (boiled) water

(P)

piano	ピアノ	N	5	piano
Pooru	ポール	N	8	Paul

(R)

rein'kooto	レインコート	N	1	raincoat
rekishi	歴史	N	11	history
repooto	レポート	N	8	report; paper
rin'go	りんご	N	11	apple
rokugatsu	六月	N	2	June
roomaji	ローマ字	N	9	roman letters
ryoori	料理	N	12	cooking; dish; food
ryoori shimasu	料理します	V	12	cook (normal form of *ryoori suru*)
Ryuukyuu rettoo	琉球列島	N	11	Ryūkyū Islands

(S)

saa	さあ	SI	7	well (hesitance) (see 7.4.10)
saizu	サイズ	N	1	size (see 1.4.9)
sakan	さかん	Na	11	flourishing; prosperous; popular
sakana	さかな	N	12	fish
(o)sake	(お)さけ	N	1	rice wine; liquor
sakimasu	さきます	V	5	bloom (normal form of *saku*)
sakura	さくら	N	5	cherry (tree or blossoms)
-sama	さま	Nd	1	polite equivalent of *-san* (see 1.4.8)
San Furan'shisuko	サンフランシスコ	N	7	San Francisco
san'gatsu	三月	N	2	March
san'koosho	さんこう書	N	8	reference book
san'po	さんぽ	N	5	stroll
san'po shimasu	さんぽします	V	5	stroll; take a walk (normal form of *san'po suru*)
sara	さら	N	12	dish
sashiagemasu	さしあげます	V	1	I give (normal form of *sashiageru*) (polite equivalent of *agemasu*) (see 1.4.4)
(o)sashimi	(お)さしみ	N	12	raw fish

seetaa	セーター	N	1	pullover
sei	せい	N	7	height; stature
seiyoo	西洋	N	12	Western (countries); the Occident (cf. *tooyoo* ''Eastern (countries); the Orient'')
sekai	せかい	N	11	world
semai	せまい	A	11	is small; is narrow; is limited (in space)
-sen'chi	センチ	Nd	7	centimeter
sen'pai	せんぱい	N	2	senior member of school, etc. (see 2.4.6)
-sen'to	セント	Nd	1	cent(s)
setsumei	せつめい	N	8	explanation
setsumei shimasu	せつめいします	V	8	explain (normal form of *setsumei suru*)
shashoo	車しょう	N	7	train or bus conductor
Shibuya	しぶや	N	2	a district of Tōkyō
shichigatsu	七月	N	2	July
shigatsu	四月	N	2	April
shigoto	しごと	N	2	work; job
shigoto shimasu	しごとします	N	2	work; do one's job (normal form of *shigoto suru*)
Shikoku	四国	N	11	Shikoku Island
shima	島	N	11	island
shimasu	します	V	12	make; decide on (normal form of *suru*) (see 12.4.14)
shimemasu	しめます	V	9	shut; close (normal form of *shimeru*)
shin'kan'sen	しんかん線	N	7	New Trunk Line (see 7.4.5)
shirabemasu	しらべます	V	8	make researches (on); check up; investigate (normal form of *shiraberu*)
shirimasu	知ります	V	2	get to know; come to know (normal form of *shiru*) (see 2.4.10)
shiro	しろ	N	13	white
shiroi	しろい	A	13	is white
shita	下	N	9	under; below
shitsumon	しつもん	N	9	question
shitsumon shimasu	しつもんします	V	9	ask a question (normal form of *shitsumon suru*)
shitsurei	しつれい	Na	5	rude
shukudai	しゅくだい	N	9	homework
shuu	州	N	11	state
soba	そば	N	9	vicinity; near
son'na	そんな	PN	5	that sort of
Soo desu nee.	そうですねえ。	(exp.)	5	Well.; Let me see.
soosoo	そうそう	SI	4	oh, yes (used when something comes into one's mind)
sugu	すぐ	Adv.	13	right (there)
suimasu	すいます	V	9	smoke; inhale (normal form of *suu*)
suiyoobi	水曜日	N	4	Wednesday
sukeeto	スケート	N	5	skate
sukii	スキー	N	5	ski
sukimasu	すきます	V	13	get scarce (normal form of *suku*) (see 13.4.3)
sukiyaki	すきやき	N	4	*sukiyaki*; beef cooked with vegetables

sukunai	少ない	A	5	is few; is little (opposite of *ooi*—are many; is much)
sumimasu	すみます	V	2	live (normal form of *sumu*) (see 2.4.11)
suppai	すっぱい	A	12	is sour
suruto	すると	SI	13	thereupon; and just then
sushi	すし	N	1	vinegar-treated rice flavored primarily with seafood, usually raw
Suujii	スージー	N	7	Susie
suwarimasu	すわります	V	9	sit (normal form of *suwaru*) (see 9.4.3)
（T）				
tabako	たばこ、タバコ	N	9	tobacco; cigarette
tabemono	食べ物	N	7	food
tabemonoya	食べ物屋	N	12	eating place
tachimasu	たちます	V	9	stand (normal form of *tatsu*) (see 9.4.3)
taihen	たいへん	Adv.	1	very (formal equivalent of *totemo*)
taihen	たいへん	Na	7	awful; hard; terrible; trouble
taishikan	大使館	N	13	embassy (cf. *taishi* ''ambassador'')
takai	たかい	A	7	is high; is tall
tama ni	たまに	Adv.	7	occasionally; once in a while
Tanaka	田中	N	13	family name
tan'joobi	たんじょう日	N	2	birthday
Tanoshimi ni shite imasu.	たのしみに しています。	(exp.)	2	Looking forward to it. (see 2.4.15)
te	手	N	8	hand
teeburu	テーブル	N	9	table
Teeraa	テーラー	N	11	Taylor
teinei	ていねい	Na	1	polite
tekitoo	てきとう	Na	8	proper; adequate
ten'in	店員	N	1	shop clerk
tenisu	テニス	N	5	tennis
(o)tera	（お）てら	N	5	temple
tetsudaimasu	手つだいます	V	12	help; assist (a person to do something) (normal form of *tetsudau*)
tokoro	所	N	2,8	place; address (see 8.4.2)
tokoro	ところ	N	9	part; section (see 9.4.4)
tokui	とくい	Na	12	proud, favorite, or strong point
toku ni	とくに	Adv.	5	especially
tomarimasu	とまります	V	13	stop (normal form of *tomaru*) (intransitive Verb) (see 13.4.12)
ton'katsu	とんかつ	N	12	pork cutlet
tooka	十日	N	2	the tenth day of the month; ten days
toori	とおり	N	13	avenue; street
torakku	トラック	N	13	truck; lorry
torimasu	とります	V	4	take (normal form of *toru*)
toshitotta	年取った	V	12	aged (person)
toshokan'in	図書館員	N	8	librarian; library clerk
tsugi	つぎ	N	1	next; following
tsuitachi	一日	N	2	the first day of the month
tsukaimasu	つかいます	V	8	use (normal form of *tsukau*)
tsukimasu	つきます	V	7	arrive (normal form of *tsuku*) (see 7.4.18)

tsukue	つくえ	N	9	desk
tsukurimasu	作ります	V	12	make; create; prepare; cook (normal form of *tsukuru*)
tsumori	つもり	Nd	4	intention; planning (see 4.4.17)
tsuremasu	つれます	V	4	take (with); bring (with); accompany (normal form of *tsureru*) (see 4.4.20)
tsutomemasu	つとめます	V	2	is employed; work for (an organization) (normal form of *tsutomeru*) (see 2.4.4)

(U)

ue	上	N	9	top; topside; on; above (see 9.4.2)
Ueno	上野	N	5	a district of Tōkyō (see 5.4.7)
ukagaimasu	うかがいます	V	2	visit; go (to someone's house) (normal form of *ukagau*) (see 2.4.9)
ukagaimasu	うかがいます	V	7	hear; inquire (normal form of *ukagau*) (see 7.4.8)
urimasu	うります	V	1	sell (normal form of *uru*)
ushiro	うしろ	N	9	behind; back
utsukushii	美しい	A	5	is beautiful

(W)

waishatsu	ワイシャツ	N	1	dress shirt
wakai	わかい	A	12	is young
wakarimasu	わかります	V	4,13	understand; find; is clear (see 4.4.24)
wasuremasu	わすれます	V	9	forget; leave behind (normal form of *wasureru*)
watashimasu	わたします	V	9	hand (normal form of *watasu*)

(Y)

yahari	やはり	Adv.	11	as I thought; as I expected (see 11.4.14)
yane	やね	N	9	roof
yappari	やっぱり	Adv.	11	colloquial equivalent of *yahari* (see 11.4.14)
yasai	やさい	N	12	vegetables
yasumimasu	休みます	V	4	is absent (from class); take leave (normal form of *yasumu*) (see 4.4.16)
yokka	四日	N	2	the fourth day of the month; four days
-yoo(bi)	曜(日)	Nd	4	day of the week (see 4.4.2)
yooka	八日	N	2	the eighth day of the month; eight days
yori	より	R	11	(more) than (see 11.4.9 and 12.4.2)
Yoshiko	よし子	N	4	girl's first name
-yuki (-iki)	行	Nd	7	bound for; for (see 7.4.9)
yukkuri	ゆっくり	Adv.	2	leisurely; slowly; take one's time
yutaka	ゆたか	Na	11	rich; abundant
yuugata	ゆうがた	N	5	late afternoon; early evening
yuumei	ゆうめい	Na	5	famous; noted

(Z)

zehi	ぜひ	Adv.	2	by all means; without fail
zen'bu	ぜんぶ	N	1	all; everything
zero	ゼロ	N	4	zero
zutto	ずっと	Adv.	11	by far; much (more) (see 11.4.12)

APPENDIX VIII
INDEX TO NOTES

346